EMPIRE LOST

Empire Lost
*Britain, the Dominions and the
Second World War*

Andrew Stewart

continuum

Continuum UK, The Tower Building, 11 York Road, London SE1 7NX
Continuum US, 80 Maiden Lane, Suite 704, New York, NY 10038

www.continuumbooks.com

First published 2008

British Library Cataloguing-in-Publication Data
A catalogue record for this book is available from the British Library.

ISBN 978 1 84725 244 9

Typeset by Pindar NZ, Auckland, New Zealand
Printed and bound by MPG Books Ltd, Cornwall, Great Britain

Contents

For my parents

Introduction: A Special Relationship

'Walk about Sion, and go round about her: and tell the towers thereof – mark well her bulwarks, consider her houses; that ye may tell them that come after'[1]

In 1958 Nicholas Mansergh finally finished a project that he had started 11 years before, a monumental survey of the British Commonwealth of Nations. He had been elected by the Royal Institute of International Affairs to the newly established chair of British Commonwealth relations, and one of the duties he assumed was the continuation of the *Survey of British Commonwealth Affairs*. From 1953 onwards, Mansergh would split his time labouring to finish his research and writing at the renowned think-tank based at Chatham House in the heart of London while also serving as Smuts Professor of the History of the British Commonwealth at Cambridge University. The result was two volumes of the *Survey* with three supporting volumes of *Documents and Speeches*. His initial volume, *Problems of External Policy, 1931–39*, offered an exhaustive study of the circumstances that had led, what at this point was still then generally termed as 'the British Empire', into its final titanic military struggle. The publication of the accompanying documents followed before Mansergh's second volume, *Problems of Wartime Cooperation and Post-War Change, 1939–1952*, was released to considerable acclaim. One reviewer described it as 'an extraordinary arrangement', a book of 'scholarship and insight, illuminated with flashes of wit'. Another, himself a great historian of the Empire and Australian by birth, viewed it as 'the most valuable contribution to the understanding of the Commonwealth of yesterday, today and tomorrow'. This noted scholar Professor Keith Hancock who pre-war had begun the task of recording the *Survey*'s assessment of the British Empire's progress, believed it to be an 'immense addition to organized knowledge' which explained fully the British Commonwealth's evolution. The story told was on a colossal scale drawn from Mansergh's wide pre-war academic studies, supplemented by his own wartime experiences. From 1941 onwards he was first the Irish expert, and then later the Director of the Empire Division within the Ministry of Information. At the war's end he moved to the Dominions Office (DO) as an assistant secretary for a short period before returning to academia. From his wartime offices in Malet Street – in peacetime the heart of the University of London – he watched the progress of the global conflict and its effect on an alliance that in 1939 had re-forged an historic bond to defeat a common foe. Now he would tell the tale of how in the process of its greatest victory, Britain had lost its Empire. In between there would be further volumes, largely on his other great passion India, and in 1969 *The Commonwealth Experience* was published, 'the centrepiece of his oeuvre' and still rightly acknowledged as the finest single book on the British Empire's progression.[2]

In 1939 there were six fully self-governing member states of the Empire: Canada, Australia, South Africa, New Zealand, Eire and Britain. Attempts to define what is now sometimes referred to as the Dominion 'concept' or 'idea', the link that bound them all together, have offered an enduring source of fascination both at the time and long after they became no more than an historical footnote.[3] A typical view was that of one post-war writer who claimed that Dominion status was something which 'white men had invented in the 1920s for other white men, in the style and practice of a gentlemen's club'.[4] This is as good a definition as any, the difficulty was though that the members were loathe to pay their contributions; during the inter-war years spending on defence made by each of them was far from proportionate to their wealth or population size and when war returned to Europe in 1939 – and two years later the Pacific – they were unprepared. In fairness much the same could also be said about the central tenet of this organization. British foreign policy during the inter-war period can rightly be said to have been 'bedevilled by illusion, naïveté, unreality and folie de grandeur', with successive leaders at the mother of parliaments in Westminster failing to recognize that the world was changing and British power was no longer guaranteed; as one historian has put it 'the policy-makers behaved likes ostriches in sand dunes'.[5] As a consequence, just three years after German forces had marched into Poland 'the British Empire appeared to be tottering on the edge of an unimaginably deep precipice'.[6] The danger was ultimately evaded and the alliance held fast. With the critical support it received from a former member of the original Imperial club, the United States, and the other allies fighting the twin Nazi and Japanese peril, in due course this British Commonwealth alliance triumphed. In victory, however, there followed defeat. Despite the assertions of celebrated post-war British writers, it is actually difficult to argue that the Second World War did not in fact speed up the erosion of the Empire's unity. The very thing which the political leadership in London had claimed it was most seeking to safeguard against, it actually helped precipitate.[7]

This book considers this 'alliance within an alliance', examining what has been an oft disregarded strand of the vast system that was the British Empire. In one of the many wartime debates that focused on Imperial themes it was said of the Dominions that they were 'not conscripted allies like the satellites of Germany', but had come into the war of their own free will and could have left at any time. The idea that they had chosen 'the nobler part of sacrifice and determined to be what Wordsworth called "the bulwark in the cause of man"' made for excellent wartime propaganda.[8] It was also typical of the florid, often overly romantic prose delivered by a generation brought up on Kipling-centric ideals. For all this it was undeniably true that this was a functioning alliance, one that prevailed over determined and ruthless foes. It is the manner in which it operated throughout the Second World War and the pressures and challenges that it faced that will be the focus of this study. Or as Lord Balfour, who played such an important evolutionary role, put it in words found on his desk after his death in 1936, 'Whence comes the cohesion of the Brit[ish] Empire?' His view was that it had drawn its basis on various factors, patriotism, loyalty, custom, religion and race being but a few.[9] What this book will question is whether such an assessment remained true in the climatic years that followed his death. In so doing it does not attempt to add directly to the undoubtedly significant debate about 'Britishness' which has developed in recent years. Bookshelves and magazine racks carry the weight of polemic – some convincing in its tone and evidence, others less so – about the British national character and the relationship with Empire. How it had developed, what it meant to live in the vast territory it covered, to what degree it was not just a nation but a society that drew its very being from the idea of Empire, each of these has been subjected to reinvigorated scrutiny. As one of these texts has effectively argued, Britain was actually never 'a convincing Imperial society' and this seemed particularly true during the inter-war years.[10] Even within this the role and place of the Dominions only occasionally feature; the references are extremely scarce, and when they do appear, they are of an almost entirely secondary nature.

This study makes no specific reference to Eire and its position within the alliance. Britain's wartime relationship with its neighbour is a complicated issue, one that has merited an ever-expanding literature of its own as more information becomes available about the relationship that existed during the war years.[11] In December 1936, the Irish government passed the External Affairs Act and, thus, only recognized the British monarch for certain limited purposes in external affairs. The following year a referendum accepted the proposal of a new constitution and a new country came into existence. The effect of the Eire Constitution of 1937 and earlier pieces of legislation was to remove all mention of the king and to abolish the office of governor-general, substituting as head of the state an elected leader. That same year the other Dominions declared that they did not regard the new Constitution as affecting the position of Eire as a member of the British Commonwealth, and this attitude was maintained, for all intents and purposes, throughout the war.[12] Even so, with this the Anglo-Irish Treaty of 1921 ceased to have any real meaning. The governor-general was duly replaced with a president elected by national suffrage, while the British high commissioner in Dublin's title also changed. However the government of Eire, headed by Eamon de Valera, neither acknowledged any allegiance to the Crown nor would it accept the Dominion conception of the unity of the Commonwealth.[13]

Neutrality was emphatically reiterated by de Valera at the earliest opportunity. A number of contemporary observers pointed to the decision not to support the rest of the Dominions in September 1939 as the most conclusive evidence that this equated fully with independent status in action. The memorandum handed to the British government by Eire's high commissioner in London less than ten days after the war had begun setting out his country's position could not be criticized by the secretary of state for Dominion affairs. He hoped that some effort could still be made to see it modified so that it was less embarrassing to the British Empire, but most other neutral countries had released similar documents clarifying their respective positions. What would not be done, however, was for any formal recognition of neutrality to be offered, an act that would formally dissolve the idea of the indivisibility of the Crown. Nor would it be accepted in London that Eire was no longer a member of the British Commonwealth.[14] Winston Churchill, as the First Lord of the Admiralty up until May 1940, was at the forefront of those who went further and questioned Eire's neutrality and the strategic limitations it placed on the British Empire. The denial of the deep-water ports of Berehaven, Lough Swilly and Queenstown could play a critical role in the coming war against the German U-boats and was pointed to as justification for a possible military response. Dublin's decision was actually of uncertain value as was made clear to the American readership of *Time* magazine with the report of an official who had released the crew of a British seaplane forced down in a remote harbour. As he said to the correspondent, 'sure, we're neutral, but who are we neutral against?'[15] At the end of war aside from Portugal, Spain, Sweden and Switzerland, Eire had managed to remain an officially recognized and respected non-belligerent yet up to 200,000 Irish citizens had actually contributed to the Allied war effort. Britain refrained from mounting an invasion although the idea was often touted and, with the American entry into the war, the Irish state became increasingly isolated and ignored.[16]

There is also no mention of India or Newfoundland. Along with Burma the first of these had been promised eventual Dominion status by the 1935 Government of India Act which followed on from the Irwin Declaration and its first offer of 'the glittering prize' for Indian nationalists. The country had been treated as 'a proto-Dominion' since the latter stages of the First World War; the war that followed would ultimately and finally remove the historic link.[17] The latter was actually a Dominion, Britain's oldest colony, and a member of the original club. It was, however, badly hit by the global economic Depression and the fall in international fish prices, and in 1933 the government was unable to pay the interest charges on its national debt. In place of responsible government it was instead administered by a 'Commission of Government', appointed by a

Royal Commission and consisting of a mixture of British and Newfoundland civil servants, technically making it no longer a Dominion.[18]

Finally there will be no attempt made to specifically explore the actual events of the military campaigns fought by Britain and its Dominion allies during the war in any chronological fashion. There is already an exhaustive literature examining in vast detail every aspect of the war; the numerous Official History volumes that were produced by all of those involved on the Anglo-Dominion side in the post-war years represent an obvious and comprehensive starting point for anybody so minded. Reference is only made to them where they are directly relevant to the struggles that were contested between the Dominion capitals and what were sometimes viewed from these distant vantage points as the twin terrors of Whitehall and Westminster. Such reference is, however, kept to a deliberate minimum; the emphasis instead is, wherever possible, on the political and diplomatic machinations that sometimes tormented the alliance and proved decisive in determining both its operation and effect.

With so little previously published material focusing on this particular Imperial theme, the records stored at the National Archives in London inevitably proved invaluable. Although there are over 40,000 listed files for the DO, the Whitehall department that was most closely involved, with the passage of the Public Records Act in 1958 a widespread destruction of documents followed. Despite the suggestions of some Dominion historians that there was a deliberate pattern in this, the intention being to hide a variety of alleged intrigues, no evidence has emerged to support such claims.[19] While a 1941 defence regulation allowed for the early destruction of sensitive documents, what instead seems to have happened is that owing to constraints of time and space the procedures for reviewing records allowed the individuals involved a great deal of autonomy in the way they conducted their review.[20] As a result certain subject areas are well covered with files copied in triplicate; in others there is virtually no saved material. The result is that in some categories and for certain years there are considerable omissions. Although it is impossible to say with any real degree of accuracy just how many files were destroyed, a cursory examination would place the figure in excess of 50 per cent. It should be remembered that many of these could have been of little or no historical value, while some were undoubtedly copies which have been saved elsewhere. Whatever gaps there were in the narrative have been circumvented by examining other government records held in London, along with a wide variety of overseas archives. A large number of personal archives both in Britain and overseas have also been examined and provided an excellent source of information. Together these largely hitherto unexplored wartime records have allowed for a comprehensive reconstruction of events.

I would like to thank the staff of the following archives and libraries for their assistance with my research: the National Archives, London; the Imperial War

Museum, London; the Liddell Hart Centre for Military Archives, King's College London; the Churchill Archives Centre, Churchill College, Cambridge University; Special Collections, Birmingham University; Special Collections, Durham University; the National Library of Wales, Aberystwyth; Special Collections, University of Nottingham; Special Collections, Cape Town University; Manuscripts and Special Collections, Victoria University, Wellington, New Zealand; National Library of New Zealand (Alexander Turnbull Library and Archives), Wellington; the National Archives, Wellington; the National Archives, Pretoria, South Africa; Special Collections, Toronto University; the Rhodes House Library, Oxford University; Library and Archives Canada, Ottawa; the British Library, London; the Australian Archives, Canberra; the National Library of Australia, Canberra; the Bodleian Library (Department of Western Manuscripts), Oxford; Senate House Library, University of London; the Institute of Commonwealth Studies, London; and finally both the King's College London Library and the Joint Services Command and Staff College Library. Lord Cranborne kindly allowed me to inspect the papers of his grandfather, the Fifth Marquess of Salisbury; in connection with this Robin Harcourt-Williams, the archivist at Hatfield House was most helpful in identifying areas of investigation. Where relevant and appropriate I must thank the trustees or similar of those archives above that have kindly granted permission for the use of selected brief quotations taken from source material within their collections. Such assistance has been gratefully welcomed and is of considerable benefit to the study.

My overseas research would not have been possible without financial assistance received from the John D. and Catherine T. MacArthur Foundation, the New Zealand Ministry of Foreign Affairs and Trade, the Irwin Fund (University of London), the Scouloudi Foundation (Institute of Historical Research, London), the University of London Central Research Fund and the Defence Studies Department Central Research Fund. For the support offered by each of these I would like to offer my sincere thanks. Ms Anne Davies assisted me in collecting various papers in Canberra while Mr Cameron Bayliss carried out a similar invaluable service in Wellington, New Zealand, and I am grateful to both. Stephen Harwood at the National Archives and Vicki Perry at Hatfield House provided valuable assistance in locating relevant pictures for inclusion. Anya Wilson and John Cox both offered editorial and proofing support which helped remove many an error from within the text.

I am indebted to Mr David Steeds who kindly read various draft versions of this work and his exhaustive historical knowledge produced many illuminating and incisive comments and much welcomed advice. Dr Robert Foley, Dr Helen McCartney, Dr Ashley Jackson, Dr Chris Baxter and Dr Kent Fedorowich gave much-needed encouragement when spirits flagged. I am of course thankful to Professor Mike Dockrill, Professor Andrew Lambert, Professor Saki Dockrill,

Professor Sir Lawrence Freedman, Professor Brian Bond and Dr Tim Moreman in the Department of War Studies and Professor Matt Uttley and Dr Stuart Griffin in the Defence Studies Department, both part of King's College London, for their support during my undergraduate studies, doctoral study and subsequent academic career. Thanks also to James Burkes, Chris Roe, Adam Simmons, Daniel Alford and Dr Mark Skidmore whose friendship has been much appreciated. There were many other friends and acquaintances that have kindly 'lent an ear' on occasion and to them I am also grateful. Bob and Joy Wilson provided the most convivial surroundings in East Hanney, Oxfordshire in which to write this book. Ben Hayes, senior editor at Hambledon Continuum, provided inspiration and advice when it was needed – my sincere thanks. Penelope Whitson oversaw the final progress of the manuscript to its culmination.

My fiancée Joanne endured the writing of this book and sacrificed a great deal to support its completion – thank you always. This book is, however, dedicated to my parents. They have supported my scholarly endeavours throughout these many years always without hesitation despite the sometimes less obvious path that I chose to follow. None of this would have been possible without them.

The analysis, opinions and conclusions expressed or implied are those of the author and do not necessarily represent the views of the Joint Services Command and Staff College, the UK Ministry of Defence or any other government agency. Any errors of fact are the responsibility of the author.

The Great Experiment

The inter-war period marked the first serious attempts to provide a scholarly answer to the question 'what were the Dominions?'[1] Although many ideas were put forward, there was, however, an obvious sense of reluctance about precise definitions; during a parliamentary debate in 1921, when David Lloyd George asked for an explanation he was told that to provide one would be dangerous.[2] A decade later, a leading Australian politician expressed what had become an increasingly familiar and commonly held view when he compared his own country's connection with Britain to that of a family relationship. As such he did not 'want the relations of myself and my children to be determined by rules written in a book, to which each of us must refer to discover who is right and who is wrong.'[3] At the same time, there also existed a sense of profound conviction that the Empire had its basis on a higher level. Lord Curzon believed that it was one of the instruments used by Providence for the benefit of mankind. Lord Rosebery, speaking to students at Edinburgh on the British Empire, saw its achievements being directed by human hands and minds but was also certain even the 'most heedless and most cynical must see the finger of the Divine' in its long history. Lord Blanesburgh, speaking publicly in January 1933, had argued that it was essential to preserve the Commonwealth of Nations as 'a civilizing force', one which would if needed be 'the final protector of Western civilization'.[4] Lionel Curtis, one of the leading Imperial thinkers, thought that the British Empire and Commonwealth would eventually evolve into a federation in which the British government would provide the central authority; once again, he believed that this would bring not only order but spiritual fulfilment.[5]

In the early days of colonial governments the Parliament at Westminster was the supreme legislative authority for all British possessions. It had the authority and jurisdiction to legislate and did so for every part of the British Empire. The refusal of settlers in what became the United States of America to recognize the right of the Westminster body to impose taxation upon them when they had their own legislature which had the power to, and did, tax them ultimately led to the American revolution and the end of the first British Empire. The catalyst for the Dominions' creation was, however, John Lambton, more commonly known as Lord Durham, who was sent to what was then termed as 'the Canadas' in 1838 to investigate two rebellions of the previous year and produced, by way of response the following year, his detailed and celebrated 'Report on the Affairs of British North America'. In his view the colonists were capable of having an elected legislature, making their own laws and generally governing themselves, in short a modified form of responsible government with a legislative union of Upper Canada, Lower Canada and the Maritime Provinces. The 'British North American Act' became law on 1 July 1867 and with it a Dominion under the name of Canada was legally established, a confederation of several Canadian provinces agreed upon by Canadian statesmen. This, at least in part, was intended to help safeguard against lingering hostility from south of the border where a Bill had been introduced into Congress proposing that Canada should be made part of the United States. A federated Australia followed although not for over 30 years; 1 January 1901 marked the establishment of 'The Commonwealth of Australia', the end of a process begun in the 1850s when the parliaments of New South Wales and Victoria had been set up by Acts passed in London. New Zealand had formally become a British possession in 1840, as part of New South Wales, a separate colony the following year and then had gained self-government in 1856 with a constitution modelled on Westminster. In 1901 it was approached to enter the Commonwealth of Australia but declined and six years later it was recognized in its own right as a Dominion. For the purposes of this study Cape Colony, Natal and Transvaal joining, officially, in May 1910 with the Orange Free State to create the Union of South Africa was the final step in this developmental process.

There were many advocates who supported such moves. The great British radical Joseph Chamberlain had told the House of Commons in London in 1900 that relations with the self-governing colonies depended 'entirely on their free will and absolute consent'. At the 1902 Colonial Conference his appeal for integration was sober and serious and his eloquence did not conceal his belief in the need to re-examine Britain's Imperial organization and how it worked. As he told his peers at Westminster, the time had come to tell the visiting statesmen that their help was needed. 'The weary Titan staggers under the too vast orb of its fate. We have borne the burden for many years. We think it is time that our children should assist us to support it.'[6] The conference held five years later was designated 'Imperial' rather than 'Colonial', and a new word entered the political dictionaries as it was agreed that the term 'Dominion' would in future be used instead of 'self-governing colonies'. This change in nomenclature was intended to help remove any sense of inferiority, and had a generally positive effect. The eventual outcome of this meeting was something approaching an organized system for collecting, analysing and disseminating information, allocating resources and pursuing a comprehensive grand strategy.[7] At the 1911 Imperial Conference this understanding was first tested as the British foreign secretary, Sir Edward Grey, warned the visiting Dominion leaders about Germany's European intentions and what, if they proved successful, this would mean for the British Empire. The message was now spread that if the centre were to collapse their future would be in jeopardy, and for the first time the Dominions had been 'initiated into the secrets of the foreign policy being pursued'.[8]

The Dominions' subsequent war efforts made it clear they were 'states that were in the process of becoming nations'.[9] In August 1914 the British government announced that it intended to defend Belgium's recently violated neutrality. Although this committed it to war with Germany, none of the Dominions hesitated in offering their broadly unconditional backing of the decision. This support came despite a period during which a number of senior Dominion figures had expressed growing anxieties about their relationship with London. Few doubts existed within the British government, however, that Dominion assistance would be offered.[10] With large populations of, in many cases, only recently arrived British settlers, emotional ties and moral concerns about the wider implications of German actions provided obvious *stimuli* for participation.[11] At the beginning of the conflict the British Empire covered some 13 million square miles, within which there were nearly 500 million inhabitants. From this total the four white Dominions alone provided over 1,309,000 men, sending troops to fight not just in France but to every front in which fighting took place, from Samoa to Siberia. Vimy, Gallipoli and Delville Wood were just some of the celebrated battles in which the Dominion forces played a prominent part. New Zealand alone voluntarily sent about 20 per cent of its male population abroad. And with such a high level of involvement casualties were proportionately large, with 150,000 Dominion troops dead or missing by the conflict's conclusion. Australia, with a total population of only about five million people, suffered more casualties than the United States.[12]

Most scholars agree the war produced confusing signals about the Empire's future for those who fought it; some saw greater cohesion, others divergence.[13] The horrendous casualty figures certainly placed enormous strains on the unity of the wartime coalition. Lloyd George's summons in spring 1917 for the Dominions' leaders to visit London produced high drama, confusion and false hopes, both at the time and during the post-war years. To federationists such as the members of *The Round Table* it seemed the great day was finally at hand. The then British Prime Minister David Lloyd George publicly transformed the discussions with Dominion leaders into what became styled as an 'Imperial War Cabinet', but this was misleading. There was intimate consultation as the Dominion leaders joined their British colleagues for 14 Cabinet meetings. But it remained only consultation; the British War Cabinet retained executive direction of the war. On the other hand few outsiders fully grasped this at the time, especially after Lloyd George added civilian and military advisers to the discussions and promoted it to a full-blown Imperial War Conference. Through 15 formal sessions those at the table discovered first-hand that even when the

British 'family' lined up shoulder to shoulder to fight a titanic struggle the idea of 'Imperial Defence' was still a complicated one. The Australian leader W. M. 'Billy' Hughes did not arrive until mid-April; he was delayed by an acrimonious general election fought mainly over the question of conscription for overseas service. Louis Botha was convinced that his fellow Dominion leaders would be 'a damned nuisance' getting in the way of a busy British government and decided not to attend at all, remaining in South Africa to make sure the fractious Union stayed in the war. He sent in his place a minister who would remain a central figure in the British Empire's subsequent development, General Jan Christian Smuts. Joining them were William Ferguson Massey from New Zealand and Robert Borden from Canada.[14]

Just in time for the Empire to fight the grim attritional battles of 1917, this Imperial War Conference produced the political commitment Lloyd George needed. Dominion power added a vital increment to British economic and military strength everywhere. But practical experience sparked more movement in arrangements for Imperial Defence. At the spring meeting Smuts posed the pivotal question 'How are we to keep together this Empire?' Borden proposed what became the official reply, Resolution IX. The British and Dominion governments agreed the war was too pressing to allow them to sit down and formally adjust 'the constitutional relations of the component parts of the Empire' but also agreed this must be done as soon as the war was over. And any adjustment must start from the agreement the Dominions were 'autonomous nations of an Imperial Commonwealth' with a right to 'an adequate voice in foreign policy' and to 'effective arrangements for continuous consultation in all important matters of common Imperial concern'. Smuts saw the problem: it would do more harm than good to try to combine formal executive centralization in an Imperial Parliament with the self-governing responsibilities of each separate Dominion Parliament. *Round Table* insiders such as Curtis soon realized that cooperation in Imperial Defence was only being pushed forward by sheer military necessity, and this was promoting Dominion nationalism and sense of identity at least as strongly as any common imperial identity.[15]

Post-war analysts focused closely on the constitutional questions raised by this public declaration. For the first time it had defined the Dominions as 'autonomous nations of an Imperial Commonwealth' who had supported the British war only as a result of 'mutual consultation'. The formal use of the new term 'Commonwealth' sparked great attention despite Lord Rosebery having pointed the way at a speech in Adelaide over 20 years beforehand.[16] The New Zealand leader saw it as a major step towards an Imperial Parliament. The Resolution in fact turned out to be a promise by the British to take more seriously Dominion demands for a voice in return for sharing the burden, and not a Dominion pledge to commit more closely to any formal imperial machinery. The British had to make such a promise; the nature of the war dictated it with the rapidly deteriorating military position. The authorities in London needed to placate the concerns of the Dominion leaders who had temporarily relocated to the Empire's capital and help them find some relief from the growing criticism they faced back at home about an increasingly unpopular war. With its formal description of what had previously been a sometime vague relationship, as Curtis and his cohorts had feared, the resolution appeared to ensure that the Dominions would approach their future political dealings with Britain in a different manner. In the Canadian case it was said that this agreement was seen as signalling that the Dominion had reached full nationhood within the Empire. One of the most recent volumes on the subject is no doubt right to conclude that four themes in the end shaped the Great War for the Dominions: their military and economic contributions and the price they paid for both; divisions in public opinion about the war; the central direction of the war; the question of status. By 1918 'the coalition of the usually willing drove to total victory – but then faced the issue of where to go next'.[17]

Following the war's end, the members of the wartime alliance lost no time in demonstrating how they intended to use their newly secured status. Resolution IX had stated that foreign policy would no longer be made solely by Whitehall but, instead, would be based upon 'continuous consultation'.[18] And for the peace conferences that followed the war's end, despite some reluctance by Lloyd George, who had first invited them to London, the right to separate Dominion representation was secured. As a consequence, for the first time, each attending delegate signed the official documents on behalf of his own government. Smuts believed this to be a critical development, equal status had been affirmed by the very fact that Dominion and British statesmen had been present together but at the same time separately.[19] Hostility from the Dominions about the British government's response to the 'Chanak Crisis' in 1922 showed that pre-war security guarantees could no longer be counted upon. Indeed, as the again separate signing of the Locarno Treaty three years later emphasized, each of the Dominion governments was now prepared to exercise to the full the autonomy from British policy it felt it enjoyed.[20]

As important as the decisions reached by the politicians was the process upon which this radical experiment was grounded, the machinery of government that would oversee its management. A pledge phrased in very general terms at the 1907 Conference by the then colonial secretary, Lord Elgin, and given largely in deference to calls from the overseas politicians present, confirmed that the British government would create a governmental body to deal exclusively with the Dominions. Much of the impetus for this move came from the knowledge that many Dominions' statesmen had grown to dislike having to deal with the Colonial Office (CO), the long-established Whitehall department that oversaw relations with them. Alfred Deakin, Australia's second prime minister, was typical in his belief that the department had 'a certain impenetrability, a certain remoteness, a certain weariness of people much pressed with affairs and greatly overburdened, whose natural desire is to say "kindly postpone this; do not press this; do not trouble us; what does it matter. We have enough to do already?"'.[21] Post-conference, a reorganization was duly undertaken and three divisions were created within the CO, one of which was to be solely responsible for administering the relationship with the Dominions.[22] Calls continued both at home and abroad for further reforms to be carried out. During the years immediately prior to the outbreak of hostilities with the Central Powers within Whitehall there was certainly a mounting sense of interest in the Dominions. The CO even found its dominant role challenged by both the Foreign Office (FO) and the Committee of Imperial Defence (CID).[23] A complete re-allocation of ministerial responsibilities and the creation of an entirely separate Dominions' department was suggested at one point but ultimately there was scant support for such proposals.[24]

The experiences of the First World War highlighted the continued need for changes to be made to the way in which the Anglo-Dominion alliance functioned but both wartime governments steadfastly rejected the need for any separate administrative body. Even the more modest suggestion that the title of colonial secretary might be altered to encompass a reference to the Dominions was roundly dismissed. One of the most significant post-war catalysts was the inability or unwillingness of successive governments in London to consult the Dominions over vital foreign policy decisions.[25] This had caused mounting tensions, most notably in 1922 during the dispute between the British and Turkish governments discussed earlier.[26] The disagreements which this caused were not the only source of complaint; Ramsay MacDonald's first Labour government's recognition of the Soviet Union in 1924, without any prior discussion with the Dominions, caused great upset. But with the announcement in November of the same year that Leopold Amery was to become colonial secretary in the new Conservative government, a substantial change in the relationship would not be long in coming. In accepting the position Amery had stipulated to Prime Minister Stanley Baldwin that he 'should be allowed to create a new and entirely separate office to deal with the Dominions'. The new secretary of state had long been a critic of, amongst other things, the CO's continuing responsibility for Dominion affairs and the manner in which it managed relations with the Imperial partners. As far as Amery was concerned the essential point to be borne in mind was that 'the Dominion and Colonial work are essentially different in character, as different as the work of the Foreign Office from that of the Admiralty. The Dominions work is entirely political and diplomatic. The Colonial work is administrative and directive. The one calls for great insight and infinite tact. The other for initiative and drive.'[27] His argument in fact called for London to make it far more apparent that it held its dealing with the Dominion governments to be 'wholly different in character from the administration of the dependent Empire', and he called for the relationship to be formally placed on an equal level.[28]

Despite his drive and passion for the project, it was not until the middle of June 1925, eight months after he had first been appointed, that the 'sudden' announcement was made to the House of Commons of the DO's establishment; a department that would be headed by Amery in addition to his continuing oversight of the CO. Much of the delay had been caused by the Westminster debate that had followed the release of the Scott Committee's report which outlined the financial implications associated with the establishment of a new department.[29] The argument put forward by Treasury Chambers was that this was merely duplicating existing duties and so adding to costs. In defending the necessity for change however, both Amery and Baldwin were quick to point to the differences in the nature of the departmental work involved in Dominion relations, on the one hand, and colonial administration on the other.[30] The colonial secretary's cause was helped, not just by the strong backing he enjoyed from the prime minister, but also the high profile he had established for himself in the public eye.[31] But it remained Amery's sheer determination to see Dominion affairs separately managed which in many ways ultimately enabled him to overcome the many obstacles he faced. Such was his passion that he even managed to persuade at least some of his opponents to soften their hostility towards the 'Foreign Office with a family feeling'.[32] It would still take another five years though before his desire for a truly separate ministry responsible for the Dominions would be fully realized.

From the date of its establishment the DO operated out of the 'Government Offices, Whitehall, North Block', a building of five floors, one below ground level, located at the corner of Whitehall and Downing Street which was the CO's home.[33] Known affectionately by those who worked within it as 'the Office', the DO remained here for the whole of its short existence. The building had originally been erected between 1862 and 1875; the famous architect Sir George Gilbert Scott presiding over a controversial project which initially suffered repeated delays from the interventions of the then foreign secretary, Lord Palmerston. In order that a self-contained area might be found for its new, junior colleague, the CO was reorganized and the DO took rooms in the basement, ground and first floors on the Whitehall front of the building. In the first-floor corridor a partition was erected, largely for the benefit of outsiders, although it was said to be difficult to point to an actual boundary between the two departments.[34] The majority of the department's staff was actually located in a cluster of rooms on the ground and first floors.[35] Some of these overlooked Whitehall and the Cenotaph, the remainder the prime minister's residence at No. 10 Downing Street.[36] Above these rooms there was the library and below the Telegraph Section, both of which were common to the two departments. Although Amery thought it would not create 'the slightest difficulty or possibility of friction', for many years to come some of those moved would 'look with envious eyes at the comparatively few rooms [the DO] occupied'.[37] Conditions were often difficult as space was at a premium and there were few luxuries. During the original construction period the CO's staff had petitioned about the unsatisfactory working conditions they faced. The greatest complaint was that 'the sky was visible through a large hole in the roof with rain and snow running down into one room'.[38] As for the room for the secretary of state for Dominion affairs, on the Whitehall front, it was said to 'lack the splendour of the Colonial Secretary's room and was apt to be noisy'. But despite expenditure on the interior being kept to a bare minimum, a report prepared just before the outbreak of the Second World War nevertheless proved quite complimentary about the building's structure and its well-built, thick, solid walls and high ceilings.[39]

From the outset the department faced considerable challenges. Perhaps the most immediate was the fact that, according to one of the DO's own people, not everybody in Whitehall was willing 'to accept the full implications of equal partnership'.[40] Put in another fashion, this meant that for the majority of the 22 years it existed, with only limited resources and manpower, the department's often difficult job was to try and reconcile the agendas of seven different governments, its own being one of them. Indeed the DO often found itself having 'to act as the conscience of the British government to ensure that they lived up to their part of the bargain'. It was widely derided by other civil servants and even the Dominions themselves were not always entirely sure as to its role.[41] Even one of its own could only conclude that there were no grounds to claim 'that the DO ever loomed large on the stage in Britain itself or that it made any dramatic impact on Parliament, the Press or public opinion. Indeed to a wider public it remained largely unknown … In Parliament, the fixed opinion died hard that [it] was nothing but a Post Office'.[42] Meanwhile its senior cousin strode like a colossus. The Canadian diplomat Lester Pearson offered his assessment from his many years spent watching from Canada House:

> The Dominions Office, in its people, its attitudes, and atmosphere, was similar to other civil service departments. But the Foreign Office was the Holy of Holies, occupied by an aristocratic, well-endowed elite who formed part of the British diplomatic service, and who saw to it that the imperial interest was protected and enlarged in accord with policies worked out in their high-ceilinged, frescoed Victorian offices, to be accepted, they usually assumed, by their political masters in Cabinet and Parliament.[43]

Making matters worse, if the new department were to have any chance of success, it was essential that it maintained a strong voice in the decision-making process of the British government, and at the earliest possible stage. Only then could it keep policy-makers informed of any difficulties that it believed their proposed approach might create. Instead, the DO found itself often faced by a certain degree of distrust and even disdain from within Whitehall, with the commonly made complaint that it was 'much too inclined to take the extreme Dominion, as opposed to the Imperial, point of view'.[44] Hostility such as this made it hard for the department to secure any real measure of influence at the critical stages of policy formulation. Certainly in its early years even some of those who were generally supportive could see the new office as no more than 'a quasi-diplomatic machine', to be short-circuited on urgent occasions.[45] Faced by growing Dominion requests for information from London, the DO almost inevitably therefore tried to achieve a compromise between those parties concerned while facing complaints from each side that its case was not being sufficiently pressed.[46]

Politically there were big developments to match the changes that had taken place in Whitehall. Lengthy negotiations were being conducted behind the scenes between London and various Dominion politicians in which some sympathy was shown towards claims that there should now be a more publicly developed role for them in international affairs. The British rationale, although it was never stated, seemed to be based upon a belief that the Dominions should take greater responsibility for their own problems, leaving the authorities in London free to focus on more important 'Great Power' issues. These negotiations were effectively made public at the 1926 Imperial Conference, with the celebrated opening address given to the Committee of Inter-Imperial Relations by the Lord President of the Council, Lord Balfour. The famous declaration, which Amery claimed to be his idea, identified Great Britain and the Dominions as autonomous communities within the British Empire, united by a common allegiance to the Crown, but freely associated and equal in status to one another in all matters domestic and external.[47] What this did was 'to emphasize the complete equality of status between the United Kingdom and the Dominions. It in fact made the United Kingdom one of the Dominions.' It did not transform self-governing colonies into Dominions, 'that particular transformation had taken place well before the war'.[48]

With the 1931 Statute of Westminster, which attempted to formalize it and other, earlier statements, the Balfour Declaration provided the basis from which analysis of the inter-war Anglo-Dominion relationship would be conducted.[49] The provisions of the statute dealt only with the removal of certain legal restrictions on the power of the Dominions. From this point on Britain could only legislate for a Dominion at its request and with its permission. The Dominions could also repeal or amend Acts that had their origin in Westminster but also affected them. As one report written much later – in 1946 – by a member of the DO put it, this document was a 'landmark' in the British Empire's constitutional development as it established legally the equality of the Dominions with Britain and 'their complete independence to this country, subject only to the binding link of the Crown'. The Sovereign was still common, Britain's king remained their king, they shared a common allegiance to the Crown and the inhabitants of the Dominions were still deemed to be 'British subjects'.[50] Crucially, in Balfour's opinion, it was 'the only constitution possible if the British Empire is to [continue] to exist'.[51] The statute would be adopted formally by each of the Dominions but it would take time. It was an offer for the Dominions to accept and, in the case of the last to do so, New Zealand, it was not until late November 1947 that the Adoption Act was passed finally in its own parliament.[52]

The importance of constitutional change remains influential in any study of the Dominions' relationship with Britain; one argument has it that the statute marked the creation of a 'Third Empire' of real partners, the ultimate triumph of the 'liberal empire' concept. British world power came to depend more and more upon this relationship, the 'economic resources, manpower reserves and political fidelity' of the Dominions turned them into vital Imperial assets.[53] On the other side of the equation migration, commerce, common ideals and sentiment were just some of the factors that kept them bound to Britain.[54] There was now both legal recognition and an administrative apparatus in place but their often complicated national characteristics presented considerable problems for Whitehall. Canada, geographically within the North American continent, contained a growing body of opinion that saw the United States as having become more important to it than Britain.[55] Added to this was the fact that by 1939 over one-third of the population were French-speaking, the vast majority of these living in Quebec. Although liberal opinion in the country as a whole was generally internationalist in outlook, this province tended to be far more isolationist, saving its energies for promoting the idea of the Canadian nation. This meant that in terms of the Dominion idea there was scant support within the province and amongst the significant proportion of the national population that it contained. In an attempt to reconcile the French-dominated province and maintain some sense of national unity, successive Canadian leaders chose to keep consultation with Britain and the other members of the Commonwealth of Nations on an informal level.

The issues attached to the Union of South Africa were much more difficult. In 1906, when he was still just A. J. Balfour, the later Declaration writer had described plans to establish the Union as 'the most reckless experiment ever tried in the development of a great colonial policy' and with good reason.[56] In the first instance, out of a total population of just over 11 million people, fewer than one quarter were of European origin, and of these some 60 per cent were Afrikaans-speaking against 40 per cent English-speaking. In proportion to numbers the latter played a comparatively small part in politics, their interests instead lying predominantly in the domination of industry and commerce. One contemporary writer noted that it was not easy for the English reader to recognize just how fundamentally apart the Afrikaans and English-speaking sections of the population were. As a consequence somebody looking from Britain would be 'apt to look upon South Africa as he does upon any other British possession that will spring like a young whelp to the defence of the Commonwealth and Empire'.[57] In a devastating report written to London in October 1932, the British high commissioner left the Dominions secretary in little doubt about the serious nature of the political situation in the Union. Sir Herbert Stanley's conclusion was stark, 'the doctrine of sovereign independence is being pressed to a point at which membership of the Commonwealth becomes barely distinguishable from an alliance between friendly but foreign Powers'. The British connection was hanging 'upon a slender thread'.[58] Many of the key figures dealing with Whitehall were men with distinctly Anglophobe outlooks who were opposed not just to the Dominion idea but to the British Empire as a whole. Generals J. B. M. Hertzog and Jan Smuts, the old Boer War colleagues, existed in an often uneasy coalition, the United Party overseeing a country which reflected the government, a sometimes unstable collection of peoples differing in language, religion and outlook.[59] Even those individuals who were committed supporters of Britain, most notably Smuts, retained doubts about how the Union should respond in the event of another war in Europe.[60] The full cabinet was only consulted intermittently; the prime minister's preferred style of leadership was to make a statement of his preferences when it met and expect its approval rather than to pursue any attempt at genuine consultation. Hertzog was secretive by nature and had 'the virtues and weaknesses of an autocrat'.[61]

The two Dominions either side of the Tasman Sea, at the south-western edge of the South Pacific Ocean, apparently presented less cause for concern in London. Australia's approach differed considerably from that adopted by both Canada and the Union as its connections with, and indeed dependence on, Britain was far more pronounced. With its 'White Australia' policy actively discouraging the immigration of non-British Europeans, by 1939 nearly 90 per cent of the country's population came from the British Isles. Although the government in Canberra remained proud of the autonomy attached to its Dominion status, during the inter-war years there was a lack of interest in foreign affairs and a general willingness to defer to British policy. The only noticeable exception to this rule was the situation in the Far East. In neighbouring New Zealand, held by many within Whitehall to be 'the dutiful Dominion', there was an even greater sense of commitment to the 'Imperial Idea'.[62] There was no mockery when a senior New Zealand government figure commented that the people of the Dominion tended to look at the Empire through English eyes – 'it is English history that has been important and the parts of the world generally coloured red. The adult

New Zealander knows more of Charles I, of Robert Clive, of Francis Drake and the rest than he does of the Treaty of Waitangi'.[63] Amery had confirmed this view when he returned to London following his 1928 Empire tour and told his cabinet colleagues that in New Zealand he had found support for the Empire to be 'a passion almost a religion'.[64] The government in Wellington was 'emotionally content to be seen as dependent'.[65] The New Zealand high commissioner in London, William Jordan, although sometimes concerned about the direction of British policy also was vehement in his support for the 'Mother Country': as he told a group of British and Dominion statesmen 'New Zealand believed in the British Commonwealth of Nations. It would be beside Great Britain always. If Great Britain was at war, New Zealand would be at war'.[66]

A key feature determining how London and the Dominions reacted to one another was finance and the global economy. In 1897 Canada had been the first of them to introduce a conditional form of 'Imperial Preference' into its tariff. From this point onwards, escalating economic dependency effectively required all of the far-flung Dominions to retain the closest possible link with the fiscal actions of the authorities in London.[67] Figures for trade between Britain and its Empire before 1914 reveal a mixed picture. Less than a quarter of all imports came from the Empire: staples were especially significant with foodstuffs such as tea, cheese and spices all being major imports; certain raw materials were also significant, most obviously jute and tin. Exports were different, however, with just under 200 million pounds, or 37.2 per cent of all goods, going to the Empire. Although India was perhaps the largest market, the Dominions also took a significant share. The Empire was useful as a market for goods that faced major international competition but the pattern of imports was such that the Empire could not offer any real measure of independence to Britain in terms of a guaranteed supply of essential imports.[68] The 'Final Report of the Dominions Royal Commission', released in 1917, recommended that there be greater exploitation of Dominion resources and it is clear that after 1919 the 'white Empire' did play a much greater role in Britain's trade.[69]

The global financial crisis that worsened at the beginning of the 1930s only confirmed this, now placing even greater emphasis on the role played by the British government. With the world's economies in turmoil, at the Imperial Economic Conference held at Ottawa in September 1932, the importance of protective 'Imperial Preference' measures was re-endorsed by all sides. This took place against a backdrop of generally deteriorating political relations and the raising of more questions about the durability of the Dominion idea.[70] But there seemed few economic alternatives to the agreements and although future commercial relations were often worse rather than better, the fiscal policies accepted by the Dominion governments kept them close to London, in mind if not always in heart. Following Ottawa there was a considerable increase in trade, with 41.2 per cent of all Britain's exports between 1934 and 1938 going to the Dominions and one-quarter of all goods imported into the British market. By the Second World War's outbreak the Dominions were effectively no less financially dependent on Britain than they had been 25 years before.

The Dominions' statesmen who visited from distant shores did not always find a warm welcome awaiting them at the Empire's heart. Walter Nash, one of the key political figures of the new administration, had publicly confirmed that 'the Commonwealth and the United Kingdom are loved by the people of New Zealand'.[71] Nonetheless, as his biographer has noted, visiting London pre-war meant dealing with people who could be difficult as 'their frame of mind was usually that of weary, impatient schoolmasters; their tone tart and superior. It did not alter much if they were dealing with a rough ignoramus or someone much better read than themselves.'[72] In light of this it seems hard to disagree with those who have wondered how the DO was able to function at all, prior to 1939, other than in 'mounting salvage operations to limit the harm caused by differences between the Dominions and the British Government'.[73] The inter-war environment had proven to be a sometimes difficult and complicated one for the department, and by the late 1930s the political relationship between the British government and its often apparently disinterested Dominion counterparts had changed. As international tensions worsened, fears grew that the emergence of a significant threat might test the unity of what some now referred to as the 'Commonwealth of Nations'.[74] When meeting in London for the 1937 Imperial Conference, with Germany's increasingly belligerent attitude much in the minds of those present, it seemed that such a challenge had emerged. As the statesmen of the various Dominions indicated that their thinking lay squarely in terms of conciliation, within the DO the focus moved to considering what might happen should this approach fail.[75]

2

War Again

Throughout much of the inter-war period little serious consideration was given to how the Dominions might respond to another European conflict. The established view was that as far as foreign policy was concerned their governments, with their undermanned, under-funded or as yet non-existent External Affairs departments, seemed content to remain dependent on London's resources.[1] Indeed, with the Union of South Africa and Canada both often preoccupied by distracting internal issues and New Zealand, and to a lesser but still significant degree Australia, captivated by the Imperial concept, public criticism of the British approach to international affairs was a rare phenomenon.[2] There had been a post-Statute of Westminster study of the question produced within Whitehall, but the resulting written memorandum focused on questions of formal procedure connected to any future declaration of war and not what form the contribution might actually take.[3] A report had also been prepared by Colonel Sir Maurice Hankey, secretary to the Cabinet and the CID, following his Dominions tour made between September and December 1934; this noted a worrying paucity of military preparations.[4] The Abyssinian Crisis had precipitated some further essentially half-hearted examination of the question the following year, but interest once again faded long before Italian troops finally marched into Addis Ababa. In February 1937 Sir Grattan Bushe, the DO's long-serving legal adviser, finally instigated a serious review when he approached the FO and told his colleagues of his concerns about how the Dominions viewed 'common belligerency'.[5] For many within Whitehall the long-held principle that the indivisibility of the King bound together each Dominion remained standard policy. There had in fact been ample evidence during recent years that this was now something of a fanciful ideal and even though it was mortified that they should be discussing such a possibility, the FO agreed that some form of contingency planning would be sensible.

Overwhelmed with arrangements for the forthcoming Imperial Conference, at this stage nothing more was done.[6] By the time the visiting Dominion ministers had left London and those government officials who had been involved had taken their summer leave, Bushe's question was more urgent. European tensions were worsening and Sir Edward Harding, the DO's most senior official, believed that the British government's most important objective was to ensure the Dominions' active support in the event of any future war.[7] In the last month of the year he therefore instructed Sir Harry Batterbee, who was both his deputy and brother-in-law, to prepare a comprehensive assessment of the Dominions' military and political state of readiness. Another senior department member, whose focus was monitoring foreign policy and defence matters, contributed to the review and shortly before Christmas a draft memorandum entitled 'Probable Attitude and Preparedness of the Dominions in the Event of War' was complete. This, the authors confirmed, was still based broadly on the earlier documents, but details had been updated and individual studies of each of the Dominions and new conclusions had been added. With Batterbee having included his final flourishes, the findings were passed to the FO for further comments and then on to Malcolm MacDonald. The Dominions secretary was also given an additional paper, prepared entirely by Dixon and reserved solely for internal DO distribution, which looked in more detail at the question of 'common belligerency'.[8]

The two documents totalled some 15 pages. A lengthy introduction made it clear that a truly definitive answer to the question was not possible at this stage. Following this was an idea about the kind of conflict that could be expected along with some thoughts on how Britain might become involved. The conclusion was stark; a war in defence of European commitments but without any direct attack on Britain in the first instance would very likely place considerable strains on the Anglo-Dominion relationship. These would be worsened if there had been no international effort to find a peaceful solution involving Britain and the Dominions beforehand. Even at this first drafting stage the authors already had few doubts that, whatever situation might develop, New Zealand and Australia would offer their support but the role that might be played by Canada and South Africa was a cause for real concern. Dixon's internal report advised his colleagues that they needed to retain 'a certain fluidity of conception' when thinking about how the Commonwealth relationship worked. Long-accepted norms did not now apply and this would need to be recognized if Britain was still to gain maximum advantage from the revised position.[9] Batterbee, however, remained more optimistic, telling the secretary of state that he believed it would be 'alright on the night'.[10] As it was impossible to say with conviction what was going to happen, he also agreed that to not make provision accordingly would be foolish. This was 'the policy of the ostrich' and the reports were therefore a sensible precaution. MacDonald clearly listened to this advice and, having no desire to be 'caught napping on this point', he asked that further work be carried out as quickly as possible on these 'important documents'.

Despite the Dominions secretary's instructions and a second meeting with the FO in just the first month of the year, throughout the remainder of 1938 little further progress was actually made towards settling on a policy.[11] It has been suggested that this was because of continuing disagreements within Whitehall over the memorandum's content and even its wording, a debate over form that

Harding had been so anxious to avoid.[12] The issue was certainly a contentious one; further complication came with the Admiralty's interest in the question and what it might mean for the various agreements that granted wartime access to Dominion port facilities. The main barrier to progress though must surely have been international events themselves as Germany pushed its claims more and more forcefully during the course of the year. Following Austria's incorporation into the expanding Nazi Reich in March 1938, MacDonald warned the foreign secretary, Lord Halifax, that his department was struggling under the pressure of the work it was handling. His staff found themselves in 'perpetual, non-stop touch with all [of the Dominions] on all international questions', leaving little spare time for other tasks.[13] Although the DO had doubled from its initial size, by 1938's conclusion the total available manpower was still fewer than 70 people. Germany's claim to Czechoslovakia's Sudeten areas later that year, and the crisis it provoked, brought still more distraction. The role played by the Dominions in helping shape British policy during this period has been well-explored.[14] According to some contemporary commentators this was the nearest they had come since 1919 to sharing a common foreign policy with Britain. Reviewing the evidence as the war drew to an end, the renowned Cambridge Don Professor E. L. Woodward, in preparing the wartime diplomatic history, concluded that the Dominions' attitude had, in fact, rarely proved decisive in helping sway the policy of the London government.[15] Certainly at the time the key DO staff concluded that only New Zealand still clung to the idea of the League of Nation's 'collective security' banner and it alone could be counted on for military support. For the others it was a policy based upon the offer of concessions to the German leadership. Australia would probably have fought, but only reluctantly, Canada after some consideration would have decided not to, the Union of South Africa would have almost certainly remained neutral.

In the face of this, Whitehall's lack of enthusiasm for a memorandum that carried with it potentially critical ramifications was quite clear and there continued to be little real progress made in its preparation. The Attorney-General finally gave his approval in late September 1938 for the British high commissioners in their respective capitals to be sent a preliminary summary of the previous year's findings. The first major development in months, even this only outlined a few of the more general thoughts that had been put forward.[16] Batterbee was certainly partly to blame. After several months of rumours, in July 1938 it was confirmed that he was being sent to New Zealand to become the first British high commissioner.[17] His personal correspondence clearly reveals the degree to which, following the announcement, his attention seems to have often subsequently been preoccupied. There were numerous arrangements to be made for the considerable relocation he and his wife were facing and the work he was required to undertake prior to his departure was significant.[18] Making matters worse was Hankey who, with his extensive knowledge of Anglo-Dominion affairs, had been asked to generally help move things forward. He singularly failed in this task and his appointment in fact served only to aggravate an already complicated process.[19]

Not until the beginning of 1939 was there finally some substantive improvement in the position. Batterbee had cleared his desk and gone, and at the first meeting held without him at the beginning of January a much greater sense of urgency could be seen. Representatives from the DO and FO, joined by colleagues from the Cabinet Office and Admiralty, debated the main question: could there be 'a half-way house between neutrality and participation' if Britain was at war.[20] Harding was in the chair and stressed the need for discretion; the Dominion governments were not to know that such a possibility was even being considered. He was worried at what the future held, wondering whether the Royal Navy might even find itself forced to seize South African ports in order to guarantee unhindered wartime access to them. His Cabinet Office counterpart was much less concerned; Sir Edward Bridges was certain that even the least enthusiastic Dominions would merely mark time before joining Britain. The FO appeared generally uninterested about the issue, as had been the case during the previous 12 months, and its recommendations were few.[21] Batterbee's departmental responsibilities had been assumed by another long-serving civil servant, John Stephenson, and he fortunately appeared a more dynamic force.[22] The high commissioners in the Union of South Africa and Canada were now provided with the complete draft memorandum and asked for any relevant comments.[23] It would take six weeks before the last of these arrived but they only served to emphasize the potential for disaster that appeared to exist.[24]

The level of cooperation from within Whitehall was still, however, at this stage far from encouraging. While the War Office and Air Ministry were 'probably willing to fall in line' with the DO strategy, the same was not true of the Admiralty which, having contemplated what it had heard at the previous meeting, now 'tended in the direction of attempting to force the hand of the Dominions'. This confrontational approach ran entirely counter to the advice of the DO but political niceties appeared not to be a concern for the First Sea Lord's department, who warned it would take its case to the CID where it clearly believed it would be treated sympathetically. In exchanges such as these it was obvious that, despite the DO's awareness and its long-running efforts to better educate its colleagues, there were few within Whitehall who recognized the true position of the Anglo-Dominion relationship. 'Common belligerency' had long since become a concept that could not be taken for granted, but few seemed to understand this fact. To echo the point, Sir Thomas Inskip, who had replaced MacDonald in January 1939, was told by Halifax that the Dominions should be expected to 'trust us to draw a just conclusion from the reports we receive'.[25] Bridges also still remained generally optimistic about the future position. Only after repeated reminders, at the beginning of March the Cabinet Office had finally submitted a formal statement and this argued that the Dominions would surely recognize that 'supreme control can only be exercised by those at the centre' if war broke out.[26] Further evidence of such thinking came with Neville Chamberlain's dramatic policy shift mid-March following the German seizure of the rump Czech state. The strategy the British leader now adopted had been decided upon without any prior discussion with the Dominions and was almost entirely at odds with what the DO thought they might have best received.[27]

The lack of any advance warning of this new approach caused considerable rancour amongst Dominions' politicians, and the high commissioners in London were the most visibly petulant. They believed their role during the Sudeten crisis had been decisive, despite there being little evidence to support such a view, and this, consequently, had led them to develop a much higher opinion of their own importance.[28] Six years previously the South African member of the group, Charles te Water, had bluntly informed the then secretary of state that if there was another war 'none of the Dominions would follow' Britain.[29] He had not altered his opinion since and buoyed by his self-perceived value, and with his Canadian counterpart Vincent Massey to support him, he now angrily urged that Germany should be given one more 'chance of saving face'.[30] Perhaps as a result of this verbal assault delivered to the unfortunate Inskip, te Water and the other high commissioners were given some degree of advance warning at the end of March that a security guarantee was to be offered to Poland. They were also told about British thinking on the future of Danzig. None of this helped mollify them.[31] When the news was made public, no formal comments came from the Dominion capitals but privately there was deep unhappiness. Jan Smuts, in his role as South Africa's deputy prime minister, was 'staggered' and felt that the decision was 'mere surrender to panic' and made war 'inevitable'. William Mackenzie King, the Canadian leader, also thought the decision amounted to 'a conditional declaration of war' but seemed more upset that it had been reached without prior consultation with Canada or any of the Dominions.[32]

At this point efforts to finalize the memorandum were once again renewed and with the Admiralty's concerns appearing to have been resolved, towards the end of April a final draft document was at last ready to be issued to the principal Whitehall departments involved.[33] Forty pages long, it still made little reference to New Zealand and Australia, the focus remained the likely reactions of Canada and the Union of South Africa but the earlier conclusions had changed.[34] Telegrams sent from mid-February onwards by the British high commissioners in Ottawa and Cape Town were said to have become progressively more optimistic in tone. 'Force of circumstances' would now dictate the Dominions response; in the Canadian case this meant almost certain participation, South Africa would 'probably' offer its support. In arriving at this new assessment any of the high commissioners' comments which could have been seen to offer cause for concern were overlooked. The clearest example of this were those warnings from Sir William Clark about almost inevitable 'delays' and 'confusion' in the Union that would follow any British declaration of war.[35] The report also chose to ignore the advice being offered by the Dominions' high commissioners in London that their respective prime ministers still held some significant anxieties. The news that a possible alliance was being considered with the Soviet Union did little to improve their mood.[36]

With the Dominion governments showing little enthusiasm to make any public declaration of support for London's increasingly aggressive stance and the high commissioners still insisting on the need for further diplomacy, at the end of May the memorandum was finally published.[37] So sensitive were its contents that distribution was restricted to those ministers who would be most concerned with the war's conduct.[38] At the same time, in the various Dominion capitals, the British representatives were also warned to make no mention of the document's existence until such time as it was necessary. Inskip appears to have had only the faintest awareness that it was being prepared; Harding sent him a copy but attached a much more optimistic view about its conclusions than he had done before. There was certainly a visible and most genuine desire amongst the senior DO staff to avoid war hence, perhaps, his hope that there would 'never be occasion' to test the findings and, if there was, those difficulties that were anticipated would 'not, in practice, prove unduly serious'.[39] The Secretary of State, by way of response to this new information, did little more than commend the quality of the work.[40]

Some of the final conclusions that were put forward made a good deal of sense. There was little reason to doubt that the governments in Canberra and Wellington would offer their support. Considerable emotional ties still existed between the two countries and Britain, which helped to guarantee that there was significant public support for British policy. Their security – there had been an almost total neglect of defence expenditure during the inter-war period – and economic welfare – neither Dominion held significant gold or foreign currency reserves – also helped safeguard their connection to Britain. This financial aspect was most critical and New Zealand's position was especially dire. The 1938 global financial depression had brought with it severe balance of payments constraints and the requirements for borrowing were consequently heavy. On the last day of March 1939 the Dominion's public debt stood at NZ£304 million, of which over half was held in Britain. Despite having pledged publicly not to do so, the socialist New Zealand government turned to London for help and Walter Nash, finance minister, was sent to negotiate directly for an agreement leaving behind him 'a tattered utopia'. He found both Whitehall and the City's financial institutions disinclined to help; the loan was eventually agreed, as much because of the coming war than any real sense of British willingness to help, but it was on stringent terms.[41] There was also a compelling argument to be made that, despite its much greater measure of economic independence and the uncertainties that accompanied Mackenzie King's leadership, Canada could most likely be counted on to fight alongside Britain. King George VI's visit to Canada earlier in 1939 had been a great success, regenerating a great deal of popular support both for the British monarchy and the 'Imperial Idea'. With the recognition, albeit tacitly in some circles, of the degree to which Canada now lay within the United States' sphere of influence, further helping the position was the hardening American attitude towards the Axis powers.[42]

By far the greatest problem, despite what the memorandum had to say, was trying to say what would happen in South Africa. There were similar economic, defensive and emotional factors to those which had influenced Australia and New Zealand. As with Canada, there was also a substantial Nationalist group to be considered which counted amongst its ranks the South African leader, General J. B. M. Hertzog. This largely Afrikaans section of the population was similar to the Quebecois of French-Canada in having no great love for the government in London.[43] The DO's fears about what all of this might mean had, however, finally spread. Within the FO there existed the 'Dominions Intelligence Department' (DID), established in 1926 to prepare information on foreign affairs to be passed to the Dominion governments. It had a small staff comprising a head supported by an assistant and three juniors who produced daily 'Intels' surveying the international situation. With the worsening European position this service had been substantially stepped up, so that by 1939 huge numbers of documents were being generated for Dominion consumption.[44] Sir Alexander Cadogan was listed as being in charge but operating at the centre of British foreign affairs he had many other more important responsibilities, and much of the daily work fell to Robert Hadow. He and the South African high commissioner's private secretary had discussed what might happen in April, and this had left him sufficiently confident to declare afterwards that South Africa would 'most certainly come in should we be involved in war'. Similar statements had been made by a number of his FO colleagues during the previous months but, following the announcement that negotiations would take place with the Soviets, Hadow began to receive information from the Dominions that made his earlier confidence evaporate.[45] He warned Cadogan that there was a risk of South African neutrality at the outset of war, 'perhaps only for a while but with dangerous possibilities'. This was dismissed as being overly dramatic and nothing more was said within the FO of the Dominion and its likely stance.[46]

The reality was that the memorandum had been broadly accepted within Whitehall as being accurate in its conclusions and an ominous lack of any discussion about what the near future might hold now settled upon the corridors of

British power. During the summer months, aside from a few messages from the Tasman governments, the Dominions also had little to say about the deteriorating international situation.[47] The high commissioners working in London were similarly restrained and appeared to have run out of angry observations to make.[48] The volume of communications passing between London and the Dominion capitals had not slowed, it was just that it had little to do with how this political alliance might function if the worst happened and the newly agreed security guarantees were tested. As the 'July rush' abated many officials in the DO went on leave but the lull was quickly shattered by the surprise announcement that Germany and the Soviet Union had concluded their non-aggression pact.[49] With the notable exception of the New Zealand representative Bill Jordan, the Dominion high commissioners found this news difficult to accept, and they were roused once again to demand that every effort be made to hold further negotiations with the German leader Adolf Hitler.[50] Even the mention of 'appeasement' remains a source of intense emotion to some historians, but in these daily meetings there was no shortage of support for the idea that the Führer should be given whatever was needed to induce him not to go to war. Any chance of securing support for this was destroyed by Stanley Bruce, and his clumsy attempts orchestrated from Australia House to apply pressure on the Polish authorities and make them accept Germany's demands. All this did was to much reduce the British prime minister's confidence in the Australian, something which was apparently 'never very high' to begin with.[51]

South Africa's support was, however, now at last a subject of very real discussion and there were serious doubts. Fortunately Clark had not shared in the general sense of stupor that had blighted the spring and summer's consideration of this potentially calamitous matter. Since the memorandum's publication his comments made to London had actually given little reason to suppose that it could be assumed automatically that the government in the Union would blithely follow the British lead. In a telegram sent during the last week of August, the DO was again warned, only now even more urgently, that this was most definitely the case, particularly as support for the Nationalists had gained ground in the preceding weeks. The Nazi-Soviet pact, it was reported, could also have a considerable impact, creating the feeling that there had been 'mismanagement' on the part of the British government, and encouraging people into the arms of those who favoured neutrality.[52] Clark's information had been consistently clear; under Hertzog's leadership there was no sense of 'common belligerency' among sizeable elements of local opinion. Many within the large Nationalist Afrikaans-speaking minority, of which the South African leader was one of the more moderate members, were openly sympathetic to German actions in Europe.[53] Hertzog had stated his position publicly at the 1937 Imperial Conference and afterwards when he had rejected the idea of his country's involvement in any future European war but such warnings had not been heeded in London. Even in the hitherto all-confident FO, there were now those willing to admit that the situation had 'suddenly' become worrying.[54]

As Smuts remained a firm supporter of the need to oppose Hitler all was not lost, however, and he quickly became the central figure in events that unfolded in Cape Town during the first days of September. Despite considerable tensions and even the apparent risk of civil war, he was able to force a parliamentary debate to resolve the impasse that had formed between him and Hertzog. Subsequently he would be criticized by the country's Nationalists for what they described as his ambiguity; he had actually been just as consistent as Hertzog in saying, from at least mid-1938 onwards, that it would be in the South African parliament where the matter would be decided, whether there would be war or neutrality. This view, as quickly became clear, was entirely at odds with that held by the prime minister, who believed that he did not need to consult parliament if he decided not to go to war.[55] The English-speaking section of the population in any case strongly supported Smuts and his endorsement of Britain's new warnings to Germany and Hitler's obvious coveting of South West Africa, the neighbouring former German colony which South Africa had administered since 1915, helped weaken the Nationalists a little.[56] What proved critical though was an administrative oversight whereby the South African Senate's life had inadvertently expired and a formal assembly was required for it to be renewed.

Clark also supported and encouraged Smuts as much as he could but this essentially took the form of moral support and the message that Britain would back him all the way. Immediately following Britain's declaration of war he had received an urgent telegram listing the minimum British requirements from South Africa. This asked that there should be no declaration of neutrality and for an expression of general readiness to cooperate in practical measures and was an indication of just how worried Chamberlain was that Hertzog would keep out of the fight.[57] Had this happened it would have been a huge propaganda victory for Hitler, one which could have had a potentially enormous adverse effect not just on the other Dominions and France but also on the United States and neutrals in general. Smuts neatly summed up the dilemma that faced him writing to a close friend afterwards: 'With us there is no enthusiasm for Poland, and less for Danzig and the corridor. Moreover neutrality is even more firmly held as faith than in the Middle West of USA. And on the other side (which happens to be my own) there is the difficulty to understand how in the long run we could possibly keep out of the fight.'[58] Hadow had noted that 'in the end – with some hesitation – I expect Smuts' view to prevail', and events ultimately proved him to be correct.[59] It was not moral ties that mattered, so much as strength of character and political experience and the South African was not found wanting when it counted most.[60] In the highly charged atmosphere that surrounded the parliament building in Cape Town, it was Hertzog who made the critical mistake. Having failed to secure a majority in favour of remaining neutral he approached the Governor-General, Sir Patrick Duncan, himself a former leading South Africa politician, and asked that he dissolve parliament. This Duncan refused to do as he believed Smuts had a majority of support still and he asked that he form a new government which he did.[61] Although pleased that he had prevailed, the newly appointed South African prime minister was clearly also saddened by the outcome of the crisis and the implications it had for the country at large. For on the other side of the political spectrum, there remained an equally entrenched view that Smuts had betrayed the country and this meant the support he could offer Britain, at least in the opening stages of the war, would be of a highly limited nature.[62]

Thus the Imperial coalition was complete once more and the Dominions again went to war in support of the British Empire and the policies of the government in London. None had been signatories to the 1936 Anglo-Egyptian Treaty or to the renewed guarantee of Belgian neutrality in the same year. Nor were any of them directly involved in the negotiations at Munich two years later. Still more recently, it has been seen that no Dominion minister had put his name to the Polish guarantee in March 1939 or to those given to Roumania and Greece in April 1939 and the later alliance with Turkey. Despite this the Dominions chose to fight and at the forefront was New Zealand.[63] Because of the time difference the war telegram from the British government did not arrive until 11.45 pm, as a result of which confirmation of its support was not announced publicly until the early hours of the following day. It was therefore decided by the Cabinet in Wellington to time the proclamation so that retrospectively it should be deemed to have had effect from the exact moment when Britain had declared war. When it reached the House of Representatives, the motion approving and confirming the declaration of a state of war was passed without a dissenting voice and immediately afterwards everybody rose to sing the national anthem. In a public address the New Zealand Prime Minister Michael Joseph Savage famously confirmed that, 'we range ourselves without fear besides Britain. Where she goes, we go; where she stands, we stand.' Robert Menzies, the Australian prime minister, also pledged his unconditional support in similarly jingoistic fashion: 'one King, one cause, one flag' was the cry from Canberra. Canada followed a few days later after having discussed the matter within the parliament in Ottawa, although Mackenzie King had formally guaranteed Canada's support even before the British declaration of war. It is alleged Hitler burst out laughing when he heard South Africa had declared war against him and if he had known the full facts about political tensions in Cape Town he may well have laughed a little harder.[64] Nonetheless it was an important fillip, and allowed for the creation of what could now be termed the Anglo-Dominion alliance.

Despite its bland and often non-urgent tone, the conclusions of the often overlooked review of the Dominion's probable reaction to another European war were, in the event, almost entirely correct. The politicians and civil servants within Whitehall could therefore offer public expressions of relief that the sanctity of the Empire had remained intact in spite of the fact that, in many cases and only up until a few weeks beforehand, they had never anticipated the level of tension that would actually occur. Probably typical of the reaction of many was that of Batterbee, now ensconsed in his official role in New Zealand. When he heard the announcement that war had been declared, one of those in the room with him described how he 'slumped sideways in his armchair, with his head bent and his hand over his eyes … a broken man overwhelmed by the tragedy'.[65] Like many of those in Whitehall, also hearing the news that British policy had failed, he had apparently remained hopeful to the last that there would not be another European war. Walking home at three in the morning in the knowledge that the British Empire was once again at war, he recalled how, at the outbreak of the First World War, it had been his responsibility to send the telegram to the Dominions advising them that the King had declared war on their behalf.[66] They were all in the fight again but the manner in which the self-governing members had shown their support had in some cases been very different to how it had been done 25 years beforehand. Although Batterbee did not say so, the omens for the alliance's future unity already did not appear entirely optimistic.

3

Controlling the Alliance

The first week of September 1939 was a tumultuous and often hectic one within Whitehall.[1] For the only recently confirmed Anglo-Dominion alliance the most significant development was the appointment of a new wartime secretary of state. Having sat on the back-benches since he resigned as foreign secretary the previous year, Anthony Eden was asked to replace Inskip. Chamberlain viewed the DO as a not 'very absorbing' department, but 'Honest Tom', as he was known by his barrister colleagues, had proven to be an almost entirely ineffective minister.[2] Eden's decision to agree to take over from him and head what was clearly held to be a lowly political department was viewed, both at the time and subsequently, as a surprise.[3] Even the new minister described his position as 'highly anomalous not to say humiliating' but he prospered in the role. Although it did not warrant a permanent seat in the War Cabinet, it was quickly announced that Eden would attend the majority of meetings of the 'inner sanctum' in order to ensure that the Dominions were properly supplied with information. Eden would even be allowed to raise Dominions related-issues when he saw fit. This understanding, confirmed at the very first War Cabinet meeting was no doubt, at least in part, designed to counter fears within official circles that to not do so would be 'a political mistake of the first order'.[4]

There was no shortage of things to do for the new Dominions secretary. The war was the most obvious and pressing question and the practical challenge of how to turn this new alliance into an effective fighting force. Germany's attack on Poland quickly demonstrated the effectiveness of a new kind of warfare as the *Blitzkrieg* shattered the Poles' resistance in a matter of only weeks. During the autumn months much of Eden's time, and that of his departmental colleagues, was therefore spent talking with the British chiefs of staff about military matters. The situation was undeniably pretty dire: the Dominions had little to offer. The best contribution they could make was on the naval side with some destroyers, cruisers and a few other smaller vessels but there were no more than 20 of these in total. There were also a number of squadrons of fighters and bombers but these were largely obsolete in design and, once again, were relatively limited in number. Finally there were troops, although these were mostly in the form of local militias designed for rudimentary self-defence rather than the professional forces needed to deter the *Wehrmacht* juggernaut.[5]

Nonetheless the Dominion governments were not short on enthusiasm and London was quickly approached for guidance; Canberra had asked the DO as early as the third day of the war what it could do to help.[6] South Africa's involvement was still considered too uncertain to gauge at this stage, so the chiefs of staff in Whitehall ordered the readying of three separate papers outlining the assistance that would be welcomed from each of the other fighting Dominions. There were separate sections for Maritime, Air and Land, and each paper was broadly the same. It was asked that, if possible, major vessels should be turned over to the Admiralty, naval bases readied as Fleet harbours and steps taken to commence ship building, especially of smaller escorts and minesweepers. The chiefs of staff anticipated there would be difficulties in finding sufficient pilots and aircrews if intensive air operations developed in Western Europe.[7] It was therefore suggested that instead of forming and training complete units for despatch overseas, the Dominions should concentrate solely on training to provide a pool of aircrew which could be incorporated into British units and then formed into national bodies when sufficient officers and personnel were ready. Finally, each Dominion was encouraged to provide an Expeditionary Force, although it was acknowledged that this might not be possible politically at the outset. This last point was critical as would become even more apparent just weeks later when the War Cabinet agreed to the Land Forces Committee's proposals that the British Army be built up to 55 divisions within two years. With the Dominions earmarked to provide a total of 14 divisions, this represented an enormous burden on their manpower and resources.[8] Speaking in the House of Representatives in Canberra, Menzies had announced that Australia would raise a force of 100,000 men but there was no date on when they would be sent.[9] New Zealand also was training troops, albeit a much smaller force and, once again, it was not clear when they might embark.[10]

Both announcements were, in fact, entirely in line with the advice issued by the chiefs of staff in London. While the Japanese position remained unclear Anzac troops were not to be despatched abroad, but should instead proceed with training within their own shores. This was not, however, what certain politicians in Westminster wanted to hear. The problem Eden faced was that a number of his colleagues seemed either ignorant or unwilling to face facts about just how little the Dominions could offer. Even when the information was put before them in considerable detail – a memorandum was presented to the War Cabinet in mid-October outlining the progress each was making – there remained a belief that more could be done. This was a view most prominently held by the First Lord of the Admiralty and the Secretary of State for War. Drawing attention to how quickly similar contingents had reached Europe during the previous war, Winston Churchill argued that Dominion troops had to be in France by the opening of the anticipated 1940 spring campaign. Leslie Hore-Belisha concurred that there needed to be a much greater land contribution from the Dominions than they appeared to contemplate as there was a critical psychological value in getting Imperial manpower to the frontline. Both ministers felt strong pressure should be exerted on the governments concerned to encourage a greater response.[11]

Whitehall opinion did not universally agree with this argument. In certain circles, mostly within the Treasury, providing greater financial and material support to help the Dominions develop some kind of credible military contribution was not viewed enthusiastically. Australian requirements, for example, were described as being 'of a much lower order of priority as compared with our own' and the point was made that the Dominions 'ought to keep within our own priority scales'.[12] Much the same was true in the case of New Zealand, while South Africa's requests, albeit admittedly wildly overstated in terms of what might reasonably be expected, were dismissed even by the War Office (WO) who suggested instead 'tokens' and 'gestures'.[13] At the very least, the Treasury urged, the government in Canberra should be encouraged to buy goods through a purchasing commission, which it was anticipated would shortly be established to prevent internal competition developing. This would mean the Dominion's lists of military requirements would be presented to London for scrutiny and a decision about what they could and could not have. A desire to prevent a drain of dollar reserves influenced much of this thinking but grudging talk of gestures and demands for oversight surely boded ill for the future.

A keenly anticipated contribution was the proposed Empire Air Training Scheme (EATS). Vincent Massey and Stanley Bruce, the Canadian and Australian high commissoners in London, had heard of the anticipated future shortages of aircrew and put forward a proposal that they felt would allow the Dominions to visibly demonstrate their support for the military effort.[14] This was warmly welcomed by ministers in London initially but soon revealed itself to be fraught with difficulties. A mission sent to Ottawa in early October to confirm the scheme's details, came perilously close to failure. Training organizations were to be established in Australia and New Zealand, but Canada was prepared to accept the lead role providing the greatest number of trainees and covering the costs this would create. There was a price in return, however, as it was made plain to the War Cabinet back in London that Mackenzie King wanted an agreement that this would be accepted as Canada's 'decisive effort'. During the First World War the scale of losses of manpower had created a huge political crisis over the need for conscription, and the Canadian prime minister was anxious to avoid there being any repeat.[15] The Cabinet reacted angrily to this demand, leaving Eden to do his best to calm his colleagues. Despite Mackenzie King's very public statements to the contrary, the Dominions secretary assured them that there was in fact considerable Canadian support in favour of sending troops.[16] In late October it was announced that the Canadian First Division would leave for England

early in December and the rancour quickly passed.[17] Mackenzie King, faced by
increasingly hostile domestic opinion, had been forced to send an expeditionary
force. Lester Pearson, a member of the Canadian High Commission in London,
recognized that his countrymen 'would countenance no such half-way involvement; Canadians would not accept a role to guard their bridges and their borders,
to produce munitions and war supplies while British soldiers did the fighting
against the Nazis'.[18] Canada's wily leader would extract suitable recompense
though when the EATS was finally agreed two months later with very favourable
financial terms for its Canadian hosts.

With the news that Canadian troops were heading for Britain it was thought
Australia and New Zealand would soon follow suit.[19] The threat from Japan and
Italy was assessed to be receding and, with this no longer preventing troop move-
ments, Chamberlain decided that the time had come to apply some pressure.[20]
The War Cabinet agreed that the sending of a second Anzac force to France
would have an effect 'on the Empire, on the French, on neutrals and the Germans'
which would be 'out of all proportion to the number of troops engaged'.[21] The
difficulty that remained was that the Australians were still uncertain of the merits
of such a move.[22] Richard Casey, a senior Australian minister visiting London
for a meeting of Dominion ministers, told the British officials that there were
lingering doubts in Canberra over Japanese intentions; an assurance that Britain
would send capital ships to Australia when necessary would remove such fears.
As will be seen, this British commitment to providing security in the Far East
and Pacific had been a long-running theme that had dominated the Anglo-
Dominion pre-war relationship. Now, while Eden urged that reassurance be given,
Chamberlain remained intent on doing everything possible to avoid any such
guarantee.

Such reluctance was not, however, shared by Churchill who seemed more than
happy to provide promises of future assistance if it meant more Dominion troops
would be available now. The Australians remained unconvinced by the First
Lord's suitably vague assurance but his oratorical soothing was better received
by the New Zealanders. The Wellington government agreed to send its troops
not because of any new confidence in London, so it announced, but because they
had insufficient training facilities left in New Zealand and had to move the first
brigade of troops. In so doing Savage, the Dominion's now seriously ill prime
minister, ignored an agreement that said he would maintain close contact with
his counterpart in Canberra about defence measures. Menzies was seriously
embarrassed, the decision by his neighbours left him little option other than to do
the same or risk what effect Australia's continuing absence might have upon his
own prestige and that of his country.[23] Ministers and civil servants in Whitehall
could, as a result, claim success in having persuaded the Tasman Dominions
finally to agree to send troops. The truth was that this was not a convincing

performance, based as it was on the back of what would later be exposed as a worthless guarantee. It was also a deal that would have hugely adverse political ramifications for the alliance in the years to come.

Dealing with military issues was not Eden's only work, there were also significant administrative matters requiring his department's urgent attention. From the outset of the war the Dominions had asked for some clear idea of what the Allies were fighting for, deeming it as essential to maintain domestic support. Chamberlain and many others within his Cabinet were wary of making such a declaration and despite the request being made repeatedly, on each occasion it was ignored. The British authorities argued that to establish the precise details of what the coalition was fighting for during the early stages of what would most likely be a long and fluid war could have a limiting effect; would the aims, for example, include a return to the pre-war European status quo, a state that was widely accepted as not only being impossible to accomplish but also extremely naïve. By the same token would the enemy be Hitler alone, Germany as a nation or Germany and the Soviet Union who were both now seen as aggressor states. Chamberlain had himself recognized that his adversary might try and weaken the Allies' resolve.[24] With the conquest of Poland completed, as anticipated Hitler delivered a speech in which a limited peace proposal was put forward. The War Cabinet played for time in order to allow the Dominions to have their say which they all did, reiterating the common theme that this was a war to defeat aggression. Menzies described the offer as being little more than 'a blustering attempt to justify the war'; the Canadian government offered no official response but the press was unanimous in its condemnation of a 'blood-stained peace', while much the same was written in the South African press, even amongst the nationalist Afrikaans newspapers.[25] The high commissioners, however, seemed keen on pursuing the option and pressed Eden for his support. Chamberlain was very upset at their attitude and the Dominions secretary found himself in a difficult position, trying to ensure his charges did not feel they were being ignored while trying to make them see sense.[26]

While this created some short-term discomfort, the debate within Whitehall about how much information should be given to the alliance partners presented a more enduring problem. It might seem incredible, but this in fact proved a highly controversial and emotive question and would remain so for the entirety of the war. Its origins, however, lay firmly during the inter-war years with the Dominions' confirmation as self-autonomous actors within the international system. At the 1926 Imperial Conference it had been agreed that they would subsequently have individual responsibility for foreign policy but, lacking money, experience and manpower, there continued to be a dependence upon London for information about events as they happened.[27] For some within Whitehall, notably Malcolm MacDonald, this was a more than satisfactory position;

Dominion leaders could be 'kept fully informed about developments' and their responses helped influence British policy.[28] The reality was something quite different, as had been demonstrated during the various guarantees and crises of recent months.[29] On several occasions even Inskip had been angered about how much was being withheld from the DO for onward distribution, so much so that one of his last acts prior to his replacement was to contact the FO and remind it that telegrams should be made available at the earliest possible opportunity.[30] His successor was in complete agreement. Although meetings between the high commissioners and the Dominions secretary had taken place before the war, most notably during the Munich crisis, Eden took responsibility for turning them into a daily and much more organized event. One of the DO officials who sat in on them believed that this succeeded in creating 'a remarkable atmosphere of reciprocal frankness and common purpose'.[31] Daily Cabinet discussions and the decisions that had been reached formed the basis of these meetings. So successful were they that the Dominions' representatives quickly turned them into an opportunity to raise matters that concerned them or their governments, and Eden relayed these to the War Cabinet.[32]

Another early change, again taken within days of war being declared, was the creation of a new series of telegrams. The 'Circular DW', issued by the DO, would ultimately remain a staple source of information for the Dominions throughout the duration of the war. A daily summary of the progress of the military situation, 'of the highest secrecy', collated from various Whitehall departments it was intended to be viewed by the Dominion representatives prior to being sent on to their respective governments.[33] Another step was the establishment of the grandly titled 'Committee for Dominion Collaboration'.[34] Its initial report concluded that improvements would be needed to strengthen how the alliance functioned. It was proposed that, in addition to the new meetings and telegrams, the high commissioners and the War Cabinet should consult directly when needed, probably once each fortnight and a meeting of Dominion ministers was also suggested.[35] It was also proposed that eventually Dominion missions should be created within the United Kingdom, similar to the Anglo-French committees which had already been established.

While the War Cabinet appeared to express its general agreement with the report's findings, in the first instance the Dominions would have little option other than to continue to rely upon the apparatus already in place.[36] The new DW telegrams would perforce be the chief source of information for them but, with its exact form and content still undecided, in many cases it was initially of only very limited value.[37] Eden was told, in a late September 1939 minute, that the Dominions should not expect them to include anything relating to future plans and, to emphasize the point, the WO insisted that copies of each communiqué were first sent to them so that they could monitor what was being passed on.[38]

This was a dangerous approach as was quickly demonstrated. The British Expeditionary Force's deployment to France was not revealed to the Dominions in advance nor even was there any mention made of it in the DW telegrams. In the British High Commission in Pretoria this cause considerable astonishment, an angry message back to London warning entirely correctly 'omission is somewhat difficult to explain and it is to be feared that the daily telegrams will lose value in their eyes if there is any implication that they contain selected items only'. There was another concern: by not including relevant information it might be taken by the Dominions that there was no confidence in their ability to keep secrets.[39] This was actually a widely held fear in Whitehall, even in the DO there was a worry that sensitive cables might be tapped.[40] Robert Hadow, who had earlier warned of the possible danger of Dominion neutrality, also wondered what might happen should a situation arise where the Dominion governments felt that London was withholding information they deemed vital to their security.[41] He argued that keeping them within the 'inner ring of events' would bring them fully in step with British policy and remove the need for 'prior consultation' and delays which could happen at some future critical stage. Cadogan was still unimpressed though and again dismissed his subordinate's concerns.[42] The result was that, at best, the DW telegrams remained highly sanitized accounts, only marginally better than Ministry of Information reports. A member of the Board of Trade who was involved in their preparation noted that they did not include anything which had 'a bearing on future plans' while the FO First Secretary who oversaw the process would later confirm that they 'never contained anything really important'.[43]

This was not lost on the high commissioners, a self-titled 'junior war cabinet' made up of forceful characters. Within DO circles, the Australian representative Bruce, himself a former prime minister, was seen as being very down-to-earth, while Massey, presiding at Canada House, was the most aristocratic. The South African, te Water, had been equally well-respected but he had resigned in protest at Hertzog's removal from power and a replacement was still awaited. This left Jordan, the New Zealander, a former London policeman, who although rarely treated seriously, was liked immensely because of his friendliness.[44] All of them had initially welcomed what they saw as the positive measures being taken to keep them better informed, ones which they believed would allow them to retain a central role in the coalition's policy-making.[45] Between the war's outbreak and the end of 1939, 83 meetings were held between them and Eden or his deputy, each of which allowed the opportunity to scrutinize official British war policy.[46] With the distances and time involved in encoding and decoding communications, at this stage comments made by the distant Dominion prime ministers could only rarely carry the same bearing. Bruce and Massey were the key figures despite the fact that both had found themselves increasingly marginalized by their domestic political leaderships. Mackenzie King was widely rumoured not to trust his representative because 'his telegrams were too English' and had asked on numerous occasions that discussions were not held with Massey that might be construed in Canada as being of an official nature.[47] With Bruce similarly marginalized, but for less obviously personal reasons, the two had little influence at home. In the vibrant political arena that was wartime London, their position appeared very different though and the potential role that they could play was quickly demonstrated when they asked for an opportunity to discuss the military situation with the War Cabinet. The resulting mid-September meeting led the Chancellor, Sir John Simon, to report back to his Cabinet colleagues that his visitors 'had taken an unwarrantable gloomy view of the situation', and as a result the 'Dominions Collaboration' committee was formed to examine the alliance's structure.[48]

They might not have had any real power or influence but the high commissioners certainly thought they did, and this was all that mattered. The idea that they were not being kept fully informed of important developments angered them and this would prove to be a long-standing complaint. They were not alone in believing this to be the case as was made clear with calls in the press and even questions tabled in the House of Commons demanding that the experience of the First World War should be repeated.[49] During this there has been two clear phases to what was termed 'consultative cooperation'. The first, from the war's outbreak in August 1914, saw frequent visits being made to London by various Dominion ministers. As the Allied strategic position on the Western Front worsened in the spring of 1917, this was deemed insufficient and an Imperial War Conference was convened chaired by the British leader, David Lloyd George, and involving all of the Dominion leaders. Experimental in both form and procedure, the authorities in London hailed the gathering as an example of Imperial unity and it continued until mid-1919 in the guise of an Imperial War Cabinet.[50] In the Dominions the reaction was not as positive; although it allowed the respective leaders an opportunity to claim they had provided assistance during a moment of great crisis for the British Empire, it also served to exacerbate some long-held concerns. There had been fears about any mechanism which could be used by the British government to make unilateral, binding decisions long before the 1911 Imperial Conference. Indeed these went back to the previous century and Joseph Chamberlain's proposals for an Imperial Council.[51] As a result the inter-war period saw a persistent reluctance to allow subsequent Imperial Conferences, now held at regular intervals, to be viewed as anything more than non-permanent meetings of a purely advisory nature.[52]

Mackenzie King was especially reluctant to be dragged into any form of what he described as an 'Imperial conclave' and already, even in the war's earliest months his sensitivities on the matter were recognized not just within the DO but throughout Whitehall.[53] Following a cursory glance at some of the telegrams received from the high commissioner in Ottawa, Eden had stated that Britain had to be careful not to appear to be setting up an Imperial War Cabinet and avoid meetings at regular intervals.[54] At the same time, however, it was also widely understood that there was a genuine need to hold some sort of gathering, if for no other reason than to 'to impress upon the Dominions that they must also pull their weight if victory is to be attained'.[55] Eden's committee therefore proposed that each should send a ministerial representative, as opposed to their political leadership, to see the vast effort that was being made by Britain. The Canadian leader was in 'a suspicious mood' and it was important to tread cautiously when considering how best to proceed. The official press release announcing the proposed meeting was consequently couched in suitably placatory terms.[56] Even though the feared *Blitzkrieg* had been re-christened *Sitzkrieg*, a reflection on the static nature of the conflict, organizing such a conference at short notice in the midst of a war was something of a Herculean task. The DO proved up to the task and by the end of October 1939 delegates from each of the four Dominion countries had assembled in London, none of whom were directly responsible for the actual war effort of their respective Dominions.[57]

Proceedings began on the first day of November 1939, with a description by Lord Halifax of the foreign political situation. His main points were that Britain should stand solidly behind France, defend key strategic positions in the East such as Aden and Singapore, while pursuing friendly relations with the Mediterranean countries and the United States of America. Questions followed and the British attempted to provide answers. Seven further meetings, each on a different theme, were conducted in exactly the same way. There were discussions on strategic policy during which British ministers encouraged the Dominions to despatch expeditionary forces. How to best conduct economic warfare against Germany, and the difficulties to be faced in maintaining current levels of merchant shipping involved in non-essential transportation provided other topics. The Chancellor chaired another in which the Dominions were asked to give all they could to help Britain overcome 'the terrible financial strain' it faced. There was also the meeting in which Churchill gave the Far Eastern security guarantee which followed on from a visit to inspect the Allied forces in France. The prevailing atmosphere throughout was generally good and no formal suggestions were offered by the delegates that there should be any change to existing arrangements.[58] There were differing interpretations as to what this meant. Harold Nicolson, the renowned diplomat, politician and author, could only lament that the visiting ministers had 'come expecting to find the Mother of Parliaments armed like Britannia, [but] merely saw an old lady dozing over her knitting while her husband read the evening paper out loud'.[59] The DO, however, was generally happy about the outcome. There was particular satisfaction gained from the fact that it had taken years during the First World War to convene a similar meeting, but on this occasion only two-and-a-half months had passed.

This is not to say that the experience was entirely free of alliance strains. Comments had been made within Whitehall prior to their arrival that each Dominion would come to the meeting not solely intent on listening passively to the lectures. This proved to be the case, the question of Britain's wheat purchases from Canada being one of the most contentious issues to be discussed on the fringes. The government in Ottawa insisted that all of its wheat be bought and at a price it set in order, it claimed, to protect both producers and consumers. This was interpreted in London as being based on purely commercial considerations and it would create an impression of 'hard bargaining between two parts of the Commonwealth'. It was consequently decided that the issue would be resolved at a special meeting involving the visiting Canadian delegation to discuss the wartime financial relationship. When this finally took place in the first week of December it was highly acrimonious. Simon, who was in the chair, found the Canadian argument to be totally unacceptable, so much so that any progress proved impossible.[60] Similar problems existed with Australia, the Commonwealth representatives making it clear they were relying on considerable financial assistance from the United Kingdom government to fund their war effort.[61] Simon saw this as being nothing more than subterfuge for Britain taking on Australia's pre-war debts. The British government ultimately would comply with both these sets of demands because it was felt there was little other option, but there was an all-too-obvious sense of shock at the tactics they had encountered. Chamberlain's experiences with the Dominion high commissioners during the first months of the war had left him 'very upset' and it can only be imagined what he felt now.[62] Nonetheless, at least publicly, after this gathering the coalition was still publicly seen to be strong, indeed the spirit of the Empire was being extolled as stronger than ever. MacDonald, speaking now as colonial secretary, told his parliamentary colleagues as the meetings drew to a close that the Dominions 'clothed with every right and privilege of the sovereign nations which they are' had chosen freely to offer their support to Britain. They had leapt into the war not as 'slaves within the British Commonwealth' but as 'free men' with the evolutionary process of gaining their freedom now complete.[63]

It was against this backdrop that the First Canadian Division began to disembark at Scottish ports, the first contingent of Dominion troops to arrive on British shores. Within weeks both the First Echelon of the Second New Zealand Expeditionary Force and Australia's Sixth Division had also sailed from their respective home ports heading for the European war theatre. With the commitment of these troops, it was widely hoped within Whitehall that the Dominions would now develop a far greater interest in the war. The reality was that, preoccupied by domestic concerns and what some London-based commentators referred to as 'strong inferiority complexes', there still remained a clear lack of willingness to actively participate in the war's direction.[64] Typical of this was Canada where, in January 1940, Mackenzie King had sensed the moment was propitious to capitalize on his earlier hard-worked intrigues and had called a general election. Privately Whitehall was alive with speculation that his defeat would be no bad thing, this in part fuelled by reports from the British high commissioner that the Canadian leader had 'dug his own [political] grave'.[65] The authorities in South Africa were also still struggling to 'come into the war' as the bitterness created by the previous September's political crisis continued to prove divisive.[66] Despite this, key figures in London had yet to grasp that their alliance partners' attention lay elsewhere. The War Cabinet was now focused on British strategy in Scandinavia, Churchill persisting with his long-standing proposals to send an Allied Expeditionary Force to secure the Norwegian port of Narvik. The Dominions' response when asked for their views about this idea and, specifically, whether a more vigorous approach was required, was guarded. Indeed they offered little other than the standard rejection of any move which might lead to a worsening of the existing situation.[67] The high commissioners were much more openly critical; Bruce had long regarded any move into Norway or its surrounding waters to be 'extremely dangerous' and instead suggested a much more vigorous propaganda campaign be conducted.[68] Eden said little to this, his attentions focused on proposals for a summer visit to Canada, but elsewhere in Whitehall there was widespread scorn among those who heard this particular contribution to the debate.[69]

The German invasion of Norway, in the first week of April 1940, surprised the War Cabinet and the Dominions who were mentally unprepared and still fixed largely on domestic concerns.[70] Menzies, who was keenest that some form of direct assistance should be provided, had recently announced the successful conclusion of negotiations with Sir Earle Page putting to an end a spat that has soured relations between the two. As a result Page's Country Party would now join in a coalition with his Australia Party. This was obviously a positive step but the political situation nonetheless still remained fragile.[71] In Canada Mackenzie King's general election victory had been assessed by the FO as leaving a leader in charge in Ottawa who would 'remain lukewarm about war measures which cannot be shown to be to [his] advantage'.[72] Sydney Waterson, at South Africa House, was almost alone therefore in responding optimistically to the recent turn of events and he felt more cheerful because the coalition needed 'a kick in the pants before we really get down to a war'.[73] As a military catastrophe unfolded on the far side of the North Sea, the most important question for him was the position of the Dominions in relation to the Supreme War Council. When this had been reconstituted in September 1939, as part of the machinery to coordinate the war effort, Eden's committee had recommended that the

Dominion governments should not be invited to join. This decision had been initially accepted without complaint and this position might well have remained unchallenged. With representatives from both Poland and Norway admitted to a Council meeting in the last week of April, Waterson now pressed for a greater Dominion involvement. Naval and air units were actively engaged in operations and a small Canadian contingent had even been earmarked for despatch to Norway, albeit without Ottawa's knowledge. This made it difficult for the South African's request to be dismissed out of hand. The response, an invitation for the Dominion leaders to visit London later in the year, was a well-calculated move which effectively deferred any further discussion for the time being.[74]

As the situation worsened further, much of the apparent stupor that in recent weeks had affected those around the South African high commissioner, now vanished. In its place was a new sense of enthusiasm as the daily meetings chaired by Eden during the first days of May 1940 once again became the venue for tense discussion about the war's progress.[75] This renewed interest was no bad thing for, if the German success against Norway had come as a shock to the Dominion governments, there was much worse to follow with the *Blitzkrieg* against the Low Countries and France. A major German attack was underway on the Continent and, with the Dominion leaders still seemingly as indecisive as ever, certainly in terms of their communications with London, it was left to the high commissioners much as had been the case the year before to question the British response. The Dominions secretary was asked to involve them much more closely in devising new policies to deal with the revised situation facing the Allies.[76] While not unreceptive to their appeals, he was, however, himself distracted by the mounting speculation about changes at the highest level of the British Empire's political machine. The implications of the Norwegian disaster were now beginning to be felt in London and, as news of the worsening military situation grew, Waterson was certain that Chamberlain would have to be replaced. Like Massey he believed that Lord Halifax was the most likely next leader of the country.[77] They were soon proven correct about a change taking place but the announcement of the identity of who would take charge was something of a surprise to the high commissioners and the Dominion prime ministers alike.

4

Standing Alone

The German attack through the Low Countries and into France struck like a hammer at the Empire's heart, and with Britain's security now clearly imperilled a major overhaul of the government was unavoidable; and the man for the hour was Winston Churchill. His appointment, against the backdrop of May 1940's darkest days, was welcomed by the distant Dominion statesmen, although not in an always entirely convincing tone. This was a reflection of the complex nature of his relationship with the British Empire which, as with most aspects of his remarkable life, has been well examined. A sort of 'romantic Disraelianism' according to one view, at the age of just 22, while serving on the North West Frontier, he had pledged that he would devote his life to the maintenance 'of this great Empire of ours'. Some of his earliest political responsibilities had been within the CO where he opposed proposals that the Colonies should be given a voice in Imperial foreign policy-making.[1] The possibility that he might return to the department in 1915 had left a fellow parliamentarian aghast, imploring the then prime minister not to agree to the move as the 'effect on the Dominions would be lamentable and possibly disastrous'. Churchill, he argued, had 'neither the temperament nor the manners to fit him for the post'.[2] A frustrated Leopold Amery agreed, noting that his standard approach to conducting diplomacy within the Empire was to make sure that 'the Colonial PMs should be given a good time and sent away well banqueted, but empty-handed'.[3]

With his preference for the term 'British Empire' as opposed to 'British Commonwealth', his approach to the Dominion idea was entirely consistent with his wider Imperial beliefs. Pre-war he had written a regular column for *The Sunday Despatch* and in March 1940 an old piece he had written some time before was published. This appeared to detail his views neatly on the Empire:

Then there are the great questions of peace and war. In the main, in these matters the Dominions trust the Mother Country, which lies so close to Central Europe and bears the brunt of Imperial Defence. But still they do not mean to take orders from anyone. They mean to judge for themselves and join in any war of the Empire as volunteers and not pressed men. What then is the new Constitution of the Empire, written and unwritten alike? It is that the self-governing Dominions are in every respect equal partners with Great Britain and that they have the same direct relation to the Crown as we have. We have in fact a seven-fold monarchy, and King George VI is seven constitutional sovereigns rolled into one. Ministers of Great Britain are his advisers in no sense superior to those of Canada, Australia, New Zealand and the others. Complete equality of status has been established. If the British Empire holds together it is only because it wants to hold together.[4]

Such apparently liberal views seemed at odds with some of his previous actions and comments. Despite a second term at the CO, this time as secretary of state, he had opposed the DO's creation from the outset, arguing that Dominion affairs required, at most 'the deliberate and reflective study of two or three selected and experienced officials'.[5] He had subsequently gone on to raise serious objections about the Statute of Westminster, 'a clumsy attempt to remove imaginary grievances', which he feared would provide an undesirable precedent for India and Eire.[6] In a letter to Lord Linlithgow a few years before the war, Churchill recognized the limits of his approach. 'Of course my ideal is narrow and limited. I want to see the British Empire preserved for a few more generations in its strength and splendour. Only the most prodigious exertions of British genius will achieve this result.'[7] For one official within the DO these were 'quaint notions about the Commonwealth' and harked back to an Empire Churchill had known in his youth.[8] One of the prime minister's wartime military advisers agreed, noting that he often forgot that his Dominion counterparts 'required handling rather differently … from the way in which they were handled thirty years before'.[9]

Personal experience was always critical in terms of how Churchill viewed those around him, and his contact with the Dominions and their leaders had been sparse. South Africa was best placed as he had gained first-hand knowledge of the country and its people from his soldiering days during the Boer War. He had also subsequently developed a good relationship with Jan Smuts which endured to the latter's death and meant that Churchill was perhaps freer with his time and information with his fellow prime minister in Pretoria than with any other Dominion figure.[10] The South African was a regular wartime correspondent and an important confidante, but he was not blind to the strengths and limitations that were a feature of his old friend's character. Hence his advice to Waterson that, 'Winston is an actor, an artist, and in this war he is playing his part and no one can stop him.'[11] New Zealand was also generally well thought of, although he had never met any of its key politicians prior to the war. Aside from its stauch backing of Britain much of the reason for this can perhaps be put down to his admiration for General Bernard Freyberg who commanded the Dominion's forces. As with Smuts, here was another individual whose exploits during the First World War, when he had been awarded a Victoria Cross, ensured Churchill's lasting respect.[12] The fact that he was British by birth might also have had some subliminal impact; as a Baron he would act post-war as the governor-general of his country.

As for the other Dominions, although he had first met Mackenzie King in London in November 1906 and had been a regular visitor to the North American continent, Churchill had little real knowledge of Canada. MacDonald, who would later go to Ottawa as wartime high commissioner, wrote that the prime minister's 'lingering Imperialist prejudices inclined him to regard Canada and the other Dominions as still partly dependent colonies, whose Ministers should accept their old British suzerain's views on all problems as the last word in wisdom'. They were no great friends, but whatever objectivity MacDonald might have lacked his assessment was based largely on what he saw. 'None of his personal messages to Mackenzie King were issued as actual orders to the Canadian prime minister, but sometimes the phraseology was couched in language which could imply some bidding.' This left Australia and with nothing else on which to base an assessment, Churchill's enduring belief in the Dominion's troops being 'brave men', which he had first gained during the Boer War and maintained, almost without exception, to his death, proved decisive. His only pre-war political contacts had come with Australian censure lambasting his Dardanelles strategy and later protests against his decision when Chancellor of the Exchequer to return Britain to the Gold Standard. This did little to endear the authorities in Canberra to him and he never really came close to grasping just how different Australian politics was to that which he experienced daily in London. He had first noted Menzies when he had supported the Munich settlement and, although post-1945 the two would profess great friendship for one another, it was often conditional at best during those war years that they worked together.[13]

The London-based high commissioners had little to say about Churchill's appointment but the same was not true about the choice as new secretary of state. Eden had been something of a mixed bag in terms of impact and effect. His profile had brought with it regular press coverage and he was an undoubted dynamic force, taking every opportunity to visit the arriving Dominion troops, first in Scotland and then in Egypt. He had also been especially keen to get out to Canada where he could better consider Mackenzie King but the plans came to nothing.[14] Waterson for one appears to have remained undecided about Eden's talents. After attending an April 1940 meeting of the Constitutional Club at which Eden spoke about Imperialism he confided to his diary: 'His delivery is poor – strangely boyish and likeable but greatly unlike what [Benjamin] Disraeli could have done with the subject … But he is the stuff of which Englishmen like their political leaders to be made: modest, sincere and well-bred. He couldn't do a rotten thing if he tried and he has courage and an indignation of which he is half ashamed.' Nonetheless his conclusion had been that he was 'not ruthless or tough enough for war', a view generally shared by his Australian counterpart.[15] The Dominions secretary's subsequent departure brought with it a more generous private epitaph from South Africa House, expressions of sorrow and the confidence that they were saying farewell to a future peacetime leader of the country. Eden himself, despite his initial reluctance at being sent to what he had feared would be a backwater, claimed to be 'genuinely sorry to leave' for the WO, although he was grateful that he no longer would have to endure 'Bruce's daily catechism'.[16]

It took three days to find his replacement. Churchill's political position was far from secure and it meant that he had to produce a balanced Cabinet acceptable to those figures within his party who continued to doubt his abilities. Eden's post was first therefore offered to Oliver Stanley, but in such a way that it was clear the country's new leader doubted his political abilities. As the unfortunate Stanley responded, it would be better for all concerned if he declined the offer, and this he duly did.[17] Later he confided to a fellow MP that he had in any case seen how Churchill had treated Eden and concluded that it would be impossible to work with him.[18] The prime minister's second choice was Inskip, now titled Lord Caldecote. Even to some of the staff at No. 10 he was a figure of fun, comparable to the barrage balloon now parked on Horse Guards Parade which, because of its rotund nature, was quickly christened 'Tinskip'.[19] His approach to ministerial life apparently even provoked some consternation among his own staff who found it generally impossible to know what he was going to say until he had actually stood up and spoken. This was because his speeches were generally dictated about an hour previous to delivery but it was not always possible to disturb him then, presumably, from his slumbers.[20]

Neither Bruce nor Massey saw any cause for amusement and they educated Waterson, who had not been there to witness it first-hand, on his pre-war performance. Among the worst incidents they highlighted was in April 1939 during the Prague crisis when 'the door mouse [sic]', as he was known, had apparently fallen asleep while sitting next to Chamberlain at a meeting. The South African was a quick leaner and developed a special dislike for the returning minister, 'a charming old man, brave and tenacious of character but legal minded and stereotyped to a degree' who delivered bad news 'like a newspaper reporter'. He was 'fatuous' and 'ineffective' and 'an insult to the Dominions as Secretary of State'. The Canadian high commissioner claimed not to dislike Caldecote personally, but he was also not happy that the senior DO role should be given as 'a consolation prize' to 'a second rate politician' but 'a good Party man'. Massey was prepared to admit, following the first meeting that 'he was more alert and more on the job than we had feared', so much so that he was willing to give him another chance. His deputy, Pearson, nonetheless remained sure that the appointment was the clearest of indications as to how the Dominions' portfolio was viewed within the Cabinet. Bruce was generally much angrier, complaining to Canberra that 'a discarded Lord Chancellor' had been appointed, a politician who 'did not possess the personality or drive necessary to put over Dominion views' and did not have 'a receptive or constructive mind'. MacDonald or the elderly Lloyd George would both have been much better appointments in his view.[21]

The business of war, now a very real one in which the German menace was no longer merely a matter of speculation, brought with it remarkably few changes in terms of how the administrative machinery of the alliance functioned. There was still considerable concern among the more junior partners about the paucity of information they were receiving and demands that improvements be made. The high commissioners complained about the 'volume and quality of the DW telegrams' but the FO remained resistant to letting them see more arguing that it would be folly to send the Dominions 'every alarmist rumour that we may receive' but the DO was strident with its view that more needed to be done.[22] There was a growing feeling, both within the department and in the overseas high commissions, that too little rather than too much was being sent, and that more was needed both of a better quality and not out of date.[23] Soothing words were soon exchanged between the two departments but it was regretfully understood within the DO's ranks that the FO would continue to tightly control the distribution of information.[24] Simply put, Cadogan could not be moved from his view that nothing should be sent that might perplex the Dominions or, much worse, 'leave them to infer that we are perplexed'.[25]

Menzies' complaints about the lack of detail contained within the reviews of Allied operations and strategy being sent to him showed that there clearly remained obvious shortcomings.[26] News that the French position might soon collapse led the Australian leader to conclude this must have been a sudden development as he had received nothing beforehand to suggest that this could happen. Churchill did now warn his Dominion counterparts of the possibility of 'an early heavy attack' but he still remained reluctant to inform them of the seriousness of the situation in France.[27] And even this was only done after Chamberlain, now Lord President of the Council, had explicitly raised the point, enquiring in front of the entire War Cabinet what information could be given to the Dominion governments. The news brought renewed messages of Dominion support. Menzies pledged 'the whole of the Commonwealth's resources to victory'. New Zealand's leader, Peter Fraser, who had replaced Savage following his recent death, also telegraphed to London with a commitment to fight to the last 'come what may'. Mackenzie King authorised the despatch of four destroyers to Britain and in another sign of support for the cause the Canadian Communist Party was outlawed 'amid a rush of Dominion feeling against Red quislings'. The South African response was more reflective, Smuts recognizing France's likely denouement would mean that the British Commonwealth would be left alone.[28]

Within Whitehall the increased tempo of the war was beginning to tell, most noticeably in the DO. Aside from its general day-to-day responsibilities and almost hourly requests from the Antipodean Dominions for strategic appreciations of

the situation, there were new tasks for the department to handle, such as finaliz-
ing what might happen were an invasion to take place.[29] For at least one of the
British high commissioners serving in the Dominions, the 'badly overworked
department' seemed to be suffering from 'a want of correlation'.[30] With Lord
Halifax continuing to extol the merits of a possible negotiated settlement with
Germany, Menzies joined in beginning what would prove to be the first of three
attempts made by him to initiate a 'peace' initiative involving the United States.[31]
The position was further complicated by the WO's confirmation that Italy would
soon enter the war on Germany's side.[32] This carried wide strategic considerations both for Britain's Middle East and Far East positions.[33] Constitutional
concerns also had to be taken into account in light of the brush with neutrality
in Cape Town the previous year with the DO's legal experts rushing to revise the
procedure by which the Dominions might declare war.[34]

For the Dominions' representatives based in London, their attention remained
firmly focused on the implications of France's demise. Their anger had not
abated nor had their belief that they were being ignored and under-utilized. So
meagre did they believe the information from the official channels to be that
they had even taken to attending the Canadian Military Headquarters on a daily
basis where it was believed they could better track developments. Bruce thought
it 'criminal' that the War Cabinet had failed to fully consider the implications
of a possible French collapse, leaving him with 'a most gloomy view of British
prospects'. The seven-page note which he produced and sent to the already
over-worked Churchill proposing an international conference to arrange a peace
settlement was, not surprisingly, very poorly received.[35] Following the British
prime minister's visit to the front in mid-June and his report back that the French
had fallen back on 'what must be regarded as their last line', the Australian high
commissioner and his colleagues emboldened themselves to make a daring
move.[36] They had become aware that the chiefs of staff had in fact prepared
reports on how to respond to France's surrender and the request was made that
they be allowed to read them. It was Caldecote who delivered this to the War
Cabinet, warning his colleagues that the Dominion governments 'must be treated
as full partners and their assent must not be taken for granted'. Two days later the
documents were made available for inspection, but they did not make for pleasant
reading as within them the degree to which British forces could be sent to the Far
East immediately following a Japanese attack was questioned. Churchill was also
clearly unhappy about having been made to release the reports and his displeasure
would be made clear in his subsequent dealings with the high commissioners.

Menzies appeared to be badly unnerved by the knowledge of the revised
British military position. Earlier in the year Britain's official figure in Canberra
had told the DO the Australian had 'no more backbone than a jellyfish' and this
now seemed to be much more obvious to those watching from London. His

insistence that, should Hitler suggest terms on which he would be prepared to conclude peace with the Allies the United States be approached for guidance, 'no matter what form it might take', was a cause of some dismay. Twenty-four hours later, however, in a note to his high commissioner in London, he stated that he was willing to follow Britain 'whatever sacrifice victory may demand'. The news that in any Franco-German peace agreement French possessions in the Pacific might be allotted to Japan had him once again desperately looking towards Washington for assistance. The DO could do little to calm him beyond thank him for his comments and pass on a report prepared by the FO which discounted the idea that the German leader would submit a renewed peace proposal at this time. A message, written in Churchill's name, was also prepared which was intended to instil in the Australian leader some greater measure of resolve.[37] Canberra's reaction was all in marked contrast to the reassurances coming out of Wellington where the government officially renewed its pledge of 'every form of assistance within our power'. The authorities in London were informed discretely, however, that there had been considerable political dismay that the long-standing premise of British assistance was now no longer guaranteed. The DO promised that there would be a review were the position in the Far East to become 'threatening' and this seemed to provide some measure of comfort.[38] Indeed the New Zealanders now seemed determined on a public display of its loyalty to Britain. An offer to send a special mission to Washington to try and secure support was politely declined in the face of FO concerns that this would be seized upon by isolationists on the other side of the Atlantic.[39]

Smuts' encouraging comments also continued to provide considerable comfort to Churchill.[40] With preparations to repel the now anticipated German invasion intensifying, he felt that there were pressing matters to be considered elsewhere. This included Operation *Catapult*, the 'necessary' attack against the French fleet anchored at Oran. Carried out by the Royal Navy in the first week of July, it was welcome by the South African leader as being both an end to France's agony and the beginning of efforts to restore it and its 'sick people' through some much-needed and no doubt British-administered 'moral nursing'.[41] This significant military operation and Churchill's offer of a union with France made the month before were not revealed to the respective Dominion governments in advance, despite the much wider political ramifications both held. The prime minister, during his celebrated 'Finest Hour' speech had told the House of Commons the opposite. The self-governing Dominions were 'absolutely devoted to the ancient Motherland' but more to the point, he claimed that they were being kept fully informed of events.[42] In both cases it had been true that very few British officials had been informed in advance but the incredulity over these claims within the DO was serious and Inskip allegedly threatened to resign in protest.[43] The reason behind his anger was well put by one of the department's most capable members.

It would be impossible for any of the Dominions to hide the fact that they had not been contacted in advance, leaving them insulted and humiliated in their home parliaments, as such omissions offered the clearest proof 'that so called Dominion autonomy was a mockery'.[44] These decisions were in fact for the most part accepted within the Dominion capitals with good grace, it being understood that the speed at which events were developing had not always allowed for any prior forewarning of British action.

Anxieties worsened either side of the Tasman, however, with closer study of the chiefs of staff 'certain eventuality' reports assessing the impact of France's surrender. Adding to the mounting tension were the reports of Japanese demands made at the end of June 1940 for the closure of the Burma Road, the only route still open to supply the Chinese government in Chungking. Sir Robert Craigie, Britain's ambassador in Tokyo, warned that war was probable unless this was carried out. The British military's chiefs concurred that failure to comply could only result in further disaster at this point and Menzies vehemently agreed.[45] Batterbee, reading the correspondence in Wellington, found it tragic that 'egged on by Bruce' Australia's leader should adopt 'so weak and defeatist an attitude'; his counterpart in Canberra could meanwhile only despair that 'Australia was still fast asleep' in terms of its war effort.[46] The high commissioners in London were, however, of a similar mind to Menzies, urging 'retreat and concessions' from the DO and making daily representations to Inskip that some form of settlement should be reached. Bruce even argued that there could be 'full and frank negotiations' with the Soviets but Whitehall's assurances that the Japanese authorities were likely to accept a proposal of a three month closure appeared to calm some of the worst fears.[47]

During the summer of 1940 the Dominion representatives – Jordan noticeable by his continuing absences – had continued to make every effort to secure a more prominent role in the direction of policy.[48] Only hours after Marshal Pétain, France's third leader in as many months, had signed the armistice with Germany, Halifax had been obliged to apologize for not being able to see two of them.[49] Caldecote had, at the same time, put in a request that Churchill himself might discuss recent events with them.[50] This was approved but in almost the same breath the prime minister informed his Dominions secretary that he would subsequently only be required to attend the War Cabinet on just two days a week, when the chiefs of staff also visited. This drew an astonished Waterson to bitterly complain that 'the PM clearly did not understand the part the high commissioners were playing'.[51] In late July Churchill finally met with the group for an hour-long discussion devoted entirely to events in the Far East. He told them that the agreement over the Burma Road had been made to gain time in the hope that a stronger American stance would emerge in the Pacific in the interim. He could also refer to *Catapult* which had freed British ships to proceed east for the protection of Australian waters should they be needed.[52] The South African attendee seemed sufficiently impressed by the encounter to note privately that their host was 'the man for the moment', his approach 'reflecting the purpose and spirit of the people'; it was clear though that he still did not really like him.[53] The Dominion leaders were less easily persuaded, and Churchill was warned that neither Australia nor New Zealand would permit the imminent despatch of troop convoys intended for the Middle East unless they were first supplied with a detailed Far Eastern appreciation.[54] The next day Halifax met again with the Dominion high commissioners to talk at length about the War Cabinet's most recent discussions, outlining what alternatives he felt existed in the Far East.[55] Following this and the promise that an appreciation of the situation would be sent to the Dominion capitals in early August, even Bruce was willing to say that Australia would now be prepared to support 'a policy of standing up to Japan', a remarkable change in light of some of his earlier comments.[56]

Standing in front of the House of Lords in mid-August 1940, Caldecote outlined how the war was progressing just three days after the first Imperial defeat and the evacuation of the garrison of British Somaliland in the face of an over-whelming Italian invading force.[57] He told his peers that there had been many uncertainties at the start of the conflict but one of them was not the 'solidarity of the free peoples of the British Empire'. Referring to Churchill's reference to blood and toil, tears and sweat, the same, he said, was true of the Commonwealth which had 'counted the cost and already paid part of the price'. With the prime minister travelling to meet with President Franklin Roosevelt, he also took this opportunity to inform the high commissioners that he intended to be more forceful in the future where the Dominions' interests were concerned. Churchill had recently formed a 'Ministerial Committee on the Middle East' chaired by Eden, the secretary of state for war, and assisted by Amery, now secretary of state for India, and Lord Lloyd, the secretary of states for the colonies.[58] At the end of July this had invited Australia and New Zealand to deploy any forces they could spare to the Middle East, but Inskip resolved that more needed to be done. Doubts persisted about whether their respective governments had been informed in advance or not about the formation of the committee and what priority would be applied to deciding upon requirements for equipment. But it was with an almost self-congratulatory tone that the high commissioners subsequently noted that Egypt was going to become the focus of attention for Australian and New Zealand forces.[59] What they did not know was that the debate about whether Australian troops already garrisoned in Britain should be despatched to the Middle East or not would actually continue at the highest levels long into the following month.[60]

Events surrounding Operation *Menace*, the attempt to seize the West African port of Dakar from Vichy French control, gave a good indication of how the alliance was actually operating. With this announcement all of the Dominions were deeply concerned about the lack of information they had received; the first reference given to them only came after the raid had failed.[61] Churchill would later admit that he had kept Smuts alone informed and even this only amounted to a single personal telegram containing a few details.[62] When the other prime ministers were finally told of the full events and, specifically, the degree to which the enterprise had proven to be a great failure, there was a strong reaction. This was most pointed from Menzies even though the political ramifications of the aborted raid appearing to be less damaging for him than for his counterparts in Canada or the Union of South Africa. While Ottawa feared what reaction the attack on French territory and shipping would produce in Quebec and Smuts was worried about emphasizing the strategic value of Dakar to the enemy, Australia could claim few such strategic concerns. The cruiser *HMAS Australia* had, however, been used without his being informed in advance and this was sufficient cause for him to at once fly into a fury, issuing criticisms which Churchill took as being a personal attack.[63] Waterson recorded that the raid had been 'an even more grisly failure than one thought', noting that 'the whole thing bears the stamp of WSC, a good idea badly executed'.[64] Fortunately there was a good deal of 'damage control' administered by the DO, supported in this instance by Bruce, and this helped ensure that the recriminations quickly subsided.[65] By the beginning of October the matter appeared forgotten, the final note from Churchill to his Australian counterpart asking that he be forgiven 'if I responded too controversially to what I thought was somewhat severe criticism'.[66]

With the high commissioners stamping outside the door of the Dominions secretary if they were kept waiting for meetings, the apparently fraught alliance was a constant source of strain within Whitehall throughout the summer months. Eric Machtig, the DO's deputy-head, recorded that his colleagues had been left 'feeling rather tired', and this was not helped by them all having to run for the air-raid shelters on several occasions. Added to this were fire-watching duties organized on a rota basis and the continuing planning for how the department would function in the event of an invasion. There was consequently a sense of relief when in August Churchill ordered that the Administrative Grade of the Civil Service should take a fortnight's leave; the sight of a pen and paper was making one of the department feel 'physically sick'. The greatest problem, even worse than the demands of the Dominions, was the serious shortage of trained personnel available to carry out the mounting range of jobs. It was hoped that the pool of those unfit for military service would provide some help, but nothing was guaranteed.

Despite these pressures, those working for him found Caldecote 'a delightful chief, completely imperturbable and cheerful in the most desperate moments and crisis', but Churchill had decided it was time he should go and Eden and David

Margesson, the chief whip, met secretly with him to discuss possible replace-
ments.[67] For some months the weary secretary of state had complained that he
was little more than 'postman and correspondent', noting with some apparent
regret that it had taken until mid-August before Churchill had sent him his first
personal minute.[68] The announcement, at the very beginning of October 1940,
that he would be taking the Lord Chief Justice's chair as part of a major reconstruction of the government following Neville Chamberlain's resignation on health
grounds, was well received within the ranks of the Dominion representatives.[69]
Sitting next to the Minister for Food, Lord Woolton, at a lunch, Waterson told
him how Caldecote had gathered the high commissioners together to tell them
in great secrecy that he would be leaving that evening. As the South African high
commissioner put it, the group was 'so embarrassed that there was complete
silence: they could not honestly say that they were sorry, because he had been
quite useless in this as in every other Government office that he has achieved'.[70]
Duncan, the governor-general in South Africa, was also pleased at the move but
could not understand why Churchill had not felt sufficiently confident to have
gone even further and removed 'some of those whose only claim to remain in
high office is that they were once fortunate enough to get there'.[71]

He was delighted, however, in the selection as new secretary of state, Robert
Gascoyne-Cecil who, as Lord Cranborne, had resigned from Chamberlain's
Cabinet in 1938 alongside Anthony Eden in protest at the government's foreign
policy.[72] The new appointee had been a popular figure within Whitehall to
everybody aside from arch-Chamberlain supporters, such as Kingsley Wood, to
whom he was one of the 'glamour boys'.[73] The connection between Churchill and
his newly appointed Dominions secretary was a long-standing one. Ever since
Robert Cecil had acted as an adviser to Queen Elizabeth I, his family had enjoyed
a significant role in British political affairs. The Third Marquess of Salisbury,
Cranborne's grandfather, held the distinction of having been prime minister on
three occasions.[74] He had also been the man who had finally destroyed the career
of Lord Randolph Churchill. For this reason, according to one who knew him well
during the wartime period, the son 'could never quite make up his mind whether
to admire the House of Cecil or resent it on his father's posthumous behalf'.[75]
Even before Cranborne's February 1938 speech to the Commons, following his
resignation as the FO's under-secretary to the Foreign Office, the next generation
of Cecils was among his closest acquaintances. On that occasion Churchill had
in fact been one of the first to offer his congratulations.[76]

To close observers, what would prove perhaps more significant in terms
of their wartime relationship, was their ability to put 'political quarrels in a
compartment entirely separate from personal friendship'.[77] This was clearly
not always the case, Churchill confiding to his son towards the war's end of the
difficulties of working with Cranborne who 'might easily be ill one fortnight

and very obstinate the next'.[78] The prime minister had presumably assumed that his new Downing Street neighbour could be counted on not to make too many waves. In July 1940 Cranborne had been offered the position of Chairman of the Advisory Committee on Aliens but had declined citing ill health as the reason. Churchill had commented at the time that if he could not take on this job because of his poor health 'there is not much in burdening him with the duties of serving as a member [of the Cabinet]'.[79] Yet now he asked him to become a minister whose responsibilities called for him to handle what already appeared to be an extremely uncertain alliance. After the fall of France in July 1940, *Punch* had published a cartoon showing two soldiers looking out to sea. One of them says, 'So our poor old Empire is alone in the world', and the other replies 'Aye, yes we are – the whole five hundred million of us'.[80] There must have been times when it was felt within Whitehall and in the British High Commissions overseas that this could not be further from the truth.

5

Coalition United

The appointment of the Fifth Marquess of Salisbury in October 1940 carried with it a significance for Anglo-Dominion relations that cannot be overstated.[1] Although it was only his second Cabinet position, and still acknowledged as being very much a junior one, 'Bobbety', as he was known to his peers, brought with him an enormous sense of enthusiasm and determination. As one of those who knew him well said of him, although 'frail in body' – the result of having been gassed in the trenches during the last war – he made up for it with 'the robustness of his spirit'.[2] One of his DO staff detected 'an unusual range of gifts and accomplishments' with a 'subtlety' to his intelligence, 'a strong sense of pride', 'a natural courtesy towards all' and 'a lively and amusing mind, with a keen sense of humour'. This left him well suited for the demands of working in the department.[3] Despite being a long-standing friend, he was not afraid to tackle Churchill on the need to provide more information to the Dominions and give them a greater say in coalition management. Cranborne was not suggesting any greater permanent presence; indeed he was particularly dismissive of the idea that a second London-based Imperial War Cabinet should be established. What he instead argued was that, if for no other reason than the progressively greater contributions of manpower and material they were providing, the British government needed to be more open with the Dominions and its leaders.

He was quick to show his resolve to resist measures which he believed might harm his new department. Both of his wartime predecessors had tried to do the same but their efforts had generally been frustrated. Cranborne was quick to try and offer reassurance, not least to the Union of South Africa and Australia, telling them that he recognized the amount of information they received was still far from adequate.[4] Shortly after his appointment he had written to Waterson apologizing that he had not been told before Eden's October 1940 visit to Egypt, a slip which had embarrassed and angered the South African.[5] This appeared to gain him little in the eyes of a high commissioner who had been critical of both of his predecessors and was uncertain about the new man, 'the usual inbred perfect gentleman, full of good qualities but really not tough enough for our purposes'. Bruce would reserve judgement, but only because he had been told that the new minister had 'ability and guts' and just needed the opportunity to prove himself.

Massey was alone in thinking him to be 'an admirable choice'.[6] Waterson's view seemed harsh indeed as the early suggestions were that a more dogmatic and pugnacious attitude now prevailed within the DO with a Dominions secretary not afraid to disagree with his Whitehall colleagues.[7]

His greatest clashes would be reserved for Churchill. This was particularly unfortunate as the rapid deterioration in relations between the two that resulted coincided with a growing political challenge based in part around the actions of one of the Dominion's leaders. During the inter-war years Australia had been alone in arguing that greater cooperation was needed, and by the late 1930s it was being said in Canberra that the level of consultation was insufficient to meet the requirements of the worsening European situation. Following the 1938 Munich Crisis, Menzies, the then Australian Attorney General, placed himself at the head of a campaign for a united British Empire foreign policy, but his proposals for a 'permanent Imperial Secretariat' were rejected by a majority of the other senior figures in Dominion political circles.[8] His appointment as the country's leader following Joe Lyons's death in March 1939 only strengthened the fervour of this self-avowed imperialist. Despite a precarious domestic political position, he had been the one Dominion leader constantly prepared to visit London during France's slow and painful collapse.[9] A telegram he sent to London in mid-June talked of the great comfort he would gain if there could be a Dominion prime ministers' conference to discuss 'empire defence'. Churchill politely declined the request but it did little to deter his counterpart in Canberra.[10]

The Dakar incident seems to have been taken by Menzies as the perfect excuse to push for improvements to be made.[11] From the war's outset he had complained that the supply of information was very meagre and that there were events happening which 'vitally concerned Australia but about which nothing was known until afterwards'.[12] Now a year later, although he was apparently dismissive of the need for an actual, enlarged Imperial War Cabinet, he still wanted a formal meeting. At this he wanted to know why Britain was 'keeping the Dominions a bit at arm's length' when it came to the war's progress.[13] His position at home looked tenuous; as one of his colleagues bemoaned to a friend in London, most of Menzies' colleagues were now 'eager for his blood'. A meeting demonstrating his statesmanlike qualities at the heart of the Empire would have been attractive; the problem that he faced was finding supporters.[14] Even the DO believed that a London conference was unfeasible and had done since earlier in the year. Half-hearted plans had been made for something, probably in July or early August 1940, but these were curtailed by the German *Blitzkrieg*.[15] A detailed summary of the various proposals that had been put forward had been prepared within the DO and, following Chamberlain's resignation, a copy had been submitted to Churchill that same month.[16] Both then and now it was felt there was no possibility of Smuts or Mackenzie King being willing to attend, but discouraging Menzies outright would have 'a chilling effect'; the War Cabinet was told that the idea might be welcomed but not the proposed timing.[17]

There were a number of political considerations to be borne in mind in Whitehall. A recent warning given to Churchill by an old political colleague had spoken of the growing parliamentary campaign to get a Dominion representative into the War Cabinet.[18] That this proposal had its backers had been made abundantly clear in the House of Lords. Gideon Oliphant-Murray, the 2nd Viscount Elibank, was a Scottish aristocrat and staunch imperialist and he was certainly the most vocal proponent of the creation of an Imperial War Cabinet. Variations on a similar theme had been referred to earlier in the summer of 1940 in both Houses but his would be the most sustained. He had told his peers that the Dominions were playing a sizeable role and asked that a 'greater unification of war direction on the part of the Empire' be considered. He proposed that the Dominions be included in the Cabinet and suggested that Bruce could prove an excellent addition. As the former Liberal chief whip reassured the prime minister, his appeal was in fact an attempt 'to induce the Dominions [to] do more'.[19] Aside from this irritation there was also the British leader's desire to demonstrate that there remained a continued resolve amongst the Allied combatants to continue the war against Germany. U-boat attacks against British shipping in the Atlantic were worsening, the Luftwaffe's aerial campaign against London showed little sign of ending, while Italy's invasion of Greece, which had begun in October 1940, further threatened Britain's Mediterranean interests.[20] Churchill wished to hold a Supreme War Council meeting to send a message to the neutrals, particularly the United States. He therefore proposed that the now Occupied Powers and Dominion governments be asked to send representatives but Mackenzie King found the idea 'distasteful'.[21] The prime minister was unmoved and warned he would press ahead regardless and when Cranborne attempted to explain possible reasons behind the Canadian leader's mood, Churchill responded angrily.[22] He now argued that it was the use of the term 'Supreme War Council' instead of the Cabinet-agreed 'Conference of Allied Representatives' which had created the problem and given Mackenzie King 'a puddle at which he was sure to shy'.[23] The Dominions secretary had in fact first sought the FO's advice before he had contacted Ottawa and it was only when Churchill was told this by a third party that he calmed down.[24]

It might have been politically expedient or a residual effect of this incident, but it was only a few weeks later, in early December 1940, that the Dominions secretary was summoned to Chequers and informed that it was now proposed to move him. Various diaries speak of his name being put forward as ambassador in Washington or even viceroy of India. He was actually asked to become the secretary of state for India and take his hereditary seat in the House of Lords where he could then also answer FO questions. This provoked a long and emotional response:

> As you know I was in the first doubtful about it, and the more I think, the more reluctant I feel, from many points of view. For one thing I am quite certain the Dominions themselves would greatly resent such frequent changes in the DO. They have already had three secretaries of state in little more than a year. If now they are asked to accept a fourth, they will draw the conclusion that they are regarded as of no account, and that the Office is treated merely as a receptacle for odd men out. They are exceedingly sensitive and the effect on them, especially at this moment when they are making so great an effort, might only too probably be deplorable.[25]

Adding to tensions was the growing anger within the DO over the question of information. During the summer Caldecote had presented the War Cabinet with a paper asking that the fullest possible account of wartime developments be given to the Dominions.[26] Now Colonel William Bishop, the department's military liaison officer, attacked the continuing official reluctance to allow 'secret' information to be sent out, in a lengthy and often bitterly critical internal minute.[27] This had been sparked by a letter from Churchill to the recently re-elected President Roosevelt outlining the war situation and the British position. Bishop thought it an outstanding review and wanted it sent to the Dominions but the proposal was rejected by the Service Departments who cited the prime minister's directive.[28] The military officer believed that the time had come when Churchill needed to be tackled directly on his policy and Cranborne agreed, confiding to his deputy his fear that the country's leader had decided on a policy of communicating 'as little information' as he could get away with and even then 'only in reply to specific requests'.[29] On one occasion it had even been suggested that a proposed telegram to his Dominion counterparts outlining the real figures for captured German U-boats should be delayed, it being better 'to let sleeping statistics lie'.[30] He was not alone with his concerns, during the preceding month the Dominions secretary had received a number of similar complaints from Whitehall colleagues. He therefore wrote to Churchill just two days before Christmas reminding him that sharing information with the other Dominion leaders helped gain their confidence and ensured their practical cooperation.[31] The oft-quoted response sent on Christmas Day 1940 took the form of a stern rebuke. There was 'a danger that the Dominions Office staff get into the habit of running a kind of newspaper full of deadly secrets' and the prime minister wanted anything 'of a very secret nature' to be approved by him in future before it was sent.[32]

Churchill was clearly angered by events, even telling Bruce that the DO was ineffectual, although he did not refer to Cranborne by name.[33] The Dominions secretary was, however, the obvious target as was clear from him being told not to attend the Tuesday meetings of the War Cabinet, the point being emphasised to him that these were reserved for those within government who made policy. He was not one of these people and his presence was therefore deemed to be surplus to requirements.[34] Bobbety could do little but accept the new arrangements despite the obvious restrictions it would place on his ability to discuss future war strategy with the alliance members. He did, however, try to offer some further explanation to Churchill as to why he had protested. The Dominions were not complaining about the lack of prior consultation about the Dakar operation – although they were privately angry – it was the fact that they had not even been informed that it was taking place and had to learn this from the Press that was the cause of their concern. They were also not claiming 'any right to supervise the work of the War Cabinet'; they just wanted to feel that they were in the full confidence of the British leadership. Few within the DO believed the prime minister would change his mind and although he soon seemed a little more receptive to requests from the department, it was nonetheless clear that the Dominions secretary was out in the cold.[35]

This was the position when, in January 1941 Menzies set out on a journey to London to carry out a 'chancy undertaking' for which he had been long planning.[36] The month before, Clement Attlee, the leader of the Labour party but also Churchill's deputy in the wartime national unity government, had told the House of Commons no Dominions' representative would be joining the War Cabinet but this did not deter the Australian.[37] The continuing difficulties he faced at home, his own political ambitions, a genuine sense of personal unease over the nature of the relationship Australia enjoyed with Britain and more general fears among his countrymen about future security in both the Mediterranean and Pacific regions all led him to make his decision to travel. Although he had assured his parliamentary colleagues that his absence would be brief, his decision to travel via Singapore and the Middle East to examine the strategic position at each of these key Imperial bastions meant that it would be nearly four months before he returned home. Menzies arrived in London in late February and was welcomed by a sympathetic press campaign, support he continued to enjoy throughout his stay.[38] Within days he had a meeting with Churchill, the first between the two men, although the visit to Chequers did not augur well for the future. The Australian politician found his host a 'tempestuous creature' whose attire and general demeanour apparently shocked him, the haranguing of the 'holy terror' eventually sending him to bed a tired man.[39] Nonetheless he chose to report back to Canberra in overwhelmingly positive tones, his host's qualities being 'much greater than we thought'. Menzies had also quickly formed the view that there was no doubt that Australia was 'Dominion Number One'.[40] Throughout the next two months he experienced events in Britain first-hand, attending War Cabinet meetings whenever possible and generally trying to place himself at the heart of the policy- and decision-making processes. By the time of his final meeting with

Churchill, the night prior to his return to Australia, he was convinced that all was not well at the heart of the Empire.

His Damascene moment was yet to come; in the meantime there was war business to consider. As has been seen, Australian and New Zealand troops had become central to the war being fought in the deserts of North Africa in so much as they formed a sizeable part of the army assembled in the region. Initially their experiences had been victorious as British Commonwealth troops triumphed against the Italians, invaders of Egypt the summer before but now in full retreat. In East Africa, British, Indian and South African troops emulated the rout and the Abyssinian capital of Addis Ababa was captured in early April. The problem came with the subsequent decision to intervene in Greece and defend Crete. Although very upset at being told by a senior British general, during his brief visit to the Middle East, that the Australian troops were 'terribly badly disciplined and caused a great deal of trouble', Menzies had agreed that his country's forces could be used.[41] The coalition now found itself facing the military might of Germany and not its more inferior Italian ally and defeat brought with it great political strains as Anzac troops suffered heavy losses of men and equipment.[42]

As it became clear that British Commonwealth forces were poised to suffer a tragic defeat on the Peloponnesian peninsula, so Menzies' attitude towards the Empire's leader changed. Despite his later description of him as a 'great warrior-statesman [and] an unrivalled benefactor to posterity', privately he was now more scathing about 'the greatest asset and greatest danger' the Empire faced.[43] There were others who agreed and as Churchill sank deeper into a growing political storm, Menzies was to be found at the heart of the intrigues complicit in the conspirators' meetings and discussions. In the final hours of his stay, he made his plans clear to Lord Hankey who had been demoted by the prime minister in May 1940 and was now centrally embroiled in the campaign opposing him. It was argued that there was only one possible course of action to be followed; an Imperial War Cabinet had to be summoned after which one of the Dominion leaders would have to stay behind. Elibank had stood again in the House of Lords in early April 1941 to raise the matter, but his peers had still generally doubted whether such a move would actually improve the conduct of the war and they were also unsure about how it might operate.[44] Menzies' cabal had the answers: there would be a similar role to that played by Smuts in the last war, 'not as a guest but as a full member' and the Australian clearly thought he was the man for the job.[45] Having discussed this with Sir John Simon, another whose loyalties to Churchill were doubtful, Hankey urged his Australian accomplice to seek one final meeting with the British leader. This was arranged but he could get 'no change' out of his host and he departed for North America and the long trip home where political crisis awaited him.[46]

His departure did not, however, mean an end to the intrigues and, in Menzies'

absence, the anti-Churchill campaign soon reached its climax. During the first
week of May 1941 a confidence debate was called in the House of Commons but
despite the best efforts of such senior figures as Lloyd George and Hore-Belisha,
the vote was won handsomely by the prime minister.[47] The following day,
Cranborne felt it prudent to warn Churchill of the true nature behind Menzies
recent visit, advising him that he should 'have the background, in case you have
not already got it'. The simple answer that came back to the DO was 'I have got
it'.[48] This was something of a rare written communication between the two. In
March Cranborne had sought approval to send to the Dominion governments
an appreciation made by the British military authorities of the likely chances of
invasion but Churchill still would not cooperate, arguing that such 'questionable
stuff' was not needed to frighten the Dominions into doing their duty. Secret
intelligence, despite the department's continuing reservations, was still not to be
sent to the Dominion governments.[49]

It was at this stage that the British leader signalled a pronounced change in
policy. He had been told by Mackenzie King that Menzies, who had just left
Ottawa on his way home, had argued passionately for a meeting of Dominion
leaders later in the year. Churchill now replied back to Mackenzie King that some
form of meeting in August or September might be in order.[50] This was perhaps a
reaction to the press campaign by Lord Beaverbrook's *Daily Express* champion-
ing a role for Menzies and the associated public support for a conference that
now existed.[51] Reminding Churchill that even basic discussion of the idea had
previously created problems, Cranborne was adamant that such a meeting would
be difficult to organize. The Canadian leader's views remained critical and he
was not interested. Within a matter of days, as the German attack began on
the Imperial forces holding Crete, the Dominions secretary received a personal
letter from Ottawa carrying exactly the same message, but Churchill remained
apparently interested in the idea of an inter-Allied council throughout that
summer.[52] Cranborne urged, in response, that serious thought was required as
Mackenzie King was 'still clearly very wobbly about coming'.[53] He had discussed
this question privately with Malcolm MacDonald who, in April 1941, had been
sent out to Ottawa as the new British high commissioner.[54] The former Minister
for Health was able to tell him that Menzies had formed the lowest opinion of
the War Cabinet and Cranborne himself. Writing back to him, the Dominions
secretary agreed with some of his arguments, especially that there should be some
kind of a 'watchdog' to champion their interests although he felt Menzies might
not 'have ability of the very highest kind'. The more obvious logistical difficulties
involved in quickly assembling the various Dominion leaders in London were
also noted as was the potential danger that calling an unexpected meeting could
lead to a popular belief that there was 'some new and spectacular development' to
discuss.

Churchill's interest in the idea was still, however, undimmed and he requested that the DO produce for the War Cabinet a case 'stating forth the pros and cons' about holding a meeting. Cranborne used this to once again press forcefully his argument that the suggestion should be deferred. At the head of his list of reasons for not issuing 'embarrassing' invitations, he placed Mackenzie King's reluctance as the most powerful and by the end of the first week of June he was able to inform Churchill that the foreign secretary agreed with him. Eden, with his own bitter personal experience of working with the Canadian leader, had been persuaded that postponement would be best.[55] With reports reaching Whitehall that Australian and New Zealand troops in the Middle East were growing unhappy, Menzies had meanwhile resumed his campaign as soon as he was back at home.[56] And in London there continued to be a considerable clamour from figures within both the political and military spectrums that he should be asked to return. Hankey remained convinced that both Menzies and Lloyd George needed to be brought into the government, 'two wise old elephants to tame the rogue elephant'. In response to the continuing intrigues Cranborne broadened his arguments and suggested that Smuts be called upon to come to London. This was a sensible proposal and one likely to find favour with the prime minister as the friendship between the two was well known. The year before one of Churchill's assistants had even proposed that were the British leader to die, his 'remarkable' South African counterpart would make an ideal replacement.[57]

With the South African leader now officially asked if he could help, his own high commissioner in London also began to try and draw him more prominently into the debate. Throughout 1941 neither Waterson nor Bruce had shown any indication of stopping their campaign to enhance their position.[58] In July they had not been given any advance warning that Iceland was to be garrisoned by American troops, a source of particular anger to them; as a result the Australian had even threatened to ignore the Secretary of State in future and make his own 'representations in highest quarters'.[59] But with the mounting calls for an Imperial presence in the War Cabinet, the two men's approach now differed. Bruce had gone on record, on more than one occasion, as doubting the wisdom of the 'impracticable' idea and he remained firm in his view that the only sensible option was to give the high commissioners a far greater role. Consequently he appeared to make every effort to keep himself close to the centre of events from where he could counter any proposals that could see his position threatened.[60] South Africa's representative had a similar agenda in regard to promoting his own role but he used a different method. With the DO asking Smuts to visit London, Waterson told his prime minister that there were continuing deficiencies in the system and it would be useful to have at least one Dominion leader present at all times sitting in the War Cabinet. He was told in response that while he shared his concerns, Smuts was mindful about any proposal that could be seen as forming an

Imperial War Cabinet. He further warned his high commissioner about becoming too closely connected to Bruce and potentially embarrassing suggestions.[61] These comments were repeated to the Dominions secretary leaving Cranborne in a position to now ask Churchill formally whether there should be a conference or not at this stage.[62] Every indication had been that the prime minister had followed this course knowing that he could count on Canadian and South African reservations. He certainly had no desire for a permanent representative in the War Cabinet as he had confirmed during a dinner at Chequers. As his secretary recorded, "'Well', said the PM, "you can easily turn the War Cabinet into a museum of Imperial celebrities, but then you have to have another body to manage it'".[63] Smuts' rejection left him free to 'regretfully' agree to a delay and reject any idea of extending an invitation to Menzies to return alone to London.[64]

There was, however, still one potential problem threatening what had proven to be an otherwise masterly strategy. Cranborne advised Churchill that the discussions with Smuts and the Canadian leader had been of a private character and, as such, there were fears about the effect of 'a blunt announcement' saying they could not attend. A telegram was duly despatched to Ottawa and the other Dominion capitals. This informed the various prime ministers that, in light of the public interest which the issue had aroused, there was an urgent need to make a statement on the matter at Westminster. It went on to advise them of what it was intended to say in light of what had been received from certain of them.[65] Faced by growing domestic hostility about what was perceived as an apparent lack of enthusiasm for travelling to London, the proposed message now upset Mackenzie King.[66] Canada's apparent tardiness in terms of mobilizing her resources during the early stages of the war had drawn the attention of the FO where, from within the American section, it was put down to 'a disingenuous – in fact dishonest – desire' which would best benefit the Canadian government and not its British counterpart. Strong stuff indeed, but it reflected a feeling within sections of Whitehall that Mackenzie King was not a great supporter of the alliance. This particular observer even felt that whatever the outcome of the war, at its end, the British government would retain no status of any kind in Canada.[67] So concerned was the Canadian leader with Churchill's suggested message that he requested mention be made that the current war was entirely different to the last and a conference was unnecessary. Churchill preferred not to give too many details beyond the inability of the Dominion leaders to attend, and largely ignored the request. Going into too many details might have kept the domestic debate going and, as it stood, he had neatly placed elsewhere the onus of responsibility for the decision not to proceed. In the last week of June 1941 he therefore stood before the House of Commons and explained how, having been invited, 'the exigencies of their work in their respective countries' made it impossible for the various Dominion leaders to visit London.[68]

This announcement was not well received in Ottawa. MacDonald sent three private notes to the DO at the beginning of August in which he detailed the events of the last few weeks. So sensitive did he feel these to be that he attached a strong plea to Cranborne not to pass on anything that might upset Churchill and lead to a serious quarrel 'between him and one or more of the Dominion prime ministers'.[69] This was a necessary warning in light of what he had to say; despite the high commissioner's reassurances that Mackenzie King admired his British counterpart enormously, there were apparently those in his cabinet who had described Churchill as a 'cad' for what he had said.[70] More significantly there had also been further proposals from Menzies for a London meeting, this time in a private telegram sent in mid-July 1941 to both the Canadian and Smuts. In this the Australian had outlined his concerns about how the war was being run from London, and reiterated the need for some form of permanent Dominion representation in the British War Cabinet. MacDonald thought the Canadian leader should attend but his host disliked what he saw as an attempt by Menzies to drag him into 'his personal ambitions'. The continuing intrigues left Cranborne angry for as he explained to MacDonald, they confirmed his own conversations with Menzies back in May. During these he had freely told the Dominions secretary, even though he knew him to be one of Churchill's ministers and friends, that he was prepared to give up the Australian leadership if necessary and enter British politics after the war with the aim of one day becoming the leader of the Conservative Party. The infuriated secretary of state roundly condemned Menzies for a 'not very pretty role' motivated 'to a considerable extent by personal motives'.[71] The Australian was increasingly desperate to be invited back to London, so much so that he asked Bruce to 'have a confidential chat with [Max] Beaverbrook' to assess his prospects.[72] Although appearing reluctant to tell Churchill the extent of Menzies' intrigues, the Dominions secretary at the same time discussed the scheming that had been taking place with Eden, one of the so-called 'Yes-Men' whom Menzies had so indiscreetly referred to on numerous occasions. The foreign secretary was asked for his comments on the potential constitutional problems that any move to include Menzies in the War Cabinet might entail. He was clearly concerned by what he heard, his secretary Oliver Harvey noting his particular worries about Menzies' potential return to London and a likely attempt 'to [try and] get into English politics via the War Cabinet'.[73]

With events in the Australian capital moving towards their conclusion, Mackenzie King arrived in London a victim of domestic public pressure that he should make such a trip. Initially scheduled for late August he had wavered to the last moment, Churchill's conference with President Roosevelt, held off the coast of Newfoundland, ultimately proving decisive.[74] Not wishing Mackenzie King to be involved, the British prime minister had deliberately kept details of his mission vague, only telling him he was going after pleas from within the

Cabinet Office in London. The Canadian had been embarrassed and now needed to save face by being seen to be briefed in person by Churchill. As MacDonald again took the opportunity to point out to Cranborne, the Canadian had been consistently critical of Menzies' schemes and he hoped that this loyalty would be highlighted to Churchill if the opportunity arose.[75] Mackenzie King, meanwhile, saw in his visit an opportunity to discuss Menzies' proposals in person with one of his Dominion colleagues. The New Zealand leader, Peter Fraser, had also been in London to meet the British government, and remained purposely to see his counterpart. Speaking privately to him he made it quite clear that he felt it would be inappropriate 'to give the impression that people here can't do the job'. He had sat in a number of War Cabinet meetings and he told Mackenzie King that he had found them to involve 'the freest and frankest discussion and expression of view'.[76] Not only did he therefore disagree with Menzies' arguments, he was adamant that there was 'no need for an Imperial Conference'. Smuts, who had recently been in Cairo, had contacted Churchill to again offer an entirely similar view, providing confirmation that three of the four Dominion leaders agreed there was no justification for calling a conference at this stage.[77]

After concluding his meeting with Roosevelt and returning home, one of Churchill's first acts had been to despatch a telegram to Canberra.[78] This made it unmistakably clear to Menzies that, were he to decide to visit London once again, he would only be permitted to attend the War Cabinet in the same manner as with his earlier visit and only so long as he remained Australia's leader. This final point perhaps reflected the degree to which Menzies' increasingly tenuous hold over his political position in Canberra had become common knowledge.[79] Now a subject of widespread debate in Whitehall, common agreement among some of the 'Yes-Men' held that he only had himself to blame. The Australian had, however, left himself with little option other than to press forward and, against the backdrop of a marked deterioration in relations with Japan, he had secured the support of his cabinet colleagues that he should return to London to try and secure a permanent Dominion seat at the highest political table.[80] While he was securing this backing, Mackenzie King and Churchill were proving to be as one in their outlook, the Canadian reassuring his host that it was the British view and not that of Australia which was viewed more favourably in his mind. So good were relations between the two leaders that Mackenzie King felt he 'would [not] be betraying any trust but rather doing my duty' in sharing the private memorandum that had been sent privately to him some five weeks before. Only later would he ask that his part not be recorded formally as he did not want Menzies 'to think I had not been square with him'. Massey, who during recent months had somewhat assiduously kept himself at a distance from the conspiracies of certain of his fellow high commissioners, felt his prime minister had pursued an excellent line.[81]

With the Australian leader's London plans thwarted, his future seemed hopeless. Although he had the backing of his cabinet, the influential Advisory War Council was less enamoured with his plans and with an even division in the House of Representatives, his detractors were effectively able to silence his pleas. According to Ronnie Cross, who had only recently arrived in Canberra as high commissioner, the desire to be rid of him had various grounds and included 'bitter personal enmities, ambitions of would be successors, Menzies' alleged lack of capacity for decision and action, and his lack of popular appeal'.[82] When he had been sworn into office in April 1939 the Australian prime minister had initially expected his government would last for only six weeks; that he was only now finally being forced to resign was therefore surely something of a success. Although he remained privately 'quite outspoken' about the degree to which Menzies had tried to get to London 'instead of staying with his own people', in front of his colleagues, Churchill appeared more forgiving, contacting him to offer his thanks for his 'courage' and 'help' during 'two terrible years'. About the Australian high commissioner on the other hand, whose fellow South African agitator was already preparing to recant some of his previous errors to Smuts, he was less generous.[83] There were few doubts though about the heartfelt thanks that Mackenzie King received from Churchill for his assistance upon his eventual return to Ottawa.[84] Massey felt that his visit to London had been a very great success and was once again glad that it was his prime minister who had 'given the quietus to the ill-thought out proposal'.[85]

The Canadian was not the only person to emerge from the episode with his reputation enhanced. From early May onwards, when he had first learnt of the full extent of Menzies' sometimes nefarious ambitions, Cranborne had maintained a scrupulously supportive stance of Churchill. Irrespective of whether this had actually improved the somewhat damaged relationship or not, he had not viewed this episode as an opportunity to 'mend fences' but, instead, an opportunity to support the prime minister and frustrate the Westminster conspirators. He was just glad to see an end to the Australian-inspired foibles, writing to a close Whitehall friend on the last day of August that it was better for all that the threat from Menzies had been removed. The Australian had made 'more of a hash of things than one would have thought possible' and throughout the summer months his 'intriguing [had been] a constant danger'.[86]

What he cannot have anticipated, however, was the degree to which the strains on the alliance were about to increase out of all proportion. A change in leadership in Canberra did not mean a change of view and the pressure on the British government to better recognize and appreciate the growing significance of the Dominions was already all but guaranteed.

6

Pacific Test

With Menzies' fall, his political challenge to Britain's leader was no more, but this did not signal an end to the tensions that had increasingly dominated relations between the two countries throughout the year. It would be down to his successor to finally secure an agreement that an Australian ministerial representative be allowed to attend the War Cabinet. Arthur Fadden had been appointed leader of the Country Party in October 1940 as a compromise candidate.[1] As Treasurer in Menzies' coalition government, during his London visit he served as acting prime minister. Many of his political colleagues viewed him as a natural choice for leader, much safer and a more popular individual than his predecessor. There is even some suggestion that he might have encouraged this view, working at the head of the Canberra-based conspiracy which helped bring about Menzies' downfall. His new position was not the strongest, parliament refused to form a 'national' government and was clearly restless for further change and he remained still entirely dependent on the support of two Independent MPs for a majority. Many observers saw the new administration as, at best, a stopgap measure and few thought it would be long before power moved into the hands of the Labour leader, John Curtin.[2] The pending Budget debate, which had to be concluded in September 1941, seemed to offer every opportunity for the opposition to mount a serious challenge but despite his weak position he lost little time in tackling the British authorities.[3] Ronnie Cross reported back that the new leader was likeable on a social level, 'you couldn't meet a better chap in a bar' where there would be 'streams of rollicking smut', and he found him to be 'good-natured' and 'shrewd'. Despite such sentiments he also warned Whitehall, although only much later, that Fadden was, professionally, suspect and had 'hardly any real thoughts of his own'.[4]

From London Bruce advised that the British leader was opposed to anybody being admitted into the War Cabinet other than a prime minister. He repeated his view that such proposals should be dropped.[5] This recommendation was ignored, Fadden telling the local press that he would soon be in a position to give them an actual name of the appointee; only a last-minute intervention from Cross, given in 'blunt terms', prevented him from going further. He could not, however, be dissuaded from contacting Churchill and telling him that an Australian minister would be sent to London on a special mission.[6] This development had been anticipated within Whitehall and the preparation of a detailed response had been begun well in advance of the news being received.[7] The new Australian leader was congratulated on his appointment before being told exactly what had been said to Menzies.[8] Each of the Dominions had been asked previously to register their views on representation and, aside from Australia, each had rejected the idea. The rest of the alliance was 'well content with present arrangements'. So far as Churchill was concerned, Fadden could send anybody he wished, they would be treated with 'utmost consideration and honour' but they would have no special access to the War Cabinet. Even Waterson felt this was the right line to have adopted as this was 'an obviously impossible proposition'. Previously an agitator for a permanent Dominion role, the South African high commissioner had come to believe that anybody other than a prime minister would prove to be 'not only useless but embarrassing' as they would be joining an executive body which could not 'wait whilst a member refers things to another body for instructions'. He doubted the long-term merits of 'the British PM telling the Australian PM where to get off' and what this might mean for the coalition, but he hoped that Fadden would take Churchill's comments in the 'right spirit'. Privately he urged Smuts to consider making 'tactful representations' to his new Australian counterpart to stop 'rocking the boat'.[9] The South African leader in turn was reluctant to intervene at this point, believing that Mackenzie King, who was still visiting London, would be far better placed to 'forestall the trouble' of potentially 'awkward constitutional questions'.

Churchill had followed up on his earlier stiffly worded telegram to Fadden with a much more restrained message.[10] There were reassurances and the promise that Britain 'would never let you down if real danger comes'. Fadden responded in turn with the barest suggestion of an apology. The earlier messages, he explained, were unavoidable as the threat to Australia became more obvious, making security the 'predominant thought in people's minds'.[11] The following day though he returned to his earlier position, now referring to discussions held during the 1937 Imperial Conference and, in the process, effectively issuing the British government with an ultimatum.[12] The Australian delegates at the meeting four years before apparently thought they had secured a firm commitment from the CID that in time of war, Dominion representation in London would be expanded to offer them a greater say. Although appreciative of the efforts made by the Dominions secretary, the authorities in Canberra now believed that the time had come for 'direct consultation' as opposed to relying on Cranborne who, they still noted, remained largely excluded from the War Cabinet. This had been noted elsewhere in the pages of *The Times* which had followed closely the summertime clamour for an Imperial War Cabinet. Allowing him access would actually make no huge difference other than 'recognize the prestige attached to the office'. But, as an editorial at the end of August stated bluntly, his role needed to be fortified and making him a permanent member of the War Cabinet would surely suffice to meet 'the very reasonable desire' of the Dominions for a closer level of participation.[13] While he would have obviously been aware of such suggestions with his relations with Churchill still uncertain, Bobbety was too discreet to be associated with them.

The secretary of state's views on what to do about Australia remained much the same as they had been throughout Menzies' summer intrigues. Fadden's first telegram had led him to suggest that the new government in Canberra should be encouraged to limit themselves to an announcement that they were sending an envoy 'on a visit of exploration and enquiry'.[14] He hoped not to have to issue any more formal, definite invitation and, although he chose not to share this view with Churchill, this remained entirely in keeping with his recent discussions with his departmental colleagues. Fadden's formal request for a larger role forced another review upon him and the DO produced a detailed assessment. This noted that it would have been better if the authorities in Canberra had maintained the same attitude as the other Dominion governments but they had not and the British War Cabinet now had to face a potentially far-reaching problem. Simply put this asked whether 'constitutional niceties or considerations of political convenience' could be cited as reasons to reject the Australian claim when to do so would 'leave a sense of rankling injustice'. This, Cranborne warned, might affect the Australian war effort and, worse, could endure and 'poison the relations between the two countries' long after the war had been won.[15] Adding to his difficulties was the British high commissioner in Canberra who had tackled Fadden and his complaints had leaked to the Australian press. Although this incident had been kept from the British tabloids, the Dominions secretary was worried about possible future 'unpleasant reactions'.[16] Reluctantly, and with the acknowledgement that successive Australian leaders had deliberately pushed Whitehall into a corner, Cranborne could only recommend that Fadden's proposal be accepted.

Churchill's response was predictable and he was left both angry and even, on this occasion, a little flustered. But irate as he was, the prime minister still recognized the wider issues at hand. 'These people', he wrote to Cranborne, 'are politically embarrassed' but they had put a 'splendid army into the field' and it was this that would dictate what happened next. He therefore authorized that the necessary arrangements be made to receive Page, the former leader of the Country Party, who had already unanimously been selected by the Australian cabinet to be sent to London. It was clearly stipulated, however, that his involvement in discussions in the War Cabinet would be restricted solely to those matters which concerned Australian interests.[17] Within the DO this decision was greeted with much apparent relief and was thought to be the best course to follow but neither Bruce at Australia House nor Cross in Canberra were to be told the department's exact position. The relevant documents dating from 1937 had been examined as part of an internal review of Fadden's argument and these made it clear that the discussions held then had in fact done no more than raise the possibility of the 'reconsideration' of the arrangements adopted during the First World War. Australia's case was obviously based on an entirely inaccurate premise but, with a solution apparently found, it was felt it would be best simply to welcome Page and keep Australian opinion satisfied.[18]

Fadden had secured his first objective but a second still remained.[19] When Menzies had arrived back in Canberra in late May 1941 the worsening military situation in the Middle East had left him facing immense pressures; following the news of Crete's fall he was described as looking 'about as happy as a sailor on a horse'.[20] His mood was not helped by local media reports that insufficient logistics support had been provided to Commonwealth forces as they retreated through Greece and speculation that this had significantly contributed to the operation's eventual defeat.[21] With the 9th Australian Division, the 18th Brigade of the 7th Australian Division and assorted other coalition forces surrounded in the North African port of Tobruk, it was hardly surprising that, following the completion of the Syrian campaign in late July, his government requested that its remaining troops in the Middle East be brought together to operate as one force. Churchill had been quick to say that he would be content to see this done so long as the position of the garrison at Tobruk was not affected; apart from the much smaller facilities at Benghazi, this was the best port along a thousand miles of North African coastline.[22] With Menzies' focus elsewhere, the garrison duly remained besieged throughout the summer despite the best efforts of General Thomas Blamey, commanding the Australian Imperial Forces (AIF) and principal advocate of the argument that Australian forces should be formed into a single force.[23] Fadden's appointment signalled much greater levels of political resolve and the new Australian leader quickly told his colleagues that he intended to resolve the matter. Pointing to Menzies' earlier comments, he informed Churchill that he wished to announce the withdrawal had been completed by mid-September. He also warned of the consequences of any further inaction and what might happen should 'any catastrophe' occur in the interim but the leadership in London remained firm in believing that 'Australia would not tolerate anything shabby' and would 'play the game' if the facts of the military situation were put to them.[24]

Churchill agreed to the move but with the condition that any withdrawal would first require confirmation from the British commander on the ground that this would not hamper his overall operations. The report back from General Sir Claude Auchinleck who, in July 1941, had succeeded General Sir Archibald Wavell as Commander-in-Chief Middle East, was far from favourable, a relief of the Tobruk garrison would not be justified.[25] Aside from Blamey there was agreement from all of the other commanders in theatre, including the other Dominion generals present, that such a withdrawal was the wrong decision. Oliver Lyttelton, who had been Minister of State in the Middle East since the end of June 1941, was even more forthright, telling the War Cabinet that no British commander would have considered the idea.[26] The reason for Australian insistence was the anxiety of the government 'to take out a political insurance policy'.[27] Similar sentiments were held by other leading political figures in London including both Eden and his private secretary.[28] Somewhat wary of 'the miserable Australians', Cranborne also appeared to concur although he warned his colleagues of a growing feeling in Canberra that the AIF was bearing the brunt of the fighting in North Africa.[29]

Drawing upon the military assessments and various other technical arguments, Churchill therefore approached Fadden again. He confirmed that if still insisted upon, the garrison would be withdrawn 'irrespective of the cost entailed and the injury to future prospects'. He had nonetheless hoped that Australia would consider a delay but Fadden could not be swayed and, despite Churchill's 'flowery phrases', his cabinet found London's case against withdrawal 'unconvincing'.[30] The British leader was willing to make allowances, recognizing the weakness of the Australian government's position, but, privately, he was 'astounded' by the refusal to offer more support. Auchinleck appears to have been even more disillusioned by Blamey's attitude and the subsequent decision by London to bow to Australian demands. So much so in fact that it was only with some apparent difficulty that he was persuaded not to resign, Churchill pointing out to him that 'any public controversy would injure the foundations of Empire'.[31] He did, however, use his commander's bitterness as an opportunity to contact Fadden one last time and ask that the two brigades that had yet to be evacuated from Tobruk be allowed to remain but he was again unsuccessful.[32] Cranborne meanwhile had contacted Cross and advised him to refuse any discussion of the matter and avoid any personal reproaches but events in the Western Desert had caused considerable bitterness in Whitehall. According to an official within the DO, writing near the war's end, the episode caused 'a great deal of fuss' and left many Australians 'feeling rather ashamed', although there is little firm evidence to support the latter argument.[33]

At the time the focus of attention in Canberra was actually Fadden's future political prospects and, following his failure to gain support for his Budget proposals, his decision to resign, a mere six weeks after he had taken power, was no real surprise.[34] The governor-general now looked to the Labour Party, which had won by far the most seats in the September 1940 general election, inviting Curtin to form a new government. Despite not having been in power for ten years, it had taken an active role on the opposition benches and retained a considerable voice in Australian politics. How it had conducted itself since the outbreak of war, however, meant that the DO had some concerns about the new government's calibre.[35] Cranborne himself lamented, earlier in 1941, that these were 'men who were entirely isolationist in their view and thought of nothing but the protection of Australia'.[36] Curtin, the former journalist and trade union organizer, who had been jailed briefly for anti-conscription activity during the First World War, had been quoted in the British press back in August 1939 as being entirely opposed to Australia's involvement in another European war.[37] By the time he took power, he had been Australia's opposition leader for five years but he had never held any high office and only two of his ministers had had any previous government experience. Cross found him very watchful and a British military visitor to Canberra reported back to London earlier in 1941 that, as a parliamentarian, Curtin 'didn't have the brains of Menzies'.[38] His earliest act as leader was to deal with yet another request from his British counterpart to postpone the final withdrawal from Tobruk.[39] Churchill pointed to the coalition's need for all available resources to support the imminent Allied operations in North Africa but Curtin was adamant that his remaining forces should be brought together. The Labour Party appeared to have entered office with few new ideas, adopting broadly similar policies to those of its predecessors.

There was, however, a much more forceful stance about the British Empire's defensive commitments in the Far East. The regional strategy had been a long-standing subject for discussion between London and the Antipodean Dominions.[40] Since 1923 successive Australian and New Zealand governments had been reassured by their London-based counterparts that the stationing of a Royal Navy fleet at the Singapore Naval Base and the safeguard of that facility ranked only second to the defence of the British Isles themselves.[41] But this guarantee had always carried with it a huge caveat, first revealed at the 1911 Imperial Conference when the Admiralty had complained about the Dominions' inability 'to comprehend the true principles of naval policy' and reiterated that the situation in the Pacific would always be 'absolutely regulated by events in the North Sea'.[42] By April 1939 increased European tensions meant a variety of previously unanticipated questions now had to be considered. One result of this was that at the Pacific Defence Conference, held in Wellington, only qualified assurances were offered to the Dominions that a fleet would still be sent and the British delegation's assurances of continuing military support were clearly greeted with some suspicion. But there was no panic, at least not at this stage. The New Zealand government publicly 'remained cool-headed', noting that the decision represented a 'departure' from the previously given assurances yet asking merely that a review of Far East strategy be undertaken.[43] The following month, in May 1939, the CID privately accepted that the 'Singapore Strategy' was no longer viable. A few weeks later a similar conclusion was reached amongst the Chiefs of Staff Sub-Committee but nothing was said to the Dominions themselves; indeed as far as they were concerned the strategy still held true.[44]

The decision of the Italian and Japanese governments to remain as bystanders in September 1939 meant that the Royal Navy could, in the short term at least, be deployed mainly in home and Mediterranean waters.[45] As has been seen, this also allowed the British government to offer renewed guarantees to the Dominion delegates who visited London two months later that the Far East remained higher on the list of strategic priorities than the Mediterranean. Churchill did this despite the private acceptances that had been reached previously. The position changed with France's rapid collapse, the subsequent entry of Italy into the war and the increasing deterioration of relations with Japan. As it had long feared it would have to do, the DO now found itself having to tell the Dominion leaders that it was most unlikely a fleet could be spared for the Far East.[46] Bruce complained bitterly on hearing the news so much so General Sir Hastings Ismay felt obliged to remind him that nobody had foreseen France's collapse, a disaster which removed both her fleet and her naval bases from previous strategic calculations.[47] Such interpretations of pre-war British strategic planning were commonplace. Back in 1923 Churchill had argued that to not defend the Pacific Dominions with a British Fleet would be 'an act of desertion, of abrogation of duty and of ingratitude both cruel and fatal'.[48] But emotive words dimmed with time; in March 1939 he had stressed to Chamberlain that 'on no account must anything which threatens in the Far East divert us from the prime objective'.[49] By the year's end, when he produced his ambiguous memorandum on Australian Naval Defence, he was even more convinced that while fighting Nazi Germany it would not be possible to make commitments in the Far East.[50] Official policy emanating from London in the months that followed seemed intent on saying as little as possible and when some form of reply was unavoidable it was given only in the vaguest terms.[51]

The worsening situation in the Far East was undoubtedly Curtin's primary cause for concern.[52] Both he and his government colleagues believed that their soon-to-arrive representative in London would help keep them much better informed of developments. Page had set out with Fadden still in charge, travelling via the Dutch East Indies on to Singapore where he attended a conference at which defence measures for the Far East region were the main subject of discussion. Here he reviewed the significant Australian contribution to the island's defence. An exhaustive review of Singapore's defence capabilities had been concluded by Menzies in October 1940, following which it had been agreed to send Australian troops to the island. This took the form initially of a single brigade from the 8th Division sent with the caveat that it was to be relieved by Indian troops, allowing it to join its parent in the North African theatre. Under the command of General Gordon Bennett, this force had in fact remained and been expanded.[53] Despite the change of government Curtin asked Page to continue and the Australian eventually reached Britain by way of the Philippines, the

United States and Canada. This choice of route meant that he would not attend his first War Cabinet meeting until the last week of October. In the meantime he looked to Richard Casey, now Australian minister in Washington, to advise him of the American assessment of the situation. Since his arrival in 1940 to take charge of his country's first foreign diplomatic post Casey had proven a great success in establishing excellent contacts in Washington and these told him that the State Department believed there to be 'very little chance' that the Japanese would attack in the near future.[54]

As Page continued his long journey Mackenzie King cabled the British leader to reassure him. He had entertained the Australian in Ottawa and believed his guest only to be interested in the situation in the Far East with 'no thoughts of urging any kind of an Imperial War Cabinet or representation of Australia in the War Cabinet'.[55] This was helpful information as fears remained in London that problems lay ahead. Page's selection was seen by one observer as 'an unfortunate choice' for, despite his being an elder statesman with considerable domestic political experience, he had 'little knowledge of defence or foreign affairs, no experience in diplomacy – he was a doctor by profession [who] owned a cattle station and was Minister of Commerce when appointed – and lacked the strength of character required to stand up to Churchill'. He was held to be 'genial' but at the same time 'fussy and rather stupid', not perhaps the best qualities for the job ahead.[56] Others who had met him in Australia were more complimentary in their depiction of a 'straight, kindly country gentleman' although even these noted that he was 'a little inclined to stress the obvious at some length and without any pause for interruption'.[57] In official circles there were undoubtedly those who considered Page's presence to be distracting and unhelpful. His bitter complaints at his initial meeting with the British War Cabinet about the poor state of the defences in Singapore and the unsatisfactory assistance he had been given during his journey did not improve the position.[58] There was also disquiet among the Dominion high commissioners who were unhappy about the apparently preferential treatment being afforded to Australia.[59] Page knew nothing of this and quickly settled down to address what he thought was his principal objective. This was influencing British policy 'while it was still fluid', so that it would bear 'a definite Australian colour and impress'.[60]

In the first instance this meant trying to obtain an agreement from Churchill to provide reinforcements for the Far East, but he was to make little progress. At the end of August 1941 Canberra had been told that the authorities in London were finally thinking that they would be able to station a naval unit in the Indian Ocean. Curtin had been pleased to hear this news, and he pressed his British counterpart to make good on some of his earlier more grandiose promises, urging that a modern ship be included in this proposed force. Churchill agreed to this, despite the opposition of his most senior naval advisors, and towards the end of October 1941 the authorities in Canberra were informed that the battle cruiser *Repulse* would be joined by the Royal Navy's latest battleship, the *Prince of Wales*.[61] Page's insistence that more should be done, at the same time drew the response that while Britain was 'resolute to help Australia if she were menaced', Japan was considered to be unlikely to invade. With his access to MAGIC intelligence decrypts, Roosevelt had known since July 1941 of the adoption of a dual policy by the Japanese Imperial Cabinet. This called for negotiations in the first instance and military action if they failed. The discussions between the two sides had subsequently proven lacklustre, at least in part because of America's decision to implement a total oil embargo as 'punishment' for the Japanese invasion of southern Indochina. This economic policy had been resolutely supported by Churchill who maintained the role of interested bystander throughout the negotiations. Believing that Japan was 'likely to pursue a policy of pinpricks' but not 'embark on total war', since late 1940 Whitehall had effectively restricted itself to sending vague warnings to the government in Tokyo. Once more the Dominions were not always fully informed, specifically when these were to be issued, despite the DO's complaints that this left their governments feeling that they were being forced into policies to which they had no input.[62]

With the alliance still beset by uncertainties, the relationship between the secretary of state and the prime minister showed little sign of improvement. Cranborne still believed not enough information was being supplied and increasingly he was of the view that the point had been reached where the DO was no longer able to function effectively. The most serious problem was the degree to which he was still being excluded from meetings, most significantly those of the War Cabinet and Chiefs of Staff Committees, as a result of which he continued to have little knowledge of the general war situation. This position was known to the London-based high commissioners who bypassed him more and more and went to other sources which talked 'more freely'. This made the Dominions secretary's position 'a farce', one which could only be remedied if he were given a free hand to pass information on as he saw fit using his discretion not to discuss operational matters or any other inappropriate issues. These comments were confirmed by Waterson in a private assessment of the British Commonwealth's position in the war sent to Smuts. In this the British War Cabinet was said to be an ineffective gathering, 'something approaching a cabinet of one who meets his colleagues twice a week and informs them of what is to be done'. As for Churchill he was undoubtedly 'a great national and imperial asset but he is not a superman'. The high commissioner nonetheless continued to remain generally optimistic about the future. He had attended a recent meeting of the local council in Lambeth: 'Proceedings were too like a council meeting to be true! Terrific arguments ... It might have been any town council in the Empire. When you see the similarity of things like these you understand why the Empire hangs together!'[63]

At the same time as Cranborne was still struggling with Churchill, he also had to keep a close eye on Menzies. Back in the summer Alfred Duff Cooper had been moved from the Ministry of Information to become Chancellor of the Duchy of Lancaster and he left the following month on a mission to the Far East, where he quickly earned the nickname 'Tough Snooper', to investigate measures for the coordination of regional defence. As part of the report he subsequently produced, he had called for the appointment of a British commissioner general based at Singapore and Menzies' name had been proposed for the job.[64] This was the second high-level suggestion in as many months that he be given a new role, the first having come from the governor-general in Canberra in early October. Lord Gowrie had proposed that a seat be found in the House of Commons in London for Menzies where 'his wide experience and knowledge of the Australian outlook would be useful'.[65] Both Churchill and Cranborne had dismissed this idea, and the new proposal from Duff Cooper found them no more receptive. It was rejected on the basis that it was uncertain how Menzies would react if he was required to implement instructions to which the authorities in Canberra were opposed.[66] Although the situation in the Far East was rapidly deteriorating, Churchill nonetheless seemed generally quite happy with how events were proceeding.[67] He was not alone; Bruce had been concerned about the British government's failure to offer any guarantee to the authorities in the Netherlands East Indies.[68] The Australian high commissioner's fears had apparently disappeared by late November and, despite having previously been one of the most vocal opponents of letting Washington take charge, he and his Dominion counterparts were now willing to accept that this was the right line to follow.[69] Page alone remained worried, largely on the basis of a 'very depressing' interview he had held with Sir Charles Portal, Chief of the Air Staff, who had told him an invasion of the Dutch East Indies might not result in Britain declaring war on Japan.[70] This, the Australian warned, would demonstrate how little the feelings of the Dominions on either side of the Tasman were understood and 'break the Empire'. This was in turn relayed to Churchill by his deputy along with the caution that there existed the potential for 'a very serious breach in empire relations'.[71] Despite the growing evidence now beginning to accumulate that Japan was poised to attack southwards, there was only silence in response.[72]

Page's concerns were the exception not the rule; where the Far East was concerned, there appeared to have emerged a surprising inclination to 'follow father'.[73] This was, in part, due to other considerations which dominated. Beginning in mid-November 1941 Operation *Crusader* had been a focus of attention throughout the Empire. British Commonwealth troops had successfully reached Benghazi only to be thrown back, and South African troops were heavily involved earning considerable praise for their bravery. During the course of the fighting the 5th South African Infantry Brigade was overrun at Sidi Rezegh, just south of Tobruk, and approximately 3,000 men were killed, wounded or captured, the worst losses experienced by the South African military in its history. Smuts never publicly criticized the British military leadership for this disaster and he reacted strongly to negative comments made in the South African media but the defeat threatened his domestic political position.[74] Meanwhile in Canada 'rampant personal quarrels' and other domestic distractions remained broadly to the fore while New Zealand's voice was also still only rarely raised and even more rarely heard.[75] Perhaps the greatest revelation was the degree to which even the Australian government appeared to have fallen noticeably more in line with British thinking. Curtin and his fellow ministers had found many domestic political distractions to occupy themselves as generally positive messages from London and Washington and the optimistic assessments of various British visitors helped ease fears of a possible Japanese attack.[76] Such was the growing optimism that parliament was even told in early November there was now no desire by the government to recall the AIF and an earlier decision to send an Armoured Division to the Middle East was confirmed.[77] Announcements such as these perhaps helped to explain why the complacency among the Australian public, which British high commissioners had referred to in the past, had if anything become worse.

High profile public criticism of London seemed to come almost solely from Dr Herbert Evatt, Curtin's Attorney-General and Minister for External Affairs. Elected to parliament in 1940, as a justice in the Australian High Court he had previously been a vocal supporter of greater federal powers. His public censure of Britain's failure speedily to declare war on Finland, Hungary and Romania, each of which had sided with Nazi Germany following the latter's attack on the Soviet Union in June 1941, was but one example of the many complaints he had to make. On this occasion though, Churchill responded with a stiff rebuke to Canberra, forcing even Curtin to apologise.[78] The reports reaching London about the attitude of the Australian leader were in fact favourable in tone, offering a far more optimistic assessment of his character and abilities than had initially been the case. In mid-October 1941 Air Chief Marshal Sir Robert Brooke-Popham visited Canberra, as commander-in-chief Far East, to offer reassurance that regional security was not being neglected by the chiefs of staff in faraway London. He subsequently provided a detailed analysis for the British authorities of what he had found and perhaps key amongst the points raised was the degree to which he had been impressed by the Australian leader. Equally impressed was Duff Cooper when, in November 1941, he was sent to Canberra to 'tell the Australians how wonderful they are and how almost as wonderful we are'. In a subsequent private letter to Cranborne he recorded that Curtin was 'a modest, sincere, intelligent and honest man and is generally regarded as such'.[79]

Despite such positive words the Australian leader actually remained greatly distressed about the security situation in the Far East. In mid-November 1941 his chiefs of staff had presented a report to him which made it clear Malaya could not be defended in the event of a major attack by Japan.[80] This led to another strongly worded telegram to Whitehall, sent on the first day of December, in which the British government was reminded of its previous promises that there would be strong defences at Singapore. Before any response could be given Japanese forces attacked the US Pacific Fleet stationed at Pearl Harbor and various other British and American targets in the Pacific and South East Asia. As Waterson put it, 'the Japs have gone over the top' and he believed there to be 'a reasonable chance of this year being the last year of the war', although it was not entirely clear who he thought would emerge victorious.[81] Churchill immediately hurried to Washington, against the advice of a number of his War Cabinet colleagues, not merely to coordinate the finer details of how the newly expanded alliance would function but also to ensure guarantees about the 'Hitler first' strategy. More commonly referred to by its short 'ABC-1' title, this proposal had originally been agreed in early 1941 during the Washington Staff Conversations. The future Allied effort was to be focused on the European theatre, not the Far East, and the prime minister did not want to see this altered despite the obvious ramifications for the menaced Tasman Dominions.[82] A young Nicholas Mansergh, serving in the public relations section of the DO, apparently agreed with the sentiment and he would later write that, from this date, the war had entered an entirely new phase. This would be one in which 'the importance of exclusively Commonwealth organizations declined'.[83] The alliance had a new member, one that could itself have been a Dominion had it not broken away, but as it had already shown it held serious doubts about the way in which this coalition was operating. Churchill went to sleep in the knowledge that the Empire was saved and Britain would prevail. There would be a price to pay though, and the long-standing relationship with the Dominions would have to be prominently included in the bargain.

7

The 'First' Dominion

During the inter-war period even innocent reference to the word 'Imperialism' was liable to generate considerable misunderstanding and hostility on the western shores of the Atlantic Ocean.[1] It was patently obvious that wide sections of American public opinion were opposed to the idea of colonies but what was less clear was the extent of the hostility to the wider imperial idea. Dominions, colonies, protectorates, names did not matter; many felt that they were evil and needed to be emancipated from the yoke of British rule. The strategies developed by successive governments at Westminster whose intention was to improve this position formed slowly and had doubtful results. There were those on both sides of the Atlantic who tried to understand why the two countries could not reconcile lingering differences on such issues, but they ran the risk of themselves being derided. Prominent among this group was the *New York Times*. Its position was typified by a question posed by one of its writers in November 1921 about the Monroe Doctrine. First announced by the president of the same name in December 1823, this was surely an imperial document if ever there was one in so much as, in formalizing a policy of resistance to European encroachment of the American continent, it carried a hidden message; the fledgling Republic would not let its continental neighbours threaten its security. As the newspaper now asked was this not also an important principle of British foreign policy, in effect constituting an Anglo-American Doctrine?[2] This was developed further in a supplement to the main publication, it being claimed that the idea had only ever worked because British governments had protected its integrity. This, they did, as a result of ties of sentiment 'based upon the principle of racial solidarity'.[3] And the modern British Empire was still doing the same: '[Britain] has constantly striven to enlarge her Dominions, not in order to exploit them – it is very doubtful, indeed, whether on balance her possessions yield a profit to the motherland – but in the instinctive desire of reserving the vast and fruitful territories of the New World to the Anglo-Saxon race'. The article's author was clear in his view that had there been an Anglo-American alliance, in 1914 there would have been no German attack. Such a link, it was concluded, was needed more than ever before following the war's conclusion, the warning being made that 'harmony and union will give peace to the world … disagreement and strife would fill the world with unhappiness and war'.

Could the distrust be overcome in the years ahead or would the mistakes of the past be repeated was therefore the question asked by many. Such warnings fell, for the most part, on resoundingly deaf ears. As one distinguished commentator has noted, the reality was that during the inter-war period 'each country turned inwards to brood upon its own troubles'.[4] American isolationism was met with British suspicion, 'the irresponsibles' who displayed 'an almost criminal neglect of Anglo-American relations'. Intellectual debate dimmed while even discussion of commerce, foreign affairs and common issues of international security were conducted in the most guarded of manner. Mutual study of law, cooperation in merchant banking and the success of British film stars in Hollywood remained the most promising avenues for cooperation and future discourse, but there was only so much that these could offer. The most celebrated example of the doubts that existed could be seen in 'War Plan Red', drawn up and approved by the American War Department in 1930 then updated at regular intervals. In the late 1920s, military strategists in Washington had developed plans for a war with Japan (referred to as 'Orange'), Germany ('Black'), Mexico ('Green') and Britain ('Red'). The 'Blue-Red' conflict, it was envisaged, would begin over international trade: 'The war aim of Red in a war with Blue is conceived to be the definite elimination of Blue as an important economic and commercial rival.' The planners anticipated a war 'of long duration' because 'the Red race' is 'more or less phlegmatic' but 'noted for its ability to fight to a finish'.[5] Sir Charles Mallet was by no means alone in his warnings that all things connected to trade and commerce were disastrous issues for the two countries to squabble over. This did not prevent the 1930 Hawley-Smoot Tariff becoming law, which precipitated, in turn, a strong Imperial response, guaranteeing that suspicion and hostility endured. While it still proved impossible to agree to a full system of Imperial Preference, at the 1932 Ottawa Conference, there was an acceptance between Britain and the Dominions of a preferential understanding of low tariffs within the Empire and higher tariffs elsewhere.[6] Essentially, in return for concessions on the part of the Dominions, the British government agreed to give them 'definite advantages' in the domestic market. For its critics, and there were many of them who engaged in an often bitter debate, Ottawa hampered free trade and placed restrictions on Britain's economic relationship with countries who were not members of the Empire but with whom she had previously maintained very close trade relations.[7]

These disagreements were watched closely in the United States but, despite Woodrow Wilson's commitment to national self-determination, for the most part political interest in Britain's imperial relationships in the inter-war period was minimal.[8] The late-nineteenth century expansion in both countries had excited very little criticism in the other, perhaps because, 'as a partner in the white man's burden the USA was indulgent, in a quite novel degree, to British colonial aspirations'.[9] It was after all an American magazine, *McClure's*, in which

Rudyard Kipling first published his 'White Man's Burden'. This understanding, if there was one, changed, however, and with the worsening situation in Europe attempts to influence mainstream American public opinion became increasingly unsubtle; the message was that the British Empire was something to be feared. Typical of such *agent provocateurs* was Quincy Howe who, according to one critic, saw 'an Englishman under every bed'. He was vocal in his criticisms and sought to deliver them to the widest possible audience. As *Time* magazine put it, writing in December 1938, since Howe had become editor of 'Simon and Schuster' it had published three books examining the 'massive, muddling, Machiavellian empire of George VI'. The last of these was Robert Briffault's *The Decline and Fall of the British Empire*, 'the most vehement book of the year' and it was said to be fortunate it would not be published in Britain as 'it consists of 263 pages of denunciation of England and all things English, her politics, smugness, selfishness, morals – even her birth rate'.[10]

Such sentiments were not confined to the western shores of the Atlantic. In January 1938 the already long-serving American leader Franklin D. Roosevelt had suggested a plan for discussing the underlying tensions that were weakening the international system. Neville Chamberlain was guarded in his response to the 'woolly and dangerous proposals'. Oliver Harvey, watching from within the FO, felt the prime minister was 'temperamentally anti-American' and the proposals ultimately came to nothing, in large part because of his obstructionism; 'it is always best and safest to count on nothing from the Americans but words' as he warned his sister.[11] It was not all doom and gloom. The visit of the royal family to the United States in June 1939 had demonstrated the degree to which there was 'an American anglophilia [that] was deeply nostalgic for a romanticized past'. The inspection by King George VI and Queen Elizabeth of the British Pavilion, part of New York's World Fair, certainly appears to have been well received. Observers were apparently dazzled by the queen's radiant smile and, no doubt for the purposes of the covering press pack, the king consumed his first hot dog. The trip, despite it having 'no discernible impact on entrenched isolationist sentiment', was deemed a great success as it demonstrated the common democratic ideals that existed.[12] It had not succeeded in calming the fears of all and elements within the American public continued to warn of the Imperial menace. Writing in his *Survey of International Affairs* the celebrated, and often controversial, British historian Arnold Toynbee was well qualified to provide the simplest explanation for this:

American feeling and policy were still governed by past facts which had already become partly or wholly irrelevant to the international situation in which the United States was now actually placed. Perhaps the most powerful of these influences from the past was the fact that over nine per cent of the living generation of white inhabitants of the

United States and the ancestors of all of them no longer ago, at the earliest than ten or twelve generations back, had, at some particular moment, deliberately pulled up their roots from ancestral ground in Europe and had crossed the Atlantic in order to start, on the American side of it, a new life free from the unhappy elements in their European heritage.[13]

The outbreak of war brought with it exacerbated tensions. Writing in October 1939 Douglas Fairbanks Jr., actor, socialite and later to become, at least temporarily, a British commando, offered the friendliest of warnings to Eden. The Dominions secretary was told an argument was being made in the United States that 'Britain is an Imperial autocracy built by plunder and wars – no better for its time than Hitler now'. To counter this he suggested it was imperative for Britain to stress 'the voluntary actions of the free dominions' as part of a strategy of making certain not to appear as 'an Imperial octopus and the more she looks like the mother of an independent but at all times cooperative family the better'. Betraying the American bent for commerce, the conclusion to this long, personal letter was that 'the British government should continue to an even greater extent to regard itself as no more that the "Chairman of the Board" of the British Commonwealth'.[14] Roosevelt had privately offered similar advice cautioning the British Ambassador in Washington, Lord Lothian, of how helpful it would be if the British could emphasize their commitment to self-government. Writing to Lord Halifax in December 1939 back in London, the former Philip Kerr repeated the President's message. The suggestion was that the British could point out publicly that the empire-building of earlier centuries had been abandoned and the lesson had been learnt that 'the only foundation for a stable international system was national autonomy'. Chamberlain wrote a marginal comment on the letter rejecting such penance, while the senior figure in the FO, Robert Vansittart, labelled it 'simply lunacy'. 'What jam for German propaganda', he wrote to his secretary of state Halifax, and for all the American isolationists, who, having goaded Britain for cowardice in the past had now 'taken refuge in the pavilion lavatory'.[15]

The cause for much of this animosity was fear about what it would cost to bring the first Dominion back into the bosom of the relationship. Frank Ashton-Gwatkin, head of economic relations within the FO had paid a six week visit to the United States the year before the war had started. His observations led him to conclude that the most that could be counted on from the other side of the Atlantic in the event of another war was 'pacific benevolence' leading to possible eventual participation if the conflict was prolonged. This certainly seemed a fair reflection of a country where a sense of isolationism so clearly reigned, both in the Congress and the national mood.[16] There were also concerns about American rivalry over air routes which had long existed in both London and Wellington and the inter-war struggle for control of air communications was often fraught.

There was lingering resentment about the Ottawa agreements and the resulting system of Imperial Preference which continued to exclude American products from Australian and New Zealand markets and annoyed many in Washington. There were also the American claims that had been made on a number of islands in the Pacific under British and New Zealand jurisdiction.[17]

Chamberlain himself was wary of the cost of American support, writing to his sister in January 1940, 'heaven knows I don't want the Americans to fight for us – we should have to pay too dearly for that if they had a right to be in on the peace terms – but if they are so sympathetic they might at least refrain from hampering our efforts and comforting our foes'.[18]

Trading practices caused a great deal of anxiety in these early wartime months and Lothian was largely responsible for helping to smooth over problems as they emerged. Indeed it has been reiterated only recently the degree to which he was 'the nexus of the Anglo-American relationship' proscribing better understanding between the two countries, the FO's response being based largely on his informed judgements.[19] Continuing British efforts to wage economic warfare against Germany – which entailed a reduction in purchases of some American goods and the introduction of a blockade – engendered a good deal of enmity in Washington.[20] The British financial position was, in fact, certainly at this stage, the critical issue of the war. Even before the first German troops had crossed into Poland the situation facing the British Exchequer was dire. The pressure placed on the pound during 1939 alone reduced Britain's war chest of gold and foreign securities by at least one-quarter.[21] The undertaking of a rapid rearmament programme begun after the Munich settlement had placed further strains on resources, and the situation was only likely to get worse.[22] And as an internal memorandum prepared by the Treasury had concluded two month's before the war's eventual start, unless the United States was prepared either to lend or give money as required, the prospects for a long war were 'exceedingly grim'.[23]

The State Department had envisaged that Hitler would follow his rapid destruction of Poland with an equally devastating assault on the Western Front and an inevitable defeat of the Allies. The opposite happened, and the 'Phoney War' helped ensure that there remained virtually no enthusiasm among the American public, and therefore its politicians, for any action beyond selling arms and equipment to those countries which might want them. The Sumner Welles mission came and went with little to be said for it other than the State Department representative formed a strong aversion to Churchill, whom he later told Roosevelt he believed to have been drunk throughout their two hour meeting; much the same tale was given by the American Ambassador in London, Joseph Kennedy.[24] There remained little chance of any direct intervention from the United States, at least until the November 1940 presidential elections had been decided. Indeed Lothian's reports, condemned as anti-imperialist by the

colonial secretary in London, talked of pessimism and a growing lack of belief
that Britain and its Empire could prevail.[25]

At the end of February 1940 Lothian posed an interesting question to
Halifax: was the British government contemplating a re-summoning of the old
Imperial War Cabinet? He believed that 'the more the Empire aspect of the war
can be visibly represented the better from the American point of view'. As the
ambassador told London, the reconstruction of the Imperial War Cabinet would
help to strengthen the argument that the Allies were fighting for the freedom of
small nations. He could not see any sense of suspicion or antipathy to be found
towards the Dominions in America and, as he continued, if his hosts were ever
going to come out of isolation and provide greater assistance 'she would be far
more likely to do so if the proposal is to cooperate with a British commonwealth
of free nations all of whom are obviously taking a hand in formulating policy
and wartime decisions than with a Britain which would seem once more to be
bossing the show'. At the DO there was little enthusiasm for the suggestion. In a
lengthy, and often insightful, minute 'constitutional difficulties' were highlighted
which would most likely result from any attempt to 'suggest the power of decision
should be entrusted to the United Kingdom War Cabinet'. As such 'anything in
the nature of a super-Cabinet ... would be unacceptable and would, indeed meet
with strong opposition'.[26]

The significance of the personal relationship that existed between Churchill
and Roosevelt has been closely examined. The British capitulation at Munich
was the greatest handicap in many American eyes and Chamberlain was at the
head of the group of those who were held to be accountable. Churchill was not
in this category, and had the added advantage of being half American; his mother
Jennie Jerome was an American heiress.[27] This did not mean that the relationship
between the two was immediately bedecked with intimacy despite the prime
minister's subsequent assertion that 'no lover ever studied every whim of his
mistress as I did those of President Roosevelt'.[28] For much of the inter-war period
he and the American leader were not friends nor were they political compatriots.
Indeed they had met only once, an encounter in London in 1918 that Churchill
completely forgot and his counterpart 'remembered with distaste'.[29] In the years
that followed the American was, however, keenly aware of the other's reputation
as a staunch opponent of Nazism and this appeared to help overcome his initial
reservations as the Anglo-Dominion position grew worse through the dark days
of Hitler's crushing of European opposition.

By autumn 1940 Britain's dollar reserves were exhausted and as the United
States continued to show few signs of offering any credit disaster appeared to
loom. A September deal had given the Admiralty 50 old American destroyers
of doubtful military value, in return for which Roosevelt gained the long-term
mortgage for a raft of prime British real estate scattered around the Empire, and

a guarantee that the Royal Navy would never be surrendered to the Germans.[30] This was only a relative success. The defeated French government had placed its gold reserves in storage in Canada but British attempts to use this as collateral for further purchases had floundered on Mackenzie King's discomfort over such an act. Negotiations with the Dutch and Belgian governments-in-exile to use the remainder of the monies and commodities that had been rescued with them as they fled the Continent had also proven unsuccessful as the repayment terms demanded were considered to be too onerous. And it soon got worse. The American Treasury Secretary Henry Morgenthau Jr. had requested a complete list of British holdings in the Western Hemisphere, differentiated according to liquidity. When Roosevelt was shown the list, he remarked, 'Well, they aren't bust, there's lots of money there.' He therefore now advised the British authorities that he had arranged for an American destroyer to sail for South Africa to arrange the transfer of some of the United Kingdom's gold held there. It was recognized that this would be virtually the last of the gold reserves available but it was also understood that there was no choice other than to acquiesce to the president's decision. Whitehall's embarrassment was all too apparent, it even being suggested that General Smuts not be told why the destroyer was visiting.[31]

Within the DO the importance of the United States was entirely recognized by Cranborne who also held that the authorities in Washington were the only ones who could deter Japan and protect the British Empire's position in the Far East.[32] He had his concerns about the extent of the relationship, however, and these drew heavily upon his knowledge of the Dominions' thinking on the matter. On the one hand there was the New Zealand high commissioner in London raging about 'toadying to a power which only acted in accordance with its own selfish and commercial interests'.[33] On the other was Canada which, even before the signing of the Ogdensburg Agreement between Mackenzie King and Roosevelt in August 1940, was recognized within Whitehall, albeit reluctantly in some quarters, as enjoying a special relationship with the Washington administration.[34] In light of its geography, history and culture, the fact that Canada should feel close to its southern neighbour can be seen today as not surprising; at the time it caused some confusion within Whitehall's more obstreperous clique. Generally speaking, as one astute commentator put it just weeks after the outbreak of war, the American-Dominions relationship would always be complicated.[35] This was because the Dominions were at the same time 'both jealous and contra-wise' admirers of all things American. They recognized that securing the support of the authorities in Washington was a prerequisite to winning the war and consequently they campaigned hard for closer links.[36]

In November 1940 Roosevelt had won the presidential election and with it came – in response to a lengthy and pointed plea from Churchill – a greater degree of confidence to provide some measure of succour. By the spring of the following year he was in a more sympathetic mood, 'We have been milking the British financial cow, which had plenty of milk at one time, but which has now about become dry.'[37] The Lend-Lease Act, pushed through Congress in the first two months of 1941 and signed into law in March saved the day in so much as it did away with the cash-and-carry policy which had obliged the British authorities to pay for all of its supplies bought in the United States in hard currency. Before its agreement Halifax had been given an ultimatum. The British must sell one of their important companies in the next week as a mark of good faith; a major subsidiary of Courtaulds was consequently sold at a knock-down price.[38] Here was the visible demonstration of the price of salvation, what was left of Britain's economic strength. According to one of those present the promise given by Harry Hopkins, the president's emissary, that he would tell Roosevelt upon his return that the United States should unconditionally support the British invoked tears in the famously lachrymose British leader and 'seemed like a rope thrown to a drowning man'.[39] According to one American reviewer US support for Britain's war effort was 'a knife to open that oyster shell, the Empire'.[40] There also remained those in Washington who saw the proposed facilities as a device that would be used by the British to sustain exports in the face of American competition; essentially having been supplied with raw materials and components free of charge these would then be sold in the global export markets.[41] This rather seemed to overlook the fact that the subsequent German attack against the Soviet Union should, if any further evidence were still needed, have amply demonstrated the enduring nature of Hitler's expansionist plans.

Roosevelt's financial promise was well received despite its apparently reserved nature. According to Cuthbert Headlam, Conservative MP for the safe seat of Newcastle North, the Americans were 'a quaint lot', prepared to do everything 'as their share in the war for democracy' but fight.[42] The Dominions, however, were often kept deliberately on the fringes of these discussions as they gained momentum throughout 1941, making them especially wary of the longer-term implications both for them individually and for the alliance.[43] This distance was in large part because the United States preferred to deal just with one set of negotiators, but there was also a desire by the British government to retain ultimate control of the distribution of loaned materials.[44] Although arrangements ultimately improved, the minimal access initially given to the newly available equipment left the Dominions angry at the DO for 'not pressing their case hard enough'.[45] As Cranborne had campaigned especially hard for them to be included, such criticism was unfair.[46] It is however clear that the lack of involvement in the first instance ensured that there was a subsequent reluctance to demonstrate any great enthusiasm for the Lend-Lease scheme. The view took hold that this economic entanglement would quite likely have potentially onerous consequences for post-war economic policy, most obviously because of an almost inevitable attack by the American government on the system of Imperial Preference.[47] As Cranborne argued, in a note written to the Chancellor in August 1941, 'it is plain that for some of the Dominions ... the abandonment of [this system], without compensating advantages which are not yet in sight, would at their present stage of development spell economic disaster'.[48] Despite subsequent criticisms of the degree to which he sought to encourage the relationship, even Churchill was not entirely blind to this danger and what it would mean for the future of the British Empire. But there was little else he felt could be done by this stage of the war.[49]

A considerable amount of squabbling followed over the exact provisions of the agreement and what they meant for each of the Dominions. The ordering and distribution of essential supplies for the Anglo-Dominion alliance had been handled in a variety of ways. Canada had, from the outset, been an exception to the rules as it was a dollar country and had its own arrangements with the United States, a provision which proved of great value not just for it but also for Britain who took full advantage of this route of purchase. The remainder of the Dominions – and indeed India and the Colonies – placed all orders for warlike stores, meaning weapons and munitions for fighting forces, through the British Purchasing Commission. The WO, in turn, was responsible for distributing these purchases based upon the appreciations of strategic necessity supplied by the General Staff. This arrangement had been put to the Dominions at the start of the war and they had agreed; for the first few years it proved a working solution but with occasional distresses. Up until April 1941 all non-warlike stores bought in the United States were again handled by Britain as the provider of dollar exchange or gold required to pay for them and at every opportunity it remained keen to limit spending. Lend-Lease brought with it a request from Washington that a similar system be maintained with all Empire needs being coordinated before submission into a single channel. Global requirements were accumulated and processed in London and Dominion supply representatives joined the Purchasing Commission. This system worked for the first few months but it soon became known in London that Casey, the Australian representative in Washington, was agitating that each Dominion should have direct dealings. The American authorities, perhaps pleased at what they saw as signs of growing agitation, seemed only too pleased to assist. According to Arthur Purvis, the head of the British mission, the degree to which the Dominions wished to make themselves involved was 'making the waters rather muddy' in Washington. His view was that the Dominions could not hope to gain either the same access to goods or the same repayment terms because the American public held no 'emotional sympathy' for them.[50] This led the DO to comment that it would be 'intolerable' if 'Dominion machinations' were found to be to blame for the trouble.[51] And by December 1941 it was now being made quite clear by the

Americans themselves that the Dominions' belief that they 'could get practically anything under Lend-Lease' was a 'misunderstanding'.[52]

To some perhaps less than objective writers in Britain it was never in doubt that the US would help, an article in the *Empire Review* in February 1941 being typical of such sentiment: 'American ideals and interests are as deeply involved as are those of Britain in the threat of Nazi domination. If Britain goes under the United States faces the loss of the most important single source of her strategic raw materials, her overseas trade and investment, the ruin of her prosperity and the end of her traditional way of living and thinking. A war to decide the fate of the British Empire cannot, therefore, be a matter of indifference to America.'[53] Watching from his vantage point in Canada House, which he used to augment the information he gained from his many connections within British society, Charles Ritchie was probably more accurate with his assessment. As he wrote in his sometime scandalous diary: 'How the English hate being rescued by the Americans. They know they must swallow it, but God how it sticks in their throats. The Americans are thoroughly justified in their suspicions of the English, and the English I think are justified in their belief that they are superior to the Americans. They have still the steadiness, stoicism and self-discipline that make for a ruling race, but what will these qualities avail them if the tide of history and economics has turned against them?'[54]

The Atlantic Charter was another challenge, a 'flop' that went down like a proverbial lead balloon in London and in large parts of the Empire but its significance in terms of Anglo-American relations and the position of the British Empire was undoubtedly greater than any of the British delegation could ever have imagined.[55] Welles, in competition with Secretary of State Cordell Hull, had been a leading force behind the idea of producing a joint declaration in which Imperial Preference would be violently censured. The actual proposal for the Charter was apparently sprung upon Churchill on the opening day of the conference by his host. Despite the leading role Sir Alexander Cadogan played in drafting the final document, it lacked any significant oversight by the Whitehall mandarins who specialized in dissecting such agreements.[56] Oliver Harvey noted in his diary that Eden 'feels FDR had bowled the PM a very quick one'.[57] The cricketing metaphor would have been lost on the American hosts; as would become more apparent later the Charter was in fact more akin to a 'Beanball' thrown to cause the opposition injury for it certainly had a considerable negative impact on the British imperial position. Article 3, which affirmed that the two governments 'respect the right of all peoples to choose the form of government under which they will live', was 'perhaps the most explosive principle of all'.[58] Churchill told the Cabinet following his return that he believed this referred to 'the restoration of the sovereignty, self-government and national life of the States and nations of Europe now under the Nazi yoke'. What it definitely did not refer to was the position of any of the many subject peoples of the British Crown. Roosevelt apparently, however, saw it as much more than just this, his understanding being that the specific promise outlined in the third article 'applied to all humanity'.[59]

Writers such as Viscount Samuel were able to gloss over the question of what the United States was actually trying to achieve during the meeting held at Placentia Bay off the Newfoundland coast in August 1941, arguing that the finer details were something to be examined at a later stage, part of a process which it was inferred would take a very long time to complete.[60] Others preferred to focus on the wider economic aspects of the document, and what was seen as the abandonment of the restrictions of Ottawa and the embracing of a more open, advantageous and international system of post-war trade.[61] Upon reading the newspaper accounts of the signing Leopold Amery, who was eminently well qualified after a lifetime considering such issues to quote on the long-term implications, rued 'we shall no doubt pay dearly in the end for the fluffy flapdoodle'.[62] His assessment was both the most alarming but also the most astute. Headlam retained a broadly similar outlook with the formal announcement of the Atlantic Charter. This was an 'eight point pronouncement' that was 'somewhat vague and woolly in character' and was likely intended for an American audience who would be 'tickled'. His conclusion though was that Britain's hoped for allies were 'a strange and unpleasing people: it is a nuisance that we are so dependent on them'.[63] As has been seen, the Dominion governments had been given only the vaguest of indications of what was proposed.[64] This led the DO to complain, 'so long as [they] are kept in the dark, they are apt to misconstrue the reasons for our actions … and to suspect us of ulterior motives which, apart perhaps from our wish to ensure absolute secrecy about future plans and operations, do not exist'.[65]

Throughout 1941 the United States edged towards war with the extension of its naval operations east of Iceland and the eventual final repeal of the most significant remaining provisions of the Neutrality Act. By this stage all bar the most myopic of isolationists recognized that the Roosevelt administration would at some stage soon become a wartime government. As Halifax confided to Amery in May 1941, 'the defeatists and non-interventionists are working very hard'. Later that month, after a visit to the Middle West, he was more optimistic that there was considerable support for a policy of supporting Britain, and that the isolationists were not so strong 'as so many people from a distance think'.[66] In August 1941 Hugh Dalton had been told that Roosevelt was 'a sick man and more and more with the mentality of an Emperor'. His source also claimed that although Halifax was now getting on better with the President, he had broken down and wept in front of him only a short time after his arrival 'because he couldn't get on with these Americans'.[67] In November of that same year Halifax was attacked by egg and tomato throwing demonstrators as he entered the chancery of Archbishop Edward Mooney in Detroit. He compared working with American government departments to being like 'a disorderly day's rabbit shooting'. 'Nothing comes out where you expect and you are much discouraged. And then, suddenly something emerges quite unexpectedly at the far end of the field'.[68] John Maynard Keynes, a regular visitor to Washington as he conducted the complicated financial negotiations, also characterized American officials as 'flying confusedly about like bees, in no ascertainable direction, bearing with them both the menace of the sting and the promise of honey'.[69] What remained to be confirmed was the exact manner in which this would take place. The President and his aides were reading intercepted Japanese intelligence and knew that in November 1941 the Nazi Foreign Minister Ribbentrop had agreed that in the event of war involving America, Germany and Japan would be in it together. Even so Hitler spared Roosevelt a tricky political manoeuvre by choosing to declare war on the United States following the Pearl Harbor attack.[70]

During the war Professor Keith Hancock, considered by one of the greatest modern historians of the British Empire and Commonwealth as 'the greatest', wrote a small volume entitled *Argument of Empire*.[71] Having previously produced the still authoritative *Survey of British Commonwealth Affairs*, he wrote as an Australian who had spent a great deal of time working and living in Britain which made him both enamoured of the way of life he had experienced but also aware of its foibles and follies. His credentials were impeccable and he used these to attack the growing American anti-colonialism stance. Published in 1943 on flimsy wartime paper, it began:

> It is difficult to conduct an argument across the Atlantic. John Bull wakes up one morning to read newspaper headlines which give him the impression that Americans are making the liquidation of the British Empire one of their war aims. John Bull growls that it's like their cool cheek and that he won't let go. John Bull's growl is cabled across the Atlantic and served up to the American citizen in bigger headlines. The American citizen gets excited and declares that John Bull is a reactionary imperialist and American boys aren't fighting for anybody's old empire but for a brave new world.[72]

Some 75,000 copies of the first run were rapidly sold, the readers being urged to 'pay attention' to the rich tapestry of ideas and examples he employed to support his premise that the British Empire might not be entirely perfect but it remained a progressive force in world affairs, and the two sides needed to cooperate much more in the future. Nonetheless, as he wrote privately to a friend at about the same time as his book was finished: 'There are of course some features of American life which are, in my view, a menace. There is crudity in American big business as well as in some methods of American thought and discussion. In this crudity there are elements of brutality, vulgarity and naïveté'.[73] It would be features such as these that would present the greatest of challenges to the cohesion of the Anglo-Dominion alliance as it entered its next crucial wartime phase.

Rupture?

The United States' entry into the war had been greeted by Churchill as the salvation of the Empire and he departed at once to visit his new coalition partner, undoubtedly *primus inter pares*. In his absence from London, and just a day after fighting had begun in the Pacific, Page had written to Canberra setting out the many deficiencies that he saw in the relationship with Britain.[1] To rectify them he wanted to find a method that would allow Australian influence to be exerted as policy was being decided. This did not mean the creation of an Imperial War Cabinet but, instead, regular visits by special representatives who would stay for two or three months, attend the War Cabinet and support the high commissioner. In short they would 'come for a special job, get it done and get away'. Page also had strong opinions about the position of secretary of state for Dominion affairs. This should be one of Britain's most senior politicians, indeed, were it not for the fact that he already had so much to do, the prime minister would be the most obvious direct link with the Dominions. The clear inference, of course, was that Cranborne was not up to the job and should be replaced. Brooke-Popham, one of the many official British visitors to Australia during the latter half of 1941, had warned Whitehall of the growing need to make his hosts 'feel that we in England look upon them as definitely part of one Empire'.[2] It was implied, somewhat prophetically, that were this not to happen there would be a risk of them 'slipping out'. This was now the danger as the Australian government insisted that better use be made of Page who, having heard that the *Prince of Wales* and *Repulse* had been sunk, had begun his own efforts to broaden his role.[3] The authorities in Canberra were told the following year, by another Australian visitor, that all Page achieved during this period was to create 'a deplorable impression' and 'exerted little influence' in terms of wartime strategy. Nonetheless guarantees were secured that troops and planes would be diverted from the Middle East as well as an agreement that he would be given access to all of the facilities Curtin had requested.[4]

With mounting press comment in London about how Australia was reacting to the expanding war, there was again unease within Whitehall about the tone of some of Canberra's telegrams.[5] Churchill was focused on his Washington meetings, but he was advised that recent messages were 'both critical and querulous' and contained 'demands and allegations made not on the basis of ascertained facts but on unspecified information and prior assumptions'.[6] The atmosphere in London had grown extremely tense as 'the old gang' of Chamberlain supporters began to sense the prime minister was becoming politically vulnerable.[7] As his deputy warned him, and as Cranborne and the DO had also long asked, calls for closer cooperation with Australia and the rest of the Dominions could no longer sensibly be resisted.[8] On Boxing Day 1941, Australia's leader told Roosevelt and Churchill that the authorities in Canberra would be happy to accept an American commander in the Pacific. The following day, in a special 'New Year' article contributed to a leading Melbourne newspaper, Curtin went even further, writing that 'Australia looks to America, free of pangs as to our traditional links and kinship with the United Kingdom'.[9] This was not the first time an Australian leader had referred to the Dominions' right to look beyond London for foreign policy guidance; Menzies had stated back in April 1939 that, where the Pacific was concerned, his government needed its own diplomatic contacts.[10] The following year he had reiterated this view when asking Roosevelt to intervene directly in the Pacific and secure a peaceful resolution with Japan.[11] The DO had ensured that these appeals received little media attention back in Britain but Curtin's new statement could not be so easily handled.[12]

To one contemporary commentator, the dissolution of the British Commonwealth was at hand.[13] Cranborne's immediate advice following this latest development remained the same as it had always been, the Dominions would have to be given a weightier political role.[14] The question of an Empire War Cabinet had again been raised in the House of Commons shortly after the Japanese attack in the Far East but the government had gone no further in response other than to say that this remained 'under constant consideration'. Having instructed Attlee to inform the War Cabinet of just how 'deeply shocked' Curtin's 'insulting speech' had left him, Churchill was not, however, in any mood for compromise. Travelling with Churchill, Sir Ian Jacob noted that although his companion had never really understood Far Eastern problems, throughout the war the Australian government had taken 'a narrow, selfish and at times craven view of events', in stark contrast to New Zealand.[15] Much of his displeasure may well have been down to the fact that Curtin's decision to make his views known publicly had generated considerable press interest in Britain, exactly what the DO had been trying to avoid.[16] The arrival of a report from Cross did little to improve the situation, the British high commissioner was downbeat about the Australian war effort handicapped as it was by a 'lack of political leadership, a shoddy and irresponsible press and a number of trade union leaders reaping a dirty harvest'. Machtig thought it all 'a desperate picture'; Cranborne noted that the report had been delayed as it had come by sea and hoped that Japan's entry into the war during the interim might have had some positive effect.[17] Nevertheless, the situation in Canberra clearly left him dejected, the government there could do little other than 'squabble, grumble and blame others, in particular us'. And his mood was made all the worse, as he told Churchill, by the British public's obvious shock at the recent Australian outburst. Indeed so negative had the reaction been that he had asked the Ministry of Information to discourage further press speculation.[18]

On the final day of 1941, Sir Earle Page talked once more with Cranborne. During the preceding three weeks his focus had remained improving Australia's position and he had enjoyed some success. Discussions with senior British political figures had yielded promises that all FO papers, irrespective of their subject matter, would be made available for him to inspect. Perhaps emboldened by this agreement, the Australian now shared his thoughts on how the Anglo-Dominion alliance should operate in future, specifically in the first instance Britain's relationship with his own country.[19] It was his view that ministers from the Dominions should join the Defence Committee, the Ministry of Supply and a man 'of considerable standing' should be embedded within the FO where they could view papers and put forward opinions. Cranborne was also left in little doubt, not for the first time by a visiting Australian, that he was much too junior and was not a suitable person to be the secretary of state. Page's considered opinion was that somebody who was a member of both the War Cabinet and the Defence Committee should fill the position, which in future would have to be 'regarded as second only to the Prime Minister'. In the face of such frank advice Cranborne remained affable, seeing 'some force' in the arguments.[20] He even circulated recommendations to the FO that, as a first step, his Whitehall colleagues should appoint a representative, with the rank of under-secretary, to act as a liaison with the DO. This would be helpful not just for the Dominions but, as he rather caustically pointed out, it would also aid a department which was still often not consulted at the earliest stages.

The Dominions secretary also correctly assumed that Page would waste little time in sending his revised proposals to Canberra. The idea that Bruce should be made the permanent accredited representative was rejected by Curtin but London was informed that an Australian politician would be sent and it was expected that he would have the right to be heard in the War Cabinet.[21] This prompted Cranborne to write directly to Eden to suggest, yet again, that the existing system needed to be changed.[22] Within the FO the reaction was decidedly unenthusiastic, Victor Cavendish Bentinck being most notable for the patronising tone in which he referred to the alliance partners; Cranborne's proposals would achieve little other than 'please the Dominions'.[23] This senior official also appeared worried that there was insufficient knowledge of 'the mentality' of the Dominion governments to allow the liaison role to function properly. One of his colleagues did, however, recognize that a clear problem existed in so much as the DO was a 'channel for the discussion of policy, the finished article', but 'does not take much hand in the processing of the raw material, in the formulation of policy'.[24] As Cranborne had passionately argued now for some months, the proposed solution was to find a method to allow the Dominion leaders to put forward amendments at a much earlier stage. It was also understood that the issue had now assumed 'big proportions' and, hence, would need to be discussed with Churchill on his return from the United States.

The prime minister was, however, already fully occupied at this stage dealing with another Australian complaint. During his Washington discussions he had agreed with Roosevelt's proposal that General Wavell be appointed supreme commander of the ABDA (American-British-Dutch-Australian) command area.[25] The authorities in Canberra seemed relatively content with this until they learned that the defence of Australia and Papua New Guinea was not to be included. Curtin and his colleagues were left angered by what was felt to be the ignoring of the Dominion's security. This was not repeated across the Tasman, however, where the reaction of the public to the worsening local situation was noted by the high commissioner as having been 'remarkably calm'.[26] As Batterbee told the DO, with some obvious sense of satisfaction, the greater distance of New Zealand from the Japanese menace could account for some of the difference. There was also 'a clear conscience', the knowledge that the authorities in Wellington had a war record beyond reproach which left no requirement 'to cover up their shortcomings by blaming other people'. From Canberra there came more angry telegrams, the net outcome being Curtin insisting that the Dominion be included within the new command area. Churchill offered soothing words about how he recognized Australia's interests but privately he remained dismissive of any criticism of his handling of the relationship with the authorities in Canberra. While recuperating from a mild stroke in Florida, his mood had been downright belligerent, highly critical of people of 'bad stock'.[27] He would not agree to any change and asked for time to reconsider the scheme's detail. Casey had been told by Canberra that this request was far from ideal and would likely receive a 'very hostile' reaction if the military position worsened. The Australian representative in Washington nonetheless saw this as a good opportunity to again press London to accept greater Dominion representation.[28]

After his three-week absence, Churchill returned to Britain to more bad news. The garrison at Hong Kong had already long since surrendered. Successive chiefs of staff appreciations had outlined the inevitably of its loss in the event of any determined Japanese assault. Churchill had himself written to Ismay in January 1941 that there was 'not the slightest chance' that it could be held or even relieved – yet when the expected collapse came he still expressed surprise:

> The worst thing that has happened is the collapse of the resistance of Hong Kong; although one knew it was a forlorn outpost, we expected that they would hold out on

the fortified island for a good many weeks, possibly for several months, but now they seem on the verge of surrender after only a fortnight's struggle.[29]

While in Washington he had remained confident that Singapore would fare much better and be able to hold off a Japanese attack for as long as two months, but the information he received now suggested otherwise. He informed Curtin that, in his opinion, the loss of Malaya had been inevitable in light of the general war situation, but urged his counterpart not to become 'dismayed or get into recrimination', nor to doubt 'his loyalty to [both] Australia and New Zealand'.[30] To his Cabinet he rejected the need for greater cooperation, arguing that it would not be possible until such time as the Australians had put to one side 'their Party feud and set up a National Government' and the sincerity of the prime minister's sensitivity towards his fellow Dominion leader was not difficult to spot.[31] An obvious example was the Far Eastern Council which it had been agreed to establish, to 'focus and formulate views' in London before passing them on to Roosevelt. Canberra had not been informed of this decision in advance and heard two days after the authorities in Wellington. When official confirmation arrived it was not surprising therefore that this was critically received. Indeed the Advisory War Council quickly declared its unanimous disagreement with the proposal and instead requested that a Pacific Council be established in Washington.[32]

Cranborne's problems in Canberra were not restricted to the criticism coming from the Australian government. In a long and often venomous telegram sent to London, Cross had launched a sustained attack on the Australian leadership. Relations in the past had always been based on 'the assumption that the Commonwealth government shared the spirit of Imperial Partnership', but in recent weeks it had become obvious to him that this was no longer forthcoming. The former British minister believed that there was clear evidence showing 'abuse of the United Kingdom authorities'. He therefore urged the DO to help him gain better access to the Australian War Cabinet and to the messages it was sending to London as 'the time [had] come to collect all our weapons and to fight for British prestige'. The greatest alarm was reserved, however, for his final recommendation, that economic pressure be applied with a British refusal to undertake 'negotiations of a commercial or financial character'. The Dominions secretary was aghast, so much so that Cross was warned that to pursue such a line would not bring Australia closer but instead 'give further stimulus to their tendency to look to the United States'. Although he was sympathetic to his high commissioner's situation, Cranborne had already acknowledged privately that he had 'taken to lecturing Australian Ministers as if they were small and rather dirty boys'.[33] Shortly after his arrival in Australia, Cross had written back to London that he was 'puzzled' by what he had found. In the intervening period he had endured a difficult time, particularly after the Labour Party had assumed power in Canberra. Much of the reason for this was an ill-advised public statement he had made in which he reminded his audience of Russia's communist heritage. In so doing even he would later recognize that he had tied 'a Tory label around [his] neck'. Duff Cooper had visited Canberra in December 1941 and been warned by no less a person than the governor-general that 'if you start wrong in Australia you can never get right again'; this was exactly what had happened to the high commissioner.[34]

Just four days after Churchill had returned to London following his Washington visit, Cranborne submitted two memoranda to the War Cabinet, both examining the issue of cooperation with the Dominions.[35] In his first paper the warning was given that 'it would ... be a great and possibly disastrous mistake ... to underestimate the strength of the feeling arising in the Commonwealth [of Australia] on this question'. Making the danger worse in his view, there was also the potential that 'a rot which started in Australia might easily spread to other Dominions'. This was therefore a genuine crisis, 'an issue not merely of machinery, but even more of status', which could be averted only through wise statesmanship. Cranborne duly recommended, yet again, that if Australia wanted to attend the War Cabinet in London it should be granted this right, 'a gesture that would pay us a hundredfold'. The other Dominions should also be invited to attend although he thought they would probably decline such an offer.[36] The caveat remained, however, that representatives would only be allowed to attend if they had authority to actually make decisions, a point upon which Churchill had been insistent.[37] Even before the War Cabinet had seen these papers, King George VI had himself read both of them. The prime minister received warning that the British Empire's sovereign had been greatly 'alarmed at the feeling which appears to be growing in Australia'.[38] In his almost immediate reply to the King's private secretary he now accepted that 'it would be foolish and vain to obstruct [Australian] wishes', offering an assurance that he had already heeded Curtin's requests.[39] This news was welcomed at Buckingham Palace and it was made quite clear that the King would remain an interested observer of how the situation developed.[40]

A more generally sympathetic mood now spread throughout Whitehall. Even Cadogan, in trying to decide how to implement Page's earlier proposals, felt that it was time something should be done. With Eden's agreement, this would lead ultimately to the defunct DID gaining a renewed role.[41] The only people who seemed less than pleased with the changes were the Dominion high commissioners. All of them doubted the merits of an Imperial War Cabinet and were even of the opinion that sending ministers to London was not practicable.[42] Massey in particular wanted it stressed that Australia had assumed the driving role and 'that it was for other governments concerned to decide whether they wished to avail themselves of the facilities'.[43] Curtin may still have wanted more but the proposals as they stood could already cause embarrassment for Mackenzie King in Ottawa. With Jordan still refusing to attend meetings with his counterparts because of his 'confirmed inferiority complex', Waterson concurred in his diary that 'it should not be made awkward for Governments not to accept the offer of Cabinet representation'.[44] Privately he was more interested in the proposals as it appeared he saw another opportunity for enhancing his position, telling Smuts that there was 'no reason why the High Commissioner should not be nominated [as] accredited representative'.[45] The South African leader's response was to send a reminder that, in his opinion, the Dominions' policy should simply be to offer Churchill 'wholehearted support in the immense dangers confronting us all'.[46]

There was still very little evidence of anything like this degree of support from Canberra and the proposed Far East Council, to be headed by the British government, had become a major source of irritation. New Zealand was also unhappy, Fraser advising that, although he was 'very sorry to worry' Churchill, his government could not accept any proposal which failed to give them 'direct and continuous' access to the United States.[47] Only days before the government in Wellington had accepted that an American Admiral would be responsible for the conduct of naval operations in the waters surrounding New Zealand.[48] Cranborne had been directly tasked to resolve the tension and he decided that Roosevelt had to be approached. The US leader was duly informed therefore that Australia and New Zealand both preferred a Pacific Council based in Washington.[49] Relations had, however, taken a dramatic turn for the worse with a new telegram from Curtin. Menzies had assured the British public that no Australian leader would 'stand on any platform and attack Great Britain'.[50] This new message carried with it the suggestion that an evacuation of Singapore would be seen by the Australian government as 'an inexcusable betrayal'.[51] This explosive charge originated from a secret communication produced by the British prime minister which mooted the possible abandonment of Singapore. Intended for the three Chiefs of Staff it had inadvertently been shown to Page who had in turn passed it on to Curtin.[52] Churchill's initial response was indignant, warning his Australian counterpart that he would 'make allowances for your anxiety and ... not allow such discourtesy to cloud my judgement or lessen my efforts on your behalf'.[53] This note was eventually not sent, but its tone made clear the extent of the British leader's renewed anger. Others in Whitehall were equally upset with the recriminations. The Australian leader, a 'wretched second-rate man ... screaming for help', found himself castigated along with his countrymen who had 'suddenly woken up to the cold and hard fact that [Australia's] very existence as a white country depends not on herself but on protection from Great Britain'.[54]

Publicly the groundswell of opinion in favour of the need for changes to take place actually appeared to be considerable.[55] A commentary published in *The Round Table* in February 1942 concluded that with the widening war, the Dominions secretary should now be a full member of the War Cabinet. *The Times* also carried an editorial endorsing a more significant role for the Dominions in formulating Imperial policy.[56] At the same time accompanying the demands for the rapid agreement of 'improved machinery for consultation', somewhat fanciful calls began to again resurface lauding the merits of an Imperial War Conference.[57] There were also vivid published accounts for British readers of how a Japanese invasion of Australia could be mounted.[58] In one version, a heavy aerial bombardment would be followed by simultaneous landings at Darwin, Cairns and Townsville. In other accounts Brisbane and even Freemantle were mentioned as targets for 'Jap' paratroopers while the so-called 'Brisbane Line' became a *cause célèbre* as the focal point of concentration of defence in the vital south-east of the country. Plans existed for a 'scorched earth' policy if there was an actual invasion. Although the Japanese had actually decided that they would isolate Australia – and ignore New Zealand altogether – in the Antipodes the worst was assumed.

In the last week of January 1942 Churchill stood before the House of Commons to make a lengthy statement. This provided a detailed analysis of the war situation and formed part of a debate that parliament was told he considered as a vote of confidence in his leadership. He also took the opportunity presented by his speech to confirm that accredited representatives of any of the four Dominions would have the right to be heard in the War Cabinet.[59] Waterson felt that the speech was 'a great performance'.[60] So much so that the South African believed if he were now 'to change his Cabinet a bit', the prime minister's position could not be challenged. Churchill's announcement was, however, heartily condemned within sections of the British media, not because it was seen as going too far but, rather, that it did not go far enough. The conclusion was that the 'Commonwealth would still be ruled by Britain alone, just as Britain is ruled by Mr Churchill'. His actions threatened to 'wipe out a hundred and sixty years or so of constitutional progress and to hark back upon the traditions of George III and Lord North, who split the English-speaking world'. One correspondent called the proposals 'humiliating' while another saw them as 'slightly ungracious'.[61] There had been an astonishing level of improvisation relied upon to make the alliance machinery work and this had 'manifestly failed'. The solution in this case was seen to be an 'Imperial Executive', one that answered to an 'Imperial Legislature' empowered to impose an Empire-wide tax to fund Imperial defence.[62] This was accompanied by continuing political debate with Cranborne, speaking in the House of Lords in January 1942, confirming that it was intended to make some changes at the formative level, the lower level of consultation over matters of defence, foreign affairs and supply.[63] Elibank understood Churchill's speech to mean that visiting prime ministers from the Dominions would no longer merely be invited to attend War Cabinet meetings but would automatically become members. He was corrected by the Dominions secretary, who told him that this membership would apply when the general conduct of the war was under discussion, allowing them to be involved in the formulation of policy. The War Cabinet was, however, responsible to the British Parliament of which they were not members.

The following day the message was formally repeated to each of the overseas Dominion governments along with the news that they were being invited to send service liaison officers to keep in contact with the chiefs of staff organization.[64] The day before there had been further warnings in the British press from Curtin that with 'too many flowery words' from Whitehall, 'patience has limits'.[65] The reaction to Churchill's speech among the Australian media had meanwhile been generally favourable, one newspaper describing it 'as a masterly political speech of a magnificent political fighter'.[66] While the government in Canberra was still far from satisfied, after some further discussion it was agreed that with the right to representation secured, they would agree to the London-based council. Curtin believed that the calibre of the individual selected to press the Dominion's claims would be crucial, and in the first instance it would be the far from convincing Page.[67] The Australian had spent the intervening weeks building a power-base. Among his supporters apparently was Ernest Bevin, who had provided 'the most stimulating and satisfactory talk [he] had with any Empire statesman since coming to Britain in the last twenty years'.[68] The Minister of Labour had suggested to him that the FO should absorb the DO making it 'the second office in government' and offered to support 'a united Empire front'.

The position in Singapore was now unquestionably the coalition's focus and further deterioration was accompanied by a lengthy debate in the House of Lords. Running over two days, it was permeated by a sense of outrage that the coming debacle should have been allowed to happen.[69] One commentator offered a typically Churchillian view: 'Clearly the defence of Singapore is not going to last much longer … One feels terribly depressed – more depressed, I think, than after Dunkirk – to be beaten and humiliated in this way by Asiatics is almost more than a Victorian Englishman can bear!'[70] The subsequent collapse of resistance in Malaya perhaps, therefore, brought with it a certain sense of release. Described by Curtin as 'Australia's Dunkirk', the well-documented defeat inflicted upon the garrison defending Singapore had a chilling effect throughout the Empire on public and political opinion alike.[71] In the days following, Churchill found himself under great pressure to implement a major restructuring of his government and when he again faced an obviously hostile House of Commons he had already bowed to the inevitable.[72] The series of changes that he announced were said to reflect the expanded nature of the war but it was clear that they were intended to help re-instil faltering confidence in the prime minister's ability to lead. Notable among them was the resignation of some formerly key figures such as Max Beaverbrook and Arthur Greenwood, the promotion of others including Oliver Lyttelton, and the overall reduction of the War Cabinet from nine to seven members.

Also included among the promotions was that of the Labour politician Sir
Stafford Cripps, who had emerged as a favoured candidate to become Dominions
secretary among certain of the high commissioners in London.[73] Seen by
Churchill as one of his most serious potential threats he instead became Lord
Privy Seal and the Leader of the House.[74] Attlee, in being confirmed officially
as deputy prime minister, a role he had been effectively fulfilling for some time,
was named as the new secretary of state for Dominion affairs.[75] This decision
marked the formal acceptance of everything that had been so passionately argued
for by Cranborne and those senior members of the DO who had supported
him throughout the previous 16 months. The now former minister, although
apparently at one stage considered as the next possible foreign secretary, had
once more been struck down by a bout of ill-health, and was instead offered
the role of colonial secretary, which he gratefully accepted.[76] His considerable
achievements at the DO, a department into which he had breathed much needed
spirit and confidence, would ensure that Bobbety would be long-remembered
after his departure. It would be up to his successor to implement the changes he
had sought to implement and help ensure that the Anglo-Dominion relationship
prospered in the environment of an expanded global conflict. Unfortunately
within the DO his replacement was seen to have neither the knowledge for his
new role nor the interest, instead appearing to those who surrounded him as
being 'somewhat aloof'.[77]

Despite the much enhanced role of the new Dominions secretary, the reaction
from the high commissioners was much the same and similar to that which had
been endured by Attlee's predecessors. He had greater seniority but both Bruce
and Massey found him dull and taciturn, talking with him was like 'a conversation
with a bronze Buddha except for the monosyllabic ejaculations which he utters
occasionally'.[78] Waterson was typically scornful: 'Went to the House to hear Attlee
on the war situation. He treated [it] to an insulting meagre string of platitudes.
The members were impatient and rather badly behaved like schoolboys when the
headmaster is away and a weak under-master is temporarily in charge.' One DO
civil servant told the South African that he now served under a secretary of state
'who would be ideally suited as an assistant manager of a bank in a small town
in the south of England'. Bruce was so disgusted with the paucity of information
still being distributed that the first week of March found him claiming to be
on the point of resigning.[79] To a man the Dominions' representatives were also
unimpressed with the expanded War Cabinet which, in their eyes, had changed
from being 'a joke' to 'a farce'.[80] They were perhaps naïve to expect more for, as
one London journal pointed out to its readership, the changes in fact offered little
that was new.[81] This was the result of a 'species of arrogant negligence' for which
the British prime minister was directly responsible meaning ultimately Britain
would continue to rule the Commonwealth.

Militarily the situation was also showing little sign of improvement. The acrimonious dispute over whether Australian troops should be sent to Rangoon showed that the coalition was not pulling together in the face of the Japanese advance. It was a cause for extreme bitterness within the parliament in Canberra, and raised questions from the British high commissioner about who was in control, Curtin or Evatt.[82] At Westminster Harold Nicolson could only lament that 'the whole Eastern Empire has gone. Australia has as good as gone. Poor little England. But I should not have minded all this so much if we had fought well.'[83] This last point was difficult to counter. At the same time, while Singapore had now passed into enemy hands it continued to poison relations within the alliance. Numerous reports continued to be received in London about the conduct of Australian troops. Although these were largely considered as still being unofficial, many talked of Anzac troops deserting en masse, throwing away their guns, rushing ships at the Kippel Harbour and generally wandering the streets of Singapore Town drunk and stealing from the local populace. Among the many devastating charges was reference to the commonly used local nickname for them, 'daffodils', so named because they were 'beautiful to look at but yellow all through'. Reviewing these the DO was concerned that censorship would not prove enough to prevent such damaging accounts from gaining a much wider coverage: 'As these stories spread throughout the Empire, they will inevitably lower the opinion in the Empire of the Australians in general and Australian troops in particular. Whether or not they are true they can only be damaging to Anglo-Australian relations.' Nobody was passing judgement, as it was recognized that there was 'no disgrace to troops to be defeated by a superior force', and no attempt was made in these Whitehall reports to ignore the fact that some British and Indian troops had also broken in the face of the Japanese attacks. The issue was that the reports all spoke of Australian forces as having been the most defeatist and least reliable and should such assessments get out the result would almost certainly be that the already strained relations which existed would likely deteriorate. Particularly as in the coming months those who had been evacuated or lost family members would likely make themselves more vocal and it was feared it would not be long before they made the charge that 'if the Australians had held we should not have lost Singapore'.[84]

The concern was not misplaced and the mood in the House of Commons was an angry one:

A lot of bitter comment in the Smoking Room today about the Singapore disaster. It seems to have been a terribly bad show if only half of what one is told is true – bad leadership and no guts anywhere – the Australians appear to have behaved abominably, giving up the unequal battle and boarding ships in the harbour – I suppose this will all be kept secret to spare their feelings – at any rate such I am told is the reason why the Government is unwilling to have an enquiry – possibly Winston fears one too![85]

Calls for a public investigation were avoided but General Wavell was asked to produce a detailed private report on events leading up to the surrender. As Machtig
rather adroitly put it, the findings made 'certain reflections upon the Australian
troops who took part' and there was little enthusiasm about letting Bruce read
a copy. Attlee felt it was inevitable that the Australian high commissioner would
find out and recommended it be shown to him but Churchill refused. If Bruce
mentioned the report he was to be told that it had been withheld to avoid 'a
controversy breaking out on such a point which would be injurious to Imperial
sentiment'.[86] This did not prevent the prime minister from also making a public
statement in which he said he could not disclose the report as it would cause
bad feeling and this was noted by the press in Canberra. Trying to defend the
Australian position in an article written for the *Daily Express* in April 1942,
Menzies told his British readership:

> Most of us like a good grumble occasionally; few of us are real haters. It is true that
> whispered anti-British agitation of a poisonous kind is going on, and good British
> Australians, the vast majority are unhappy about it. But I am convinced that these things
> are superficial and temporary; a resounding British success in some theatre of war would
> clear them. They are not a deep rooted condition; they are a skin irritation – a sort of
> eczema of war. You must also remember a little bit of human nature – that it is in many
> ways desirable to argue with a fellow bigger than yourself. It builds you up, even if it
> does not pull him down.[87]

It would be many months before Cross could write back to London with a more
encouraging report about the Australian attitude.[88] The fact that the war had
come to Australia's very doorstep probably had had the greatest impact on public
awareness. On the morning of 19 February 1942 nearly 200 Japanese planes had
bombed the town of Darwin and 242 civilians and military personnel had been
killed. The raid only lasted 45 minutes but the harbour was devastated with
25 ships sunk or damaged, among them an American destroyer. Many of the
townspeople thought it to be the start of an invasion and panic resulted. The
town was abandoned as civilians and deserting military fled along the road south
in what later became known as the 'Adelaide River Stakes'; by the following day it
was estimated that no more than 500 people were left.[89] A new sense of seriousness was made clear when the South Australian government finally decided to
ban all horse-racing and close the betting shops. There would, as a result, be
virtually no sport organized for public amusement in the state, the first within
the Commonwealth to take such a 'draconian' step.[90]

   Matters were not helped by the worsening situation in the Western Desert.
Here British Commonwealth forces found themselves forced to retreat in the
face of a determined attack by Rommel's *Afrika Korps* and renewed Imperial
disaster and humiliation followed. On 21 June 1942, after a final assault that

lasted less than a day the port of Tobruk surrendered; garrisoned by South African, British and Indian troops, 33,000 men were captured along with vast amounts of supplies and equipment. For Churchill it seemed the British Army's morale had crumbled and he would later describe Tobruk's loss as one of the heaviest blows of the entire war.[91] For his wartime coalition government it also presaged a serious parliamentary challenge although, in due course, this was easily seen off. The military commander on the ground, who Churchill would ultimately hold personally accountable for the disaster, was Auchinleck, and he complained back to London in July 1942 that he was hampered by his inability to detach subordinate Dominion formations for their parent divisions. In a sign of their growing independence, Dominion commanders refused to allow units to fight as piecemeal formations. The British general understood this was down to past events and political necessities but it hindered his flexibility and he reportedly never felt comfortable with troops he could not rely on not being suddenly removed from the fight.[92] His deputy during the fighting around El Alamein in June and July 1942 even concluded that if there been three British divisions present prior to Tobruk's defeat as opposed to a largely Dominion force, 'we would have done better than we did'.[93] The Empire appeared on the verge of collapse and nobody seemed to know how this might be stopped.

9

Holding the Imperial Line

The British Empire faced its nadir in 1942 as military defeat was followed by further military defeat. At its emotional centre outrage and dismay had followed the 'Channel Dash', the escape of a German naval fleet consisting of *Scharnhorst, Gneisenau* and the *Prinz Eugen*, supported by a number of smaller ships, through the Straits of Dover to their German home ports. An editorial in *The Times* of London reported that 'nothing more mortifying to the pride of our seapower has happened since the seventeenth century'. The event signalled 'the end of the Royal Navy legend that in wartime no enemy battle fleet could pass through what we proudly call the English Channel'.[1] The Far East position had collapsed and the massed Commonwealth armies that had been assembled in North Africa appeared to be faring little better with Tobruk gone and the final line of defence established near a small railway station at El Alamein. None of the alliance members were immune. The raid on Dieppe in August 1942 was the greatest amphibious attack since Gallipoli and the first European battle fought by the Canadians since the last war. Contemporary accounts and articles written shortly after the subsequent Normandy landings portrayed it as having been 'a symbol and an experiment' that provided important experience and allowed ideas to be trialed for future operations. The official Canadian historian would record that 907 of his compatriots died – nearly one-fifth of the total who had embarked on the raid – over 1,000 were wounded and nearly 2,000 more taken prisoner. The casualty rate was in fact the heaviest sustained in any Allied attack during the entire war.[2]

Success at the third Battle at El Alamein in November 1942 appeared to save the day and represented what Churchill described as 'the end of the beginning'. The polemic is one of his most famous, delivered as part of a speech at the Mansion House and it was during this that he also told his audience he had 'not become the King's First Minister in order to preside over the liquidation of the British Empire'. As his most eminent biographer has pointed out his next remark is seldom quoted, that if this were to take place 'someone else would have to be found' to carry it out, a declaration of his belief in Empire, 'not a political statement that the Empire would never be dissolved'.[3] This sentiment was noteworthy as debate about the alliance's future was becoming increasingly fever-pitched. Even a cursory reading of the sessions in the House of Commons that same month, following the

King's Address, gives a flavour of the arguments that were being put forward. The Empire's role in the war was widely praised but there was dismay at the growing practice of referring not to the 'British Empire' but to the 'British Commonwealth of Nations'. Sir Edward Campbell believed that 'it is a horrid term for the greatest Empire the world has ever known' and, despite being informed that the phrase had been first used over 40 years ago, the irate parliamentarian resolved that he would continue to use 'British Empire'. Flight-Lieutenant Raikes, by his own description a right-wing member of the House, was of a similar mind. He welcomed the continuing use of the term and believed that there had been 'a gasp of relief' from many countries upon learning that 'the British still believe in something which they are prepared to hold and fight for'. Mr Emmott, the Member from eastern Surrey, was also troubled and as he put it: 'Are the British not to be permitted to acknowledge their pride in the British Empire, their determination to defend it against those who would destroy it and their will to make all sacrifices for it?' He believed that the British public was actually mystified by 'a pestilent doctrine which teaches men to be apologists for the British Empire, to be ashamed of it, to explain it away as part of the old world'. As he concluded: 'Are we to deny, to disown that Empire which has given peace, justice, humane administration, and good government to countless human beings throughout the habitable globe? … How odious, how shameful is this doctrine!'[4]

As this debate should have made clear, while there was no shortage of interest much of it remained hopelessly uninformed about how the Imperial alliance was changing. This was nothing new; the father of all the parliaments scattered around the Dominions had a pretty indifferent record when it came to debating about them. There were a number of parliamentarians who were keen to discuss Imperial matters but they were definitely in the minority. Edgar Granville had been born in Britain but had served in the AIF during the First World War and was one of the most vocal questioners of government policy relating to the Dominions. He served briefly as a captain in the Royal Artillery before returning to Westminster, first as a National Liberal but from 1942 until the war's end as an independent. Another leading protagonist was Emmanuel Shinwell. A leading member of the Labour Party, in May 1940 he refused a position in the Ministry for Food in the National Coalition Government but two years later became party chairman. In June 1941 both of these parliamentarians rounded upon Churchill for not having organized an Imperial War Cabinet.[5] Two weeks later Granville was asking another question about the functioning of high commissioner meetings; the week after he was enquiring about methods of increasing the amount of information being supplied to the Dominions; six weeks later yet another question on the possibility of an Empire War Cabinet.[6] Another in this category was Beverley Baxter, a Canadian-born journalist-turned-politician who held the suburban London seat of Wood Green for the Conservatives. In a May

1942 debate about the war situation he criticized Churchill and his parliamentary colleagues for their apparent lack of interest in the Empire. Many felt deeply about the subject but he wished that the prime minister, one who 'had done so much to bring the English-speaking people together', would appear more visibly interested and that in Britain as a whole there could be a far greater appreciation of what the Dominions were doing in the war.[7]

Inevitably the figure of Churchill loomed large over the debate. As he told a Party meeting on 9 October 1940, convened to discuss the question of Chamberlain's successor, he had always 'faithfully served two supreme causes – the maintenance of the enduring greatness of Britain and her Empire and the historic certainty of our Island life'.[8] Indeed, an American correspondent in London wrote later that same year, Britain's wartime leader was undeniably 'the son of Jennie Jerome of New York City, American in his directness but otherwise British as bully beef' but while his 'blood is half American when it begins to boil, a chemistry of ancient loyalties makes it all British – exultant, proud, superior, unbeatable even in defeat'.[9] Massey referred to him in often critical terms as the 'Headmaster' for this was how he sometimes appeared to deal with his errant pupils.[10] Although a staunchly self-professed imperialist, his views continued to draw their basis from an era that was drawing to a close. Indeed to certain commentators in London, he was 'Eighteenth century in many respects' and even his undoubtedly closest Dominion confidante, Smuts, could only lament the degree to which Churchill remained 'obsessed with 1776'.[11] Even the British leader's own trusted secretary thought that his boss was 'in the main oblivious to the growth of nationalism as a force in British imperial affairs'.[12] As an exponent of Empire in nineteenth- rather than twentieth-century terms, he was determined that nothing should be surrendered.[13] The Empire was 'an instrument that gave to Britain a world position that she would not otherwise have had'.[14] Malcolm MacDonald, in his draft handwritten memoirs talking about Britain's wartime relations with Canada, detailed the 'certain difficulties' that arose 'now and then'. Sometimes this was because of the prime minister's 'old fashioned notions'. He was inclined to regard Canada and all the other Dominions as still a partly, if not wholly, dependent colony of Britain, whose Cabinet ministers should accept – and indeed obey – the British government's views on all problems at all times as 'the last word in wisdom'. He recognized their constitutional status but tended to view this as 'a matter of polite, and somewhat ridiculous theory rather than undeniable fact'.[15] With this highly romanticized, but often conditional view of the Empire, he found it hard to view the Dominions as equals.

If Churchill loomed, Cranborne's was a much more munificent presence. He may no longer have been at the helm at the DO but he had only moved to the larger, sister CO department situated in the same building. From here he remained a key presence, a contender for the mantle of the Empire's most important wartime statesman. He saw the Commonwealth of Nations as a living organism in which the grown-up children were the self-governing Dominions and what pains there were could best be described as 'growing pains'. In July 1942 Lord Elibank had once again begun another debate on the question of the future unity of the British Empire. Together with Viscounts Bennett and Bledisloe, these grandees of the 'Imperial Idea' detailed what they considered the post-war world might hold. Cranborne was called upon as secretary of state for the colonies to respond for the government and employed a familial relationship to put across his argument. He told the Peers that during a family's early days, 'children are young and inexperienced, and not able to face problems themselves'. This meant that they had to be protected and educated but as they grew up they could 'begin to take their own line – to think for themselves'. Eventually they would become independent entities, independent personalities and, finally, self-supporting. 'They are no longer dependent upon their parents, but they remain members of the family still bound to each other by ties of affection, and still having a responsibility to help and protect each other.' He concluded his passionate account with the assertion that the Empire was 'neither dead nor even going into decline'. Instead, with sensible and sympathetic treatment, it would emerge 'wiser and more united than it has ever been in its long history'.[16]

His new position left him well placed to focus on what he considered to be the most critical areas of deficiency blighting the relationship. Cranborne had written to the high commissioner in Ottawa in early summer 1942 detailing his thinking on Imperial issues. He believed that relations between Britain and the Dominions needed to be closer and the job being undertaken by MacDonald and his counterparts in the other overseas capitals was 'invaluable'. The danger as he saw it was that there were 'centrifugal tendencies' and these increased the strain on future unity so much so he believed that its structure was on the point of collapse.[17] He was also concerned about the way in which the Dominions thought of the Colonial Empire. Commenting on a report on the subject prepared by the DO he noted that it was an aspect of Imperial policy that had been long neglected. As he went on:

> So long as the Dominions regard the Colonies as our private property they will take no interest in them – although, as a matter of fact, they are just as much involved as we ourselves. We must manage by hook or by crook to make it clear to them before the end of this war that the British Empire is not a number of very loosely connected units; it is an inter-dependent whole; and that the loss of or even unsatisfactory condition in any portion of it must affect not only the prosperity but the international influence of the whole. The Australians I feel, are particularly bad about this. They want all the advantages of the Imperial connection without any responsibilities. We must by some means manage to make them realise that this is not possible, and that it is not even to their own interests that they should divorce themselves from the affairs of the Empire as a whole.[18]

There seemed to be a growing view that the Colonial Empire was being over-looked and a wish to break down stereotypical images of what the English were about. A joke repeated in the *Empire Review* in January 1943 seemed to say as much: 'We all know the story of the six men wrecked on a desert island. Two Scotsmen, two Irishmen, and two Englishmen. The two Scotsmen immediately went over to a cave and formed a Caledonian society. The two Irishmen began to fight and the two Englishmen walked up and down the beach waiting for somebody to introduce them.' The writer's comment on this was that the rather 'snooty' impression was misplaced and it was actually shyness that was the problem. The article's message was that the future lay not with the Old World but with the New, those states that had been colonized by Britons.[19] Throughout the 1930s Empire and colonization had been a largely marginalized issue in the British Labour Party; not until the war years would ideas of long-term colonial development became much more visible, ones in which the white dominions played a central role.[20] Home Secretary Herbert Morrison told the House of Commons that he held out the twin prospects for the colonies of greater atten-tion to their economic welfare and eventual self-government. He also thought though that it would be 'sheer nonsense – ignorant, dangerous nonsense – to talk about grants of full government to many of the dependent territories for some time to come. In these instances it would be like giving a child of ten a latchkey, a bank account and a shotgun.' According to the *Economist* it was clear that the government was 'building up an apologia for the Empire', one that represented 'not only the timely riposte of bludgeoning from abroad but also a new and welcome upsurge of popular interest in the responsibilities of Empire rule'.[21]

This was certainly a debate that was closely followed by the media. A long piece written by a *Time* correspondent in London in April 1942, in seeking to identify the current character of the British people, examined the role of Empire. It argued that it was something that had been taken for granted, the assumption being that it would always be there and the conclusion for the American readership was that 'England as a whole simply did not have any serious thought whatever about the Empire. England was unanimously non-imperialist – and unanimously unprepared for the break-up of her Empire.' It perhaps took an American to identify the problem:

> The English people themselves are principally to blame for the weakness of their Empire. The English people blame their various rulers – including the Old School Tie. But the average Englishman has for a decade or two exhibited an almost total lack of interest – even a lack of ordinary curiosity – in great affairs of Empire. He and his countrymen had an Empire – and they were just plain not interested. That, perhaps, is the whole truth, as nearly as it can be stated in one sentence.[22]

A survey on the public's opinion conducted by the BBC's Listener Research Department reached similar conclusions. One of the findings of the January 1943 study was that there was widespread ignorance as to the differences between a Colony and a Dominion, hence the habitual use of the term 'the Colonies' to denote any part of the Empire other than Britain. There was, however, a much better understanding that the term 'British Commonwealth of Nations' covered the Dominions; 10 per cent, however, did not think this included the British Isles.[23]

The intensity of the debate could be seen in something as apparently innocent as the correct use of language. There was often little distinction drawn between 'Commonwealth' and 'Empire'; as was made clear in a post-war memorandum the two were considered 'strictly speaking interchangeable' and sometimes they were used together, sometimes separately. But the meanings could vary depending on the circumstances and those using them.[24] Churchill was a leading advocate of the importance involved and had rounded on more than one member of the House of Commons for 'pedantic divisions about nomenclature'.[25] During his second wartime visit to London in the spring of 1944, Mackenzie King had asked for some explanation as to what was meant by 'Commonwealth and Empire'. Cranborne told him that Churchill himself had coined the phrase and everybody had followed suit. 'The Commonwealth meant the five completely self-governing countries: Britain being one of the five. I said: "the Balfour Declaration". He said: "Yes". That Empire meant the Colonial Empire – Colonies and India.'[26] There is of course the well-known anecdote about the British leader's address to a group of Americans among whom was Senator Arthur Vandenberg, a leading anti-imperialist. During this he made it clear that 'British Empire' or 'British Commonwealth of Nations' were merely titles, taunting the senator with a mischievous suggestion that he maintained 'trade labels to suit all tastes'.[27]

He was not alone in such opinions. Keith Hancock, although an Australian by birth, with his long historian background, was perhaps better qualified than any to comment on the nature of the Dominions. In his wartime mini-polemic, *Argument of Empire*, he put the case in his usual informed fashion. For him Dominion status meant 'sovereignty but not separation, independence but not interdependence'. There might be those who disagreed or found it odd but his view was that 'the Dominions are free to separate from the British Commonwealth if they choose' but the reality was that they did not choose to do so.[28] He was also prepared to add a word – or two – on the correct use of language:

> Some people have become ridiculously self-conscious even about words. If, for example, I use the old-fashioned term British Empire, there are progressive people who will write me down as a Blimp. If, on the other hand, I use the new-fashioned term British Commonwealth, there are plain blunt men who will think me hypocritical or high-

falutin. I intend to use both forms of speech just as I please: indeed, I can't properly get along without using both, for each signifies an essential aspect of the living reality. British Empire connotes the historical tradition, which is alive and real: British Commonwealth connotes the progress and the programme, which are also alive and real. There are many people who mistake words for things. Some people use the same words to signify different things. The word 'Imperialism' is a good example. In one morning I once counted up ten different meanings given to it by ten different writers: to some of them it meant federation between Great Britain and the Dominions, to others it meant military expansion, to others it meant 'dominion over palm and pine', to others it meant the 'monopoly stage of capitalism', to others it meant the government of primitive peoples. Its connation was at one time political, at another time military, at another time economic, at another time racial. Words are good servants but bad masters.

There was also a considerable public debate about the future of the Commonwealth alliance and this reached its crescendo again in 1943 as various politicians, some still influential, others less so, sought to promote the value of the imperial connection. It had begun the year before with an address by Attlee, in his role as Dominions secretary, to the *Royal Empire Society*. His speech provided a typically impressive array of facts and figures detailing how grand and important the role of the alliance partners had been in fighting the war so far, outlining 'a common battle with common ideals'. As he concluded, 'the British Commonwealth stands today as an example to the world of the unity of democratic nations who have learnt how to achieve unity and common action while retaining individual freedom'. The enthusiastic questioning that followed agreed with the theme, indeed expanded upon it, that the war had been fought effectively by an alliance that had adapted to the necessities it encountered.[29] Barely a month later Duff Cooper – a late replacement for Sir Walter Monckton, a much more acknowledged imperialist – was the guest of the lunch-time meeting at the same venue, his task being to consider the make-up of the post-war world.[30] He introduced to his audience a new idea of international relations: 'interdependence'. This involved a future based upon closer cooperation and there was no better example than the British Empire, 'a binding together of a vast community of peoples'. Richard Law followed a week later. A key FO figure, he had been considered in early 1940 as a potential Dominions secretary and would lead the committee examining American understanding – or lack of – of the Empire. His theme was 'The British Commonwealth as a World Power' and his aim was to consider how this 'unique' organization would fit into the proposed post-war international system. Here was a model for a global organization, the only one that was already worldwide, allowing it to 'form a bridge of understanding and influence between one continent and another'. In his vision it would take a central position with each of the members taking a key role in their particular region. Once more this provoked an outburst of mutual self-congratulation. Geoffrey Whiskard, who had been an 'eventful' high commissioner in Australia until 1940, thought that the British had used their genius to evolve 'a new relationship between completely free and independent nations'; previously, independent states had existed only with the fear of war between one another.[31]

The debate extended to the *Empire Review* which was full of stories that same year on a broadly similar theme, what would be the fate of the British Empire. Aside from Richard Law's speech, which was apparently considered to be sufficiently important to be repeated, Lord Elton, Lord Hailey and Sir Charles Petrie, 3rd Baronet, each of whom was an established commentator on imperial matters, produced polemics which were published with great prominence.[32] Elton was full of praise for 'the only League of Nations which has ever worked'. The Dominions had banished the idea of war yet they had gone to the rescue of victims of aggression. If the post-war world was to work it would do so only because it had its core the British Commonwealth and other like-minded states which had 'gravitated towards it'. Both of the other writers were content, meanwhile, to develop upon popular, emotive themes typical of which was the claim that 'if it had not been for the British Empire the swastika would be triumphant in the world at the present time'.

In the background and pervading much of this discussion and debate, the United States was as a sometimes malevolent presence that had many in London almost looking over their shoulders while creating tensions for the Anglo-Dominion alliance. The sense of anti-American prejudice which Dalton detected within the FO and Treasury was accounted for by one of his sources as 'the jealousy of the old British governing classes at "the passing of power"'.[33] It was perhaps an intrinsically and peculiar American vice, certainly in the eyes of those living in the shadow of the British imperial sun, to question British imperial motives. Lord Swinton, the Resident Minister in West Africa, reported back to London that he was having considerable problems in the Gold Coast with the Americans. The Headmaster of the National School in Accra wrote to the Governor-General to complain about 'the most reprehensible conduct and hooliganism' being displayed by many of the visitors.[34] This did not at all 'reflect any credit on the Americans as cultured people' and there was a widespread rumour that they 'had come to be lords of the Africans, to exploit them and treat them as "hewers of wood and drawers of water"'. As the writer warned, there was a danger 'that the rude and bratish behaviour of the American may have a tendency to impair the whole structure and fabric of amity and goodwill which have been built up with so much tact and patience by many generations of British men and women on the Gold Coast'. Of greater concern for the British authorities in London, however, would undoubtedly have been reference to 'some stupid loose talk by irresponsible Americans to African about the desirability of Americans taking over the country'.[35] Such 'anti-colonial whispering' and the message it contained had fortunately been quickly rejected out of hand by the African audience.

There were other more serious examples of American indiscretions and these directly affected the Dominions. Perhaps foremost amongst these was the alleged case of Colonel Frank Knox, the United States Navy Minister, news of which reached London through a tortuous route involving the interception of a letter sent back to Britain from the French Cameroons. During a tour of the Pacific area in 1943 he had apparently given an impromptu speech to a group of Australians and New Zealanders during which he had expressed the view that they would no doubt want to 'quit the British Empire and join us after this war'. The audience's response was less than complimentary, leaving the minister 'with a very red face'. As the correspondent concluded, aside from being amazed that an American politician should say such a thing, it seemed clear that there was a section within the United States 'who seem to think that we should liquidate the Empire – God forbid we ever do!' Across the Tasman Antipodean hostility in response to similar American sentiments had extended beyond strong language. The British high commissioner in Canberra had reported in December 1942 that riots had broken out in Brisbane and the behaviour of even quite senior US officers, particularly in the US Air Force, had become a cause for real concern. The Australian military was clearly unhappy with its American counterparts, in part because of a failure to fulfil promises of material support but also because of the often disparaging attitude displayed by the visiting forces to their new allies.[36] Orders had apparently been issued by Generals Eisenhower and Clark that any member of the US forces in North Africa heard making derogatory remarks about Britain or British forces were to be sent home.[37] This did not apparently extend, however, to the South Pacific.

From his vantage part at the heart of the British Embassy in Washington it was Gerald Campbell who had precipitated much of the debate about American thinking on the Empire with the reports he sent back to the FO. Previously Britain's other representative in Ottawa, after Mackenzie King had fallen out with him, he had been moved to become senior British Minister to Washington where he had been warmly welcomed, in at least some circles.[38] Typical of his warnings to London was that written in August 1942 discussing Australia's position. In a lunch with Roosevelt his host had told him that the Australians 'had been rather a nuisance' in their efforts to gravitate closer towards him. Campbell apparently enjoyed taking the opportunity to tell the president that the Australian attitude made little sense: 'I have often noticed that Americans think the Australians like them, and therefore their country, much better than us and our country, and that they only have to beckon for them to come: and I have also noticed that when Australians, who rather play up to this idea initially, are beckoned, they are furious.' The same conclusion was held among the FO's mandarins, 'a distant flirtation is one thing but [the Australians and Canadians] would both recoil violently from embraces which would, in their view, shortly be of the possessive kind'.[39]

The 'Open Letter to the People of England', published by *Life* magazine in October 1942 and running to some 1,700 words, is perhaps the most visible wartime example of American disdain for British imperialism. It famously pronounced: 'One thing we are sure we are not fighting for is to hold the British Empire together. We don't like to put the matter so bluntly, but we don't want you to have any illusions. If your strategists are planning a war to hold the British Empire together they will sooner or later find themselves strategizing alone.'[40] There was also the worldwide tour made by Wendell Wilkie, the defeated 1940 Republican presidential candidate, the focus of which was the condemnation of colonialism at every opportunity, apparently with Roosevelt's tacit approval. Amery thought his strategy to be a 'mischievous and silly effusion', telling Cranborne that he had become angry 'about our worthy allies, who are no doubt good at mechanical production, but slightly ignorant in other domains'. His suggestion was that the secretary of state for colonies should broadcast to America 'saying that Wendell Wilkie is an ignorant and mischievous ass'. Bobbety agreed that there could indeed be more productive use made of propaganda and assured his colleague that he favoured 'a sturdier attitude' than had been the case previously promising 'we will not stand before our Allies in a white sheet'.[41] The Wilkie tour certainly had an impact, spectacularly backfiring as Stalin, whilst pleased to see his two key allies bickering, used the visit to Moscow as an opportunity to chastise Roosevelt and Churchill. As for the principal target, the British prime minister responded to Wilkie's call from Chungking for an end to imperialism – and Roosevelt's subsequent endorsement of the statement – with his most explicit public defence of Empire policies with his previously referenced speech at the Mansion House.[42]

The reaction to all of this American interventionism was generally hostile, even amongst the Dominions and their representatives overseas. The London-based high commissioners were notably critical about the degree to which there was an American sense of defeatism about the future of the Empire. Attlee wrote to Churchill in June 1942 to warn him that they were growing restless and were 'considerably exercised in their minds as to the habit of prominent American, including members of the Administration, of talking as if the British Empire was in the process of dissolution'. He went on: 'It would be well for the Americans, whose knowledge of Dominion sentiment is not extensive, to be aware that the British Colonial Empire is not a kind of possession of the Old Country, but is part of a larger whole in which the Dominions are also interested.' There was also reference to the aggressive commercial activities of the Empire's main strategic ally, with the Dominion representatives also being disturbed by 'the economic imperialism of the American business interests which is quite active under the cloak of a benevolent and avuncular internationalism'.[43] Smuts received his own lengthy assessment of the position as it was understood by his representative. The commonly held view in Whitehall, and one with which the South African high commissioner agreed, was that 'the average American is convinced that Great Britain rules the Empire (in which is included India and the Dominions) direct from Downing Street, derives large revenues in direct taxation from everywhere and that the Empire is peopled with subject races to whom the glorious freedom enjoyed by every American is unknown'.[44] Massey returned home distinctly anti-American, at least in terms of his private outlook. His biographer speculates that this might have been as a result of American over-assertiveness in Newfoundland and Canada or over-glorification of the role that the American military had played in Europe.[45] Or, more simply, it might have been as a result of having to deal with the American Ambassador Joseph Kennedy 'or the complacent self-satisfaction of visiting American movie stars and politicians'.[46]

From the war's earliest stages there had been many besides Churchill and Cranborne who had recognized that maintaining Imperial unity in the post-war world was an absolute prerequisite if Britain was to have any hope of keeping a powerful voice. Perhaps the three most celebrated contributions to the debate came not from parliamentarians at Westminster. The first was a speech given by John Curtin who, speaking in Adelaide in mid-August 1943, had proposed the creation of a supreme body to govern the entire post-war Empire. He had appar-ently re-embraced the 'Imperial Idea', conveniently forgetting his earlier emotive 'looks to America' statement. The United States had subsequently mishandled the war, and Curtin had become 'no lover of the Yankees'.[47] No doubt buoyed on by the positive reaction he received, the Australian expanded upon his proposals during the following months. An Empire Council could be a permanent body with a permanent supporting secretariat. Its regular meetings could be held in the various Dominion capitals and so on. It was an apparently far-reaching argu-ment, although of course, as commentators in Canberra were quick to point out a similar series of proposals had been first put forward during the 1911 Imperial Conference and resoundingly rejected.[48] Various Australian speakers made the journey to the *Royal Empire Society* in London where they repeated a broadly similar message – Australia was determined to assist in maintaining the British Empire.[49] In the DO Paul Emrys-Evans was particularly pleased at the visit by a Parliamentary Delegation from Canberra. He thought they returned home impressed by what they had seen and hoped they believed Britain was 'more conscious of the Commonwealth and Empire than we have been for over 25 years'.[50] There were also regular written contributions from sympathetic writers which lauded the Australian role in the wartime alliance and painted a picture of a post-war future dominated by strong political and economic relations.[51] This was all good for public consumption and helped dampen some of the hostile reaction to Curtin's actions immediately following the Japanese attack.

Jan Smuts gave another speech not many months later to the Empire Parliamentary Association at Westminster. This was perhaps the most noted wartime comment made by any Dominion statesman, with its twin themes of Britain's position in the post-war world and the general position of the British Empire. Titled 'Thoughts on a New World', it was given to about 300 parliamentarians who had gathered in Room 17 of the House of Commons. According to his son, who accompanied him on his wartime visits to London, Smuts, who said he was 'merely thinking aloud' himself, referred to it as his 'Explosive Speech'.[52] He spoke from brief notes to an audience who cheered enthusiastically at the end of the address. He told them that Britain would emerge victorious but poor and if it was to play a significant position as a world power it would be necessary to strengthen the Empire and Commonwealth, to look to its inner strength and see to it that it would be safeguarded for the future, his over-riding message being that there should be some way to bring the two closer together. He doubted the prospects of a closer union with the United States. Instead he proposed the forging of new links with some of the smaller European powers, specifically the Scandinavian states. He proposed that some of the colonies might be combined to form more economically viable groups and these might then become self-governing Dominions under white leadership. The Empire and Commonwealth was the best missionary enterprise that had been launched in a thousand years and such a move would help tighten up the whole system. Of some interest also was his conclusion that neither France nor Germany would emerge as significant post-war powers.[53] The speech was poorly received in Canada, where it was seen as advocating a single British Commonwealth foreign policy and a return to the centralization of the machinery of government within the Commonwealth and Empire. It was noted, however, that it should have been unusual that the speech should have caused 'so much excitement' when Curtin's not entirely dissimilar proposals had generated relatively little interest.[54]

The final, and perhaps most controversial of these contributions, was given by Lord Halifax in January 1944 at the Empire Club in Toronto. Essentially this speech argued that the Dominions should fortify their relationship with Britain and with one another so that, as a group, the British Empire could claim a degree of substance and equality with the United States and Russia. In his own words, the speech argued that 'while the Statute of Westminster had given us all equality of status, we had to be thinking quite hard upon the problem of how we were to get real equality of function and responsibility in such fields as Foreign Policy and Defence'.[55] Mackenzie King was 'simply dumbfounded' and saw it as an Imperialist conspiracy, a plan worked out with Churchill to push through a 'centralization' in which future policies would again be made in London. He even considered resigning and forcing an election with the question of British interference his main theme. His initial explosion abated as it became clear that the official British response was one of concern that he should be so distressed and renewed expressions that this was not the time to discuss Empire policy.[56] The British ambassador was distraught that his 'wretched speech', the giving of which had completely 'bored' him, could have caused 'a slight extra headache' for London.[57] Cranborne was quick to respond with soothing words. The speech had not caused any headache but was instead read with 'admiration and agreement'.[58] Churchill, however, had disowned it and the ideas it represented but, along with Smuts and Curtin, Halifax had publicized still further the importance of this issue and the debate which existed.

The continued close cooperation of the Dominions was clearly paramount to Britain, and this could only be secured if they were satisfied that their interests and position were being safeguarded. This was the conclusion of a memorandum issued by the FO in December 1943 the specific focus of which was the British Commonwealth's future. Eden had produced another War Cabinet paper in November 1942 in which he stated that if the British Empire and Commonwealth could not be maintained Britain could no longer exist as a world power.[59] The new document, barely three pages in length, incorporated a vast sweep of the subject. Its aim was reportedly to help stimulate debate in overseas missions about how foreign relations involving the Empire – specifically methods of exchanging information, consultation and cooperation – might be conducted post-war.[60] Caveats were added about how difficult it was to foretell the future and that in order to safeguard brevity the Dominions had been treated as one when in fact it was recognized that 'each has its particular characteristics, interests and problems, and will increasingly develop and assert its own national individuality'. The DO had little involvement in its preparation, a draft being submitted for comments, some of which were adopted. The result was that it was distributed without any departmental objection but, equally, without its endorsement. Attlee doubted whether the Dominions would be willing to accept the idea that Britain might be a member of the proposed post-war international organization, the so-called 'Four-Power Council', without there being any separate representation for them.[61]

This first warning had been made at the beginning of 1943 and would remain a much repeated one throughout the discussions that continued on the matter over the coming months.[62] As Attlee, in his dual role as deputy prime minister and secretary of state, put it to those present at a meeting in the DO held on April Fool's Day 1943 – two of the four Dominions high commissioners being amongst them – the problem was that both the United States and the Soviet Union were only prepared to accept a single voice in discussing questions of general policy.[63] There were obvious areas for which this presented a potential clash; most notably in terms of the route by which any future declarations about the surrender of the Axis powers and the post-war world might be settled upon. The group recognized that, in terms of resources and population alone, the United Kingdom would struggle to lay claim to a seat at the 'top table'. Its association was as a result of war effort, colonial possessions and relationship with the Dominions. It was therefore argued by successive British speakers that it would be best if one voice could be presented. While Massey and Bruce were willing to accept certain merits to the proposal, they would not countenance any suggestion that the Dominions might sacrifice their hard-earned separate nationhood. There was clearly something of an impasse of thinking, and while the commonly expressed sentiment was to hope for some form of compromise, nobody appeared to have any idea as to what this might be or how it might operate. What few anticipated was that the solution would actually come from Canberra and it would not prove a particularly palatable one for the British government.

10

The Private Anzac Club

It has been highlighted the degree to which 1944 was the year when both Australia and New Zealand made it clear that, while they still believed strongly in the idea of Commonwealth unity, they would no longer blithely accept the British view of the post-war security system.[1] The Australian-New Zealand Agreement signed at Canberra in January of that year was certainly the first visible indication of some sense of devolution towards greater regional control. The first Cairo Conference, held the November before and attended by Churchill, Roosevelt and the Nationalist Chinese leader Chaing Kai-shek, is often pointed to as the catalyst for the Tasman Dominions thinking on post-war organization. Neither was consulted about decisions that were reached and each of them only learned from the official communiqué that Japan was to be stripped of all of the islands it had seized in the Pacific. This and other decisions such as the announcement that Korea would become free and independent in due course led them both to worry that post-war settlements would be concluded without them, despite their military contributions and their interests in the region.[2] From the High Commission in Canberra, Ronnie Cross, had written back to London in December 1942 warning that he was hearing 'ambitious ideas' about Australia's future role in the South-West Pacific and South Asia.[3] At this stage this even extended to the Commonwealth being involved in the post-war administration of the Netherlands East Indies but the Dutch reaction had been such that this was dropped. This had not stopped Evatt from developing similar themes throughout the year. His goal was that Australia would take a far greater role up to and including the development of security zones which would involve the trusteeship of Pacific islands. Within the British High Commission this was seen as an attempt by Evatt to 'achieve something of historical significance and value with which his name would be particularly identified'. But, at the same time, it was wondered whether the minister's ambition 'had not somewhat overwhelmed his sense of proportion'. Highlighting the junior nature of Australia in terms of its political development there were said to be advantages that could be reaped by 'boys' which 'would prove impossible if the maternal partner were consulted'. Evatt was known to want to take over the administration of the British Solomons and it was not doubted that he had 'a predatory eye towards other islands not in British possession'.

As Cross had warned shortly after his arrival in Canberra, while there were few real doubts about the strength of the cultural bonds, it remained more difficult to judge wartime political ties with Australia. One post-war view held that it needed to be regarded not so much as an alliance as 'a multi-purpose and adjustable but enduring entente cordial' in which shared sentiments, common culture and personal affection each had a part to play.[4] At the time though, these were not always that transparent on both sides. A long-serving member of the DO, Walter Hankinson, had been in Australia on two previous occasions, first in a fairly junior capacity in 1931 and then again four years later as acting high commissioner before returning once more in a wartime deputy role. He found himself asked on numerous occasions, as a self-avowed 'Aussie-phile', what he thought of his friends and their sometimes apparently petulant attitude towards Britain and the Empire. Although he had actually been back in London during the angriest exchanges he had more than enough knowledge of the relationship to offer an informed opinion. As he wrote some years later, his response was, apparently, always the same, answering the leading question with a question of his own. 'Had my questioner ever met a man who had suddenly had all the things he fervently believed in and on which he based his life, swept away one by one in exorable succession? Such a man said many things in his bitterness which he did not really mean and which, in due time when his hurt was healed, he regretted.'[5] Some of the difficulties were put down to the high commissioner who often struggled ever since his initial gaffe. Within the nascent Department of External Affairs there was a hostile view towards him; Cross saw his role to be not just an ordinary diplomat but 'a guide and mentor with whom the colonials should seek to have consultation.'[6] In the process, however, he managed to develop a previously unimagined level of cordiality with Curtin based on 'intimacy, understanding and friendship' and a long despatch sent back to the DO in December 1943 contained a glowing account of the recent parliamentary session and his performance. This led Cranborne, who had been re-appointed as Dominions secretary a few months before, to reaffirm his growing respect for the Australian leader, 'a man of character and good sense', and he was clear that everything possible should be done to work with him and better gain his confidence.[7] There continued to be some disagreements but Cross considered these largely a thing of the past. The triumph at El Alamein had helped greatly, 'a victory for British arms' that he believed now enabled the Australian public to 'exalt the fair name of United Kingdom forces'.

The relationship with New Zealand was much more uncomplicated, particularly once it became clear that there was no actual military threat from the Japanese.[8] Batterbee's great fear, from shortly after his arrival in Wellington in February 1939, was American motives in the Pacific region. Remote from the European war, he continued to see the invidious growth of American influence all around him. He even felt one reason why New Zealand had not been fully geared for war when Japan attacked was the belief that existed locally that Washington would come to its aid in the event of an invasion. His anxiety had remained throughout 1943, warning the DO that there was a growing sentiment in the local press that responsibility for the defence of Australia and New Zealand had been 'abdicated' in favour of the United States.[9] His fears waned soon thereafter as it became more obvious that the initial 'outburst of emotion' that had greeted the arrival of American troops had been replaced by something else. It was the visitors themselves who were responsible with their 'natural habit of bragging and, I am sorry to have to add, the anti-British talk of many of their officers and men'. In spite of an apparently reckless habit of 'flinging their money about' they soon began to alienate the staunchly pro-Empire locals. The high commissioner also remained a little concerned about the effort and application being shown by his Dominion. He still noted that Christmas 1943 had seen 'Wellington close down for a fortnight and there was a holiday air everywhere'. As he went on: 'It is generally the habit to regard New Zealand as the good boy of the Commonwealth family, but even the best of boys is not perfect and it may well be that from time to time visitors from the United Kingdom report when they get home that New Zealand is not making as much of a total war effort as is commonly understood.'[10] He put this in context, however, as the general tone of his long report was almost entirely supportive of the New Zealand effort and he was full of praise for the Dominion's fighting record. That parliament in Wellington had unanimously declined to press for the return of the New Zealand Division from the Middle East the previous year, when Australian forces had all been withdrawn to the Pacific, had been just another instance of the resolute support; out of a total of 43,500 men sent to the Middle East by the late autumn of 1942, 18,500 were dead, wounded or captured.[11]

The British government had first heard, indirectly, at the end of November 1943 that there were Australian plans afoot to hold some form of a conference, and that an invitation had been sent to Wellington. The following month saw an official announcement by Evatt confirming that Fraser would visit Canberra in the near future and discussions would be held between the two countries. Still, however, the authorities in London were given little idea as to what it was intended to discuss. It had been suggested to Cross that the conference was not being organized with serious policy goals in mind. Curtin told him in early December that there were local matters that required settlement, such as New Zealand's making of Army boots for American troops and the resulting shortage of hides this was creating across the Tasman. This proved to be 'misleading' yet, as the high commissioner concluded, 'it was quite possible that the prime minister in mid-December knew next to nothing of what Evatt was planning'. It was also clear that firm instructions had been given by someone in Canberra that British officials were to be given no prior information about what was to be discussed. This order, it was concluded, had been down to Evatt in the first instance with Curtin supporting the strategy once he had discovered the extent of the conference's remit.[12] As a result, Cross and his staff in Canberra proved unable to discover even the broad subjects that it was intended to discuss. Attending meetings Britain's token observer remained entirely in the dark, so much so that he did not even know there was to be a formal agreement signed until two days before it took place.

The reality was that Curtin saw it as a far-reaching gathering, to consider wartime lessons and plan strategies for the future. There were two primary goals to be achieved by those present: demonstrate that it would be Australia and New Zealand who would take the lead in guaranteeing regional security and in the process enhance the international standing of both of them. Fraser agreed but clearly viewed it far more as an opportunity to demonstrate that the two Dominions would have agreed permanent principles of cooperation in the post-war world thereby avoiding repetitions of the instances during the war where the Canberra government had 'squealed'. A joint statement recorded that both countries saw their future security based around an island screen which would need to be suitably developed to make full use of sea and air power. It was recognized that this could only be done in concert with other regional powers; aside from the resources of the British Empire, the Netherlands, Portugal, the United States and France were all mentioned at some stage.[13]

The outcome of the meeting was the Anzac Pact, signed at the same table at which, in 1900, Queen Victoria had given her royal assent to a Constitution for Australia. The *Time* correspondent saw this new document as a possible 'Charter of the Southwest Pacific', a common foreign policy produced while London 'dallied' which offered a translation of the proposed Smuts doctrine into 'a dynamic program [sic]'.[14] It certainly appeared to provide for closer consultation on matters of common interest, with a proposed full exchange of information and measures to develop cooperation for defence. These included joint planning and the organization of equipment as well as training of the Dominions' armed forces based on a common doctrine. In short, the two governments were agreeing to speak with one voice in the Pacific and to coordinate both their war effort and, implicitly, their post-war security. They reaffirmed their desire to be involved in the membership and planning of the proposed United Nations organization, reference to which had been made in the October 1943 Moscow Declaration. Within this framework it was proposed that there would be a regional defence zone comprising the South and South West Pacific Areas. Until such time as this could be established they were willing to take on its management.[15] The two were also opposed to any final settlement until hostilities with all the Axis powers had been concluded. Their requested representation on all armistice planning was meant not just for those discussions relating to Japan but to all the other Axis powers as well. Nor would they accept any change in the control or sovereignty of Pacific islands or enemy held territory in the Pacific without their involvement in the negotiations. The two governments declared that the wartime construction of bases by another power – in other words the United States – gave no basis for territorial claims after the war. In a meeting with Cross on the first night of the conference, Evatt indicated that it had been vital for the two Dominions to hold talks in the face of potential American expansion into the Pacific.[16] This anxiety was again repeated a week later as being the primary motivation.[17] Added to this was the remark that the British government tended to concede too easily to proposals made in Washington; the comments made at the meeting were intended to forestall anything similar taking place which might have an effect on the Pacific region. In short, as Evatt told Cross, 'it needed saying. You couldn't say it. We could.' And with this in mind Australia took the initiative in calling for an all-power conference to be held in Canberra to discuss Pacific security, post-war development and native welfare, after the gathering of the Dominion prime ministers in London.

Although there had been no British delegate present at the Canberra meetings one of the members of the New Zealand Department of External Affairs gave a fulsome account of what had happened to his friend in the High Commission in Wellington.[18] His record noted that

> the conditions in which the conference opened were typical of the un-businesslike atmosphere that pervaded the whole proceedings. Mr Curtin, after keeping the representatives waiting for some time in the appointed committee room, thought on his arrival that the room was too small and insisted on the company adjourning to the House of Representatives, where, however, it was found that the lights had been removed for cleaning. The lights could not be restored for some time and the conference began an hour later. From that point onwards the proceedings were extremely rushed, and many of the subjects received practically no consideration. Dr Evatt dominated his colleagues, who took little part, and the agreement may be regarded as his handiwork.

According to this Curtin was apparently not much interested, his mind focused on domestic matters, while Evatt was looking 'to make a splash' that would bring glory both to him and the department he led. The British official, having heard the account, thought Evatt's main idea was 'the putting of Australia on the map as an independent power'. He also thought that relations between these two most senior figures were not good, 'there is a tendency for them to work in watertight compartments', and this, in his view, was an important factor in explaining recent events. This view was apparently shared by other British officials based in the Australian capital. They were reported by another New Zealand observer as

affecting to be amused by the agreement: 'two of the children playing amongst
themselves' requiring 'adult supervision'.[19] As Cross put it, writing to London in
January 1944, 'it was Dr Evatt who developed and led the chorus of snarls that
emanated daily to the papers from ministers' press conferences, which in time
became accompanied by another note, a note of superior wisdom – after the
event'.[20] Batterbee also had been able to report back to London the results of a
'long and frank talk' with Fraser that had taken place immediately following his
return back to Wellington. This confirmed that the New Zealand ministers had
been rushed by Evatt and Fraser had been uncomfortable with, and even reluctant to agree to, the language used in the final document. The official secretary
in the High Commission had dubbed it 'the Anzaxis' but his boss had concluded
that there was in fact no anti-British intention, 'if it was anti-anything, it was
anti-American'.[21] And while the apparent American determination to retain New
Caledonia at the end of the war was the basis for many of the shared concerns
that existed within the two Dominions the New Zealand leader was worried in
terms of how Washington might react.

Using these accounts, Cranborne was able to produce a detailed summary for
his Cabinet colleagues of the background to the agreement and the main terms
it entailed. He also outlined his concerns. He reiterated the degree to which there
had been little prior knowledge of the conference. Indeed it had been thought
that it was the Dominions' intention merely to hold 'mutual consultation' of a
preliminary character prior to talking with the British authorities more formally.
In fact there had been no references at all to there being future discussions with
the British government on these subjects. There were, however, potentially 'some
useful results'. The fact that there should now have been a public statement made
by the Dominions highlighting the significance of Pacific defence was valuable
as it could have implications for post-war arrangements. In addition, the idea of
regional collaboration in the Pacific was one that had been already raised publicly
in Whitehall. And, of course, the fact that Australia and New Zealand were seen
to be enjoying closer cooperation was 'all to the good'. Aside from the other
positives and negatives he also drew his colleagues' attention to another section
of the agreement in which the two governments asked for representation at the
highest level on all armistice planning and executive bodies. This, he thought,
might lead to problems as recognizing such claims could have an 'awkward' effect
in regard to discussions over the United Nations.[22] London was also particularly
disturbed at the suggestion that an early conference should be called, termed as
a South Pacific Regional Commission, to discuss Pacific security issues involving
all those countries with territorial interests in the region.

The official response sent by the DO to both the Dominion governments
contained mixed messages. On the one hand there was some praise for the
strengthening of relations between the two and platitudes about them having

taken such a bold step. There were also lots of concerned references about the United States which was clearly central to most of the matters raised.[23] In essence it was asked that all of the matters of substance, particularly the call for the creation of a South Seas Regional Council, be held in abeyance to be discussed at the prime ministers' conference which was due to be held in London in a few months time. In the DO's eyes this meant Canada and South Africa could be included in the discussions and they could probably be counted upon to scupper the worst elements of the Australian plan. Evatt was disappointed at the reaction. He felt that there was collusion between Washington and London in their rejections of his call for an international conference and hoped that the British view might come to recognize that time was of the essence.[24] He told Cross that it was necessary to 'stake a claim' and argued that it might have been embarrassing to Britain to have been consulted in advance. Of course what he did not say was what both parties knew full well, that if London had been told of the plan in advance, considerable embarrassment would have come from its almost certainly negative reaction. Evatt's anger still seems to have been based as much on the outcome of the Cairo Conference, Cross reporting that the concessions made to China at this meeting between the Allied leaders the previous year still 'rankled'; whether it was the nature of the concessions or the fact that there had been no prior consultation with Canberra was not so clear.

While the FO was upset that the draft reply had been produced without it having been consulted, the agreement itself was generally viewed much more favourably.[25] It was felt the process could have been handled in a better manner, but the practical result was helpful from the point of view of enhancing the world position of the Commonwealth.[26] The two governments were in a position to be able to say things that would be 'much less convincing' if they had come from London. It demonstrated to Washington that Australia and New Zealand were independent-minded states and 'not mere appendages of Great Britain'. It also was felt it should serve notice that some of the comments being made by American commanders in the Anzac area had been poorly received.[27] Indeed, the concerns about the manner of the publication aside, the conclusion within the FO was that the Pact had done more good than harm and had made clear to the United States certain points which British diplomats could never have made.[28] This was, of course, just as the Antipodean politicians had claimed. A more detailed analysis was provided by the DID who viewed parts of the agreement as being likely to lead to delay and confusion and being much more helpful to Australia than New Zealand. The proposed consultative machinery would be dominated by Canberra's more experienced officials who would see to it that their view became heard as the common Anzac view. The hope was that Carl Berendsen, the New Zealand high commissioner in Canberra, who was noted for being extremely tough and capable and 'who dislikes and despises the

Australians', would be able to ensure that this was not the case. The conclusion was that the agreement would have to be accepted in good grace and monitored to see what, if any, positive lessons could be learnt for the future.[29]

Elsewhere, among the other Dominions, only Canada offered an opinion about the agreement, focusing on its perceived anti-Americanism. From London, Canada House thought the discussions in Canberra had been rashly handled – it was doubted that the British government had not been consulted beforehand – while the outcome was bound to be offensive to American opinion. Only the year before, the Australians had professed, very publicly, their wish for closer integration of the Commonwealth and yet, with this decision, they had broken from the long-established principles of inter-Imperial consultation. As it was Curtin who had 'raised his voice more than most' it was odd that he now appeared 'a trifle inconsistent'.[30] Pearson, who had moved to Washington to become the Canadian Counsellor, was alone in thinking it a good thing, an indication of progress in the evolving Commonwealth relationship, and was perhaps of a similar mind to the FO; to him it demonstrated an increased independence of mind, something that would prove significant in the discussions about the post-war world that were yet to come.[31] It was reported from Ottawa that *Le Devoir*, the leading French-language newspaper published in Montreal, had described the Pact as a new form of foreign policy. It highlighted the degree to which this marked the declining British imperial role; Australia still wished though to retain its position in the alliance so long as this did 'not place her again in the tragic position of 1941 and 1942'.[32] An editorial in the *Sydney Morning Herald* described the agreement as 'a remarkable achievement' while recognizing that both the Tasman Dominions still relied upon the United States and Britain for their security and had to be 'wary of appearing too importunate, or too ambitious'. Later assessments talked of the agreement being 'ambitious' but a realistic conclusion that Britain could no longer defend itself and its distant imperial outposts. Menzies and the opposition were bitterly critical of the Pact, saying that it set a 'new standard of crudity in international approach' and stressing that it would not be binding on future governments. Indeed, in parliament, he went so far as to say that all the bases needed to dominate the Pacific and ensure security should be given to the United States. In New Zealand there was, initially, a reserved public response but with some more general 'mild sarcastic criticism' of those proposed actions that affected Britain and the other great powers.[33] It proved, however, to be of only limited interest to the press and in a few days ceased to be front-page news.

An immediate impact of the agreement was that Fraser now believed that he could no longer discuss related questions freely with the British government without first discussing them with Curtin.[34] He was, at the same time, also evidently uncomfortable with this and the manner in which the agreement had been reached; he therefore chose to circumvent any possible restrictions by talking informally to Batterbee, who was then free to pass the views exchanged back to London. Indeed he seemed to go out of his way in the days that followed to speak in a 'most frank and friendly nature', stressing how pleased he was with the British response and how important it would be for Britain to remain in the Pacific. He even hoped that British forces might yet be deployed to New Zealand.[35] This was the method used to send to London the full text, accompanied by Fraser's response and his assessment of what it meant, of the message sent to the US charge d'Affaires in Wellington from Cordell Hull which was generally critical of the proposed measures. Indeed both leaders either side of the Tasman were contacted by the American secretary of state and told that neither Washington nor London thought the stage had been reached where formal discussions should be held about possible post-war regional developments. This could spawn a rash of such conferences in the process, inhibiting efforts to achieve a general system of world security.[36] The British high commissioner sensed Fraser's relief at the way in which the Americans had responded as this, theoretically, made Australian pressure all the more difficult to maintain. He was also perhaps a little pleased that the Americans had immediately reacted as he had warned that they would.[37] The New Zealand leader also worked hard to ensure that Evatt's initial proposed response to Washington was not sent as he thought it would be likely to cause offence.[38]

The idea of pursuing the proposed Regional Commission continued to be badly received both in London and Washington well into the spring. In the South Pacific also it was reported that senior American naval officers interpreted the Pact as an attempt to exclude the United States from the region; as a result forces from the Dominions were not used in operations against the Marshall and Caroline Islands to prevent any subsequent claim for a say in what should happen to them post-war.[39] There was some barely disguised glee within the FO at Evatt's vitriolic response to Hull's polite admonishment, it being noted that the Australian 'did not mince his words' but had instead 'violently attacked' some of Roosevelt's 'ill-considered theories and rash remarks'.[40] During Curtin's visit to Washington on his way to the prime minister's gathering in London he met with Cordell Hull and an 'informant' had passed on to the British Embassy the outcome of the conversation. Curtin, who had initially begun by saying he did not think there to be 'much harm' in the agreement, was 'all at sea' about the intensely negative reaction he encountered. His host had left him in no doubt that the Canberra meeting and the decisions taken there, particularly calling for a Pacific conference, had not been appreciated.[41] A meeting with the president produced similar results; as a result of this Roosevelt had concluded that responsibility for recent Australian initiatives lay squarely with Evatt and Curtin seemed content 'to wash his hands of it'. This overtly hostile response helped guarantee that there would be no conference about regional security prior to the Dominion leaders meeting in London.[42] At the same time Cranborne's efforts, both with the summary and the subsequent manner in which he had sent detailed responses and messages to Canberra and Wellington, were also welcomed within Whitehall as having helped ensure that 'this tiresome incident appears after all to have turned out well for us'. Pointing to the Cairo communiqué as providing some sort of justification had proven to be an especially misguided gambit; as one member of the FO commented, this had actually been 'sprung' on the British attendees by the Americans 'at short notice after prior consultation with the Chinese' and was not designed as a slight against the Dominions.[43] Another member of the FO noted in April 1944, 'how indignant the Australians would be if the UK behaved as they have done. I don't think any harm has been done and they – or at least Mr Curtin – may now be a little ashamed.'[44] The reality was that the Pact would have little more than 'a token effect', an attempt at a naked land grab, in the old imperial style.[45]

Success or otherwise, the two Dominions had agreed that they would establish a secretariat to provide for a more permanent means of continuous consultation and planning. They would also subsequently hold two annual conferences, a development seen at the time in London as having been 'unfortunate'.[46] The discussions held in Wellington in November 1944 were the first to take place under this agreement and they caused further difficulties within Whitehall and a fair degree of additional embarrassment.[47] The main problem lay with declarations that were made connected to the question of future colonial administration. As has been seen, the role of the Colonial Empire had been a particular area of concern for the DO. Paul Emrys-Evans's memorandum had been based upon the Dominions' own views which they themselves had submitted to Whitehall.[48] Having reviewed these there was some concern that they had not fully considered the part they might be expected to play in the proposed post-war policy. Developments during the pre-war years had seen the relationship between the Dominions become gradually looser. In so doing, their interest in the Colonial Empire, one which they should have thought of 'as a joint heritage' laying upon them 'a common obligation', had reduced to the point where it was not certain if it existed at all. The mandated territories they had received at the end of the First World War – all except Canada – had not absorbed their energies nor proven a particularly successful venture. South Africa alone had maintained an existing policy, but here racial prejudice meant that there could only be anticipated a 'small measure of cooperation'. The war, the author felt, had changed the situation and it was likely to be the case that the various members of the Commonwealth would have greater interest in the post-war position; the time had arrived 'to ask our partners to share some of the burdens as well as to enjoy the advantages of the British connection'. Indeed, it would be necessary for the British government to construct a new Imperial Policy, one in which the Dominions would be expected to play their part.

This message had apparently been taken fully onboard by at least some of the Dominions. During the Wellington discussions it was stated firmly that there should be set up an international body to which Colonial powers should undertake to make reports on the administration of the territories they controlled. This would be empowered to visit these territories, such supervision being binding on trustee states, and publish their completed reports, all as part of the 'spirit of trusteeship for dependent peoples'. Seen within the context of the proposed United Nations organization, both governments were willing to support any such proposal as it might affect both colonies and mandated territories. In addition, and as had already been revealed at Canberra at the beginning of the year, they also wished to promote a regional commission, involving in addition Britain, the United States and France, to consider specifically the South Seas area. Here they hoped it would be possible 'to pool their experience and collaborate in furthering the welfare of dependent peoples'.[49] The response was instant and terse; as it was commented in London, 'they have issued without consultation with us or with the other Commonwealth Governments a declaration of policy on matters affecting us all'.[50] This judgement was based on the understanding spelt out at the 1923 Imperial Conference: 'a Government contemplating any negotiation should consider its effects upon the other Governments and keep them informed'.[51] Bruce even wrote to Curtin advising him that this had put 'the cat among the pigeons' and caused great annoyance.[52] He warned of an 'electric atmosphere of tension' as a result of the lack of consultation before the embarrassing statements were announced and suggested the proposals should be 'quietly dropped'.[53]

The violent reaction was particularly unfortunate in light of the efforts that had been made in Wellington to avoid any repetition of the offence that had arisen at Canberra. They had endeavoured to keep Batterbee advised of developments, despite the irritation this caused the Australians, and the high commissioner had been led to believe that there would be nothing of any great significance discussed; indeed he doubted that Fraser really wanted it to take place at all.[54] Cranborne had still been suspicious about the invitation for Batterbee to attend only a formal meeting at the conference's end, without having heard any of what had been discussed beforehand. This he deemed to be 'an odd way of avoiding the impression that they took place behind closed doors'. There was also some recognition among New Zealand officials that talking about the future of the Pacific without inviting the British representative to attend would probably make London believe that the Antipodean Dominions were 'behaving a little queerly'.[55] Nonetheless the Dominions secretary concluded that the authorities in Wellington would manage a meeting much better than had been the case in Canberra and he thought Fraser was trying to do the right thing.[56] This was indeed probably the case as Batterbee certainly enjoyed a better relationship with his government than Cross across the Tasman.

With his direct assurances that 'nothing except of the most anodyne character would appear in the published statements' Batterbee was shocked when a copy of the speech to be released to the press was handed to him at the last moment.[57] Evatt had insisted that a big statement be made and Fraser had been unable to resist. The high commissioner's best efforts to have the offending statement removed from the end-of-conference published statement proved to no avail; the responsibility for this lay with the Australian delegation and Batterbee thought it 'pretty monstrous'.[58] Worse, the New Zealand authorities initially tried to claim that they had consulted with him beforehand about the nature of the statement and he was anxious to ensure that the DO did not think this was actually the case.[59] There was in fact a great deal of sympathy across Whitehall for the way in which their colleague in distant Wellington had been treated.[60] The instigator was recognized by all involved as having been Evatt; Cranborne thought it 'a bad story', particularly as far as the Australian politician was concerned.[61] The high commissioner had written back to London immediately after the incident with a detailed account of the Australian's behaviour and an assessment of why he had followed this course; while having 'the profoundest admiration for Mr Churchill' he apparently believed that the government in London was inclined 'to overlook the independent nationhood of the Dominions'.[62] He seemed particularly aggrieved that Australia had not been represented in the discussions about the armistice terms to be imposed upon Germany. If the same were the case when considering the terms for Japan there would be 'deep resentment'. Despite such criticisms, Evatt was keen to stress that the Tasman Dominions would be prepared to 'to act as a unit' in certain cases and wished to work with Britain in all matters relating to the Pacific. He recognized, though, that South Africa and Canada continued to approach the issue of the future relationship from a different viewpoint and there remained much discussion to be had about how the British Commonwealth might function in the post-war world.

An official response was sent by the DO and the words 'surprise', 'concern' and 'regret' were all mentioned. London felt that the Wellington conference was espousing a form of international control where colonies were concerned and the British authorities would now likely have to issue their own statement by way of response. In so doing this would inevitably highlight the difference in outlook which existed within the coalition. Both Dominions, in turn, produced long defences not just of their actions but also of their respective attitudes and approaches towards Colonial matters, to an extent which should have caused concern in London about future international discussions which might include the matter. Evatt, as was his want, went further, complaining about the tone of the telegram sent from London which he claimed 'recalled Colonial Office despatches of the distant past'. Cranborne was more than content to defend the manner in which his department had dealt with the spat. As he told the Minister for External Affairs in Canberra, there had been numerous 'very frank telegrams' received from the Australian government during his time as secretary of state and he had appreciated these as 'frankness is the necessary basis of close and cordial collaboration'. On this most recent occasion, however, the unilateral statement on colonial policy had caused embarrassment in London. Not only had the British view been known in Canberra beforehand, and apparently ignored, there had been no prior warning or attempt to find common ground. For Cranborne to have not indicated the depth of dismay that this had caused in Whitehall would 'not have been fair to you nor to us'; indeed he thought the exchange had done some good and, even, cleared the air. Evatt did not agree and responded once again, this time petulantly pointing to occasions where the British government had embarrassed him, adding discussions about Polish boundaries to his now traditional complaints about the Cairo Conference, although it was not entirely clear how either had directly involved Australia. The Dominions secretary recognized these had taken place but they were a result of 'the emergencies of war' which sometimes required the making of rapid decisions. Where the future settlement of policy was concerned there was always time available for consultation with those countries that would be involved: this had not been forthcoming with the Wellington declaration.[63] By way of conclusion he thanked both Dominions for their views and told them that British post-war Colonial policy had not yet been formulated. Batterbee was happy to report to London that he and Evatt had actually kept on good terms with one another, parting in 'the most friendly fashion', and the Australian seemed sincere in looking forward to next visiting London.[64]

There was, however, some anger in Wellington at what was considered to be the high commissioner's unnecessary interfering and his efforts to change the wording of the final resolution.[65] Alister McIntosh was secretary of the War Cabinet and also secretary of the new Department of External Affairs. He noted that New Zealand had been 'soundly slapped on the wrist'; a British friend who had been the official secretary in Wellington, but was now back at the DO, wrote to him referring to it as 'a fairly hefty clout on the ear'. The recipient did not, however, object as he thought the admonishment was deserving and told the same to his former boss Berendsen, who was just settling in as the New Zealand minister in Washington. As he told him, if Britain had published something similar without prior consultation, he was pretty certain that Australia, at the very least, 'would have up and left the Empire, and the scream would have been heard all the way to Whitehall without benefit of submarine cable or wireless aerial'. He thought the DO faced an 'impossible job' and that New Zealand was not entirely without blame in terms of what had happened.[66]

The quarrel was ultimately resolved, but the message coming out of the discussions could not be so easily ignored, containing as it did an inexorable movement

away from London and the pre-war Imperial system.[67] One view, promoted by a
renowned post-war Australian historian, saw it as 'not an aberration in Australian
foreign policy but its logical outcome'. A former member of the Department
of External Affairs described it as an 'explosive protest' challenging the Anglo-
American domination of power.[68] At the time two articles were printed in the
London *Evening Standard* in January 1944 just after the initial announcement of
the agreement that had been signed at Canberra. The author of these, the Rhodes
Professor of Imperial History at London University, asked his readership whether
the British Commonwealth could be kept together at the war's end. He provided
a detailed review of how this grouping had historically operated, its basis being
'the principle of voluntary collaboration'. It went on to provide a critique of
Curtin's proposals of the previous year for a standing Empire Council and offer
a more detailed account of the Anzac Pact and what it meant for the Empire.
His conclusion was to refer to Halifax's speech, given just days before, and the
unavoidable fact that the in the post-war world only a Commonwealth speaking
with one 'united, vital and coherent' voice could hope to be heard. Speaking to
a meeting of the Royal Empire Society the learned Professor Harlow went still
further. He told his audience that there existed 'a most appalling ignorance' about
the Dominion, a level of ignorance which terrified him. He might not have said
explicitly but it had become undeniably clear. As Whitehall's attention focused
on a long-anticipated meeting of the Dominion leaders to be held in London, the
British Commonwealth's unique development had reached a critical stage.[69]

11

A Family Council

In May 1944 the various prime ministers from the Dominions finally assembled at the centre of the British Empire to meet face-to-face, discuss the war's progress and begin considering how the post-war world might look. This was the first time in seven years that such an assembly had taken place and it would be the only time during the entire global conflict that all of them would be gathered together in one room. As has been seen, for a variety of reasons some of the central figures involved were previously unable or unwilling to attend such a formal event, one that carried memories of meetings of the last war and discussions not merely of Imperial unity but of sacrifice of power. The idea that such a meeting might take place had been put forward almost immediately the war had started but it had taken this long to organize and, in the process, proven to be one of the most contentious questions that had faced the Anglo-Dominion coalition. The first detailed proposal had come in the spring of 1940 but it contained a reference to it being an Imperial War Conference; Mackenzie King, the most suspicious of the group, objected and with Smuts, in any case, unable to attend the idea was dropped. Menzies' efforts in the summer of 1941 had seen the proposal revived, first in the June and then in the August, but these ultimately proved disastrous for the Australian.[1] With each of the leaders preoccupied during the following year's military and political turmoil, it would not be until 1943 that any really serious discussion of the matter would once again resurface and, perhaps surprisingly, it was Churchill who took the lead.

That he, Britain's magnificent wartime leader, should suggest the Dominions visit London to help formulate high strategy could have been anticipated at any stage during the war. It would have been a big idea from the colossus of the Empire's political world but, rhetoric aside, he had actually given every indication of loathing such a proposed gathering. Perhaps, in keeping with Amery's warning of many years before, he did not feel that he had the time spare to entertain his colleagues to tea when there was so much other pressing business to be managed. This did not prevent visiting Dominion ministers being welcomed to meetings of the War Cabinet, or some other suitably impressive gathering, as a visible manifestation of the greater access that they and the other members of the Commonwealth alliance were now said publicly to enjoy. In early April 1943, however, Churchill had written to his Canadian counterpart to say that more was needed, suggesting that an Imperial Conference should be held later that year. Mackenzie King, constantly suspicious of Whitehall orchestrated Machiavellian plots, was still unconvinced about something so formal but he did agree that a meeting involving the Dominion leaders would be sensible.[2] With this approval, efforts to bring the various prime ministers together took on a greater sense of urgency and, mindful of Ottawa's caveats, Whitehall's intention was that it would only be the key men invited. Various dates when each could attend were submitted from the distant capitals: it was noted at this initial stage that Curtin was unlikely to be prepared to travel and Evatt would probably appear in his stead; Smuts also was unwilling to leave South Africa until the back end of the year. This meant that November was quick to emerge as the most obvious date but Churchill preferred something earlier although he indicated to the DO that there should be some margin given; September made the greatest sense in his mind.[3] Despite his initial acceptance the difficulty still lay with Mackenzie King and his continuing hesitancy about publicly endorsing a date.

The British leader was clearly angered at this, telling the DO that there was no reason to wait 'indefinitely' for a response from Ottawa and that the delay should not be allowed, effectively, to veto a meeting of the whole Imperial body.[4] But, with no sign of consensus emerging, it was reluctantly decided to again, at least, temporarily curtail the planning. The eventual decision to hold the meeting in May 1944 can in fact though largely be attributed to Smuts. He told Cranborne that he could not travel any earlier and he thought it would be a more convenient date for his fellow Dominion leaders; also he believed, crucially, that the war would be within a few months of its end, allowing for more relevant talks about the future.[5] As a basis for reaching a final consensus this seemed to do the job and proved the culmination of the long-running attempts to settle on a date.[6] On this basis the British political class could now become more fully involved. Cranborne had first asked at the beginning of January 1944 that he be allowed to submit a short memorandum on the subject to the War Cabinet. A very tentative agenda for a meeting in London involving all of the Dominion prime ministers had first been set out in the summer of 1943; there were at this point two items for discussion, 'short term problems, mainly in Europe' and 'long term problems of world organization'. Inevitably the changing nature of the war had quickly made this redundant, but this gave the DO a start-point with which to sit down and produce a more comprehensive document. The Dominions secretary envisaged that the main subjects for discussion would be the immediate military situation, questions arising from the probable defeat of Germany prior to Japan's capitulation, outlines of the post-war settlement and cooperation within the Commonwealth following the war's end. There would also likely be special subjects such as colonial policy, migration and civil aviation. He did not want any 'elaborate preparation of documents', but felt that there would be advantages in giving certain material in advance to the Dominion leaders, noting that Smuts had asked that this might be done.[7] With the desire being to stress that it was not an Imperial Conference, Cranborne was keen that the South Rhodesian prime minister should not be invited and the Indian representative in the War Cabinet should only attend if there were any special subjects affecting India.[8]

This departmental study resulted in a Cabinet paper that was discussed at an evening meeting of the War Cabinet held later that month, although it was actually a much shortened and more general document than had been prepared by the Whitehall officials. Churchill concluded the very brief discussion with the comment 'we should be at pains to make it clear that the note of the meeting was to be an effort to establish still more strongly, closely and recognizably the unity of the structure of the Commonwealth and the Empire'.[9] Privately he had let it be known among his senior colleagues in Westminster that the agenda for the meeting was to be reduced to a minimum. The senior official in the FO responsible for Dominion affairs recorded that he understood Churchill did not contemplate a series of formal meetings and that any agenda, if one was even prepared, would be extremely restricted.[10] It was proposed that a Ministerial Committee be formed, headed by Cranborne, whose aim would be to scope out the parameters of the proposed conference, who would be attending, the views of other government departments – notably the FO – as to the suggested agenda and whether the political discussions might be followed by talks amongst the respective military chiefs about future cooperation post-war.[11] To do this the Committee would need to have memoranda on various subjects commissioned from the departments concerned and then make recommendations to the War Cabinet about what line to take during the subsequent meetings. The memoranda could, if they were agreed upon, be communicated to the Dominions in advance.[12]

From the first meeting of the Ministerial Committee there had been some argument over how best to proceed. At the centre of it all was a prolonged discussion about the best strategy for dealing with Curtin's proposal made the previous year. Cranborne felt that ignoring it and waiting was the best approach; if the Australian leader wanted to discuss his views he could do so in front of the other Dominion prime ministers and let them express their opinions back.[13] The FO agreed that this was too complicated a subject and it would be best to leave the initiative to the visiting Dominion leaders. Any discussion on the subject would have to avoid the use of the word 'machinery' as this would likely lead to misgivings in Canada; 'methods' was the specific word to be adopted. There was also an argument from the FO that securing an understanding on how collaboration at the lower level might function was possibly more important than any other; discussions among civil servants, and any agreement that could be reached, was deemed to commit the respective Dominion governments to given courses of action. The proposal therefore was for a meeting of officials to take place after the conference had finished. Apparently taking the lead on the question, the FO recognized the need to improve the current position although with the considerable caveat 'as far as circumstances permit'. As the intra-Whitehall discussions gathered pace it even proposed that some form of discussion about improving methods should be encouraged among the Dominions themselves as this would 'help to overcome inertia'.[14]

Despite this keen interest it was Cranborne who actually produced the memorandum which considered the question of future cooperation within the British Commonwealth. The Dominions secretary felt that Curtin would raise his proposals, but doubted whether they would find much support. The official policy so far from the British government had been to refrain from committing itself. While Australia wanted a more effective voice in the framing of policy, Mackenzie King, as he had made clear with public responses to the Curtin proposals and Halifax's Toronto speech, was satisfied with the existing system and was opposed to any alterations. He wanted to ensure that Canada could influence world policy and did not believe that this could be achieved by closer linkage with the Commonwealth. His preference was for a worldwide organization in which Canada could play a leading part. Smuts had indicated his support for the idea of another great Power to counter-balance the Soviet Union and United States and was prepared to see closer links, not just with the nations of the Commonwealth but also with other countries in North-Western Europe. New Zealand had made no public comment on the matter but it was likely that there would be some support for its Tasman neighbour. Changes in machinery would be considered with an open mind but would need to be approved by all. He proposed therefore that some compromise suggestions be offered. These entailed a regular annual meeting of ministers concerned with foreign policy, subject to three of the four Dominions splitting the portfolios of 'external relations' and prime minister, something that was thought likely to work more effectively in the post-war international political system. The other option was for some kind of formalization of the meetings with the Dominion high commissioners or expanding the number of liaison officers who could maintain stronger links within Whitehall.[15]

Responding to Cranborne's paper at the next Ministerial Committee meeting, Amery was critical of this proposed permanent secretariat, 'an Empire post office' whose role would merely be to exchange and collate information and prepare the agenda for more formal meetings. He could not see anything wrong with Curtin's proposal. The FO's representative also stressed that the Australian leader's ideas should not be dismissed as impracticable. While Mackenzie King might be opposed to the idea he judged that the other Dominions were not and with 'the benevolent neutrality of His Majesty's Government' it was possible that Canada might drop some or all of its objections.[16] Within the FO there was also little real support for any possibly higher profile for the London-based Dominion representatives who, it was considered, would be unlikely to 'add any weight to the Councils of the Empire'.[17] J. D. Greenway who, pre-war, had served in the British Embassy in Moscow, giving him something of an established diplomatic pedigree, was prominent with his criticism. He thought that progress was 'disappointing and somewhat timid' and was certain some form of machinery could be devised that would not be hamstrung by Canada choosing not to join. Curtin's proposed permanent secretariat did not seem such a bad idea.

If this was the most important issue to be addressed before the Dominion leaders arrived in London, the question of military cooperation was not far behind. From the Committee's earliest meeting the DO's argument was that it would be best to try and secure some form of approval for continued joint planning at the staff level in the hope that this might lead eventually to planning on the political or ministerial level. As Eric Machtig put it, 'we would be wise, particularly in view of Canadian idiosyncrasies, not to fly too high'. Proposals put forward by Bevin were, therefore, considerably more than had been envisaged. A letter from him to the Chairman recommended that the Empire be split into zones: Australia and New Zealand would be the Pacific Area; South Africa would be the nucleus of an area stretching as far north as Kenya; Canada would take responsibility with America for the Pacific and the Atlantic; Britain would accept responsibility for the defence of the Commonwealth in relation to Europe. Such a scheme, he argued, would also see benefits in terms of promoting trade and intra-Imperial immigration. The FO saw various potential issues with the suggested Canadian role – specifically how the US might respond and the danger that the government in Ottawa might choose not to be involved – but they appreciated its 'big' nature. The DO deemed this to be going much too far when it would be difficult enough simply to secure a continuance of the existing liaison machinery that had developed during the war. Amery also had written to Cranborne stressing that future defence collaboration needed to be considered as a matter of priority but many of his ideas were also a little too enthusiastic.[18]

The determining answers would come from the experts and Cranborne had approached the chiefs of staff asking that they prepare papers on the main issues involved by the end of March. It was proposed that the immediate military situation, the war against Japan, the military aspect of the post-war settlement and the coordination of defence within the post-war British Commonwealth would all be raised during the conference. As the meeting would be short they could only be tackled in a general fashion without any detailed arrangements, and the committee was anxious to avoid placing any 'cut-and-dried proposals' before the visitors.[19] With papers submitted by the chiefs on 'Policing of Europe' and 'United Nations' Bases in Relation to General Security Organisation',[20] the main memorandum reviewed the system of Imperial Defence and examined how it had worked before 1939 and the changes that had taken place as a result of the war. On the whole, the comments it had to make about future collaboration on defence were positive. Australia and New Zealand were felt to have recognized the need to strengthen their links with the centre, 'they see the advantages of securing that the whole weight of the British Commonwealth shall be applied in future situations in which they might be involved'. It was anticipated that the Tasman Dominions would require inclusion in the central formulation of any future world security system but, also, that they would be prepared 'to take their full share' of ensuing responsibilites. The South African view was less clear but was felt likely to be broadly similar. Canada, however, was recognized as being different because of its relationship with its southern neighbour and the corresponding desire to retain a more independent stance. One WO reviewer of a draft of this paper had complained that it did not really bring out the need for a strong British Commonwealth as part of the post-war system, what he saw as 'the big point' that needed to be made to the Dominion leaders when they visited. To him it was clear that Australia, New Zealand and South Africa could be counted upon to adopt closer ties and commitments within the British Commonwealth. The authorities in Ottawa could, perhaps, be persuaded to look favourably upon the existing system by being told that they would have no voice if they stood alone and telling them that they must choose between London and Washington. By a neat calculation it was assumed, therefore, that remaining within the Commonwealth would be recognized as the only solution 'if she is to make her voice heard'.

Ultimately these two issues would appear to have been the most heavily worked on with political and civil service input coming from far and wide. That is not to say that there were not other important areas that were highlighted. Other papers were submitted on education matters, post-war shipping policy and the disposal of former Italian colonies. As the committee secretary noted, these were only part of a rather 'formidable array'; 'International regional bodies in colonial areas', 'Future of the French Colonial Empire', 'Migration' and items focused on the actual mechanics of how the conference itself would be run were all included.[21] Investigations were also made about a possible appreciation of American thinking over its future role in the Pacific but this proved too difficult to arrange beyond a series of unofficial comments.[22] There was also the question of the future intentions of the Soviet Union to be considered, a subject of particular interest to Smuts.[23] Additional preparations also needed to be made, Eden being asked to prepare a statement on the proposed post-war settlement under two headings, the political aspect of post-war organization and the future of Germany.[24]

The curtain raiser to the Dominion prime ministers' visit took place the month before when, in April 1944, a two-day debate on Dominion affairs was held in the House of Commons. This offered an opportunity for parliamentarians to express their opinions while the press coverage recognized that it could not be seen as 'an occasion for a declaration of Imperial policy'. This was the first time since he had become prime minister that Churchill would speak specifically on the Dominions and, as such, Cranborne was asked to prepare him a lengthy briefing paper. The Dominions secretary was asked to identify any points that critics of the government might raise and, while he considered this a difficult challenge, he did offer seven areas that he thought were of greatest concern. These included any suggestion that the government should take a lead in pressing the Dominions to enter into closer cooperation. There was also a chance that the levels of pre-war cooperation – both in terms of defence and foreign policies – might be criticized as having been inadequate or that participation by the Dominions in any future war could not be counted upon. Curtin's proposal was an obvious subject that could be raised, migration, Imperial Preference and the Dominions' interest in colonial affairs made up the list. Cranborne was able to provide simple single sentence rejoinders to deal with any questions that might focus on these issues; just to be on the safe side, he also provided another ten pages of notes and reference material.[25] The line it was suggested Churchill take was that the meeting was an informal discussion, nothing more and nothing less, and it would be wise not to advocate to any particular suggestion or proposal in advance.

The debate itself was recorded as having been marked by some 'plain and straightforward speaking'. There were 27 speakers on the first day, drawn from all the parties, including in their ranks Messrs Winterton, Granville and Shinwell, each notable contributors to the wider debate that had taken place throughout the war. Added to these was an intriguing mix, some from rural wards, others from large cities, some self-avowed Imperialists, others talking of the shameful exploitation that had been suffered by the Colonial Empire. At the end of this opening salvo Hugh Dalton finished on behalf of the government. Time and again he returned to the central position, the forthcoming meeting was to be informal in nature 'conducted between equals at the family council table'.[26] Fourteen new speakers rose the following day to add their observations, reflections and, more often than not, their advice as to how the 'Imperial Idea' should be developed in the years to come. Beverley Baxter, Canadian by birth, journalist by trade and Conservative by calling, made perhaps the most telling observation when he noted: 'The neglect of the Empire over the last 25 years is not one of the proudest moments of this great Assembly. It did not matter in those fateful days between the two wars what the particular subject of foreign affairs was, it drew this House like a striptease revue. But once the Dominions or the Empire was being discussed, the indifference was chilling to a degree.' As he concluded, all sides had been as bad as one another and if there had been greater interest in all things Empire, both at home and abroad, it might have been the case that Hitler would have been restrained and the Nazi party would have collapsed.

When Churchill finally rose he did so to tell the House that the debate had been a great success. There followed an opportunity for him to wax lyrical on his understanding of Empire, ideas extolling the spirit of Kipling and sprinkled liberally with historical and anecdotal metaphor. It was the by now traditional *tour de force* although low on harangue, instead much more soothing in tone and structure. The British Commonwealth and Empire had never been more united but the system needed to be modernized so that those nations involved could be better advised of world events and better aware of what each was thinking. It was a surprisingly progressive speech, in light of many of his wartime observations and instructions, and would appear to have augured well for the conference soon about to begin. According to *Time*, 'for two days men of all parties hailed Commonwealth and Empire' and it had provided the prime minister with 'a jubilant stage ... in his imperial role'. Even Shinwell, previously noted for his clashes with Churchill on Empire-related questions, seemed prepared to offer him his support. As the magazine noted: 'Every Churchillian turn got a cheer [as] he beamed, waved, chuckled ... Ever jealous of Empire, and now equally committed to world association, Churchill hoped for the best.' Nonetheless it was clear from his comments and the tone of his speech that he was still thinking of a Commonwealth centred in London where the British government could bring greatest influence to bear.[27]

The gathering of Dominion prime ministers followed shortly afterwards. Because the emphasis was on it being a personal exchange of views and not a full Imperial Conference, they did not bring any ministerial colleagues and were accompanied by a small staff. Fraser and Curtin travelled via the United States. The Canadians flew direct. Smuts flew in his own aircraft to Cairo, accompanied in the end by Sir Godfrey Huggins, the Southern Rhodesian leader, to whom it had been decided to extend an invitation; there Churchill's personal plane was waiting for both of them to complete the journey to London.[28] The seven-strong Canadian delegation were centred at the Dorchester Hotel, the Australians and New Zealanders, 18 in total including the prime ministers' wives, settled into the Savoy, while the much smaller South African party, just four in total, made do with the Hyde Park Hotel. Special telephones with scrambler equipment were installed in the suites of each of the Dominion leaders. In addition Curtin and Fraser were allotted offices in the War Cabinet Rooms; Mackenzie King and Smuts preferred to work in their hotels and arrangements were made to assist them.[29]

The Dominion leaders were invited to attend the Monday War Cabinet and any other war-related meetings that were deemed appropriate. In addition there would be two meetings a day of the actual Conference both held in the Cabinet Room at No. 10 Downing Street; the only exception was the two general reviews of the war situation which took place in the Prime Minister's Map Room at the War Cabinet office.[30] The timetable covered ten days, but there were plenty of gaps with only eleven specially convened sessions and the invites to attend the War Cabinet gatherings; on seven of the days there was just a single meeting. A draft schedule showing a two-week programme was also given to each of them upon their arrival, but it was subsequently found to be impracticable to adhere to these plans. The Dominion leaders made various suggestions as to the order on which the subjects should be discussed and it proved impossible to forecast with any degree of accuracy how long would be spent on each. As a result the detailed agenda issued the night before a meeting was the only firm indication of arrangements. To keep each of the prime ministers fully informed it was agreed that, aside from messages received from their home governments, that they would receive various FO telegrams and the weekly résumé of the military situation during their stay. Ultimately no papers were circulated in advance, only the main points for discussion were sent to them. Ten papers were circulated during the course of the meeting and several of these were intended as providing further clarification about points that had arisen during the discussions. A reviewer of the events that took place, writing some time afterwards, commented that because it had not been intended to produce a series of formal resolutions this 'made it all the easier for discussion to be developed on broad lines and unnecessary detail to be avoided'.[31]

Socially no effort was spared to impress the Imperial guests. The Conference opened with a dinner party at Buckingham Palace; the King had asked before-hand for a briefing of the current political situation in each of the Dominions and this was augmented by a personal report from Cranborne in late April of the most recent developments.[32] Each of the overseas leaders was also the guest-of-honour for their own hosted lunch as Cranborne was keen to ensure that they would all have an opportunity to make an important public speech. Smuts would visit Birmingham where he would receive the Freedom of the City. In addition Mackenzie King was invited to address members of both Houses at Westminster – he was said to 'excel' in parliamentary surroundings – while both Curtin and Fraser had the Freedom of the City of London conferred upon them in a grand ceremony at the Guildhall.[33] Initially it had been agreed that private individuals and bodies were to be discouraged from extending social invites to the assembled leaders. The official record noted that 'in the event it turned out that the prime ministers were rather embarrassed by the number of invitations they received to attend official or semi-official parties'. The problem was that many of these were issued by Whitehall departments with no reference to what other engagements were taking place. Also it was clear that the secretariat had been largely ignored.[34]

At the first meeting there were 28 British ministers, military officers or civil servants present; the Dominions between them – not including representatives from India and Southern Rhodesia who had also been invited – mustered 15

in total. The number of British officials – with the exception of those most
directly connected – was supposed to be based on the number of Dominion
officials present; the rule was that they should not attend unless specially needed.
Dominion high commissioners were also to be discouraged from attending. As it
had been repeatedly stressed that these were to be intimate meetings, some of the
Dominion guests were a little annoyed at the consistently large numbers of British
officials who tried to attend subsequent meetings. So much so that Churchill was
asked to offer a soothing comment or two along the lines of how important the
topics were and how important it was thought to hear the views of the visiting
statesmen from the Empire.[35] The meetings were recorded in the normal form
used for War Cabinet Conclusions with the possibility of additional confidential
annexes being added at a subsequent date. The draft minutes were sent to each of
the prime ministers for them to make amendments but very few were forthcoming;
a bound final version was available for when Mackenzie King, the first to leave,
departed for Ottawa. They also received a completed set of records as did members
of the War Cabinet, the Service ministers and chiefs of staff in London and the
DO and supporting secretariat. Copies with the confidential annexes removed
were given a much wider distribution. Finally, the Ministry of Information was
responsible for dealing with the media. This was clearly an important part of
a meeting for which the intention was to demonstrate Imperial unity and the
arrangements had been discussed in some detail as part of the pre-conference
committee process. Cranborne held four press conferences during the period and
the Dominion leaders also spoke individually, both to correspondents from their
own Dominions and to the British press.[36] The Conference's opening was reported
prominently in *The Times* and the other leading newspapers, and regular stories
were published throughout the meetings and in leading journals.[37]

The most detailed account of the Conference is provided by the meticulous
summary sent the following month to British Heads of Mission. Understandably
this was dominated by references that had been made to foreign affairs and it was
stressed to the readers that accounts of the proceedings had been given a most
restricted distribution in London and should therefore be regarded as being
'most secret'.[38] The Conference began at noon exactly on 1 May with a brief
address from Churchill on the immediate war situation. He told his audience
that they had gathered to take stock of affairs and whilst he did not expect them
to reach conclusions to all the problems that 'confront the British Empire and
vex mankind' this would be an overdue opportunity to exchange views and ideas.
More than that, it would allow them to show the watching world and the 'very
powerful Allies' with whom they had fought, what they were about. With a typical
flourish he had concluded that the meeting would demonstrate that the British
Empire and Commonwealth 'stands together, woven into one family of nations
capable of solving our common problems in full loyalty to the supreme cause for

which we have drawn the sword'.[39] Mackenzie King thought these comments to be 'most impressive' and 'reassuring'.

Eden's review of foreign affairs followed. According to the comments given to Britain's ambassadors these were well received with general praise being given for the way in which wartime foreign policy had been handled. It was further, pointedly, noted that there was 'entire satisfaction with the arrangements that had been made to keep them in close and effective touch with developments'. These comments were 'particularly gratifying'. Fraser thought that British policy had been right; Curtin did not know how it could have been done better than it had; even Mackenzie King thought that difficult situations had been 'handled marvellously' and in such a way as to command 'the strongest possible admiration'. All this seemed very different to some of the stinging comments that had been received on the DO's deciphering systems during the course of the war. While brief reference was made to the other meetings – monetary and commercial, colonial policy, shipping and migration – special mention was also given to the two full meetings that had been devoted to the post-war settlement. Even in the flowery diplomatic prose of the Foreign Service, it was clear that there had been some tensions during these discussions despite these having been confined to 'broad principles'. Mackenzie King had made it clear that there could not be a single Commonwealth spokesman at any future discussions; each would speak with their own voice. He was willing to offer British representatives the 'fortification' that the Dominions would be 'of one mind with them', and the knowledge that this was 'a body of nations that normally acted in concert'. But such balm would only be given if adequate consultation had taken place beforehand.

The issue identified beforehand as being potentially the most contentious, future Commonwealth cooperation, was saved for the penultimate meeting. Curtin began by announcing he no longer intended to pursue his proposals of the previous year which he now recognized were clearly unacceptable to Canada and also possibly to South Africa. This, in the end, was not entirely unexpected. Curtin had given a press conference soon after his arrival in which he extolled some of his thinking about a permanent secretariat. It was reported back to the FO by somebody who had been present that at this the Australian leader was 'very frank throughout' and had said that he would be prepared to take what he could get and explained that 'if three would agree, why then, let's have a secretariat for three'.[40] Discussion had followed among the Dominions about the idea, the result of which seemed to be that he was now prepared to confine himself to ideas for improvement based on generally informal means such as periodic meetings of ministers and expansion of liaison staffs; not a permanent executive group as had been contemplated in the text of the Anzac agreement. His final proposal was very similar to that which the FO had argued for, that a small technical committee might be formed including representatives from Britain and the Dominions to

consider the whole question of cooperation.[41] He would later confide that he had
been disappointed that his plans for closer unity did not receive more of a hearing
and it was noted that neither Churchill nor Smuts had attended the meeting that
discussed the proposals.[42] He was though prepared to accept the inevitable and
the conclusion following the meeting was that the prime ministers seemed most
satisfied with the existing methods of consultation.[43]

The conclusion of the FO's long review of the Conference sent to the overseas
diplomatic corps was that it had been 'successful beyond our hopes'. The atmosphere had been 'strikingly friendly' and discussions had been completely frank.
There had, however, been one striking exception to this and, unsurprisingly,
it had come from Churchill. With their enthusiastic support for the League of
Nations, the New Zealanders were especially interested in ideas regarding any
future world organization and it had been the British leader who had submitted
the relevant paper. His ideas for Regional Leagues under a World Council had
been politely dismissed even by Cranborne who, having seen them at the draft
phase and in his attempt to dissuade the prime minister from introducing them
to the Conference, had pointed to his knowledge of how the League of Nations
had failed. He had spent a long period at Geneva while serving in the pre-war
FO and had seen first-hand how it had worked, but this did little to improve the
merits of his observations.[44] Churchill was pressing for a United States of Europe
with a Council in which Britain, the United States and the Soviets would all be
members. While Fraser was prepared to recognize the British paper as 'a valuable
contribution', Berendsen was said to be highly critical of the British proposals.[45]
A protest ensued forcing the FO to convene a special meeting at which it was
agreed that the British leader would withdraw his paper. The alternatives of 'the
supreme body versus general mob' would be reconsidered by the professional
Whitehall bureaucrats who would put the argument in a more balanced way to
produce a revised version that would be amenable to all of the Dominions. The
DO was upset at this outcome, believing the FO to have adopted an 'unfortunate'
approach; Machtig thought that the contents of the revised paper were quite
different from what had been agreed at the Conference. The DO believed that
it was entirely clear that the Dominions had rejected both of Churchill's key
suggestions, the unitary representation of the British Commonwealth and the
idea that regional organizations would act as representatives on any future World
Council.[46] Yet the new document still supported Churchill's point of 'capital
importance', and that there should be some European regional machine.[47] The
re-draft was savaged when it was put before the Dominion diplomats who had
been left behind in London to discuss such matters, the allegation being that it
contained ideas which had not been approved at the full conference. The proposal
that Britain alone might represent all of the Dominions on any future World
Council was particularly abhorrent to the overseas representatives.

For each of the Dominion leaders, their visit to London had a different effect. The FO's summary had noted that Curtin in particular had conducted himself in a praiseworthy fashion, his visit having been remarkably successful in demonstrating his ability to stand out among his fellow prime ministers. He had 'hit it off' well with the British leader and admitted his 'boundless' admiration for the British war effort. Fraser also, despite some doubts about the conduct of the war in the Mediterranean and Italy, was assuaged by Churchill's exposition and left in a positive frame of mind. It was noted that Mackenzie King had proven as reluctant as had been expected to commit Canada to specific Commonwealth proposals. He had, however, remained throughout 'most helpful, friendly and enthusiastic' and it was believed that he had returned home well satisfied. Smuts was 'as always a source of strength and inspiration'. The South African had commented in his closing address to the Conference that while it had not been a formal meeting, what had been achieved was successful and 'amazing' under the conditions prevailing in an atmosphere and spirit unlike any he had experienced at previous gatherings. As another writer put it, it had not been expected that Curtin would be such a success; aside from Smuts, 'an international statesman of the Churchill-Roosevelt calibre', his performance was judged to have placed him 'head and shoulders above the other PMs'.[48]

Some of the doubts about what to expect had been based on the warnings received by the DO beforehand that the Australian leader had been in 'a far from cheerful mood' about the Conference. Indeed, in February 1944, a visiting DO official returned from Canberra with the news that Curtin was not interested in international affairs and would likely still refuse any invitation to visit London. According to Cross, he was apparently apprehensive about the prospect of meeting with Churchill and uncertain about how he would compare to the other Dominion leaders, both in terms of his statesmanship and his stature. He returned home full of self-assurance, feeling that he was 'in every sense one of the brotherhood'. He was also particularly pleased to have formed a strong friendship with the British leader and extolled the degree to which it was vital for the Commonwealth and the Empire that he remained in power for the duration of the war. He felt 'the hatchet had been buried' over 1942 and the high commissioner believed that Australian cooperation would in future be 'more sympathetic' and 'pliant' than in the past. Overall the experience was likely to introduce a new degree of understanding and cordiality and greatly enhance Anglo-Australian relations. Press correspondents who had returned to Canberra brought with them the message that 'Curtin is now as British as Churchill'.[49]

Curtin briefed the Australian parliament in mid-July on what he had learnt during his trip. It was an upbeat and optimistic review in which he made quite apparent his renewed support for the need to maintain the appearance of a unified Commonwealth. He stressed that the smaller members should offer their views in a discrete fashion allowing them to be discussed within the group who might then develop 'a friendly acceptability' to them. As he concluded, 'we cannot approach by a crude and blatant declaration the problem of getting other countries to see our point of view'. However sincere the sentiment, this all seemed a little ironic in light of the events surrounding the Anzac agreement and the controversy it had caused. It was commented on in the local press about it being axiomatic that Britain should take the initiative in British Commonwealth relations in Europe, but it was appreciated the way in which the main partner 'refrained from trying to assert any political domination'.[50] After some reflection the value of Curtin's speech was in fact generally doubted, and the lack of new information it provided was widely criticized. There was, however, some agreement that the promise that large and powerful British forces would soon be fighting in the Pacific region had offered a practical indication of how the power and prestige of the Empire would be restored.[51]

Mackenzie King's biographer claimed that the Canadian approached his second wartime visit to Britain in a much more positive frame of mind. His position at home was now secure, while he and Churchill had become quite friendly and he had no uneasiness about his reception in London. His diary entries during his stay at the Dorchester, never noted for their brevity, were fulsome as is reflected in the length of the relevant chapter in the volume.[52] This seems at odds with the view of one official in Canada House who recorded that his prime minister believed such meetings should be 'for consultation and cooperation but not for the formulation or preparation of policies'. He did not want to work through the Empire towards broader affiliations and, as a result, was said to 'mistrust the whole thing'.[53] The Canadian might have arrived in an apprehensive frame of mind but he left reassured by the results of the Conference, although nothing could remove the view that the speeches by Halifax and Smuts expressed the official views of the British government. His speech to the combined House of Commons and Lords was recognized as a warning not to mess with the existing system. The Commonwealth was not founded on racial ties but on the ideals of freedom and justice. This was seen as evidence that if any attempts were made to strengthen political and economic ties Canada would not offer its support. The Canadian leader was widely seen to have 'won on points', he had got his message across to the Whitehall crowd.[54] In fact, for Mackenzie King the Conference was a great public relations coup and on his return to Ottawa airport he was greeted by members of the public and politicians of all sides; ovations and civic receptions followed. This was all due to his having been seen to have spoken on behalf of all Canadians, successfully pleading the Dominion's case. It was deemed astonishing within the British High Commission that a man who had considered holding a divisive election on 'the Empire issue' following Halifax's speech only a few months before should have enjoyed his visit so much and returned with such apparently fond sentiments, telling all that he had 'never been more proud to be a citizen of the British Commonwealth'.[55]

Smuts' visit had re-emphasized the degree to which he was treated differently than the other Dominion leaders. Instructions had been given by Churchill before he arrived that the South African was to be allowed to view any documents of interest as there was nothing seen by the British prime minister that could not be seen by the field marshal. It was stressed that, in this respect he was to be 'treated on an entirely different footing' from his counterparts. As a result, every morning and afternoon a pile of sensitive documents were despatched to South Africa House in Trafalgar Square; included among these were copies of Churchill's personal telegrams, Heads of State telegrams in their special locked boxes, along with any other papers he wished to see connected with military operations. Whenever the South African leader had visited London he had been allowed such apparently unrestricted access to Whitehall's documents; the other Dominion leaders had been given much less.[56] The younger Smuts had once again accompanied his father and noted in his diary at the Conference's conclusion: 'The Conference has been largely exploratory and no real resolutions have been thrashed out, but it does indicate for the future that we can at least get together and discuss contentious subjects in a friendly mood. The range of subjects covered was very comprehensive and most of the delegates will leave with a sound background to current world affairs ... There has been much mutual patting on the back. So we are all happy and beaming.'[57] While his counterparts went home, Smuts stayed on and took great pleasure in accompanying Churchill on visits to the coalition forces who were preparing for the imminent invasion of Normandy.

As for Fraser, he had repeated Savage's pledge that 'where Britain goes, we go; where she stands, we stand'. He had also made himself and his country heard about how the Empire should approach the question of a future international security organization. He left London to visit New Zealand troops fighting in Italy and stood at the ruined site of the monastery at Monte Cassino, before going on to Egypt and then home via the United States. On his return to New Zealand he had travelled over 8,000 miles and once again demonstrated that he had a gift for oratory that could, on occasion, rival that of Churchill himself. As he told the House of Representatives in a fitting example of this talent, 'here is a paradox the world outside the British Commonwealth finds it difficult to understand – the paradox that, the freer we become, the closer we draw together; the more our constitutional bonds are relaxed, the more closely we are held in bonds of friendship ... the more truly we are one in sentiment, in heart, and spirit, one in peace, as well as in war'.[58] This in many respects was an entirely fitting epitaph for the Conference, far better than the flowery final statement that each of the leaders had signed at its conclusion.[59]

Speaking in the House of Lords in the first days of January 1945, Cranborne was still finding reason to praise the meeting that had taken place the previous year. Those pessimists who had prophesied that the Statute of Westminster would mean the beginning of the dissolution of the Empire had been proven visibly wrong. He could claim that there was a different reality in which material and spiritual ties were actually stronger than ever before. He also proposed that the Dominions could build on this in peacetime by having an annual prime minister's meeting.[60] To British writers at the time the Conference had been a 'milestone in history'.[61] More intriguingly, the largely American readership of *Time* was told that Churchill 'had neither qualified nor abandoned Britain's belief that she must have the Commonwealth and Empire behind her in order to remain a Great Power'.[62] The idea that the Dominions might form a bloc had been – at least temporarily – abandoned. Instead, those assembled had publicly agreed that there should be a world organization which would allow them to 'gather around Britain as closely or as loosely as they pleased'. Despite the apparent success of the London meeting and the renewed vows of loyalty and unity of Empire that had spewed forth, the process of creating this United Nations would demonstrate just how much the wartime experience had changed the Anglo-Dominion alliance.

12

Losing an Empire

The Parliament in Westminster dispersed for its summer vacation after hearing the prime minister's survey of military and diplomatic affairs, delivered with an unmistakeable note of victory. In June 1944 Allied military forces liberated Rome, Operation *Overlord* successfully began the re-invasion of occupied France and in Eastern Europe Russian troops were advancing along a huge front. In Burma Commonwealth forces – not just British but also Indian and native African troops – were pushing the Japanese onto the defensive. American-led forces were on the point of expelling the Japanese from northern New Guinea and Admiral Nimitz had defeated the Imperial Japanese Navy in the Philippine Sea. Although there was still a great deal of fighting ahead the end could be seen and the Dominions were centrally involved: New Zealand and South African troops were heavily committed in Italy, the large Canadian land force was playing a key role in north-west Europe, Australian forces were proving their worth in New Guinea. This did not include, of course, the continuing efforts of Dominion sailors and airmen who had fought the longest war on the seas and in the air in various theatres throughout the course of the global conflict.[1]

Adding to Churchill's sense of well-being, the meeting of the Empire's prime ministers had also been a great success and the unity of the coalition never appeared to have been stronger. The British leader had himself described it as the 'highest pinnacle' to which this 'worldwide family organization' had yet reached. As *The Round Table* warned, however, great as the achievement had been, there was a need to beware, the danger being that 'hope and resolve' might turn into 'complacency and inaction'. This august monitor of Imperial affairs had detected a problem, the relationship of the last five years had been based upon a common goal, defeating the aggressor, but post-war Commonwealth relations would be different. Each of the Dominions was bound not just by the value which it attached to its historical position in the Empire but also its regional position and the development of a future international security organization. 'As nations they pursue their separate national interests; as members of the group they share the group responsibilities as well as the group resources.' It was indeed potentially something of a paradox.[2]

The recent London meeting had been keenly watched on the other side of the Atlantic. Halifax had telegraphed back from Washington just before its start to say that the decisions that were reached would likely have considerable influence on American policymakers. As he put it, 'if the result demonstrates Commonwealth solidarity respect for us will increase and vice versa'. He cautioned, however, that any reference to Imperial Preference, or indeed economic questions in general could prove disastrous, having a negative impact on willingness to consider plans for cooperation and the attitude towards Lend-Lease. If this could be avoided he believed it would encourage a desire to work with the Commonwealth. He believed 'a good deal would depend on this' and the FO generally agreed with his comments. Post-Conference the department concluded that American opinion thought Mackenzie King had triumphed in defeating calls for the Commonwealth to be more coordinated and centralized. He had also successfully opposed the efforts of those Dominion leaders who wanted the Commonwealth bloc to have a bigger say in the discussions about the post-war organization. Nonetheless it was also believed that the outcome should have been satisfactory to both American and the British alike, confirming that 'the Commonwealth can no longer be regarded as an end in itself' and showing the rest of the world that 'the Commonwealth is far from moribund'.[3]

The only concern was that the American press was judged not really to have realized the Conference's significance; radio comments monitored in the British Embassy had included 'a certain amount of talk about "glittering phrases of which people have begun to grow tired"'.[4] MacDonald in the High Commission in Ottawa therefore took it upon himself to double his efforts to better explain to the North American audience what the Empire stood for or at very least his interpretation. He had produced a series of rough notes in the spring of 1943, later titled as 'Some Thoughts on the Post-War Position of the British Commonwealth of Nations', which had been distributed throughout Britain's overseas posts.[5] Following Lord Halifax's Toronto speech he had promised London that he would provide a more detailed study of Imperial cooperation and his new treatise, which covered 22 tightly typed pages, was delivered in April 1944 with apologies for the long delay in its production.[6] This new document had generated scant praise in Whitehall, but it did not appear to deter him from his self-appointed role. Taking the message directly to the target, he told an audience in Boston in October 1944, it would be best for everybody if the ignorance which existed could be overcome and both Americans and Britons could be better informed about each other. The main purpose of British Imperial rule, as it now stood, was to extend freedom 'to all the peoples of the British Colonies, Burma, India and the Dominions, whatever their race, colour or creed'. It might have been more akin to propaganda than education but it was considered to be of stalwart value by those reviewing it – and no doubt helping prepare it – within the High Commission who extolled London to read these excellent speeches being made by MacDonald. Examining the speeches in the DO, what was noted was the undesirable tone and content and Emrys-Evans was clearly upset. This most recent speech was 'altogether too apologetic about the British Empire. It is not good from a historical point of view and merely confirms the Americans in the view held among a large part of the population that the United States introduced constitutional government into this country and the Commonwealth.' He believed that such speeches did not help to improve Anglo-American relations or 'bring any light into the darkness of American ignorance of our Imperial developments'. Cranborne was less scathing but he also could not agree with MacDonald's almost sycophantic praise of American political institutions. In the Dominions secretary's view, the reality was that 'they learned almost all they know on this subject from us, and if they had modelled their constitution more closely on ours, they would be in a much happier situation today'.[7]

The quest for unity dominated discussions and debate throughout what was to prove to be the penultimate year of the war and a commonly heard theme was the danger that the rest of the world faced if the alliance collapsed. A speaker at the Empire Club in Toronto – where Halifax had ignited a crisis – believed at least one of the causes of the two great conflicts of the century had been that Britain's enemies had believed the Dominions were 'so unconcerned for her interests, so remote if not actually hostile in purpose, as to be negligible in a forecast of comparative fighting strength'. The challenge would be to ensure that this never happened again.[8] Elsewhere a contributor to *Empire Review* was convinced that a united Commonwealth would 'save the world future torture', all that was needed to secure this was realistic diplomacy and straight-speaking.[9] Mackenzie King's address to the combined House of Commons and Lords in May 1944 was pored over in the FO for clues as to his thoughts on the subject. As a result of this analysis, it seemed the only way to maintain the Commonwealth was the successful establishment of an international authority, one in which unity could be preserved in so much as the Dominions, although associated with other powers, would likely act together. Were there to be no organization, the Whitehall reviewers feared that the Commonwealth 'would gradually cease to exist', or it would 'exist only in part'. Some form of continental isolationism would be encouraged in Canada and South Africa, while Australia and New Zealand would be 'driven into the arms of the United States'. Although such conclusions were seen elsewhere in the same department as being unduly pessimistic, here was evidence of the gloom that existed.[10]

Another key tool in this research process was the FO's memorandum on the future of the Empire which had been distributed the previous year and was generating a 'flood of suggestions' from the overseas embassies. Perhaps the most incisive of these came from Halifax, fresh from his recent brush with Dominion sensitivities.[11] He offered a both perceptive and far-sighted view, taking issue with the central idea that Britain could preserve its 'Great Power' status without the support of the Dominions. He recognized the changing nature of the relationship, even if some of his colleagues in London did not, and disagreed with the notion that there could remain 'any lingering tendency to assume that the members of the Commonwealth are in any way less than equal'. He counselled that there should no longer be talk of 'preserving' or 'maintaining' the Commonwealth 'as if it were a venerable but hoary building which has to be shored and buttressed if it is not to tumble down'. Not until October 1944 was a précis available of all the responses, and it took the form of a draft FO programme for promoting better Commonwealth cooperation. All new candidates for the Foreign Service would be encouraged to spend part of their training period in a Dominion and refresher courses of lectures on the British Commonwealth and Empire would be given to serving officials. It was also agreed that members of the DO would, in appropriate cases, be attached to British Embassies where other Commonwealth governments were represented and junior FO staff would be attached to the High Commissions in Canada and South Africa. Even nomenclature was considered. Reminding the reader that the term 'Commonwealth' actually connoted Britain and the Dominions, it was stressed that it whenever possible would be well received. One oft-advanced suggestion which it was agreed not to include was that the DO and FO should be amalgamated; despite the obvious lingering contempt shown by many of the ambassadors it remained official policy that relations with the Dominions required special handling and their own Whitehall department.

The DO was generally content with the submission. There were, however, some reservations about the 'somewhat patronizing tone' in places and the degree to which the special nature of the relationship between Britain and the Dominions was not necessarily brought out. The British high commissioners in their distant outposts had also been asked for their views about this document. From the High Commission in Ottawa, despite not agreeing with all of the points that were made, it was seen as encouraging that the FO should be taking an interest in Commonwealth matters. There were, however, some telling criticisms. The paper appeared to have been written from a 'superior standpoint', one which seemed 'to regard the Dominions as strange animals which require special treatment'. The Dominions were in fact 'good friends or ours', who if treated in an adult way as being able to 'form their own views' could be of great help, not only in terms of defining the future relationship but also helping find common ground with the United States. There were also some agreement with Halifax and his doubts that Britain could be a Great Power without the Dominions. Batterbee thought it to be generally sound both in terms of the picture it presented and the conclusions it reached. He did, however, note that the memorandum failed to carry any disclaimer saying that it did not represent the official view of the government and worried about this omission presumably because of how it might have been interpreted by certain of his diplomatic colleagues. In his view Britain held its position in the world because it had 'long been regarded as the champion of political liberty'. In order to maintain its position at the head of the Commonwealth, enabling in the process 'the Commonwealth to endure', there was a need to show a much greater interest in social and economic liberty and this was entirely overlooked in the FO's conclusions.[12]

Wider public attention was inevitably increasingly focused on the myriad discussions to determine the nature of the post-war international system. One of these was the meeting held in Chicago in November and December 1944 involving delegates of 52 nations to plan for international cooperation in the field of air navigation in the years following the war's end. As Attlee had explained at the beginning of a long debate in the House of Commons the year before, Britain's need was urgent as it was at the centre of a great Commonwealth and Empire, a quarter of the world's inhabitants 'scattered over every Continent'.[13] What he did not say was that concerns about American rivalry over air routes, which had existed since before the war, had worsened as its attempts to dominate had become much more obvious. A November 1944 high commissioners' meeting in London was dominated by bitter warnings that the United States now regarded the air as 'something created by divine providence for them to dominate' and it degenerated into 'a chorus of anti-Americanism'.[14] In this light the International Conference on Aviation might not have been the best venue to test the cohesive nature of the alliance. This proved to be the case; following the meeting a long and secret report was produced by the DO's representative and it made for difficult reading. It was a 'depressing' account for Cranborne to read, who claimed to have had no idea of 'the divergences in the British Commonwealth' when the intention should have been to settle on 'a united Empire policy'. The Canadian delegation had been especially difficult and it was feared that there might be a rift as an outcome. It was believed that the Ottawa attendees were more concerned with modifying the British viewpoint to meet that of the United States' delegation than arriving at a common Empire policy. The result was that they were 'unfortunately mistrusted', and not just by the British but also by the other Dominions. There were nightly meetings of the British Commonwealth delegates to discuss progress and future policy but the Canadians declined to attend and generally appeared to have a tendency to disappear for long periods of the conference.[15] It was recognized that there had in fact been a breakdown of the alliance during these discussions, the Canadian delegation being in much closer touch with its American counterparts than the British.[16] The conclusion was that relations with the Dominions had in this case been adversely affected, and what Cranborne read certainly made him pessimistic in terms of preparing for future meetings.

The major focus of the many proposed conferences facing him was obviously to bring together an effective post-war global security organization. It has already

been seen that Churchill favoured regional councils and blocs and proposed a
network of them. It is difficult to avoid the conclusion though that the British
leader's policy towards such ideas was prone to sporadic bursts of imaginative
energy but lacking in any real substance or, for that matter, a policy that was
coherent and workable. Planning on the British side was achieved in spite of his
efforts while his most consistent characteristic was that of 'obstinate apathy'.[17]
There was also little reference to Gladwyn Jebb's Economic and Reconstruction
Department within the FO, which had been tasked with planning for the post-
war organization. As Jebb commented, the prime minister was quite allergic to
any proposals for post-war action that he had not himself engendered, or at least
discussed personally with his American counterpart.[18] An obvious example had
been when Roosevelt apparently proposed the term 'United Nations' because
'Associated Powers' sounded flat and when he tested it on Churchill, who was
taking a bath at the time, he concurred.

The Moscow Declaration, signed in October 1943, had reaffirmed the
announcement of the previous year relating to the 'United Nations' and marked
the official recognition of the need for an international organization to replace
the League of Nations. The earlier 'Four Power' Declaration, authored by the
United States, had already necessitated the Dominions be approached for their
views and they had broadly agreed with the proposal but with some anxiety
about the role to be played by the non-'Great Powers' such as themselves. As
the Cabinet in London were told Australia had a further recommendation; the
'British Commonwealth of Nations' as a whole should be treated as one of the
four 'Great Powers' and not just Britain alone. This was in keeping with Curtin's
proposals for closer political integration but, despite its superficial attractiveness
to the DO – the idea was after all no different than had been adopted at the Paris
Peace Conference in 1919 – it was once again recognized as being untenable.
Aside from the fact that Canada and South Africa were unlikely to endorse such
an idea, it was felt that each of the Dominions would insist on retaining a final
say on questions affecting their foreign policy and considerable time would be
consumed during any future international negotiations in trying to secure their
complete agreement.[19]

At the Dumbarton Oaks Conference, held near Washington in August and
September 1944, the four 'Great Powers' attempted to draft specific proposals for
a charter for the new organization. It was clear that there were considerable differences of opinion, particularly over the issue sponsored by the Americans that
the Permanent Members of the proposed Security Council should have a right of
veto on any decision which potentially affected their own interests. The Soviets
had a different view and were adamant that only the four principals should have
any form of vote.[20] So great were the disagreements that it proved necessary to
hold another series of discussions about the structure of the proposed World

Organization. This was held at the Crimea resort of Yalta in early February 1945; once again the Dominions were not represented in person but, instead, had to rely upon Britain to safeguard their interests.[21] One of the British officials who had been at the Dumbarton Oaks talks admitted that the attitude of the British delegation there changed 'in a rather remarkable way' during the course of the talks. Initially there was strong indignation at what were considered to be 'disreputable' proposals from the Russians that would 'place the Great Powers above the law'. In time the British came to see that this view was actually quite 'realistic' and that to oppose it would have been hypocritical and akin to the worst days of the League of Nations.[22]

Cranborne had striven at every opportunity to cajole Churchill into keeping the Dominions fully informed about developments affecting the proposed post-war security organization. They had been equally forceful in turn in making it clear how much they disliked any system under which the smaller powers were to be treated differently. The Dominions secretary's argument, that he had made repeatedly to the prime minister, was if they were consulted on the proposals at the formative stage it would not then later appear that they were being approached merely for their acquiescence in a policy that had already been settled in London.[23] This was sage advice as it remained the issue about which the Dominions had indicated from the outset of the war that they were most sensitive. As Cranborne now noted, any suggestion that the British government endorsed the idea of regional blocs would likely make it 'most difficult' to bring the Dominions into line. The announcement from the White House in the spring of 1945 that it had been agreed at Yalta that it would be acceptable for the United States and the Soviet Union to have three votes each only served to make the situation worse.[24] The British government had not actually been consulted about this proposal in advance, not for the first time. The British delegates at the conference realized that there remained a popular belief that the Dominions would actually perform as a bloc and there was still little understanding of the British Commonwealth and how it functioned.

It had been decided that final talks involving delegates from around the world would be held in San Francisco in April 1945 to establish the United Nations organization. In preparation for this a group of Commonwealth politicians met in London for ten days to discuss associated issues. Chaired by Cranborne, the meetings included some now big 'Imperial' hitters, notably Smuts, Evatt and Fraser. The Dominions secretary was keen that these talks should not be viewed by the press and public at large as anything more than 'a perfectly normal feature of the routine working of Commonwealth cooperation'.[25] The opening session would, however, include a series of speeches which would be released and during these he stressed that what would follow would merely take the form of 'conversations' – Mackenzie King was not present so it had to be clearly stated that they were informal – concerned mainly with the plans for the new World Organization. As Cranborne told the delegates, it was quite possible to be a citizen of the world and a member of a family. 'We are a family and it is natural that we should wish to deliberate together so as to ensure that, as far as possible we see eye to eye on the difficult problems we have to face.'[26] Cadogan was also centrally involved but found himself harassed by the 'bloody Dominions' who took up so much of his time and he was left uncertain in his own mind whether the Anzac representatives were 'more stupid than offensive'.[27]

The sensitive issue of the Colonial Empire which had been so exposed the previous year had not gone away and the question of trusteeship remained a bitter one. In late December 1944 it appeared that an official British position had finally been reached with a long memorandum entitled 'International Aspects of Colonial Policy'. There was little within the document that differed from the statement made by Oliver Stanley to the gathering of the Dominions' leaders. It did not raise any issues that were considered controversial with regard to the proposed establishment of a number of regional organizations, including those in the South Pacific and South East Asia which had been highlighted by Curtin. The question of 'accountability' was, however, different and would need some specific explanation to the Dominions. It was recommended that an International Colonial Centre be created through which each Colonial power could publish an annual report outlining economic and social progress in their respective territories. As this would not have any supervisory or executive powers this was deemed as not going far enough to appease the views on the subject expressed by the Tasman Dominions.[28] Churchill was much less enthusiastic about such talk of colonial trusteeship. There was no question of Britain being 'hustled or seduced' into making any declarations that affected sovereignty in the Dominions or Colonies. He had no opposition to the Americans taking Japanese islands which they had conquered, 'But "hands off the British Empire" is our maxim and it must not be weakened or smirched to please sob-stuff merchants at home or foreigners of any hue.' Eden reassured him that there was not the slightest question of liquidating the British Empire, Stanley's paper instead represented 'a constructive policy', one which safeguarded both the sovereignty and admin-istrative responsibility of the powers involved. It was an attempt to persuade the Americans to accept the British version of colonial administration and 'not to go in for half-baked international regimes' in the ex-enemy held territories they occupied.[29] Churchill nonetheless remained vehement in his opposition to any American-inspired move which might weaken his Empire, erupting at regular intervals at Yalta in a grand old imperial fashion, famously advising his audience that under no circumstances would he ever 'consent to forty or fifty nations thrusting interfering fingers into the life's existence of the British Empire'.[30]

The position changed dramatically in the run-up to the San Francisco

Conference. It was clear that it was unacceptable not just to the United States but also New Zealand and Australia, who had indicated that they remained advocates of the existing mandate system. Added to this it was unlikely that much in the way of international support could be garnered. But most importantly it was now obvious that this subject would not be discussed in private but in open session, in front of a 'motley assembly', where the future of Britain's colonies would no doubt be painfully scrutinized. A new memorandum, released to the War Cabinet in March 1945, recommended that the continuation of mandates be therefore endorsed in principle but with some insistence on revisions to remove their worst features. Ideally discussions about trusteeship could be avoided and resolved later by an ad hoc, and presumably less uncertain and potentially emotive body. The great danger remained that American elements would demand that the whole of the Colonial Empire be placed under international review and, potentially, pressure would be applied that it be placed under trusteeship.[31] Attending the London meetings the following month the Dominions had been informed of the changes which, once again, had been reached without any prior communication with them and they remained unconvinced.[32] Despite Cranborne's best efforts the alliance departed for San Francisco in questionable spirit.[33]

The Conference was conducted on a typically American grand scale and as one commentator put it, 'confusion reigned at almost every level'. No less that 2,636 journalists were accredited as part of the propaganda campaign orchestrated by the authorities in Washington. A total of 282 delegates represented their countries and were assisted by staffs and a secretariat totalling over 2,500 people. At 4.30 pm on the afternoon of 25 April 1945, American Secretary of State Edward Stettinius Jr. struck his gavel three times on the podium to convene the first plenary session of the United Nations Conference on World Organization. The Conference opened on the same day as American and Russian troops met on the banks of the River Elbe. For working purposes the Conference was divided into 12 committees with sections of the Dumbarton Oaks documents assigned to each for review and revision. These committees reported in turn to one of four Commissions, which in turn reported to plenary sessions of the entire Conference. Coordination was theoretically the responsibility of a Steering Committee supported by a smaller Executive Committee. In reality the most important work was done by the informal group made up of the representatives of the four Great Powers, joined later by France. Along with China, however, the French delegate had little real voice; power rested with 'the Big Three'.[34]

The part played by the Dominions during the Conference and their relationship with the British delegation can be gauged from a series of 'racy and interesting' letters that had been sent back to London by a member of the British delegation. In the summer of 1944 it had been proposed that Ben Cockram, who had been the Political Secretary to Lord Harlech in South Africa, should move to the Washington Embassy as the DO representative. With the rank of Counsellor, he would replace Stephen Holmes who was departing for the High Commission in Ottawa. He was to be considered a full member of the embassy staff with full diplomatic privileges and an impressive array of allowances.[35] Cockram held an Oxford doctorate and had been part-educated at an American university. With nearly 20 years' experience of Dominion affairs he was well-respected and there was no opposition from the FO to his appointment. His role would be to act as the DO's 'eyes and ears', working within the Embassy to gather what information he could about specific issues that involved or affected the Dominions. Having previously prepared a detailed analysis of the Dominions' likely attitude to the Conference, he was well qualified to provide this new commentary. His letters arrived at the DO approximately a week after each was sent from San Francisco and provided an excellent and well received account of events as he experienced them.[36]

The British delegation only arrived the night before the Conference began and were, therefore, thrown in 'head first'. The opening days were spent squabbling over who would take the Chairmanship and listening to plenary speeches. Cockram judged the British delegation to be more efficient in organization and ahead in planning than any of the other delegations present and this had helped them to secure a leading position on the important Steering Committee. He was happy to report that, at the outset, relations with the Dominions' delegation were 'admirable', with all of them appearing to be 'as helpful and cooperative as possible'.[37] Having delivered their initial speeches the delegations quickly settled down to business and the two weeks that followed proved 'unconscionably grim and earnest'. Problems were encountered due to a lack of experience amongst many of the smaller states and Cockram estimated that only one committee was effectively presided over, the 'success' being Sir Ramaswami Mudaliar, the former Mayor of Madras and leader of the Indian delegation.

Much of Cockram's time was spent trying to reconcile the proposed amendments to the draft Charter that had been submitted by each of the various Dominion delegations. From a long initial list of concerns this was whittled down to just four questions that needed to be referred for further negotiation. The first of these, as had been widely predicted, was trusteeship.[38] Ultimately, however, the solution proved much less intractable than had thought would prove to be the case. Discussions between Eden and his American counterpart, who had taken over from Cordell Hull the previous November as the American secretary of state, produced an accord that appeared to safeguard British interests and was also sufficient to overcome New Zealand reservations on the issue.[39] With the other three outstanding issues, the adoption of regional agreements, the manner in which the Council might call upon any member to use armed forces and the respecting of domestic jurisdiction, it was agreed that the British delegation would try and seek amendments. Cockram felt that it should prove possible to secure the agreement of the sponsoring powers to make the changes required by the Dominions, leaving the prospects for a common British Commonwealth line not unfavourable. The greatest challenge, however, remained Evatt, 'the biggest thorn in the flesh of all the British Commonwealth delegates and officials'. He had already caused considerable offence to the Americans and an official from the State Department told the British delegate privately that so long as Evatt was a member of the government in Canberra there was not 'the slightest chance of Australia being elected to the Security Council'. In Cockram's view, he was probably 'the most generally disliked man at the Conference' and had been outmanoeuvred at every turn but, with his potential supporters alienated, he had come to realize that he would have to cooperate with the British rather than work against them.[40]

Cockram's hopes that an early conclusion to proceedings might prove possible proved overly optimistic, two weeks later the now 'Big Five' were still struggling on the issues of regionalism, trusteeship and domestic jurisdiction. At this point hopes of an early conclusion had collapsed and events had gone 'haywire' with all sides degenerating into squabbles over those issues closest to their own national interests. At the heart of the tumult remained Evatt who had become steadily more disgruntled. His many amendments had either been voted down or emasculated; the fact that those sponsored by the other members of the British Commonwealth were generally accepted seems to have increased his ire. The State Department prophecy had also reached his ear which only served to strengthen the vitriol and within a short space of time he succeeded in further offending the Americans, upsetting the French, and annoying both the Russians and Chinese, in short all of the major players. His explosion at Cockram late one evening was returned in kind and this was judged as having had something of a positive modifying effect on the Australian's attitude. Field Marshal Smuts had, in the meantime, also lost faith with the discussions and was threatening to go home. He had been appointed President of the General Assembly from where he grew steadily more impatient with proceedings, comparing them unfavourably to the 1919 Peace Conference.[41] His departure would have been hugely embarrassing and only a personal intervention by Lord Halifax persuaded him to stay. Despite this Cockram thought that inter-Commonwealth relations were better than at any stage of the Conference.[42] The bureaucrats from the respective Dominion foreign affairs departments tasked with organizing the management of their respective delegations seemed content with the manner in which the alliance functioned. A number of them were pleased that the Dominion delegations had demonstrated that they had their own ideas.

The Conference itself, however, remained in a state of flux as it proved impossible to move the Russian position on the fundamental idea that the United

Nations Organization should first 'discuss and consider' disputes without the automatic application of the proposed veto which was to be offered to each of the Big Powers. This issue had proven particularly difficult, Evatt believing it was 'a negation of democracy'. Although the self-appointed champion of the smaller powers could no longer count on Fraser's support about trusteeship, the New Zealander would still listen to the 'poison' being 'distilled into his ears'. The rest of the Australian delegation remained generally moderate though and it was clearly hoped that its leader's dissenting voice could be controlled. South Africa and Canada had been 'helpful and cooperative throughout', and what votes they had registered against the British position had been well considered and served to demonstrate the degree to which the Commonwealth was not a single block. The finding of a successful resolution to the domestic jurisdiction dispute proved this to be the case but in a fashion that was acceptable to the British delegation as 'the battle was fought and won'.[43]

With the Conference now hopefully drawing to a close Cockram could look back at the analysis he had provided earlier in the year. He had been proven correct in most regards not least in his warning that the great difficulty would be the Australian delegation. He had worried that it would be likely to find itself 'disunited and split by personal ambitions and dislikes', leaving it 'an unpredictable factor' upon which the British could not necessarily count for support.[44] Headed by the deputy prime minister, Frank Forde, soon to become the shortest serving leader in Australian history, he and almost all of the other officials had been anxious to cooperate. There had been fatal division, however, as Evatt had often been 'hasty and suspicious'. In the view of those who accompanied him from Canberra, in many ways the Conference was both the high and low point of the Australian minister's career. He had successfully lobbied at the outset for Australia's inclusion as a member of the Executive Committee, an opening which 'gave so many opportunities'.[45] From this position he assaulted those aspects of the agreements at Dumbarton Oaks that were deemed the most reprehensible. For this the small powers accorded him a vote of thanks at the Conference's end. What he had wanted, however, was the acclaim of the lead nations. His fruitless efforts to amend the Great Power veto in the Security Council did little more than extend the gathering's life by several weeks and ensure that he would be subsequently viewed with considerable suspicion by both the United States and Soviet Union.[46] And in a clear sign that the Australian position had been weakened as a result of some of his antics it was noted that Stettinius had apparently deliberately kept the Australian off the list of speakers for the final session of the Conference. Cockram would subsequently note that Forde's visit to Washington to discuss supply difficulties had also apparently met with little success and he concluded that this was an indication of the likely nature of post-war relations between Canberra and Washington.[47]

The Conference had amply demonstrated that 'the Commonwealth countries breed independent and vigorous personalities' and, it was hoped, dispelled any lingering illusions that Dominions' representation actually meant six votes for Britain. Halifax was concerned as the end approached that there had been perhaps too much success in demonstrating the independence of each of those involved and that the dangerous impression might have been created that 'the British Commonwealth was less united than it really was'. The Dominions' delegation heads disagreed and thanked him for the support he and Cranborne had given them. There was, however, considerable criticism about many of the more junior British representatives who had treated their Dominion counterparts 'with lofty superiority'. The DO participants had been 'unfailingly helpful', but FO officials appeared to think that 'the Dominion delegations should be seen but not heard'. Halifax pointed, by way of a defence, to the general election that had been called in Britain and the impact that this had had. Eden and Attlee had been called home to defend their seats, leaving officials to sit on committees who lacked experience of parliamentary practice and procedure. Cranborne was also anxious to correct Evatt's claims that there had been a departure from conclusions that had been reached at the April meetings held in London. There had been no conclusions reached beforehand about what line might be taken, the pre-Conference gathering had taken the form of discussions that had been intended solely to gain a better understanding of each Dominion's point of view.[48]

At the end of this final meeting of Dominion representatives the Australian minister had gone out of his way to thank Cockram for the support that had been given to his delegation, a 'superb gesture' that had left its recipient 'slightly deflated'. He also felt that it would be wise to put this commendation on record just in case Evatt should 'at a later date, have second thoughts and come seeking our hides with a boomerang or whatever they use for scalping purposes at Walleroo'. This decision revealed just how well the British official had come to know his character for, as he had feared, Evatt still had a card to play. Four days later he gave on off-the-record briefing to the British press correspondents covering the Conference. Those present were left with the impressions that he was trying to discredit the work of the British delegation in order to claim greater credit for Australia. He criticized a number of members of the British delegation by name, including Halifax and Cranborne, and had complained that Britain had not supported Australia. This was all a clear breach of the one of the guiding principles of inter-Commonwealth relations, that one country of the Commonwealth does not interfere with the affairs of another.[49] The matter was reported in the Australian media and debated in the House of Representatives in Canberra where every effort was made to dampen excitement about any potential damage to imperial relations.[50] Forde, having returned from the Conference, specifically refuted the idea that there had been any British criticism. The truth was that Cranborne had written to Evatt complaining at his actions and had also forwarded a copy to the deputy Australian leader. He, in response, had issued his usual 'forceful' rebuttal; clearly this in large part was because Forde had been copied into the correspondence. Cranborne had been so stunned by the language and argument employed in this that he at once wrote back refusing to accept the version of events put forward by Evatt and suggesting that no good would come from continuing their correspondence.[51]

Shortly following the conclusion of the San Francisco gathering a new nuclear age dawned and Hiroshima and Nagasaki's destruction was swiftly followed by the end of what had proven to be the Empire's final war. One FO commentator noted that recent events did not mean the Dominions' attachment to the Commonwealth was impaired. It was, however, clear that 'the lead did not rest with the UK in the same way as before the war'.[52] Traditional impressions of Dominion independence had been adapted as a result of events at San Francisco. The Canadians, whose performance had been so warmly applauded by the British, had been anxious that this should be the case and were pleased with the results; reports reached the DO confirming that senior Canadian officials thought 'the myth of unity' had now been broken.[53] Such a position was entirely as some felt should be the case. British Labourite Frederick Pethick-Lawrence was a conscientious objector during the First World War who was destined to become post-war secretary of state for India and Burma. The previous December, during the debate on the King's Speech at Westminster, he had responded to criticisms that the Dominions were displaying a policy of their own which differed from that of Britain, by rising to defend them. He saw this as a source of strength, the fact that there was a unity based around loose bonds, and attempts to turn them into something more rigid would not work. He held the Dominions to be 'a magnificent partnership of free nations, the constitution of which we certainly would not desire to see altered'.[54] The war had certainly seen all of the Dominions grow increasingly more confident of their abilities to manage their respective foreign policies. It had also provided them with levels of fiscal and military strength that had been hitherto unimagined and a sense of independence that would not now be surrendered. Canada and South Africa had shown this on numerous occasions before the war had begun; now they were joined by even New Zealand, the most loyal of Dominions, but a member in its own right of the United Nations of independent states.

Batterbee, writing for the last time as the high commissioner before he left Wellington in the summer of 1945 for retirement, warned that Britain needed to show the will and ability to take the lead in the new world. His lesson for London was that 'as soon as peace comes again Great Britain, if she is to retain her prestige, must show that she belongs to the future and not to the past, and that she is determined not to follow but to lead the world in all matters of social and economic progress'.[55] The final word must, however, go to the figure who had laboured longest to try and keep this sometimes difficult but nonetheless crucial coalition working. Following the defeat suffered by his Conservative Party colleagues in the July 1945 general election, Cranborne wrote to Emrys-Evans with a long appraisal of the DO's wartime performance. He was modestly pleased with the role he had played and the successes that had been achieved but he was less happy with the situation that now prevailed within the Empire, generally concluding that there had actually been little improvement during the last five years. As the figure who had been most intimately involved in the management his is a fitting epitaph.

First Canada, and now as appeared at San Francisco, Australia and New Zealand, are beginning to show most disturbing signs of moving away from the conception of a Commonwealth acting together to that of independent countries, bound to each other only by the most shadowy ties. Dr Evatt is only a particularly repulsive representative of a not at all uncommon point of view in his own and the other Empire countries. I wish that I could see the answer to all this, but I don't. It may be that we ought to speak more frankly to Dominion governments. Whenever, however, we have tried this, the only result has been to irritate them and strengthen the voices of independence. I really, during the last few months, sometimes felt at my wits' end. Perhaps that is a sign that I had been at the DO quite long enough, and that what is needed is a fresh mind, both at the Dominions and Foreign Offices, and perhaps most of all, at No. 10. For I think that Winston, with all his great qualities, always tended to look at Foreign and Empire policy as if they were in watertight compartments whereas they are in fact mingled. Our prestige with the other countries of the Commonwealth is dependent on our prestige in the outside world. Today we are regarded abroad as very much the junior partner of the Big Three and this inevitably and immediately affects the attitude of the Dominions towards us.[56]

Britain had lost its Imperial position and the unquestioned leadership of the Empire and, in his mind, if this could not be regained it would now have to look to Europe to demonstrate it still maintained a strong global role. This would not be a challenge Churchill would have to face, but instead would be one for Attlee and his new Labour post-war government. It would quickly discover that the Anglo-Dominion alliance had in fact seen its best days.

Conclusion: Brave New World

War had come again in September 1939, and once more the call had gone out to the Empire's scattered millions. The Australian Minister Richard Casey was reportedly fond of G. K. Chesterton's remark that Commonwealth members were like passengers on a London omnibus; as a rule they ignored one another until such time as there was a crisis, when they all pulled together.[1] On this occasion the same was once again true, leaving London overrun with 'bold-eyed Canadians with a slouch and a swagger, New Zealanders with overcoats hanging untidily, Australians often with girls', an 'invading armies of irresponsible younger brothers' who, according to the observer who was working in Canada House, 'the English soldiers looked at not unkindly but with a sober ironic air – puppies and old hound dogs'.[2] Speaking at a lunch of the United Wardens of the City of London in February 1942, Attlee had reminded his audience that 'in the dark days of 1940 after the fall of France when Hitler's blow fell on Britain, Britain was not alone because she had with her the British Commonwealth and Empire'.[3] They had come not to fight a war of survival, as many seemed to think, but as a demonstration of their loyalty to a far greater cause. This fortitude was shared by a Colonel in the Royal Army Medical Corps, writing in May 1940 before Dunkirk, who did not feel his Empire was threatened by ultimate defeat. The idea had never entered his head because the British Empire, what he termed as 'the domination of the world by the English-speaking nations in consultation', was in fact in its infancy.[4] This all seems at odds with the recent research which, by examining British society and cultural trends, has sought to demonstrate that there is little evidence to suggest that public opinion necessarily still held such views. None of this is a new argument: to some 'the Empire penetrated the emotions of millions'; to others 'the British Empire vanished quietly and almost imperceptibly'.[5] This is perhaps today most obviously to be seen in the debate on 'Britishness' and the commonly perceived national ignorance about British history and the country's origins that exists among contemporary society.[6]

Undoubtedly at the war's end a reflective period had begun, examining the wartime alliance for clues about what it had achieved and it started even before the Japanese emperor's final agreement to restore the conquered British Imperial territories to their pre-war suzerainty. Another Australian by birth, Professor Hessel Duncan Hall was another of the pre-war historians who had dedicated themselves to unravelling the secret of the Dominions. He had worked at the League of Nations and spent the war years at the British Embassy in Washington, from where he published an article in the highly respected *Foreign Affairs* entitled 'The British Commonwealth as a Great Power'.[7] In this he noted varying interpretations that had been offered by way of description as to what was the British Commonwealth; perhaps most notable among these was an American view that it was 'little more than a mystical expression of spiritual affinities'. Events during the pre-war years could in his mind be seen as signifying separate legal sovereignty, 'the coming of age of a family of states'. Dominion status he saw as a thing of the past because the Commonwealth had passed out of its adolescent stage. It was a family relationship united by its common allegiance to the Crown. The FO read the article keenly and noted the points made. The article was said to show that Australia and New Zealand were most loyal, Canada was the most likely to take an independent line and disliked being regarded too often as 'part of the Commonwealth' and Smuts was loyal, but the reaction of the rest of the Dominion he led was uncertain. There was particular satisfaction, still, in recording that when the vote had been taken in Britain, Canada, Australia and New Zealand in September 1939 only a single member of parliament had failed to offer his support for the Empire's war; conveniently the South African example was put to one side.

The long, exhausting struggle that followed had not just been about defeating tyranny in Europe. The defence of their autonomy and sense of equality and a lingering allegiance to the Crown were ideals put forward as helping determine why the Dominions had done what they had done. It had actually been a massive battle for 'hearts and minds' where the ultimate goal was the maintenance of Imperial unity. That there was such a contest, not to mention the rules it adopted, had been often overlooked by the vast majority of those subconsciously involved. Among the ranks of the guilty were the respective parliaments, the aristocracy, the media, academia and various assorted think-tanks and conference attendees. Only a few recognized the true nature of what was happening. The most obvious of these was often not able to exert much influence; the Dominions secretary should have been the most powerful man in the 'white' Empire, but it was not always the case. Some of this came down to the quality of the individual. All of them tried in their own way but their motivation was not always compelling. Cranborne, despite his often poor health, was undoubtedly a key figure who encouraged those around him to do their utmost to maintain the sometimes fragile coalition. He was susceptible to the often Machiavellian intrigues of Westminster and ultimately his interventions led to his removal from office; during his absence it seems clear that the department over which he presided was seriously undermined.[8] When he said in a House of Lords debate that 'the British Commonwealth of Nations is today one of the greatest, one of the main elements of stability in a distracted world, and any division of opinion would only tend to weaken counsels and prolong our ordeal', he was speaking with conviction and passionate knowledge.[9]

The machinery of the Imperial system was kept working by a dedicated Whitehall organization. The size and complexity of the British Empire was recognized by the number of different departments required to oversee its management. Each had their role and their titles appeared self-evident, the India Office dealt with India, the CO the colonies and the FO everything else.[10] The creation of the DO added to this team although at the war's outbreak this constituted fewer than 100 people administering the needs of the Dominions from a ramshackle collection of offices, surrounded by considerable prejudices from many of their Whitehall peers. The regular warnings it issued about the potential that existed for confusion were often misunderstood or ignored. In part this was down to the many complicated and conflicting agendas which existed among the Dominion governments and the questionable degree of interest which these distant Imperial outposts generated in Whitehall corridors. The added challenge, certainly in the initial war years, of dealing with the Dominion high commissioners in London did little to improve the position. Tasked with securing the unity of the British Commonwealth of Nations, this meant the department faced a constant and often lonely struggle. This did not inhibit its response and there was quick condemnation when it was deemed necessary.[11] Perhaps the best critique of the impact the DO made came from Gerald Campbell who, prior to taking his position in Washington, had been Britain's representative in Ottawa. Not originally from the department, he had gone to Canada with little knowledge of the country other than the generally negative Whitehall view. Upon his subsequent departure for his new role in Washington, he could only conclude that 'other UK departments ... would have produced secession any day of the week if what was once described to me as the "bloody Post Office" had not done a most useful job'.[12] It might have been fair to claim that, pre-war, the DO had to 'concentrate on tactics rather than strategy' because it lacked political muscle.[13] During this final conflict, while the general view appears to have been a blissful ignorance of its activities or even existence, it is undoubtedly the case though that this was a department that played a major, if largely unrecognized, role in the successful wartime management of the British Empire.

The power within this alliance lay with the prime ministers, specifically those of Britain, Canada and Australia, and their closest acolytes within government. *Primus inter pares* was obviously Winston Churchill and here lay a good deal of the problem. Amery, the founder of the DO and a father-figure in terms of the Anglo-Dominion relationship, was undoubtedly better placed than most – albeit with an overly passionate and generally biased eye – to comment on the performance of the British leader. He lamented that he 'never really sympathized with any of the developments in Imperial relations during the present century' and begged the Dominions secretary to see to it before the 1944 visit by the Dominions' leaders 'that Winston does not let loose some passage of old-fashioned Victorian Imperialism' on his visiting Canadian counterpart.[14] As Churchill had himself said at the height of the Battle of Britain, he had always faithfully served two 'supreme causes': the first was 'the historic certainty of our Island life'; the other 'the maintenance of the enduring greatness of Britain and her Empire'.[15] Despite such typically bombastic rhetoric the truth was that he clearly did not find it easy to preside over a free Commonwealth at a time when the pace of wartime events meant action had to be taken quickly and, often, secretly. He still lived in the days of the old Empire, a single unified whole bound together by romantic attachment to British ideals and pride in British accomplishments. The system that existed in his mind did not question the direction issued from the centre and he sometimes appeared unable to understand why the modern version was not the same.

And then there were the Dominions. Australia had been by far the most pronounced in both its support and, in equal measure, its criticism. The position it felt it occupied within the corridors of power and influence in London and the actual situation were, however, often quite different. The reality was that the self-perceived 'blue-eyed boy amongst the Dominions' was often in fact sometimes loathed. Menzies came and went and caused trouble in the process and bore much of the blame for this state of affairs. His successor was then largely instrumental in causing the political clash between the British and Australian governments following the Japanese attack in December 1941, which proved to be perhaps the most serious threat to Anglo-Dominion relations during the entire war. Bitterness and recriminations persisted for many months, the tensions becoming so visible that *The Times* was moved to comment on the unfortunate impression that 'Australian plain speaking is synonymous with empty grumbling and futile fault-finding'. Churchill apparently later claimed that he generally liked Curtin, 'this eminent and striking Australian personality', and it was certainly true that in time he was thought of favourably within the DO, both generally and by US senior figures. But at the time of Singapore's denouement the significance of the shock, both physical and mental, caused by the rapid collapse of the alliance's military position could not be denied. The repercussions were devastating, the value of the British connection was open to question and with the raising of doubts about whether it could ever be restored an opportunity presented itself for the United States to exploit the discord. Subsequent aid from Washington was as much mischievous as sincere. Australia's primary function in their new ally's strategy proved to be as a base from which to mount operations across the Pacific and South East Asia in driving Japan back; when this role receded from mid-1944 onwards, American leaders paid correspondingly less heed to Australian wishes.

In turn disenchantment led to Curtin's London 1944 proposals, a demonstration that his country was not in fact chained to any 'American imperium'.[16]

The oldest and largest Dominion, Canada, maintained an often subdued approach to its relations with 'the Mother Country'. William Mackenzie King remained highly suspicious of Whitehall's motives. Backed by advisers who also, in some cases, had serious doubts about Britain's intentions, his fear was that the war would be used as a pretext to challenge the idea of Dominion autonomy. This ensured that, certainly until his visit to London in August 1941, his support could appear far from enthusiastic and wherever possible he kept comment on how the alliance should proceed to a minimum. The sizeable French-speaking population in Quebec had no real sympathy with the British Empire even when Vichy's fall meant that their support should have been unquestioned. Fully aware of the potential dangers this held, particularly if there were to be any repeat of the First World War's casualty figures, he fought a sometimes lonely war, one in which he was ever conscious of the growing significance of the United States. Ritchie noted in his diary in March 1941 that the average Englishman looked upon the Canadian military as 'an army of friendly barbarians who for some incomprehensible reason have come to protect him from his enemies'. Canadian troops were indeed the first to arrive on British shores and the contribution they made to the coalition war effort during the decisive campaigns in Italy and North-West Europe could not be criticized. Popular opinion in Canada though appeared to empathize with the sometimes mercurial leader in Ottawa; a *Gallup* opinion poll conducted in June 1942 showed that just 52 per cent of those questioned definitely wished to remain within the Empire.[17]

In the Union's case, the controversial manner in which Jan Smuts had become prime minister in September 1939 was always likely to place restraints on the degree of active support he could offer, a point fully understood by the DO if not always elsewhere in Whitehall. It was much more commonly accepted that the South African effort and Smuts were symbiotic; as the British high commissioner in Pretoria put it in July 1942, 'the further contribution that South Africa can make to the Allied cause depends all too absolutely on the life, health and continued leadership of Field Marshal Smuts'. Throughout the war he faced an organized nationalist opposition that, in many cases, openly sympathized with Nazi Germany's objectives. Wartime instructions from the WO for Army educators stipulated that they were to stress in their briefings that the Union was 'an independent sovereign state' and that Britain had no control over 'internal or external policy'.[18] The South African military was obliged to operate on two levels, with only those who wore 'Red Tabs' on their uniforms willing to serve outside of the African theatre of operations; this ultimately did not prevent them from marching all the way through Italy. Indeed the Dominion's military played a full part, in all about 200,000 of its citizens served during the war, nearly half of whom were Afrikaans-speakers, and there were 35,000 killed, wounded or captured. Following the loss of Tobruk Smuts considered what a retreat from Egypt would entail and the wider impact it would have. Such an eventuality, he concluded, would lead to his removal from power and a political change which would see the Dominion 'cease to be a line of Empire communication'. His proposed fighting retreat to the Sudan or the Eritrean highlands proved unnecessary and, militarily, the position was quickly restored but this was indicative of the difficulties he faced. Indeed the South African leader was obliged to maintain a consistently cautious line and, despite his 1943 electoral triumph, his post-war demise proved unavoidable.[19]

Last but by no means least, there was New Zealand. Out of a total population of 1,630,000 at the war's beginning, some 355,000 were 18–45-year-old males. By the end of 1943 mobilized forces including full-time home defence stood at 129,000, with a further 284,000 taking a part-time home role, a remarkable effort. With the exception of the Soviet Union, battle casualties were expressed as being the highest in proportion to population of any member of the United Nations.[20] With its predominantly British-drawn population, its distance from the European theatre and the relative inexperience it had in foreign affairs, the general acquiescence it showed to the British government was not surprising in the early years of the struggle. The historically intense dislike of fascism that successive governments in Wellington had held was also significant, helping to further strengthen its endorsement of British policies. Only with Japan's attack on the Far East, which brought the region directly into the expanding global conflict did first private doubts, and then more serious public questions begin to emerge. Peter Fraser's calls for a greater direct role for his country in wartime planning were critically received by Churchill but the Dominion's previous unflinching support helped ensure that its standing in London still remained strong, and would continue to do so until the war's end. Certainly the eagerness with which the idea of an international security organization was welcomed did not mean that New Zealand would lead the charge to distance itself from the 'Mother Country'. In the years immediately following the war's end the country still enjoyed the reputation of being the 'good boys' of the Commonwealth family. It would be the last to ratify the Statute of Westminster in 1947 and another forty years would pass before the official use of the description 'Dominion of New Zealand' was ended.[21]

Watching all of this from the sidelines with some apparently malevolent intent was the United States with its criticisms of the British Empire. Militarily its contribution obviously proved decisive, without it there would likely have been no need for a post-war debate about unity as there would have been nothing left to hold together.[22] There was a price to pay and this was an almost incessant rumbling from the western shores of the Atlantic, a crescendo that had begun long before the war's outbreak and would continue long after its end.[23] They did, however, present a serious danger; Richard Law, the under-secretary of state for foreign affairs, visited Washington in September 1942 and reported back to the British War Cabinet that it might not prove possible to instruct the American people in the real nature of the British Empire because 'the ghosts of Lord North and the Hessian troops still haunted their thoughts'.[24] In response three months later a 'Committee on American Opinion and the British Empire' was established under his chairmanship and its initial meetings concluded that Americans were 'extremely ill-informed' about Empire. They did not, for example, grasp that the Dominions were as autonomous as one another, and it was recorded as being still quite usual to be asked by American hosts when visiting the country '"how much do you make Canada pay towards the cost of your Navy?" or "will you reward the Australians for their efforts in the war by treating them better afterwards?"' Considerable time and resources were devoted in an attempt to correct such impressions, but it is questionable how far these efforts succeeded and the degree to which prominent Americans were encouraged to talk less 'as if the British Empire were in the process of dissolution'.[25] Lord Snell, present at a speech given at the Royal Empire Society in January 1943, had argued that it was better for America to be critical of the Empire than indifferent as if it was interested differences could be explained away. They should not think of it as 'something completed'. 'The Empire was not breaking up, it was growing up.' There were others who were more indignant; one writer put it that the hint that perhaps the British Empire was doomed beyond recall would be 'greeted by a storm of abuse, spluttering futility, or humorous evasion'.[26] The 'Special Relationship' endured despite such fears and suspicions; today the debate centres increasingly on which of the two has been more 'imperial' in the way in which it dominated the international system of its day.[27]

This all came at a price, the financial cost of the British effort to hold its position was simply staggering. The taxpayer had funded the war, and in the process the country had become a debtor nation, by the war's end the largest in the world: it owed £15 billion to the United States and a further £3 billion to other members of the Sterling Zone. Here was ample demonstration, if more were needed, of how the alliance had changed. The individual fiscal burden to the British was enormous, no less than 42 per cent of the whole of the personal income from the outbreak of war up until victory in Europe had been taken in taxation or out of savings to finance the government's expenditure. The country had sold almost everything it had, including £1.1 billion of foreign assets, but accumulated debts around the world totalled £2.7 billion. Churchill had not been afraid to tell Stalin at the Potsdam conference in the summer of 1945 that Britain 'came out of this war as the greatest debtor in the world' and that the country was in effect bankrupt. When Lend-Lease was abruptly ended that following September

Britain had received over £31 billion of supplies; Washington decided to issue an invoice for just £650 million but this was still money that Britain did not have.[28] Militarily the cost was just as high.[29]

Much thought had been devoted throughout the last years of the war to how the alliance could move forward intact and with a sense of Imperial unity that would provide Britain a voice in the new international system greater than its shattered economical position should allow. Even with a change in government – the new Labour government was determined to maintain British influence in the world – the Empire was not to be surrendered. It was seen as the solution to most problems in the post-war period, what one writer has described as 'a convenient framework for projecting a certain image of Britain'. Broadly speaking it was still a British Commonwealth; out of a population of about 87 million spread around the globe, about 15 million were not British and these were predominantly in South Africa and Canada. Unfortunately this goal did not materialize as the nature of the Dominion idea quickly changed. Sweeping political changes were about to take place and this would alter the balance beyond all pre-war comprehension, in the eyes of some commentators actually giving the Dominions a key role in preserving the Empire's future. It would also bring with it issues of British citizenship and allegiance to the Crown and the realization that none of the new club was prepared to unhesitatingly follow the ideas developed by British officials. Some of this had been foreseen by Lord Halifax in the spring of 1944, when commenting on the FO memorandum discussing the alliance's future. He had already identified that the use of the terms 'Dominions' and 'Dominion status' would likely cease at some future point as 'they may be held to imply that there is some difference in status between the United Kingdom and the other Dominions'. His conclusion was that some other phrase would be required such as 'nations of the Commonwealth' or 'Member States of the Commonwealth'. This prediction came to pass with the London Declaration, the result of the April 1949 gathering of Heads of State from the Commonwealth, which has been said to have marked the birth of the modern organization and formally changed the name from 'British Commonwealth' to 'Commonwealth of Nations'.[30] This was a collapse that, with hindsight, some saw as being inevitable. One post-war view held that the 'white' commonwealth had always represented 'a triumph of sentiment over strategy'.[31] Many years later the same author argued that with British armed forces reduced during the inter-war years to operational impotence, *realpolitik* should actually have dictated that the Dominions were told that they would need to defend themselves. Instead sentiment intervened and the result was that 'strategic overstretch of Empire ended in strategic collapse, and Australia and New Zealand passed under American protection'. Of the many factors that kept it together so long, the most enduring was the idea that these distant people, while not always faithful to the idea that they owed some sort of fealty to the parliament in Westminster, were prepared to defend their monarch who lived a few streets away. This point was illustrated in a lengthy and effusive March 1944 portrait of King George VI published in *Time* which referred to a recent speech by Richard Law given to the American Chamber of Commerce in London in which he talked of 'the British Commonwealth'. As the widely read American publication put it, 'what Statesman Law calls "Commonwealth" practically all Britons call, without shame, "Empire"'. The war had 'at once tightened and loosened the bonds of Empire' and the link that undeniably held it together was 'the King-Emperor'.[32] Even Churchill, speaking post-war as the Leader of the Opposition, was prepared to agree with this assessment. He argued that the Statute of Westminster had swept away what he termed 'constitutional safeguards' and left the unity and cohesion of the British Empire reliant solely on the link to the Crown. What he did not go on to say was the degree to which he thought this still existed.[33]

Speaking a few months after the article referred to above was published in a Westminster debate Lord Cranborne had taken the opportunity to praise the British Commonwealth: 'that strange, unprecedented combination of self-governing nations, bound, not by visible bonds, but by ties of spirit is in a unique position at the present time'. He saw a great future as while there were bigger nations there was no other Power of a similar nature. 'Sprawled over the whole world, the British Commonwealth partakes of the qualities both of the Old and of the New World. It is firmly based in the past by its traditions and Constitutions, and it looks out fearlessly into the future.'[34] The reality was that at the war's start the Dominions had still been relatively inexperienced in diplomacy but their international recognition, self-confidence and connections had all quickly grown in the years that followed. Their active participation in various wartime theatres had been accompanied by marked signs of British military weakness. By the time church bells were rung throughout Britain, for the first time since the summer of 1940, to celebrate the final victory at El Alamein in November 1942, the alliance had already altered beyond any hope of repair.[35] For the most part at this point British leadership was still accepted, but on occasions even this was qualified or more obviously carried overt reluctance. The establishment of the United Nations organization effectively signalled political emancipation and the DO warned that in the post-war system the ideal policy for dealings with the Dominion govern-ments would be based on 'private wisdom and public silence'. While South Africa and Canada had shown a readiness to put up with this guarded approach when it suited them, even before the game of chance really got started Australia and New Zealand had shown that they seemed determined to take the opposite line.[36] The exertions shown by each of them in the war enhanced their national pride and, by something of a paradox, eroded imperial unity. An alliance that had started the war as 'Dominions' had ended it as a 'British Commonwealth', and in the process an Empire had been lost.

Notes

*All references to archive documents are taken from the National Archives, Kew, unless otherwise stated.

Notes to Introduction: A Special Relationship

1 Psalm 48:12, the injunction to which Mansergh was apparently mindful when undertaking his study; Nicholas Mansergh, *Survey of British Commonwealth Affairs: Problems of Wartime Cooperation and Post-War Change, 1939–1952* (London, 1958), p. xvi.
2 Mansergh, *Survey of British Commonwealth Affairs: Problems of External Policy, 1931–39* (London, 1952); Mansergh, *Documents and Speeches on British Commonwealth Affairs 1931–1952: Vols. 1&2* (London, 1953); W. K. Hancock, 'Nicholas Mansergh: Some Recollections and Reflections' in Norman Hillmer (ed.), *The First British Commonwealth: Essays in Honour of Nicholas Mansergh* (London, 1980), pp. 3–9; Ronald Hyam, '(Philip) Nicholas Seton Mansergh (1910–1991)', *Oxford Dictionary of National Biography*; Kenneth E. Miller, 'Book Review', *The Journal of Politics* (Vol. 21, No. 3; August 1959), pp. 549–51; K. C. Wheare, *International Affairs* (Vol. 35, No. 2; April 1959), p. 227.
3 John Darwin, 'A Third British Empire? The Dominion Idea in British Politics' in Judith M. Brown and Wm. Roger Louis (eds), *The Oxford History of the British Empire: Volume IV – The Twentieth Century* (Oxford, 1999), pp. 64–87 [hereafter 'OHBE4']; W. David McIntyre, 'The Strange Death of Dominion Status' in Robert D. King and Robert Kilson (eds), *The Statecraft of British Imperialism: Essays in Honour of Wm. Roger Louis* (London, 1999) pp. 193–5; Fred Nash, '"Salutem adferre reipublicae" (Cicero): The Dominion Concept and the Empire', *BISA/PSA Political Science Group Workshop Conference*, July 1998.
4 John Darwin, 'The Fear of Falling: British Politics and Imperial Decline Since 1900', *Transactions of the Royal Historical Society* (Vol. 36, 1986), pp. 28–9.
5 A. P. Thornton, 'The Transformation of the Commonwealth and the "Special Relationship"' in Wm. Roger Louis and Hedley Bull (eds), *The 'Special Relationship': Anglo–American Relations since 1945* (Oxford, 1986), p. 367.
6 Bill Nasson, *Britannia's Empire: Making a British World* (Stroud, 2004), pp. 164–70.
7 John Gallagher, *The Decline, Revival and Fall of the British Empire* (Cambridge, 2004), p. 141.
8 'Migration within the Empire', 24 May 1944, *House of Lords Official Report* (Vol. 81), pp. 931–41.
9 H. Duncan Hall, 'The British Commonwealth of Nations', *The American Political Science Review* (Vol. 47, No.4; December 1953), pp. 997–1015.
10 Denis Judd, 'Britain: Land Beyond Hope and Glory?', *History Today* (April 1999), pp. 18–24; David Cannadine, *Ornamentalism: How the British Saw Their Empire* (London, 2002); Cannadine, 'Ornamentalism', *History Today* (May 2001), pp. 12–19; Bernard Porter, *The Absent–Minded Imperialists: Empire, Society and Culture in Britain* (Oxford, 2004); Porter, 'What Did They Know of Empire', *History Today* (October 2004), pp. 42–8.
11 Clair Wills, *That Neutral Island* (London, 2007); T. Ryle Dwyer, *Irish Neutrality and the USA, 1939–1947* (Dublin, 1977); Donal O'Drisceoil, 'Neither Friend nor Foe? Irish Neutrality in the Second World War' (Book Review), *Contemporary European History* (Vol. 15, No. 2; 2006), pp. 245–53.

12 'Constitutional Relations between the United Kingdom and the Dominions', Note prepared by Charles Dixon, August 1946, DO35/1112.
13 Dierdre McMahon, 'Ireland and the Empire–Commonwealth, 1900–1948', in OHBE4, pp. 155–8; Mansergh, *Problems of External Policy*, pp. 270–328.
14 'The Neutrality of Eire', Memorandum by Eden, 16 September 1939, CAB66/1.
15 'All In', *Time*, 18 September 1939.
16 Andrew Baker, 'Anglo–Irish Relations, 1939–1941: A Study in Multilateral Diplomacy and Military Restraint', *Twentieth Century British History* (Vol. 16, No. 4; 2005), pp. 359–81.
17 Denis Judd, *The Lion and the Tiger: The Rise and Fall of the British Raj* (Oxford, 2004), pp. 148–65; Judith M. Brown, 'India' in OHBE4, pp. 421–46; Robin J. Moore, 'India in the 1940s', in Robin W. Winks (ed.), *Historiography: Oxford History of the British Empire, Vol. 5* (Oxford, 1999), pp. 231–42.
18 Empire Information Service, *Origins and Purpose: A Handbook on the British Commonwealth and Empire* (London, 1946), pp. 66–8.
19 E. M. Andrews, *The British Commonwealth and Aggression in the East, 1931–1935* (Sydney, 1987), p. xi.
20 Anne Thurston, *Records of the Colonial Office, Dominions Office, Commonwealth Relations Office and Commonwealth Office* (London, 1995), pp. 57–9, 63–7.

Notes to Chapter 1: The Great Experiment

1 W. Y. Elliot, 'The Riddle of the British Commonwealth', *Foreign Affairs* (Vol. 8, No. 3; 1930), pp. 442–64; W. K. Hancock, *Survey of British Commonwealth Affairs: Problems of Nationality, 1918–1936* (London, 1937); K. C. Wheare, *The Statute of Westminster and Dominion Status* (London, 1942); D. K. Fieldhouse, 'Autochthonous Elements in the Evolution of Dominion Status: The Case of New Zealand', *Journal of Commonwealth Political Studies* (Vol. 1; 1961–1963), pp. 85–7.
2 Wheare, *The Constitutional Structure of the Commonwealth* (London, 1960), pp. 10–11.
3 J. D. Latham speaking in the Australian federal parliament in 1931; cited in W. R. Brock, *Britain and the Dominions* (Cambridge, 1951), pp. 415–16.
4 Viscount Bennett, 'The British Commonwealth of Nations: Its Constitutional Development', *United Empire* (Vol. 35, No. 2; March–April 1944), p. 43.
5 Lord Blanesburgh, 'The Statute of Westminster', Lecture at Royal United Service Institution, 18 January 1933.
6 Joseph Chamberlain, House of Commons Debate on Commonwealth of Australia Bill, 14 May 1900; Handwritten Note on 'Inter Commonwealth Relations', Patrick Duncan, n.d., (Duncan Papers, University of Cape Town), A15.4 (BC294).
7 Mansergh, *South Africa 1906–1961: The Price of Magnanimity* (London, 1962), pp. 15–35; Mansergh, *The Commonwealth Experience* (London, 1969), pp. 84–9; D. Judd and P. Slim, *The Evolution of the Modern Commonwealth, 1902–1980* (London, 1982), pp. 11, 21; Donald Gordon, *The Dominion Partnership in Imperial Defense, 1870–1914* (Baltimore, 1965), p. 194.
8 Martin Kitchen, *The British Empire and Commonwealth* (London, 1996), pp. 61–3; Judd, *Empire: The British Imperial Experience* (London, 1996), pp. 214–25; James Joll, *The Origins of the First World War* (London, 1985), pp. 148–54; Robert Holland, *Britain and the Commonwealth Alliance*, (London, 1981), pp. 1–4; James Williamson, *Great Britain and the Commonwealth* (London, 1965), pp. 178–80; BBC Research Manuals, '*Number 4, The Development of Self–Government in the British Empire*', Abrams Papers (Churchill College, Cambridge), ABMS1/7/9, p. 3.
9 Mansergh, *The Commonwealth Experience*, p. 21.
10 Hyam, 'The British Empire in the Edwardian Era' in OHBE4, pp. 56–7.
11 Paul Hayes, 'British Foreign Policy and the Influence of Empire, 1870–1920', *Journal of Imperial and Commonwealth History* (Vol. 12; 1984), pp. 113–14.
12 Max Beloff, *Imperial Sunset, Vol. 1: Britain's Liberal Empire, 1897–1921* (New York, 1970), pp. 191–3.

13 Judd and Slim, *The Evolution of the Modern Commonwealth*, pp. 39–40; Porter, *Britain, Europe and the World*, (London, 1987), p. 79; Porter, *The Lion's Share*, (London, 1975), p. 228.
14 C. P. Stacey, *Canada and the Age of Conflict Vol. 1* (Toronto, 1983), pp. 203–11; R. C. Brown, *Robert Laird Borden* (Ottawa, 1975), p. 85; I. M. Cumpston, *The Evolution of the Commonwealth of Nations, 1900–1980* (Canberra, 1997), pp. 4–5; Heather Harvey, *Consultation and Cooperation in the Commonwealth: A Handbook on Methods and Practice* (London, 1952), pp. 90–2; Sir Percival Griffiths, *Empire into Commonwealth* (London, 1969), p. 250.
15 Judd and Slim, *The Evolution of the Modern Commonwealth*, pp. 38–40; Holland, 'The British Empire and the Great War,' in OHBE4, pp. 127–30.
16 The speech in January 1884 included the comment that 'there is no need for any nation, however great, leaving the Empire, because the Empire is a commonwealth of nations'. He is subsequently said to have forgotten the phrase but in his Rectorial address in Glasgow on 'Questions of Empire' delivered in November 1899 he used 'commonwealth' three times as a synonym for Empire which he acknowledged had acquired 'some taint of disagreeable association'. Adopted by Liberals and Fabians for similar reason from this point the term became freely used. Smuts also pointed to his reference to 'the British Commonwealth of Nations' in a 1917 address to the members of the House of Commons in London, a descriptive term which was subsequently endorsed by Imperial Conferences. This, he argued, became the official name for 'Britain plus the free Dominions' but it was not officially used until 1921 when it featured in the Irish Treaty; Hancock, *Survey of British Commonwealth Affairs: Vol. 1, Problems of Nationality, 1918–1936* (London, 1937), p. 54; Mansergh, *The Commonwealth Experience*, pp. 7, 122; Duncan Hall, 'The Genesis of the Balfour Declaration', *Journal of Commonwealth Political Studies*, pp. 169–70; 'The British Colonial Empire', *Life*, 28 December 1942.
17 Brian Farrell, 'Coalition of the Usually Willing: the Dominions and Imperial Defence, 1856–1919' in Greg Kennedy (ed.), *Imperial Defence, 1856–1956: The Old World Order* (London, 2007), pp. 251–302.
18 Frank Underhill, *The British Commonwealth* (London, 1956), pp. 46–53.
19 'Memorandum by General Smuts on Constitutional Relations', 1921, DO117/33.
20 Darwin, 'The Dominion Idea in Imperial Politics' in OHBE4, pp. 67–9; Robert Holland, *The Pursuit of Greatness, Britain and the World Role, 1900–70* (London, 1991), pp. 87–120; Norman Hillmer, 'The Foreign Office, the Dominions and the Diplomatic Unity of the Empire, 1925–29' in David Dilks (ed.), *Retreat From Power, Vol. 1* (London, 1981), pp. 64–5.
21 Cited in 'Whitehall and the Commonwealth: The Distribution of Department Responsibility', *The Round Table*, (Vol. 45; 1954/1955), p. 234.
22 'Lord Elgin's Despatch on CO Reorganization', September 1907, Cd.3795; Cross, *Whitehall and the Commonwealth* (London, 1967), pp. 14–16; Holland, *Britain and the Commonwealth Alliance*, pp. 40–5.
23 The latter had been created in 1904 as a purely advisory body headed by the British prime minister, its role being 'to investigate, report [and] recommend' on matters which affected the Empire; Cecil Hurst (et al.), *Great Britain and the Dominions* (Illinois, 1928), pp. 39–41.
24 Frederick Madden and John Darwin (eds), *Select Documents on the Constitutional History of the British Empire and Commonwealth, Vol. VI, The Dominions and India since 1900* (London, 1993), pp. 16–26; I. R. Hancock, 'The 1911 Imperial Conference', *Historical Studies* (Vol. 12, No. 47; October 1966), pp. 156–172.
25 Philip Wigley, 'Whitehall and the 1923 Imperial Conference', *Journal of Imperial and Commonwealth History* (Vol. 1; 1972–1973), pp. 223–36.
26 David Walder, *The Chanak Affair* (London, 1969), pp. 215–16, 229–30, 353; Mark Arnold-Forster, 'Chanak Rocks the Empire: The Anger of Billy Hughes', *The Round Table* (Vol. 58; 1968), pp. 169–77.
27 'The Dominions and Colonial Offices – Proposals for Reorganisation', Memorandum prepared by Amery, 20 February 1925, DO121/1.
28 L. S. Amery, *My Political Life: Vol. II, War and Peace 1914–1929* (London, 1953), p. 335.
29 'Report by R. R. Scott, H. P. Hamilton and R. V. Nind-Hopkins to Baldwin', 20 February 1925, DO121/1.

30   Mansergh, *Problems of Wartime Cooperation,* pp. 398–401; Joe Garner, *The Commonwealth Office* (London, 1978), pp. 10–12; John Rimington, 'Sir Warren Fisher's Civil Service', *The Source Public Management Journal* (19 January 2000).

31   For example Amery to General Sir C. Ferguson, 19 March 1925, DO121/1; ibid., Amery to Bruce and Massey, 19 March 1925; Wm. Roger Louis, *In the Name of God Go! Leo Amery and the British Empire in the Age of Churchill* (London, 1992), pp. 88–9.

32   Sir Walter Runciman cited in Gerald Palmer, *Consultation and Cooperation in the British Commonwealth* (London, 1934), p. 24.

33   Memorandum prepared by Robinson (CO),12 May 1937, CO886/32.

34   Garner, *The Commonwealth Office,* p. 15.

35   Amery to Baldwin, 23 May 1925, DO121/1.

36   Parkinson, *The Colonial Office from Within* (London, 1947), pp. 12–13; Garner, *The Commonwealth Office,* pp. 15–16; 'The Buildings of the FCO', http://193.114.50.10/directory/dynpage. asp?Page=61.

37   Amery to Baldwin, 23 May 1925, DO121/1.

38   'Memorandum prepared on the Building of the Colonial Office by Sir Frank Baines, Office of Works, 9 October 1925', CO886/32.

39   'Memorandum prepared by Ministry of Works', January 1938, DO35/548D.

40   Garner, *The Commonwealth Office,* p. 26.

41   Typical of such sentiments were those offered by the Canadian High Commissioner Vincent Massey in March 1936: 'The machinery of the DO instead of keeping us in close touch with foreign crises at present seems somehow to provide an obstacle or rather delay in getting news which we could get and sometimes do receive informally from the FO. What good purpose does the DO serve?'; Vincent Massey, *What's Past is Prologue* (Toronto, 1963), p. 236.

42   Garner, *The Commonwealth Office,* p. 137.

43   Lester B. Pearson, *Through Diplomacy to Politics: Memoirs, 1897–1948* (London, 1973), p. 108.

44   Hubert Montgomery to Foreign Secretary, 23 July 1926, FO372/2216.

45   H.V. Hodson, 'British Foreign Policy and the Dominions', *Foreign Affairs* (Vol. 17; July 1939), pp. 762–3.

46   Garner, *The Commonwealth Office,* p. 26.

47   Patrick Walker, *The Commonwealth* (London, 1962), pp. 97–116.

48   Amery to Colonel Sykes, 13 October 1941, Amery Papers (Churchill College, Cambridge), AMEL2/1/33; Ridgway F. Shinn Jr, 'The King's Title, 1926: A Note on a Critical Document', *English Historical Review* (Vol. 48, No. 387; April 1983), pp. 350–2.

49   A. Berriedale Keith, *Speeches and Documents on the British Dominions, 1918–1931* (London, 1932), pp. 16–47; B. E. Dugdale, *Arthur James Balfour, First Earl of Balfour, 1906–30* (London, 1936), p. 381; Mansergh, *Problems of External Policy,* pp. 1–88; Mansergh, *Problems of Wartime Cooperation,* pp. 11–16; Heather Harvey, *Consultation and Cooperation in the Commonwealth* (London, 1952), pp. 1–10.

50   'Constitutional Relations between the United Kingdom and the Dominions', Note prepared by Charles Dixon, August 1946, DO35/1112.

51   Speech at Edinburgh, 27 January 1927, cited in George Bennett (ed.), *The Concept of Empire* (London, 1953), pp. 398–402.

52   'Constitutional Legislation Affecting Commonwealth Relations since 1931', Central Office of Information, London (March 1952), pp. 1–2.

53   Darwin, 'The Dominion Idea in Imperial Politics' in OHBE4, pp. 66–7.

54   Darwin, 'Imperialism in Decline? Tendencies in British Imperial Policy between the Wars', *Historical Journal* (Vol. 23, No. 3; 1980), pp. 661–6.

55   Stacey, *Canada and the Age of Conflict,* p. 117.

56   House of Commons debate cited in Mansergh, *Problems of External Policy,* p. 18.

57   Martin Chanock, *Unconsummated Union: Britain, Rhodesia and South Africa, 1900–1945* (London, 1977), p. 13; 'South Africa: The British', *The National Review* (No. 116; January 1941), pp. 23–4; G. H. Calpin, 'South Africa and the War', *The Nineteenth Century* (September 1940), p. 266.

58 Stanley to Thomas, 11 October 1932, DO121/101.
59 W. K. Hancock, *Smuts, The Fields of Force, 1919–1950* (London, 1968), pp. 318–25; C. M. Van der Heever, *General J.B.M. Hertzog* (Johannesburg, 1946), pp. 278–83.
60 W. H. Clark, 'Race Relations and Political Trends in the Union of South Africa, 1935–1940', April 1940, Clark Papers (University of Cape Town).
61 Mansergh, *Problems of External Policy*, pp. 381–2.
62 Angus Ross, 'Reluctant Dominion or Dutiful Daughter? New Zealand and the Commonwealth in the Inter–war Years', *Journal of Commonwealth Political Studies* (Vol. X; 1972), pp. 28–44.
63 W. B. Sutch, 'New Zealand and World Affairs', *International Affairs* (Vol. 16, No. 5; September 1937), p. 721; this article was written by Walter Nash's secretary–economist.
64 'Notes on Mr Amery's Tour in Australia and New Zealand', 8 February 1928, CAB24/192.
65 Garner, *Commonwealth*, p. 49.
66 'Comments by William Jordan at meeting of Dominion delegates at Geneva', 12 September 1938, DO114/94.
67 Walter Phelps Hall, *Empire to Commonwealth* (New York, 1928), pp. 165–82; Edward Porrit, *The Fiscal and Diplomatic Freedom of the British Overseas Dominions* (London, 1922), pp. 141–8.
68 D. K. Fieldhouse 'The Metropolitan Economics of Empire', in OHBE4, pp. 98–102.
69 Correlli Barnett, *The Collapse of British Power* (London, 1972), pp. 117–20.
70 P. J. Cain and A. G. Hopkins, *British Imperialism: Crisis and Deconstruction, 1914–90* (London and New York, 1993), pp. 96–135; Judd and Slim, *The Evolution of the Modern Commonwealth*, pp. 73–78; L. E. Davis and R. A. Huttenback, *Mammon and the Pursuit of Empire. The Political Economy of British Imperialism, 1860–1912* (Cambridge, 1986), pp. 160–3, 189–91, 303–6.
71 Walter Nash, 'New Zealand and the Commonwealth', *United Empire* (Vol. 28, No. 1; January 1937), p. 31; McKinnon, *Independence and Foreign Policy* pp. 23–6.
72 Keith Sinclair, *Walter Nash* (Auckland, 1977), p. 137.
73 John O'Brien, 'Conditional Loyalties: Australia, Ireland and the Decline of the Dominions Office', *Institute of Commonwealth Studies Seminar Paper* (1990), p. 2.
74 Keith Middlemas, 'The Effect of Dominion Opinion on British Foreign Policy, 1937–1938', *Institute of Commonwealth Studies Seminar Paper* (1971), p. 47.
75 David Carlton, 'The Dominions and the Gathering Storm', *Journal of Imperial and Commonwealth History* (Vol. 6, No. 2; January 1978), pp. 172–5; Max Beloff, *Dream of Commonwealth, 1921–42* (London, 1989), pp. 270–98; Ritchie Ovendale, 'Why the British Dominions Declared War' in Robert Boyce and Esmonde Robertson (eds), *Paths to War: New Essays on the Origins of the Second World War* (New York, 1989), pp. 276–96; Ovendale, *Appeasement and the English Speaking World* (Cardiff, 1975), pp. 38–63.

Notes to Chapter 2: War Again

1 John Hilliker, *Canada's Department of External Affairs, Vol. One* (Montreal, 1990), pp. 111–213; R. G. Neale (ed.), *Documents on Australian Foreign Policy, 1937–1949: Vol. II, 1939* (Canberra, 1976), pp. 13–14; Paul Hasluck, *Diplomatic Witness: Australian Foreign Affairs 1941–1947* (Melbourne, 1980), pp. 3–16; Lorna Lloyd, 'Loosening the Apron Strings: The Dominions and Britain in the Inter–War Years', *The Round Table* (No. 369, 2003), pp. 279–303.
2 MacDonald to Halifax, 23 March 1938, DO35/576; Keith Sinclair, *A History of New Zealand* (London, 1959), p. 277; F. L .W. Wood, 'The Dominion of New Zealand at War' in Duncan Hall and William Elliot (eds), *The British Commonwealth at War* (New York, 1943), pp. 407–12; Mansergh, *Problems of Wartime Cooperation*, p. 16.
3 Dixon to Batterbee, 14 December 1937, DO35/543/28/5; ibid., letter from Malkin to Bushe, 18 February 1937, DO35/543/28/2.
4 Ann Trotter, 'The Dominions and Imperial Defence: Hankey's Tour in 1934', *Journal of Imperial and Commonwealth History* (Vol. 2; 1974), pp. 318–32.
5 Bushe to Malkin, 8 February 1937, DO35/543/28/2.

6   Ibid., Malkin to Bushe, 18 February 1937.
7   Ibid., minute by Harding, 18 September 1937; Garner, *The Commonwealth Office*, p. 20.
8   Dixon to Batterbee, 14 December 1937, DO35/543/28/5; ibid., 'Memorandum prepared by Batterbee', December 1937; Sir Charles Dixon, 'Memoirs on Service in the Colonial Office, the Commonwealth Relations Office and the Commonwealth Office from 1911 to the 1970s', (n.d.), Sir Harry Batterbee Papers (Rhodes House Library, Oxford), Box 20/5; Dixon to Malkin, 23 December 1937, DO35/543/28/4; Garner, *The Commonwealth Office*, pp. 91–3; in comparing his account of events with that contained within the DO's original correspondence files, Garner, who had no involvement in the preparation of these documents, seems to have become a little confused in his narrative, at least in the earlier stages.
9   'Memorandum prepared by Batterbee', December 1937, DO35/543/28/5; ibid., 'Note prepared by Dixon – "Position of the Dominions on the Event of War"', December 1937 .
10 Ibid., Batterbee to MacDonald, 7 January 1938.
11 Ibid., minute by MacDonald, 21 January 1938; ibid., Malkin to Dixon, 11 January 1938; as part of the ongoing review process of internal files adopted by the DO, in 1957 the majority of files D28/6 to D28/20 contained within DO35/543, covering approximately one year of the memorandum's progress, were deemed to be of insufficient historical interest to merit not being destroyed; see Anne Thurston, *Records of the Colonial Office, Dominions Office, Commonwealth Relations Office and Commonwealth Office* (London, 1995), pp. 62–4.
12 Garner, *The Commonwealth Office*, p. 94.
13 John A. Cross, *Whitehall and the Commonwealth: British Departmental Organisation for Commonwealth Relations, 1900–1966* (London, 1967), p. 52; G. M. Carter, *British Commonwealth and International Security* (Toronto, 1947), pp. 300–2; MacDonald to Halifax, 10 April 1938, CAB123/246; MacDonald, 'Interview to the Oxford Colonial Records Project' (Rhodes House Library), p. 3.
14 R. A. C. Parker, *Chamberlain and Appeasement: British Policy and the Coming of the Second World War* (London, 1993), pp. 156–82; Keith Middlemas, *The Diplomacy of Illusion* (London, 1972), pp. 21–3; Duncan Hall, *Commonwealth* (London, 1971), pp. 753–62; Middlemas, 'The Effect of Dominion Opinion on British Foreign Policy', *Collected Seminar Papers on the Dominions between the Wars* (Institute of Commonwealth Studies; October 1970–March 1971), pp. 51–4; Barnett, *The Collapse of British Power*, pp. 228–9; Holland, *The Commonwealth Alliance*, pp. 200–2; Ovendale, *Appeasement and the English Speaking World*, pp. 210–11; Michael Graham Fry, 'Agents and Structures: The Dominions and the Czechoslovak Crisis, September 1938', *Diplomacy and Statecraft*, (Vol. 10, Nos. 2 and 3; 1999); 'The Influence of the Commonwealth on British Foreign Policy: The Case of the Munich Crisis' in D. C. Watt, *Personalities and Policies* (London, 1965), pp. 162–3; Duncan Hall and Elliot, *The Commonwealth in War and Peace*, p. 13; The Earl of Halifax, *Fullness of Days* (London, 1957), pp. 197–8; Robert J. Beck, 'Munich's Lessons Reconsidered', *International Security* (Vol. 14, No. 2; Autumn, 1989), pp. 161–91.
15 Bridges to Machtig, 28 September 1944, DO35/1482; ibid., Machtig to Bridges, 30 October 1944; Bridges to Woodward, 17 November 1944.
16 DO to British High Commissioners, 28 September 1938, DO35/543/28/8.
17 Liesching to Batterbee, 28 July 1938, Batterbee Papers, Box 9/1.
18 Minutes and correspondence regarding supply of papers to the UK High Commissioner in New Zealand, October/November 1938, DO35/548F.
19 'Hankey, whose mother was Australian and who, unlike most of the British politicians who paid lip service to the idea, genuinely desired participation by the Dominions in Imperial policy making'; P. G. Edwards, 'The Rise and Fall of the High Commissioner: S. M. Bruce in London, 1933–45', in A. F. Madden and W. H. Morris (eds), *Studies in Commonwealth Politics and History: Australia and Britain* (London, 1986), p. 54; Batterbee to MacDonald, 7 January 1938, DO35/543/28/5.
20 Batterbee to Clark, 4 January 1939, Clark Papers (London School of Economics); 'Note of a meeting on 5 January 1939', DO35/543/28/21; although it is not within the remit of this study, Harding's warning extended as far as to also keeping the information from the Irish authorities.
21 Donald Lammers, 'From Whitehall After Munich: The Foreign Office and the Future Course of

British Policy', *The Historical Journal* (Vol. 16, No. 4; 1973), p. 832; Malkin to Dixon, 10 January 1939, DO35/543/28/21.

22   Ibid., minute by Stephenson, 26 January 1939; Bridges to Dixon, 24 January 1939.

23   Harding to Campbell/Clark, 1 February 1939, DO35/543/28/21.

24   Clark to Harding, 20 February 1939, DO35/543/28/23; Whiskard to Inskip, 16 March 1939, DO121/46; Campbell to Inskip, 24 March 1939, FO800/310.

25   Bridges to Harding, 13 February 1939, DO35/543/28/21; Harding to Batterbee, 18 February 1939, Batterbee Papers, Box 6/4; Halifax to Inskip, 2 March 1939, FO372/3315.

26   Bridges to Minister, 1 March 1939, CAB21/488.

27   Dixon Memoirs, Batterbee Papers, Box 20/5; Parker, *Chamberlain and Appeasement*, pp. 201–2; P. M. H. Bell, *The Origins of the Second World War* (London, 1986), pp. 252–4.

28   During the Munich crisis MacDonald had found himself obliged to agree to requests by the hitherto largely dormant London-based Dominion high commissioners for meetings, 'sometimes more than once a day', to brief them fully on developments. These daily gatherings were in addition to the overwhelming flow of messages and telegrams already being provided by the DO to the Dominion governments. And, requiring a good deal of advance preparation by a variety of officials, not to mention actual attendance by others, they accounted for much valuable time; Dixon Memoirs, Batterbee Papers; Malcolm MacDonald, *Titans and Others* (London, 1972), pp. 80–1.

29   Minute by Harding, 2 May 1933, DO35/100.

30   High Commissioner's Meeting (hereafter 'HCM'), 21 March 1939, DO121/5; Campbell to Inskip, 24 March 1939, FO800/310.

31   HCM, 30 March 1939, DO121/5.

32   Smuts to Duncan, 25 April 1939, Sir Patrick Duncan Papers (University of Cape Town); Smuts to Gullet, 6 April 1939, Jan Smuts Papers (National Archives, Pretoria); Mackenzie King Diary, 31 March 1939, Mackenzie King Papers (Library and Archives Canada, Ottawa), MG26, J13, Fiche 129–130; J. L. Granatstein and R. Bothwell, 'A Self–Evident National Duty: Canadian Foreign Policy, 1935–39', *Journal of Imperial and Commonwealth History* (Vol. 3, No. 2; January 1975), p. 228.

33   Harding to Bridges, 6 April 1939, DO35/548D/1/57; Harding to Creedy (WO), 19 April 1939, CAB104/19; he would soon be hospitalised by an attack of piles which may well have been the cause of his apparent distraction, Harding to Batterbee, 6 August 1939, Batterbee Papers, Box 6/4.

34   Op. cit., 'Memorandum', April 1939; Campbell to Stephenson, 19 April 1939, DO35/543/28/23; ibid., Clark to Harding, 20 February 1939; Clark to Harding, 28 April 1939, CAB104/19.

35   Clark to Harding, 20 February 1939, DO35/543/28/23; Clark to Harding, 13 March 1939, CAB104/19.

36   Parker, *Chamberlain and Appeasement*, pp. 216–46; John Charmley, *Chamberlain and the Lost Peace* (London, 1989), pp. 180–5.

37   HCM, 23 May 1939, DO121/5; 'Position of the Dominions in the Event of War', May 1939, DO35/543/28/32.

38   Minute by Dixon, 24 May 1939, DO35/543/28/32; ibid., minute by Stephenson, 27 May 1939.

39   Garner, *The Commonwealth Office*, pp. 88–9.

40   Minute by Harding, 25 May 1939, DO35/543/28/32; ibid., minute by Inskip, 25 May 1939. Just a month earlier Harding had written to his brother-in-law in Wellington and referred to the Secretary of State as 'not having the knowledge or the temperament [for the job]', Harding to Batterbee, 16 April 1939, DO35/543/28/32.

41   Australia, it was felt, would not be far behind with a similar request for help. Carl Bridge, 'Poland to Pearl Harbor' in Carl Bridge (ed.), *Munich to Vietnam: Australia's Relations with Britain and the United States since the 1930's* (Melbourne, 1991), pp. 39–41; Lloyd Ross, *John Curtin* (Melbourne, 1977), p. 41; Cain and Hopkins, *British Imperialism*, pp. 511–14; Minute by Machtig, 25 February 1939, DO35/548A; Sinclair, *Walter Nash*, p. 177; T. K. Bewley, 'Memorandum on New Zealand', n.d., CAB21/489.

42   Beloff, *Dream of Commonwealth*, pp. 284–5.

43   Hancock, *Smuts: The Fields of Force*, pp. 318–25; Van Der Heever, *General J.B.M.Hertzog*, pp. 278–83.

44 The DID virtually ceased to exist 'in the stress of war' and by mid-1940 it no longer provided any real coverage of events; minute by Sir Basil Newton, 25 November 1942, DO35/1002/52/10; handwritten comment, 'Foreign Affairs', 17 July 1942, DO35/998/7/48.

45 Minute by Hadow, 19 April 1939, FO372/3314; ibid., minute by F. H. Cleobury, 26 January 1939, FO372/3314; minute by Cleobury, 6 April 1939.

46 Ibid., minute by Hadow, 24 May 1939; minute by Cadogan, 31 May 1939, FO800/310; Ovendale, *Appeasement and the English Speaking World*, p. 275.

47 Batterbee to DO, 23 May 1939, CAB104/19; Fairburn to Earl de la Warr, 9 May 1939, DO121/46.

48 'Index of HC Meetings', DO121/5.

49 'Minutes of a meeting to discuss security', 5 August 1939, DO35/548D/3/126.

50 Inskip to Lord Chatfield, 23 August 1939, CAB21/2464.

51 HCM, 22 August 1939, DO121/5; Dairy, 23 August 1939, Lord Hankey Papers (Churchill College) HNKY1/7; Diary, 25 August 1939, Sir Thomas Inskip Papers (Churchill College) INKP; 'Index of HC Meetings', DO121/5; 'Germany and Great Britain, Settlement', note by Massey, 31 August 1939, Massey Family Papers (Library and Archives Canada).

52 Clark to Harding, 24 August 1939, DO114/98; minute by Hadow, 9 August 1939, FO371/23964.

53 Andrew Crozier, *Appeasement and Germany's Last Bid for Colonies* (London, 1988); D. C. Watt, 'South African Attempts to Mediate Between Britain and Germany, 1935–1938' in Bourne and Watt (eds), *Studies in International History* (London, 1967); Albert Grundlingh, 'The King's Afrikaners? Enlistment and Ethnic Identity in the Union of South Africa's Defence Force During the Second World War, 1939–45', *Journal of African History* (Vol. 40; 1999), pp. 353–4; Van der Heever, *Hertzog*, pp. 278–3.

54 Minute by Scott, 31 August 1939, FO371/23965.

55 Deneys Reitz, *No Outspan* (London, 1943), p. 237.

56 A document discovered in Berlin in 1945 by Allied investigators revealed that Hertzog had considered accepting German offers to negotiate about the future of South West Africa in 1937/38. Although he had kept the DO informed, the post-war department was worried about what effect the news might have on imperial relations and suppressed the information; DO35/1517/211/1.

57 Chamberlain to Clark (Telegram), 3 September 1939, FO371/23964.

58 Smuts to Gillett, 28 September 1939, cited in Hancock, *Smuts*, p. 314.

59 High Commission (Pretoria) to DO, 29 August 1939, FO371/23964.

60 Thornton, *The Imperial Idea and its Enemies* (London, 1959), p. 323.

61 Andrew Stewart, 'The South African Neutrality Crisis', *English Historical Review* (Vol. CXXIII, No. 503; August 2008); Duncan was left distraught at what had happened and what it would mean for his country. Smuts had prevailed but the Dominion was now split on racial and political lines. When the Governor-General died only a few year's later, tributes from all sides of the political spectrum were sincere and fulsome, but for some months after the crisis he had been publicly reviled by the worst elements within the Nationalist ranks. This was because as the King's agent he remained firmly loyal to the Crown he represented despite his previous political career and natural allegiances. Duncan to Lady Duncan, 4 September 1939, Duncan Papers; *The Round Table* (No. 117, December 1939), pp. 200–14; Harlech to DO, 20 July 1943, DO35/1120.

62 Chamberlain's old friend in Cape Town, Abe Bailey, wrote to him twice in the first part of 1940 in extravagant praise of Smuts, 'he has proved the saviour of South Africa – goodness only knows what would have happened here'. The answer to his question would come some years later following the war's end. Sir Abe Bailey to Chamberlain, 3 February 1940, Neville Chamberlain Papers (University of Birmingham), NC7/11/33/15; ibid., Sir Abe Bailey to Chamberlain, 1 April 1940, NC7/11/33/16.

63 H. V. Hodson, 'British Foreign Policy and the Dominions', *Foreign Affairs* (Vol. 17; July 1939), pp. 753–63; H. V. Hodson, 'Collective Security and Empire Defence', *United Empire* (Vol. 30; 1939), pp. 745–7; Eric Siepmann, 'The Neutrality of South Africa', *The Nineteenth Century* (September 1939), pp. 279–94; Duncan Hall, 'The British Commonwealth of Nations at War' in Duncan Hall and Elliot, *The British Commonwealth at War*, pp. 19–27; ibid., Lucretia Ilsley, 'The Union of South

Africa in the War', pp. 426–32; Geoffrey Cox, 'The Commonwealth' in Arnold Toynbee and Veronica Toynbee (eds), *Survey of International Affairs 1939–1946: The Initial Triumph of the Axis* (London, 1958), pp. 300–3; Ovendale, *The English Speaking Alliance*, p. 5; Ovendale, 'Britain, the Dominions and the Coming of the Second World War, 1933–9' in Wolfgang J. Mommsen and Lothar Kettenacker (eds), *The Fascist Challenge and the Policy of Appeasement* (London, 1983), p. 335.

64 Nicholas Mansergh, *Problems of External Policy, 1931–39* (London, 1952), p. 379; Andrew Stewart, '"The Liquidator": Sir Harry Batterbee and the British Wartime High Commission in New Zealand' in Chris Baxter and Andrew Stewart (eds), *Diplomats at War* (Leiden, 2008), pp. 171–94; Inskip to Chamberlain, 1 September 1939, PREM1/300; Lewis Gann, 'South Africa and the Third Reich', *The International History Review* (Vol. 14; 1992), p. 518.

65 W. G. Stevens, 'Recall Without Repining', W. G. Stevens Papers (Alexander Turnbull Library, Wellington), 84–006–2/3, p. 147.

66 'Diary of a Crisis: Sunday, 3rd September 1939', Batterbee Papers, Box 9/5.

Notes to Chapter 3: Controlling the Alliance

1 D. C. Watt, *How War Came* (London, 1989) pp. 601–4; Parker, *Chamberlain and Appeasement*, pp. 337–42.

2 Holland, *The Commonwealth Alliance*, pp. 198–199; Diary, 17 January 1939, Inskip Papers INKP1/2; Inskip to Simon, 31 January 1939, Sir John Simon Papers (Bodleian Library, Oxford), Box 85; publicly it was understood that Inskip had been made the scapegoat for increasing dissatisfaction over government policies. Privately though it appears that much of the reason for his demotion was because he had come to believe that war was now certain to happen, leaving him at odds with Chamberlain; Sean Greenwood, 'Caligula's Horse Revisited: Sir Thomas Inskip as Minister for the Coordination of Defence, 1936–1939', *Journal of Strategic Studies*, (Vol. 17, No. 2; June 1994), pp. 17–38; 'Cato', *Guilty Men* (London, 1940), p. 79.

3 Earl of Avon, *The Eden Memoirs: Vol. 3, The Reckoning* (London, 1965), pp. 62–8; V. Rothwell, *Anthony Eden: A Political Biography* (London, 1992), p. 51; David Carlton, *Anthony Eden: A Biography* (London, 1981), pp. 151–3.

4 War Cabinet 7(39), 12 September 1939, CAB65/1 (hereafter 'WCM'); Yates to Tucker, 3 September 1939, PREM1/384; he exercised this right a total of 27 times during his period at the DO.

5 'Relative strengths of each of the Dominion Armed forces at the outbreak of war, September 1939', prepared by Miss Y. Streatfield, n.d. (1945?), CAB101/275; Cox, 'The Commonwealth' in Toynbee and Toynbee (eds), *The Initial Triumph of the Axis*, pp. 304–6.

6 R. G. Neale (ed.), *Documents on Australian Foreign Policy, 1937–49, Vol. 2, 1939* (Canberra, 1976), p. 232 (hereafter 'DAFP'); 'Action taken by the Dominions', 6 September 1939, WP(R)(39)5, CAB67/1; Campbell to DO, 20 September 1939, DO35/1003/3/1/2; Whiskard to DO, 12 September 1939, DO35/1003/3/2/3.

7 'Canadian Cooperation–Report by Chiefs of Staff Committee', 4 September 1939, WP(39)4, CAB66/1.

8 The Land Forces Committee consisted of Hoare, Chatfield, Burgin, Churchill and Hore-Belisha, CAB65/1, 23(39), 22 September 1939; J. R. M. Butler, *Grand Strategy: Vol. 2* (London, 1957), p. 32.

9 'An Australian Army of 100,000', *Daily Telegraph*, 20 September 1939; Most Secret Cablegram, 8 September 1939, DAFP, p. 249.

10 'Action taken by the Dominions', WP(R)(39)50, 17 October 1939, CAB68; there were 6,600 troops earmarked in the first instance but it was later confirmed that the intention was to send an expeditionary force of a fully equipped division to any theatre within eight months, the British identifying France, Burma, India, Singapore or Fiji as the best locations. The New Zealand Navy's assets were placed under the Admiralty's command and RNZAF personnel in Britain were permitted to serve in the RAF adding 500 to its numbers with an order for 30 Wellington bombers also being waived; Fraser to Jordan, 3 October 1939 (National Archives, Wellington) EA1 63/2/2 pt.1; W. David McIntyre, *New Zealand Prepares for War* (Canterbury, 1988), pp. 337–54.

11 WCM(39)50, 19 October 1939, CAB65/1; WCM(39)75–78, 8–10 November 1939, CAB65/2; telegram from R. Campbell, 25 November 1939, CAB21/952; Michael Dockrill, 'The Foreign Office and France During the Phoney War, September 1939–May 1940' in M. L. Dockrill and B. McKercher (eds), *Diplomacy and World Power, Studies in British Foreign Policy 1890–1950* (Cambridge, 1996), pp. 181, 192; the fact that these divisions would require armament from British supplies has added credence to the argument that the Dominions were a burden on Britain. This was the case at this stage of the war but the long-term benefits of the Dominions' support were plainly considerable; G. C. Peden, 'The Burden of Imperial Defence and the Continental Commitment Reconsidered', *The Historical Journal* (Vol. 27, No. 2; 1984), pp. 405–23; Michael Howard, *The Continental Commitment* (London, 1972), pp. 123–49.

12 Bewley to Machtig, 26 October 1939, CAB21/490.

13 Price to Dykes, 25 October 1939, CAB21/677; ibid., Antrobus to Porter, 25 October 1939; General Smuts had suggested that a total of two army divisions and fourteen air force squadrons be raised and trained for service in Northern or Eastern Africa.

14 Andrew Stewart, 'The British Government and the 1939 Negotiations for the Empire Air Training Plan', *The Round Table: The Commonwealth Journal of International Affairs* (Vol. 377; October 2004), pp. 739–54; Cecil Edwards, *Bruce of Melbourne: Man of Two Worlds* (London, 1965), pp. 277–80; Butler, *Grand Strategy*, pp. 39–40; William Stevenson, *The Origins of the British Commonwealth Air Training Scheme from 1923 to December 1939* (University of London, 1981) unpublished manuscript; F. J. Hatch, *The Aerodrome of Democracy: Canada and the British Commonwealth Air Training Plan, 1939–45* (Ottawa, 1983), pp. 1–12; W. A. B. Douglas, *The Creation of a National Air Force: The Official History of the Royal Canadian Air Force, Vol. 2* (Ottawa, 1986), pp. 200–4.

15 WCM(39)49, 10 October 1939, CAB65/1.

16 Halifax had informed Eden of a report he had from the Washington Embassy of comments by Herridge, the Canadian minister in Washington. 'Everything [in Canada] had become rather drab. Volunteers had been told they were not immediately required, no stirring appeal had been made to deeper Canadian feeling that wished to be convinced that it was engaged upon a holy war. Herridge told me that the Canadian contribution to the Air Force made little popular appeal. The great majority of his friends would prefer conscription'; Report no. W15706/10478/68, 30 October 1939, FO371/23966.

17 WCM(39)58, 24 October 1939, CAB65/1.

18 Pearson, *Through Diplomacy to Politics*, p. 140.

19 WCM(39)68, 2 November 1939, CAB65/2.

20 Sir Llewellyn Woodward, *British Foreign Policy in the Second World War, Vol. 1* (London, 1970), pp. 20–2.

21 WCM(39)68, 2 November 1939, CAB65/2; French tension over Britain's contribution was still increasing as witnessed in the tone of the telegrams being despatched by Ronald Campbell, the British ambassador in Paris, 'the French estimate that the French Empire is bearing a burden of war expenditure equal to that of the British Empire although it is only one third as wealthy … the fear persists that Great Britain will insist upon a peace which will contain what France would not consider adequate political and military guarantees against any further threat', Campbell to FO, 25 November 1939, CAB21/952.

22 Report no. F11951/4108/23, 18 November 1939, FO371/23572; Cavendish Bentinck, reading the relevant telegrams in the FO, complained that, 'the Australians remain terrified of the Japanese, refuse to give any undertakings as regards an expeditionary force, and are concentrating to an excessive extent on home defence'; Report no. W14977/14472/68, 18 October 1939, FO371/23967.

23 Dominion High Commissioners Wartime Meeting (69), 22 November 1939, DO121/6 (hereafter 'HCWM'); High Commissioner, Canberra to DO (No. 301), 24 November 1939, FO371/23967.

24 As he wrote to his sister, 'As you know, I have always been more afraid of a peace offer than of an air raid, but I did feel that if Hitler made it himself it would almost certainly be in such a form as to be plainly acceptable', Chamberlain to Ida, 10 October 1939; cited in Iain Macleod, *Neville*

NOTES TO PAGES 31–34

NOTES TO PAGES 31–34181

Chamberlain (London, 1961); Christopher Hill, *Cabinet Decisions on Foreign Policy* (London, 1991), pp. 100–45.

25 'Views of the Dominions', *The Times*, 9 October 1939.

26 WCM(39)43, 10 October 1939, CAB65/1; ibid., WCM(39)46, 13 October 1939; HCWM(29), 10 October 1939, DO121/6; Diary, Wednesday 11 October 1939, Lord Avon Papers (University of Birmingham), AP20/1/19.

27 Mansergh, *The Commonwealth and the Nations* (London, 1948), pp. 32–46.

28 MacDonald, 'Interview to the Oxford Colonial Records Project' (Rhodes House Library), p. 1.

29 Minutes by Lord Halifax and Cadogan, 11 February 1939, FO372/3315; Hankinson to Harvey, 28 March 1939, FO800/310.

30 Minute by Hadow, 12 September 1939, FO371/23966; Hankinson to Jebb, 7 September 1939, DO35/548D/3/128.

31 Notes by Norman Archer, 29 May 1962, Avon Papers, 27/1.

32 Diary, 14 September 1939, Lester Pearson Papers (Library and Archives Canada), MG 26, N8; the majority of the information comes from Norman Archer who worked as Eden's secretary and helped him with the relevant section of his memoirs. As a young naval officer he had served with the Russian fleet during the First World War and entered the DO as part of the post-war reconstruction stream. In his post-war correspondence with his former boss he refers to 'personal and secret letters which you used to write to Mr Chamberlain on matters arising out of the high commissioners meetings' but it has proven impossible to trace copies of these; Archer to Eden, 29 May 1962, Avon Papers, 27/1/62A.

33 Telegram to Dominion governments, 7 September 1939, DO35/548D; HCWM, 8 September 1939, DO121/6.

34 WP(G)(39)10, 14 October 1939, point 3, CAB21/874.

35 The Committee also agreed that the Dominions should not be invited to attend meetings of the Supreme War Council, restricting discussion to just themselves and the French. For a description of the War Council see Butler, *Grand Strategy*, p. 9.

36 WCM(39)17, 16 October 1939, CAB65/1; there were some reservations, most notably that meetings with the high commissioners should not take place very frequently 'in view of the heavy pressure on the members'.

37 Price to Barnard (Board of Trade), 14 October 1939, CAB104/247.

38 Thomas to Eden, 20 September 1939, CAB104/247; ibid., Graham (WO) to Jacob (Cabinet Secretariat), 16 September 1939.

39 Clark to DO (No. 162), 15 September 1939, CAB104/247.

40 Report no. W13797/9831/68, 20 September 1939, FO371/23963.

41 Minute by Hadow, 17 September 1939, FO371/23963; minute by Hadow, 12 September 1939, FO371/23966.

42 Minute by Cadogan, 27 September 1939, FO371/23963.

43 Barnard to Price, 17 September 1939, CAB104/247; Patrick Howarth, *Intelligence Chief Extraordinary* (London, 1986), p. 145.

44 Massey, *What's Past is Prologue*, pp. 297–98, 303–6; Garner cited in I. M. Cumpston, *Lord Bruce of Melbourne* (Melbourne, 1989), p. 159; Mansergh, *The Commonwealth Experience*, p. 283; Garner, *The Commonwealth Office*, p. 90; Holland, *Britain and the Commonwealth Alliance*, p. 204; Edwards, *Bruce of Melbourne*, pp. 277–80; Lorna Lloyd, *Diplomacy with a Difference: the Commonwealth Office of High Commissioner, 1880–2006* (Leiden, 2007), pp. 63–74.

45 HCWM(2), 8 September 1939, DO121/6.

46 Eden attended all of them with the exception of six in November, when he was conducting the Dominion minister's meeting to France. Of the Dominion high commissioners, the two most regular attendees were Massey, the Canadian representative, and Bruce from Australia who missed only one meeting.

47 Diary, 29 October 1940, Sydney Waterson Papers (University of Cape Town).

48 HCWM(5), 12 September 1939, DO121/6 – it was recorded the day after discussion; WCM(39)15, 14 September 1939, CAB65/1; Ismay to Simon, 15 September 1939, CAB104/247.

49   'Question by the Rt. Hon. Ellis-Smith to the Prime Minister', 21 September 1939, CAB21/874; the issue was also debated in the Dominions, Whiskard, high commissioner in Canberra, warned Whitehall that Menzies had told him, 'there was a growing opinion amongst his colleagues that the supply of information was very meagre … things were happening and would happen which vitally concerned Australia but about which they knew nothing until afterwards'. Surprisingly Lester Pearson viewed them as 'admirable for information'; 'Wartime Inter-governmental Consultation and Communication', n.d. (1940?), Pearson Papers, MG26, Vol. 71.

50   Duncan Hall, 'The British Commonwealth of Nations at War' in Duncan Hall and Elliot, *The British Commonwealth at War*, pp. 29–32; W. David McIntyre, *The Commonwealth of Nations: Origins and Impacts, 1869–1971* (London, 1977), p. 177; Madden and Darwin (eds), *The Dominions and India since 1900*, pp. 34–49; A. J. Stockwell, 'The War and the British Empire' in John Turner (ed.), *Britain and the First World War* (London, 1988), pp. 36–48; Beloff, *Imperial Sunset*, pp. 218–220; Maurice Hankey, *The Supreme Command, 1914–18, Vol. 2* (London, 1961), pp. 657–63; Hall, *Commonwealth*, pp. 160–76.

51   Op. cit., Hall, pp. 21–5; Judd, *Empire*, pp. 214–25; Porter, *The Lion's Share*, pp. 134–40.

52   Holland, *The Commonwealth Alliance*, pp. 1–151, 167–209.

53   Diary, 21 September 1939, Mackenzie King Papers.

54   Wilson to Chamberlain, 12 September 1939, DO35/1003/3/16.

55   Minute by Cavendish Bentinck, 4 October 1939, FO371/23963; WP(G)(39)10, 14 September 1939, CAB21/874.

56   Bickersteth to Euan Wallace, 1 October 1939, Hankey Papers; Campbell to DO, 5 October 1939, FO371/23967; DO to High Commissioners in Australia, Canada, New Zealand and South Africa, 4 October 1939, CAB21/489.

57   'Meetings with Dominion Ministers', November 1939, CAB99/1; Garner, *The Commonwealth Office*, pp. 197–8; there were six Canadians, two each from Australia and New Zealand and a single South African.

58   'Minutes of First Meeting', 1 November 1939; ibid., 'Minutes of Eighth Meeting', 20 November 1939. One of the delegates described his experiences of the meetings: 'The British are a phlegmatic race … it might have been the meeting of some suburban county council discussing the rates', Reitz, *No Outspan*, p. 248.

59   Diary, 2 November 1939 in Nigel Nicolson (ed.), *Harold Nicolson, Diaries and Letters 1939–45*, (New York, 1967), p. 41.

60   'Questions relating to Canadian War Finance', 1 December 1939 CAB21/490; 'I wrote in my diary, "So now it's to be a fight between a monopoly seller in Canada and a monopoly buyer here. Bad business this in wartime. Both sides are to blame"', Pearson, p. 145; London's suspicions seem not to have been misplaced in light of the following: 'It is not always wrong to turn other person's misfortune to one's personal advantage. And by the same token, it is not wrong for Canadian enterprises to turn to profitable account their advantageous position and opportunity in respect of the current war … our enterprises would be blameworthy if they failed to use the present opportunity to sell, to the maximum of possibility all they can … and to sell at prices established by the law of supply and demand', J. C. Kirkwood, 'The War and Business', *The Quarterly Review of Commerce* (No. VII; Autumn, 1939).

61   'A Discussion between the Chancellor, the Secretary of State for Dominion Affairs and Bruce and Casey', 24 November 1939, CAB21/490.

62   Diary, 11 October 1939, Avon Papers.

63   'Debate on the Address', 30 November 1939, *House of Commons Official Report* (Vol. 355), pp. 405–8, 761–2, 1, 341–2.

64   Peake (FO News Department) to Eden, 1 February 1940, Avon Papers, AP20/8/286; 'Research Draft prepared by Mrs Agnew', August 1945, CAB102/33; Diary, 24 April 1940, Pearson Papers.

65   Minute by Dixon, 26 January 1940, FO371/25224; ibid., minutes by Bentinck, 12 and 26 January 1940.

66   Minute by Dixon, 21 February 1940, DO35/1003/3/4/32; minute by Dixon, 26 January 1940, FO371/25224; ibid., minute by Bentinck, 26 January 1940.

67 Winston Churchill, *The Gathering Storm* (London, 1948), pp. 373, 569; S. Roskill, *The Navy at War, 1939–1945* (London, 1960), pp. 59–61; William Manchester, *Winston Churchill: The Caged Lion* (London, 1988), p. 572; David Reynolds, 'Churchill in 1940: The Worst and Finest Hour' in Roger Blake and Wm. Roger Louis (eds), *Churchill*, (London, 1993) pp. 241–5; Churchill to Chamberlain, 25 December 1939, Neville Chamberlain Papers; Clive Ponting, *Churchill* (London, 1994), pp. 416–28; Richard Collier, *The Years of Attrition* (London, 1993), pp. 18–32, 34–48; Martin Gilbert, *Finest Hour: Winston S. Churchill, 1939–1941* (London, 1983), pp. 127–284; David Irving, *Churchill's War, Vol. 1* (Australia, 1987), pp. 205–54; Campbell to Machtig, 27 February 1940, DO35/1072/276/124; Whiskard to Eden, 22 February 1940, DO121/111.

68 HCWM, 22–29 February 1940, DO121/7; 'October 1939', Lord Bruce's War Papers (National Archives of Australia, Canberra) AA1969/275/1; DO Minute, 16 March 1940, DO35/1000/1/101.

69 Machtig to Eden, 2 April 1940, DO121/66; ibid., Chamberlain to Mackenzie King, 8 April 1940.

70 Earl of Avon, *The Eden Memoirs*, pp. 95–6.

71 Minute by Dixon, 13 March 1940, FO371/25222; ibid., minute by Dixon, 20 March 1940.

72 Minute by Mason, 7 April 1940, FO371/25224; HCWM, 10/11 April 1940, DO121/7; J. W. Pickersgill, *The Mackenzie King Record: Vol. 1, 1939–44* (Toronto, 1960), pp. 77, 107.

73 Diary, 10 April 1940, Waterson Papers; Waterson had been an early beneficiary of Smuts' victory in September 1939 and his decision to take control of the External Affairs Department in Pretoria and purge the officials with a pronounced anti-British outlook who had dominated it pre-war. Another former minister turned diplomat, much as was the norm for Dominions who lacked a professional cadre of such officials, he was moved from Paris to London and it was made clear to the British government that the new man could be trusted; *Evening News*, n.d. (September 1939?), Waterson Papers; minute by Dixon, 6 March 1940, FO371/25224.

74 Diary, 3 April 1940, Waterson Papers; HCWM, 22 April 1940, DO121/7; 'Note on Supreme War Council', 16/24 April 1940, DO35/998/7/13; WM(39)15, 14 September 1939, CAB65/1; Gilbert, *Finest Hour*, p. 250; Diary, 24 April 1940, Pearson Papers.

75 HCWM, 1 May 1940, DO121/7; ibid. 4 May 1940; ibid., 6 May 1940.

76 Eden to Halifax, 9 May 1940, DO35/1000/1/110.

77 John Colville, *The Fringes of Power: Vol. 1* (London, 1985), pp. 139–44; John Charmley, *Churchill: The End of Glory* (London, 1993), pp. 395–434; Robert Blake, 'How Churchill Became Prime Minister' in Blake and Roger Louis (eds), *Churchill*, pp. 257–74; Sir John Wheeler–Bennett (et al.), *Action this Day: Working with Churchill* (London, 1968), pp. 203–4; Diary, 8 May 1940, Waterson Papers.

Notes to Chapter 4: Standing Alone

1 Ronald Hyam, 'Churchill and the British Empire' in Blake and Roger Louis (eds), *Churchill*, pp. 167–86; Watt, *Personalities and Policies*, p. 162; Machtig had 'some most interesting stories' about Churchill's relationship with the Dominions but he could not be induced to share them, instead preferring to keep them to himself, even after Churchill's death, Dixon to Batterbee, 21 March 1968, Batterbee Papers, Box 20; Gilbert, *Finest Hour*, p. 81; Sir Evelyn Wrench, 'Churchill and the Empire' in Charles Eade (ed.), *Churchill by His Contemporaries* (London, 1953), p. 288.

2 Alfred Emmott (Churchill's fellow MP at Oldham in the 1900 parliament) to Asquith, 20 May 1915, cited in Roy Jenkins, *Churchill* (London, 2001), p. 275.

3 Leo Amery, *My Political Life: Vol. 1, England Before the Storm* (London, 1953), p. 196. Although they were friends of a sort, the two men often clashed. So much so the individual who can take much of the credit for creating the DO would later complain that the wartime prime minister, 'Congenitally Little England' as he once referred to him, 'never really possessed an "imperial" or "commonwealth" intellect'; Roger Louis, *In the Name of God Go!*, p. 89; Roger Louis, 'Churchill and Egypt' in Blake and Roger Louis (eds), *Churchill*, p. 486.

4 Winston Churchill, 'The Mystery of Empire', *The Sunday Dispatch*, 17 March 1940 [N.B. written before the outbreak of war] Chartwell Papers (Churchill College), CHAR8/666.

5   Roger Louis, *Imperialism at Bay: The United States and the Decolonization of the British Empire* (London, 1978), p. 16; Churchill to Amery, 7 December 1924, DO121/1.

6   Winston Churchill, 'The Statute of Westminster', (n.d.) Chartwell Papers, CHAR8/565.

7   Martin Gilbert, *Winston S. Churchill (Vol. 5, 1922–39)* (London, 1976), p. 584.

8   Garner, *The Commonwealth Office*, pp. 13, 55, 153.

9   Sir Ian Jacob cited in Lord Normanbrook (ed.), *Action this Day: Working with Churchill* (London, 1968), p. 204.

10 'Winston Churchill', *The Round Table* (March 1965), p. 104.

11 Diary, 3 November 1942, Waterson Papers.

12 I. Stewart, *The Struggle for Crete* (London, 1966), p. 51.

13 'Memoir written for the Mackenzie King colloquium at University of Waterloo 1975', MacDonald Papers, 109/7/48; Roland Quinault, 'Churchill and Australia 1899–1945', *War and Society*, (Vol. 6, No. 1; May 1988), pp. 41–9; Robert Menzies, 'Churchill and the Commonwealth' in Sir James Marchant (ed.), *WSC: Servant of Crown and Commonwealth* (London, 1954), p. 92.

14 Typical were his comments to a Foreign Press Association lunch in March 1940 at the Savoy, when he had told his audience that the scope and significance of the Dominions' support had 'no parallel in history' and would prove decisive when it was fully developed; 'Dominions' Own Cause', *The Times*, 14 March 1940. The FO had been enthusiastic supporters of what was viewed as an opportunity to be seen to be more visibly supportive of the Dominions' effort. The DO were uncertain as to whether this would be such a good idea in light of the Canadian's recent obstructions and did their best to stall; it was perhaps fortunate therefore that the German attack against Norway and the change in government this precipitated should have forced a cancellation; Charles Peake (head of FO News Dept.) to Eden, 1 February 1940, Avon Papers, AP20/8/286; ibid., 'Handwritten note by Eden', n.d. (1962?), 27/1/62B; Notes by Archer, 29 May 1962; Chamberlain to Mackenzie King, 2 April 1940, DO121/66; ibid., Machtig to Eden, 2 April 1940; Stephenson to Eden and Machtig, 30 March 1940, DO35/998/7/1; ibid., Machtig to Eden, 2 April 1940; Mansergh, *Problems of Wartime Cooperation*, p. 40.

15 Diary 17 April 1940, Waterson Papers; ibid., 17 April 1940; 'Conversation with Neville Henderson', 13 October 1939, Bruce Papers.

16 'Eden leaves us for the WO. I'm sorry: it has been most interesting and agreeable working with him for eight months, seeing him every day. He is a delightful fellow and I should say certain to be PM one day. In about 10 years time he will make an ideal Conservative peacetime PM. He is able, receptive, liberal and I think quite incapable of any kind of intrigue or dirty work – the type of man an Englishman likes – but he is not ruthless or tough enough for war'; Diary 11 May 1940, Waterson Papers; Diary, 12 May 1940, Avon Papers.

17 Oliver Stanley to Churchill, 13 May 1940, Chartwell Papers, CHAR20/11/62–64.

18 Ben Pimlott (ed.), *The Second World War Diary of Hugh Dalton, 1940–45* (London, 1986), pp. 190–1.

19 Memoirs, May 1940–April 1943, p. 6, Sir John Martin Papers (Churchill College) MART.

20 Minute by Garner, 18 September 1940, DO35/1012/40/1; this was an apparently common difficulty, during a September 1940 High Commissioner meeting he had gone to sleep 'peacefully' whilst the DW telegrams were being read; Diary 30 September 1940, Waterson Papers.

21 HCWM, 17 May 1940, DO121/8; Diary 15 May 1940, Waterson Papers; ibid., Diary 17 May 1940; Diary 3 June 1940; Diary, 23 June 1940; HCWM, 25 June 1940, DO121/8; Diary, 15 May 1940, Massey Papers (University of Toronto); Dairy, 15 May 1940, Pearson Papers; Bruce to Menzies, 15 May 1940, in R. G. Neale (ed.), *Documents on Australian Foreign Policy, Vol. 3, 1940* (Canberra, 1979) (hereafter 'DAFP III').

22 HCWM, 4 May 1940, DO121/8; Bentinck to Dixon, 1 May 1940, FO371/25218.

23 Ibid., Parkinson to Cadogan, 7 May 1940; Cadogan to Bentinck, 7 May 1940.

24 Parkinson to Batterbee, 16 May 1940, Batterbee Papers, Box 7/3.

25 Ibid., Cadogan to Bentinck, 9 May 1940; David Dilks (ed.), *The Diaries of Sir Alexander Cadogan, 1938–1945* (London, 1971), pp. 276–86.

26 Minute by Bentinck, 13 May 1940, FO371/25222.

27 Menzies to DO, 23 May 1940, DO35/1003/2/11/1/1B; Churchill to Dominion Prime Ministers, 23 May 1940, PREM4/43B/1; WCM(40)140, 26 May 1940, CAB65/13.

28 Whiskard to DO, 27 May 1940, DO35/1003/2/11/1/1B; ibid., Batterbee to DO, 27 May 1940; Harding to DO, 27 May 1940; John Robertson and John McCarthy, *Australian War Strategy 1939–1945* (Brisbane, 1985), pp. 75–80; Diary, 24 May 1940, Mackenzie King Papers; 'We Shall be Together', *Time*, 27 May 1940.

29 Hill, *Cabinet Decisions on Foreign Policy*, pp. 156–63, 169–73; HCWM, 28 May 1940, DO121/8; 'Memorandum', May 1940, DO35/548E/22/9/3.

30 Harding to Batterbee, 5 June 1940, Batterbee Papers, Box 6/4.

31 P. G. Edwards, 'R.G.Menzies Appeals to the United States, May–June 1940', *Australian Outlook* (No. 28; 1974), pp. 64–70; P. G. Edwards, 'S.M. Bruce, R.G. Menzies and Australia's War Aims and Peace Aims, 1939–1940', *Historical Studies* (Vol. 17, No. 66; 1976/77), pp. 10, 11.

32 Eden to Inskip, 3 June 1940, DO35/1003/2/11/1/1B; ibid. WO to Archer, 30 May 1940; New Zealand troops were reported to have cheered when they were told of Italy's entry into the war as it 'put an end to a trying period of uncertainty'; 'Reaction in the Dominions', *The Times*, 13 June 1940.

33 'Memorandum by the First Lord of the Admiralty on Australian and New Zealand Naval Defence', WP135(39), 23 November 1939, CAB67/3; WCM(39)92, 23 November 1939, CAB65/2.

34 Dixon to Ronald (FO), 10 June 1940, DO35/1003/8/13; ibid. minute by Garner, 13 June 1940; minute by Stephenson, 14 June 1940; Mansergh, *Problems of Wartime Cooperation*, pp. 43–4.

35 WCM(40)141, 27 May 1940, CAB65/13; Edwards, *Bruce of Melbourne*, pp. 286–99; Gilbert, *Finest Hour*, p. 435.

36 Telegram to Dominions, 12 June 1940, DO35/1003/2/11/1/1B; Telegram for Dominion Prime Ministers only, 14 June 1940; P. M. H. Bell, *A Certain Eventuality* (London, 1974), p. 31–54; HCWM, 12 June 1940, DO121/8; WCM(40)165, 13 June 1940, CAB65/7; ibid., WCM(40)165, 13 June 1940; HCWM, 13 June 1940, DO121/8; Chiefs of Staff Report, June 1940, WP168(40), CAB66/7; Chiefs of Staff Report, June 1940, WP201(40), CAB66/8; Dairy, 3 June 1940, Waterson Papers.

37 Robert Menzies, *Afternoon Light* (London, 1967), pp. 17–19; Whiskard to Eden, 22 February 1940, DO121/11; Menzies to DO, 16 June 1940, DO35/1003/11/3/3; ibid., FO to DO, 19 June 1940; Menzies to Bruce, 17 June 1940, DO35/1003/11/3/4; ibid., Churchill to Menzies, 23 June 1940; Menzies to DO, 18 June 1940, DO35/1003/1/3/7; ibid., DO to Whiskard, 21 June 1940.

38 Batterbee to DO, 15 June 1940, DO35/1003/11/4/1; Governor-General to Caldecote, 15 June 1940, DO35/1003/11/4/2; ibid., Machtig to Phillips, 22 June 1940; Batterbee to DO, 18 June 1940, DO35/1003/11/4/4. Wellington's support was welcomed within the FO: 'On the night of 15 June [1940], heart-warming messages reached 10 Downing Street from Australia and New Zealand. Both offered their unconditional support. "If HM Government in the United Kingdom decide to fight on" said the telegram from Wellington, "we pledge this Dominion to remain with them to the end, and we are confident this policy is unchangeable in the Dominion ... whatever the decision ... in these most difficult circumstances, it will be understood, accepted and supported by us to the end". Churchill replied at 3.30am: "I am deeply touched by your message, which is only in keeping with all that the Mother Country has ever received in peace or war from New Zealand"', David Dilks (ed.), *The Diaries of Sir Alexander Cadogan*, pp. 302–3.

39 Caldecote to Batterbee, 26 July 1940, Batterbee Papers, Box 6/1; Mason to Garner, 19 June 1940, DO35/1003/11/4/2; ibid., Garner to Stephenson, 20 June 1940; Machtig to Caldecote, 21 June 1940, DO35/1003/11/4/4; Anne Orde, *The Eclipse of Great Britain, The United States and British Imperial Decline, 1895–1956* (London, 1996), pp. 130–1.

40 Harding to DO, 19 June 1940, DO35/1004/11/5/3.

41 Smuts to Churchill, 12 July 1940, DO35/1003/11/1/36; ibid., Churchill to Smuts, 13 July 1940; A. J. Marder, *From the Dardanelles to Oran* (London, 1974), pp. 206–88; Bell, *A Certain Eventuality*, pp. 38, 152–6; Warren Tute, *The Deadly Stroke* (London, 1973), pp. 36–62; Churchill, *Their Finest Hour*, p. 573.

42 Winston S. Churchill (ed.), *Never Give In!: The Best Of Winston Churchill's Speeches* (Pimlico, 2004), 'This Was Their Finest Hour', 18 June 1940, p. 227.

43   Garner, *The Commonwealth Office*, p. 201.
44   Minute by Liesching, 17 June 1940, DO35/1003/11/1/4.
45   David Day, *Menzies and Churchill at War* (New York, 1988), pp. 25–7; Churchill, *Finest Hour*, p. 214.
46   Batterbee to Whiskard, 6 July 1940, Batterbee Papers, Box 7/5; ibid., Whiskard to Batterbee, 22 July 1940.
47   Ibid., Batterbee to Whiskard, 6 July 1940; HCWM, 6–18 July 1940, DO121/9.
48   Harding to DO, 19 June 1940, DO35/1004/11/5/3.
49   Halifax to Massey, 23 June 1940, DO121/8.
50   Diary, 23 June 1940, Waterson Papers; HCWM, 25 June 1940, DO121/8.
51   Diary, 28 June 1940, Waterson Papers.
52   Ibid., Waterson to Smuts, 26 July 1940.
53   Ibid., Diary, 26 July 1940.
54   WCM(40)214, 29 July 1940, CAB65/14.
55   HCWM, 31 July 1940, DO121/9.
56   'Note of a Meeting', 31 July 1940, DO35/1000/1/124; Robertson and McCarthy, *Australian War Strategy*, pp. 146–9.
57   'Progress of the War', 20 August 1940, *House of Lord Official Report* (Vol. 67), pp. 272–3.
58   HCWM, 8 August 1940, DO121/9; *The Memoirs of Lord Ismay* (London, 1960), p. 192.
59   HCWM, 23 August 1940, DO121/9; ibid. 26 August 1940; ibid., 29 August 1940.
60   Eden to Churchill, 18 September 1940, PREM3/63/13; ibid. Eden to Churchill, 20 September 1940.
61   Gilbert, *Finest Hour*, pp. 747–52, 787–90, 804–10; Irving, *Churchill's War*, pp. 385–6, 420–4; Churchill, *Finest Hour*, pp. 390–4, 569–72; HCWM, 24 September 1940, DO121/9; WCM(40)259, 26 September 1940, CAB65/16.
62   Churchill, *Finest Hour*, pp. 389–90; minute by Holmes, 1 October 1940, DO35/1003/11/1/74.
63   Bruce to Menzies, 26 September 1940, DAFP III; ibid., Menzies to Churchill, 29 September 1940; 'Minute', September 1940, Lord Bruce's War Files, AA1969/275/1; HCWM, 26 September 1940, DO121/9; Churchill to Menzies, 2 October 1940, DO35/1003/11/1/74; ibid., 'Note by Bruce of talk with Churchill', 2 October 1940; ibid., Bruce to Menzies, 2 October 1940; ibid., minute by Holmes, 1 October 1940; Diary, 3 October 1940, Waterson Papers.
64   Ibid., Diary, 25 September 1940.
65   HCWM, 1 October 1940, DO121/9; Menzies to Churchill, 4 October 1940, DAFP III; Whiskard to DO, 1 October 1940, DO35/1003/11/1/74.
66   Churchill to Menzies, 6 October 1940, PREM3/63/13.
67   Garner, *The Commonwealth Office*, p. 199; Machtig to Batterbee, 28 August 1940, DO35/1000/1/124; ibid., Liesching to Batterbee, 3 September 1940; Machtig to Batterbee, 28 August 1940; Diary, 2 September 1940, Avon Papers; Machtig to Batterbee, 28 August 1940, Batterbee Papers, Box 7/2.
68   Caldecote to Batterbee, 26 July 1940, Batterbee Papers, Box 6/1; Churchill to Caldecote, 15 August 1940, Chartwell Papers, CHAR20/13/8.
69   Ibid., Churchill to Caldecote, 2 October 1940; he would now be the Lord Chancellor's effective deputy, serving as the second most senior judge in the country after Lord Simon.
70   Diary, 31 October 1940, Lord Woolton Papers (Bodleian Library, Oxford), M. S. Woolton.
71   Duncan to Lady Selbourne, 8 October 1940, Duncan Papers.
72   A. R. Peters, *Anthony Eden at the Foreign Office, 1931–1938* (New York, 1986), pp. 258–60; Lord Todd, 'Robert Arthur James Gascoyne Cecil, Fifth Marquess of Salisbury, 1893–1972', *Biographical Memoirs of Fellows of the Royal Society* (Vol. 19; Dec. 1973), pp. 621–7.
73   Amery to Smuts, 16 October 1940, cited in Jean Van der Poel (ed.), *Smuts Papers, Vol. 6* (Cambridge, 1973), p. 256; Pimlott, *Diary of Hugh Dalton*, p. 53; 'Neville [Chamberlain] was in a rage yesterday and in the morning whilst he was going over questions he delivered himself of an angry tirade against the "Glamour Boys". More particularly, Bobbety Cranborne who is the most dangerous of the lot. "Beware" he said "of rampant idealists. All Cecils are that"'; 5 May 1939, cited in Robert Rhodes James, *Chips: The Diaries of Sir Henry Channon* (London, 1967), p. 244.

74 In being appointed as leader of the House of Lords he took an office which both his father and grandfather had held before him. An article in *Commonwealth and Empire Review* some years later commented not just on this unique family record but also the manner in which he resembled his most celebrated ancestor, Sir Robert Cecil; 'Commonwealth Consultations', *Commonwealth and Empire Review* (March–May 1945), pp. 37–8.

75 John Colville, *Winston Churchill and His Inner Circle* (New York, 1981), p. 223; if there was the potential for family animosity, from an early age, Churchill had nonetheless established what would prove to be a lasting friendship with Lord Hugh Cecil, 'the most intimate friend he ever had' and his best man at his wedding; Rene Kraus, *The Men around Churchill* (New York, 1941), pp. 72–4; Colville, *The Fringes of Power: Vol. 1*, p. 382.

76 Churchill, *The Gathering Storm*, p. 222.

77 Colville, *Inner Circle*, p. 227.

78 Churchill to Randolph, 18 April 1944, Chartwell Papers, CHAR1/381/21–31.

79 Churchill to Halifax, 28 July 1940, Chartwell Papers, CHAR20/13/8.

80 *Punch*, 17 July 1940.

Notes to Chapter 5: Coalition United

1 Garner, *The Commonwealth Office*, pp. 193–4; Mansergh, *Problems of Wartime Cooperation*, pp. 45–6.

2 Ronald Tree, *When the Moon was High* (London, 1975) pp. 54–5.

3 Garner, *The Commonwealth Office*, pp. 163, 176–9.

4 Stirling to Department of External Affairs, Canberra, 5 October 1940 in W. J. Hudson and H. J. W. Stokes (eds), *Documents on Australian Foreign Policy, 1937–1949: Vol. 4, July 1940–June 1941* (Canberra, 1980), p. 206 (hereafter 'DAFP IV').

5 Cranborne to Waterson, 17 October 1940, Waterson Papers.

6 Ibid., Diary, 3 October 1940; Diary, 4 November 1940; Diary, 3 October 1940, Massey Papers; Bruce to Menzies, 3 October 1940, Bruce Papers.

7 Cranborne to Halifax, 24 October 1940, FO371/25224.

8 Skelton to Wrong, 2 March 1939, Pearson Papers.

9 Note by Costley-White, May 1940, DO35/998/7/11.

10 Menzies to Bruce, 17 June 1940, DO35/1003/11/3/4; ibid., Churchill to Menzies, 23 June 1940.

11 Day, *Menzies and Churchill at War*, pp. 30–4.

12 Whiskard to DO, 20 September 1939, DO121/46.

13 Whiskard to DO, 23 October 1940, DO35/998/7/11.

14 Sir Frederic Eggleston to Mackay, 8 October 1940, Eggleston Papers (National Library of Australia), MS423/1/143.

15 DO to Dominion Governments, 22 April 1940, DO35/998/7/1; Garner to Parkinson, 16 May 1940, DO35/998/7/9; DO to PM, 20 May 1940, PREM4/43A/11; Peck (PM's Office) to Costley-White, 27 May 1940, DO35/998/7/9; ibid., Machtig to Secretary of State, 31 May 1940; ibid., DO to Peck, 6 June 1940; Machtig to Cranborne, 24 October 1940, DO35/998/7/11.

16 Note prepared by Costley-White, May 1940, DO35/998/7/11.

17 Ibid., memorandum by Stephenson, 26 October 1940; ibid., memorandum by Cranborne (for War Cabinet), 28 October 1940.

18 Josiah Wedgewood MP to Churchill, 25 October 1940, Chartwell Papers, CHAR20/8/122. This he had been advised to strongly reject on the grounds that '[the Dominions] would get swelled head; we are the Power House and pander to them enough already'.

19 'The War Situation', 8 October 1940, *House of Lords Official Report* (Vol. 67), pp. 402–8, 453–6; ibid., Lord David Davies, Question 'Dominions and the War', 8 August 1940, p. 161; Elibank to Churchill, 10 October 1940, PREM4/43/A/13; Mansergh, *Problems of Wartime Cooperation*, p. 93.

20 Churchill, *Finest Hour*, pp. 422–38; Gilbert, *Finest Hour*, pp. 876–90.

21 Stephenson to Machtig, 30 October 1940, DO35/998/7/13.

22 Mackenzie King to Churchill, 31 October 1940, DO35/998/7/13; ibid., Prime Minister's Personal Minute (No. M282), copied to Cranborne, 4 November 1940; ibid., Cranborne to PM, 8 November 1940.

23 Ibid., PM to Cranborne, 10 November 1940.

24 Cranborne to PM, 11 November 1940, DO35/998/7/13; ibid., Bridges to Cranborne, 11 November 1940; PM to Cranborne, 13 November 1940.

25 Cranborne to Churchill, 21 December 1940, CHAR20/11/114–116. Suggestions that he would be moved to Washington persisted into the following year and were clearly a source of annoyance to Cranborne: 'What an absurd idea about my going to Washington! I am glad to hear that there is nothing in it. Apart from everything else, it would be the greatest possible mistake for Edward to throw up the sponge after less than six months. Every ambassador takes at least a year to settle down to a new post. He cannot expect to be known and liked before that. And especially in this time for Edward, who is by nature shy and fastidious. I hope we shall hear no more of such nonsense'; Cranborne to Emrys-Evans, 31 July 1941, Emrys-Evans Papers (British Library), Add. MSS 58240.

26 'Information for the Dominions', 5 June 1940, WP192(40), CAB66/8.

27 Colonel Bishop to Holmes, 15 December 1940, DO35/1003/2/11/25.

28 Bishop to Machtig, 10 December 1940 within 'Information for the Dominions', WP466(40), December 1940, CAB66/14.

29 Machtig to Cranborne, 20 December 1940, DO35/1003/2/11/25; Pimlott, *Diary of Hugh Dalton*, pp. 120–2.

30 Churchill to Cranborne, 12 November 1940, Chartwell Papers, CHAR20/13/8; ibid., Churchill to Cranborne, 1 December 1940; Churchill to Cranborne, 21 December 1940.

31 Ibid., Cranbourne to Churchill, 23 December 1940.

32 Ibid., Churchill to Cranborne, 25 December 1940.

33 Note by Bruce of conversation with Churchill, 18 December 1940, Bruce Papers.

34 Churchill to Cranbourne, 7 January 1941, DO121/119.

35 Minute by Holmes, 30 December 1940, DO35/1003/2/11/25; ibid., minute by Stephenson, 1 January 1941; ibid., Machtig to Cranboune, 9 January 1941; Cranbourne to Churchill, 8 January 1941, DO121/10A; minute by Cranbourne, 12 January 1941, DO35/1003/2/11/25.

36 Diary, 11 January 1941, Menzies Papers (National Library of Australia), MS4936.

37 Mansergh, *Problems of Wartime Cooperation*, p. 90.

38 Day, *Menzies and Churchill at War*, pp. 33–40, 63–171; *Daily Telegraph*, 22 February 1941 and *Sunday Times*, 23 February 1941; an excellent account of the visit made to Britain by Menzies can be found in Galen Roger Perras, 'Hurry Up and Wait: Robert Menzies, Mackenzie King, and the Failed Attempt to Form an Imperial War Cabinet in 1941', *Working Papers in Military and International History* (No. 3, September 2004), Centre for Contemporary History and Politics, University of Salford, pp. 2–42.

39 Diary, 22 February 1941, Menzies Papers.

40 Menzies to Fadden, 25 February 1941, DAFP IV; ibid., Fadden to Menzies, 26 February 1941; Menzies to Fadden, 4 March 1941.

41 Ismay to Brooke-Popham, 15 June 1941, Brooke-Popham Papers (Liddell Hart Archives), V/1/13.

42 Major-General I.S.O. Playfair et al., *Official History of the Second World War: The Mediterranean and Middle East Vol. 2: The Germans Come to the Help of Their Ally, 1941* (London, 1956), pp. 1–40, 153–72; Martin van Creveld, 'Prelude to Disaster: the British Decision to Aid Greece, 1940–41', *Journal of Contemporary History* (Vol. 9, No. 3; 1974), pp. 65–92; Field Marshal Earl Wavell, 'The British Expedition to Greece, 1941', *The Army Quarterly* (Vol. 59, No. 2; January 1950), pp. 178–85; David Day, *The Great Betrayal, Britain, Australia and the Onset of the Pacific War 1939–42* (Melbourne, 1988), pp. 110–41; David Horner, *Inside the War Cabinet* (NSW: Allen and Unwin Ltd., 1996), pp. 48–59; Sheila Lawlor, *Churchill and the Politics of War, 1940–41* (Cambridge, 1994), pp. 167–259; Mansergh, *Problems of Wartime Cooperation*, pp. 96–101; General Freyberg

to Churchill, 25 March 1949, Sir G.S. Cox Papers (Alexander Turnbull Library, Wellington) 2003–005–15/10; Callum MacDonald, *The Lost Battle: Crete, 1941* (London, 1993) pp. 87–113, 186–307; Antony Beevor, *Crete: The Battle and the Resistance* (London, 1991), pp. 30–82, 82–226; Brigadier A. T. J. Bell, 'The Battle for Crete – The Tragic Truth', *Australian Defence Force Journal* (No. 88, May/June 1991), pp. 15–18.

43 Sir Percy Joske, *Sir Robert Menzies: A New, Informal Memoir* (Sydney, 1978), p. 115; Diary, 17 April 1941, Pearson Papers.

44 'The Empire and the War', 2 April 1941, *House of Lords Official Report* (Vol. 118), pp. 952–73.

45 Diary, 30 April 1941 and 1 May 1941, Hankey Papers; Irving, *Churchill's War: Vol. 1,* pp. 550–6.

46 'Curtin Falls on Menzies', *Reynolds Illustrated News*, 27 April 1941.

47 Gilbert, *Finest Hour*, pp. 1083–4.

48 Cranborne to Churchill, 12 May 1941, PREM4/43A/12; ibid., Churchill to Cranborne, 13 May 1941.

49 Churchill to Cranborne, 25 March 1941, Chartwell Papers, CHAR20/13/8; minute by Holmes, 13 April 1941, DO35/1012/28/1/1.

50 Churchill to Mackenzie King, 11 May 1941 in Churchill, *The Second World War: Vol. 3, The Grand Alliance* (London, 1949), p. 595.

51 Ibid., Churchill to Mackenzie King, 10 May 1941; Day, *The Great Betrayal*, p. 134.

52 Cranborne to Churchill, 12 May 1941, PREM4/43A/12; Mackenzie King to Lord Davies, 19 May 1941, DO35/999/8/3; ibid., Mackenzie King to Cranborne, 20 May 1941.

53 Churchill to Foreign and Dominion Secretaries, 30 May 1941, PREM4/43A/12; ibid., Cranborne to Churchill, 30 May 1941.

54 Cranborne to MacDonald, 31 May 1941, Malcolm MacDonald Papers (University of Durham), 14/4/13.

55 Cranborne to Churchill, 3 June 1941, PREM4/43A/12; ibid., Cranborne to Churchill, 6 June 1941; Minutes of Advisory War Council Meeting, Canberra, 28 May 1941, cited in Horner, *Inside the War Cabinet*, p. 62.

56 Halifax to FO, 12 June 1941, FO371/27575; Menzies had told his colleagues in Canberra upon his eventual return, 'Mr Churchill has no conception of the British Dominions as separate entities. Furthermore, the more the distance from the heart of the Empire, the less he thinks of it'; cited in Christopher Thorne, *Allies of a Kind: The United States, Britain and the War against Japan, 1941–1945* (London, 1978), p. 63.

57 Diary, 5 June 1941, Hankey Papers; General Ismay to Brooke–Popham, 15 June 1941, Ismay Papers, V/1/13; Cranborne to Churchill, 6 June 1941, PREM4/43A/12; Diary, 6 June 1941, Hankey Papers; General Auchinleck to Ismay, 29 September 1941, Ismay Papers, IV/Con/1/1A; Garner, *The Commonwealth Office*, p. 203; this idea was, indirectly, forwarded to King George VI but his reaction was not recorded – Diary, 20 October 1940, Colville Papers (Churchill College), CLVL.

58 Diary, 5 June 1941, Waterson Papers.

59 WHC, 8 July 1941, DO121/11; Diary, 10 July 1941, Waterson Papers.

60 Casey to Menzies, 30 May 1940, DAFP III, p. 361; Bruce to Menzies, 29 June 1940, Bruce Papers; ibid., 'Speech given by Bruce at a dinner for Sir Ronald Cross', 18 May 1941; Cranborne to Churchill, 5 June 1941, DO35/1009/446/1/21.

61 Churchill to Smuts, 13 June 1941, PREM4/43A/16; Waterson to Smuts, 11 June 1941, Waterson Papers; ibid., Smuts to Waterson, 16 June 1941; Smuts to Duncan, 16 June 1941, Duncan Papers; Cranborne to Churchill, 17 June 1941, DO35/99/8/2.

62 Cranborne to Churchill, 17 June 1941, PREM4/43A/12.

63 Colville Diary, 21 June 1941/p. 480.

64 Churchill to Cranborne, 17 June 1941, PREM4/43A/12; Colville to Garner, 18 June 1941, DO35/999/8/2; Colville, *His Inner Circle*, pp. 174–5.

65 Cranborne to Churchill, 18 June 1941, PREM4/43A/12; ibid., Churchill to Dominion Prime Ministers, 21 June 1941.

66 Pickersgill, *The Mackenzie King Record*, pp. 216–17.

67 Minute by P. Mason, 15 October 1940, FO371/25224.

68   Mackenzie King to Churchill, 22 June 1941, PREM4/43A/12; ibid., Statement to the House of Commons by Churchill, 24 June 1941.

69   MacDonald to Cranborne, 1 August 1941, DO121/68; ibid., 'Note No. 1', 1 August 1941.

70   In the draft of his memoirs, the British high commissioner later asserted that, in his view, Churchill generally regarded his Canadian counterpart as 'a pygmy [and] with a touch of contempt'; Draft Memoirs, n.d., MacDonald Papers, 121/10/10.

71   Diary, 16 July 1941, Mackenzie King Papers; Garner to Martin, 14 July 1941, Chartwell Papers, CHAR20/27/36; ibid., Churchill to Cranborne, 18 July 1941, CHAR20/27/38; ibid., 'Note No. 2', 1 August 1941; Mackenzie King to Menzies, 2 August 1941, DO121/68; ibid., Cranborne to MacDonald, 11 August 1941; Pickersgill, *The Mackenzie King Record*, p. 235.

72   *The Times*, 13 August 1941; Menzies to Bruce, 8 August 1941 in W. J. Hudson and H. J. W. Stokes (eds), *Documents on Australian Foreign Policy, 1937–1949: Vol. 5, July 1941–June 1942* (Canberra, 1982) (hereafter 'DAFP V').

73   Diary, 14 April 1941, Menzies Papers; Diary, 17 April 1941, Pearson Papers; Diary, 1 May 1941, Hankey Papers; DO to Eden, 14 August 1941, FO954/4; Diary, 15 August 1941, Harvey Papers (British Library, London), ADD.MD.56398.

74   'Extracts of a telegram dated 2 August 1941', MacDonald Papers, 14/5/11–16; Orde, *The Eclipse of Great Britain*, pp. 135–6.

75   Churchill to Attlee, 7 August 1941, Chartwell Papers, CHAR20/48/2; Bridges to Churchill, 5 August 1941, PREM3/485/3; MacDonald to Cranborne, 19 August 1941, MacDonald Papers, 14/5/9.

76   Batterbee to Cranborne, 29 April 1941, Batterbee Papers, 6/1; Diary, 30 June 1941, Waterson Papers; Diary, 22 August 1941, Mackenzie King Papers.

77   Smuts to Churchill, 23 August 1941, DO35/1009/446/1/38; Attlee to Churchill, 14 August 1941, Chartwell Papers, CHAR20/23.

78   Churchill to Menzies, 18 August 1941, Chartwell Papers, CHAR20/38/112.

79   Diary, 20 August 1941, Harvey Papers; DO to Eden, 14 August 1941, FO954/4; Diary, 25 August 1941, Mackenzie King Papers.

80   J. J. Dedman, 'Defence Policy Decisions Before Pearl Harbor', *Australian Journal of Politics and History*, No. 13 (1967), pp. 343–4; Australian Cabinet Minutes (Vol. 7), 19 August 1941, (National Archives, Canberra) CRS A2697; Paul Hasluck, *The Government and the People* (Canberra, 1973) pp. 495–6.

81   Diary, 22 August 1941, Mackenzie King Papers; ibid., Diary, 24 August 1941; Diary, 5 September 1941; HCWM, 22 August 1941, DO121/11.

82   Cross to Cranborne, 13 August 1941, CAB120/20; A. W. Martin, *Robert Menzies, A Life: Vol. 1* (Melbourne, 1993), pp. 364–5, 373–8; Menzies, *Afternoon Light* (London, 1967), pp. 14, 52–4.

83   Churchill to Menzies, 29 August 1941, DO121/19; Waterson to Smuts, 30 August 1941, Waterson Papers.

84   Diary, 5 September 1941, Mackenzie King Papers; ibid., 16 October 1941; Churchill to Athlone, 12 September 1941, PREM4/44/10.

85   Diary, 22 August 1941, Massey Papers; Massey to Pearson, 12 September 1941, Pearson Papers.

86   Cranborne to Emrys-Evans, 31 August 1941, Emrys-Evans Papers.

Notes to Chapter 6: Pacific Test

1   Fadden to Bruce, 29 August 1941, DAFP V; Martin, *Menzies*, pp. 364–5.

2   Sir Earle Page, *Truant Surgeon* (London, 1963), p. 298.

3   Hasluck, *The Government and the People*, pp. 505–7.

4   Cross to Cranborne, 20 January 1942, Emrys-Evans Papers.

5   Bruce to Fadden, 29 August 1941, Bruce Papers.

6   Cross to Cranborne, 13 January 1944, DO121/11; Bruce to Fadden, 29 August 1941, DAFP V.

7   Garner, *The Commonwealth Office*, p. 211.

8   Churchill to Fadden, 29 August 1941, PREM4/50/4A.

9   Diary, 25 August 1941, Waterson Papers; ibid., Waterson to Smuts, 30 August 1941; Diary, 2 September 1941; Waterson to Smuts, 30 August 1941; Smuts to Waterson, 2 September 1941.

10 Churchill to Fadden, 31 August 1941, DAFP V.

11 Fadden to Churchill, 4 September 1941, DO35/1010/476/3/30.

12 Fadden to Churchill, 5 September 1941, DO35/999/8/15.

13 'Dominions and the War: Voice in Direction', *The Times*, 12 June 1941; ibid., 'The Dominions and the War Cabinet', 13 August 1941; 'Dominions' Part in the War: Question of Cabinet Representation', 28 August 1941; 'The Dominions' Part', 25 August 1941.

14 Cranborne to Churchill, 4 September 1941, PREM4/50/5.

15 Cranborne to Churchill, 6 September 1941, DO35/999/8/13.

16 It also left him unsure about his high commissioner: 'I really don't know what has happened to Ronnie. Apart from telephoning every day to say that he must have a new car or two new bathrooms, 'on public grounds', he has now taken to lecturing Australian Ministers as if they were small and rather dirty boys. The air of the Antipodes seems to have gone to his head …'; Cranborne to Emrys-Evans, 31 August 1941, Emrys-Evans Papers.

17 Churchill to Cranborne, 6 September 1941, PREM4/50/5; '[Page] was no polished Bruce. He was a country doctor, who, having made good in Macquarie Street as a very fine surgeon, got into politics and stayed there by a remarkable shrewdness in anticipating which way the cat was going to jump, and jumping before it'; 'Our Best Men Must Go to Singapore and London', *Sydney Daily Telegraph*, 23 December 1941.

18 Minute by Stephenson, 8 September 1941, DO35/999/8/13; Machtig to Cranborne, 9 September 1941, DO35/999/4; ibid., Cranborne to Machtig, 10 September 1941.

19 Sir Arthur Fadden, *They Called Me Artie* (Melbourne, 1969), pp. 73–8; Sir Arthur Fadden, 'Forty Days and Forty Nights: Memoir of a Wartime Prime Minister', *Australian Outlook* (Vol. 27; 1973), pp. 9–11.

20 Cranborne to Churchill, 22 April 1941, PREM3/206/1–3; Fadden, *They Called Me Artie*, pp. 58–9; Judith Brett, *Robert Menzies' Forgotten People* (Australia, 1992), pp. 250–1.

21 Day, *The Great Betrayal*, pp. 153–5; Horner, *High Command, Australia and Allied Strategy* (Sydney, 1982), pp. 100–13; Halifax to FO, 12 June 1941, FO371/27575.

22 Menzies to Churchill, 20 July 1941, DAFP V; ibid., Churchill to Menzies, 9 August 1941.

23 Horner, *High Command*, pp. 104–17. Blamey was even willing to make the dubious claim that his troops in Tobruk should be replaced because they were no longer medically capable of its defence; Blamey to General Auchinleck, 18 July 1941 cited in Robertson and McCarthy, *Australian War Strategy*, pp. 125–6; Duffy (Acting Official Secretary) to DO, 25 February 1946, DO35/1767.

24 Sebastian Cox, '"The Difference between White and Black": Churchill, Imperial Politics and Intelligence before the 1941 Crusader Offensive', *Intelligence and National Security* (Vol. 9, No. 3; July 1994), pp. 413–15; Fadden to Churchill, 5 September 1941, PREM3/63/2; ibid., Churchill to Auchinleck, 6 September 1941.

25 Auchinleck to Churchill, 10 September 1941, DO35/1009/446/1/40.

26 Diary, 3 October 1941, Massey Papers.

27 Lyttelton to Churchill, 11 September 1941, PREM3/63/2.

28 R. James (ed.), *Victor Cazalet* (London, 1976), p. 264; Diary, 15 September 1941, Harvey Papers

29 Cranborne to Emrys-Evans, 31 August 1941, Emrys-Evans Papers; WCM(41)92, 11 September 1941, CAB65/23.

30 Churchill to Fadden, 11 September 1941, PREM3/63/2; ibid., Fadden to Churchill, 15 September 1941; Fadden, *They Called Me Artie*, p. 77.

31 'Auchinleck Overruled During Tobruk Siege: Australia Insisted On Relief of Her Troops' (Lt-Gen H. G. Martin, Military Correspondent), *Daily Telegraph*, 22 August 1946.

32 Churchill to Fadden, 29 September 1941, PREM3/63/2; ibid., Fadden to Churchill, 4 October 1941; Churchill to Cranborne, 15 September 1941.

33 Ibid., Churchill to Lyttelton, 18 September 1941; minute by Pugh, 25 July 1945, DO35/1767; ibid., DO minute, 13 September 1945; Holdgate to Antrobus, 13 September 1945; minute by Antrobus, 13 September 1945.

34   Hasluck, *The Government and the People*, pp. 510–18.

35   Ross, *John Curtin*, pp. 214–19.

36   War Cabinet Defence Committee, 5 March 1941, cited in J. M. McCarthy, 'Australia: A View from Whitehall, 1939–1945', *Australian Outlook* (No. 28; 1974), p. 325.

37   Horner, *Inside the War Cabinet*, pp. 21–2; Horner, *High Command*, pp. 137–40; *The Times*, 25 August 1939.

38   Cross to Cranborne, June 1944, Machtig Papers, DO121/111; Brooke-Popham to Ismay, 28 February 1941, Brooke-Popham Papers.

39   Day, *The Great Betrayal*, p. 188; Cox, 'The Difference between White and Black', pp. 416–17; Horner, *High Command*, p. 123.

40   It is easy to see why it has been described as a long, slow game, one that wavered between, conciliatory diplomacy, economic blackmail and downright appeasement at the basis of which lay the panacea, 'Main Fleet to Singapore', John Gallagher, *The Decline, Revival and Fall of the British Empire* (Cambridge, 2004), pp. 130–1; John McCarthy, 'Singapore and Australian Defence, 1921–1942', *Australian Outlook*, (Vol. 25; 1971), pp. 165–79; Ian Cowman, *Dominion or Decline: Anglo–American Naval Relations on the Pacific, 1937–1941* (Oxford, 1996), pp. 37–9.

41   For example the *Review of Imperial Defence* and the *Far Eastern Appreciation*, two major documents produced by the British chiefs of staff as preparation for the 1937 Imperial Conference; W. David McIntyre, *The Rise and Fall of the Singapore Naval Base* (London, 1979), pp. 129–31; A. C. Welburn, 'The Singapore Strategy: Half–Truths, Evasion and Outright Deception', *Australian Defence Force Journal* (No. 100; May/June 1993), pp. 39–48.

42   'Imperial Naval Policy', Committee of Imperial Defence (Minutes of 123rd Meeting) cited in Donald Gordon, *The Dominion Partnership in Imperial Defence, 1870–1914* (Baltimore, 1965), p. 279.

43   W. David McIntyre, *New Zealand Prepares for War* (Canterbury, 1988), pp. 193, 203–16, 241; McIntyre, 'Imperialism and Nationalism' in Geoffrey W. Rice (ed), *The Oxford History of New Zealand* (Melbourne, 2002), pp. 338–47; Air Chief Marshal Sir Arthur Longmore had been part of the British delegation and confirmed publicly four years later that Frederick Jones, the NZ defence minister, 'had not appeared to be convinced' by his assurances that New Zealand would be all right as long as Singapore was held, 'Speech given at the Royal Empire Society, London by The Hon. Frederick Jones, MP', 8 June 1943, *United Empire* (Vol. 34, No. 5), p. 128.

44   Committee of Imperial Defence (Minutes of 355th Meeting), 2 May 1939, CAB2/8; Report of the Chiefs of Staff Sub-Committee (53rd Meeting), 20 June 1939, CAB27/625; 'Appreciation on the Far East', June 1939, CAB104/70; Raymond Callahan, 'The Illusion of Security, Singapore 1919–1942', *Journal of Contemporary History* (No. 9; April 1974), pp. 77–81; Ovendale, *Appeasement and the English Speaking World*, pp. 243–9; Lionel Wigmore, *Australia in the War of 1939–1945: Army Vol. 4, The Japanese Thrust* (Canberra, 1957), pp. 6–12; S. Woodburn Kirby, *The War Against Japan: Vol. 1, The Loss of Singapore* (London, 1957), pp. 1–22.

45   Malcolm Murfett, 'Living in the Past: A Critical Re-examination of the Singapore Naval Strategy, 1918–1941', *War and Society* (Vol. 11, No. 1; May 1993), pp. 91–3.

46   DO to Dominion Prime Ministers, 13 June 1940, DO35/1003/2/11/1/1B.

47   Bruce to Menzies, 3 July 1940, Lord Bruce's War Files; Ismay to Bruce, 4 July 1940, DAFP IV, pp. 13–15; Dixon Memoirs, Batterbee Papers, Box 20/5.

48   'Singapore and the Empire', 1923, Chartwell Papers, CHAR8/338.

49   Churchill to Chamberlain, 25 March 1939, cited in A. J. Stockwell, 'Imperialism and Nationalism in South-East Asia' in Brown and Roger Louis (eds), OHBE4; Robert O'Neil, 'Churchill, Japan and British Security in the Pacific, 1904–1942' in Blake and Roger Louis (ed.), *Churchill*, pp. 279–86; ibid., Churchill to Chamberlain, 23 August 1939, cited in D. C. Watt, 'Churchill and Appeasement', p. 202.

50   Minutes of Meeting with Dominion Representatives, 20 November 1939, CAB99/1.

51   Murfett, 'Living in the Past', pp. 94–5; Callahan, 'The Illusion of Security', pp. 82–6.

52   War Cabinet submission by Curtin, 13 October 1941, DAFP V, pp. 133–6 .

53   Jeffrey Grey, *The Military History of Australia* (Cambridge, 1990), pp. 160–3.

54 Whiskard to Inskip, 19 June 1939, DO121/46; T. B. Millar, *Australia in Peace and War* (London, 1978), pp. 137, 140–1; Casey to Evatt, 25 October 1941, DAFP V.

55 Mackenzie King to Churchill, 25 October 1941, DO35/999/8/18.

56 Garner, *The Commonwealth Office*, p. 211.

57 Brooke-Popham to Ismay, 10 October 1941, Brooke-Popham Papers; the media in London meanwhile preferred to dwell on 'his hearty laugh, which he use[d] remarkably well as an evasive instrument when embarrassed by a touchy question', *Evening News*, 28 October 1941, DO35/999/8/18.

58 Page, *Truant Surgeon*, pp. 310–13; Diary, 5 November 1941, Cadogan Papers (Churchill College), ACAD1/10.

59 Diary, 3 December 1941, Massey Papers.

60 Memorandum on 'Machinery of Consultation', Sir Earle Page Papers (National Library of Australia, Canberra), Item No. 641.

61 Minute by Cranborne, 25 August 1941, DO35/1079/5; Churchill to Fadden, 31 August 1941, DAFP V, pp. 92–3; Advisory War Council Minute, 12 September 1941, DAFP V, pp. 106–108; ibid., Curtin to Cranborne, 16 October 1941, p. 149; Churchill to Curtin, 26 October 1941, pp. 153–4.

62 WCM(41)112, 12 November 1941, CAB65/24; John Pritchard, 'Winston Churchill, the Military and Imperial Defence in East Asia' in Saki Dockrill (ed.), *From Pearl Harbor to Hiroshima* (London, 1994), pp. 42–4; S. Hatano and S. Asada, 'The Japanese Decision to Move South' in Boyce and Robertson (eds), *Paths to War*, pp. 399–403; Thorne, *Allies of a Kind*, pp. 51–85; 'Note of a Meeting between Halifax and the Dominion High Commissioners', 31 July 1940, DO35/1000/1/124; Minute, 28 August 1941, DO35/1010/476/3/29.

63 Waterson to Smuts, 11 November 1941, Waterson Papers; ibid., Diary, 31 October 1941; Diary, 27 September 1941.

64 Duff Cooper to Churchill, 31 October 1941, PREM3/155; Glen St.J. Barclay, 'Singapore Strategy: The Role of the United States in Imperial Defense', *Military Affairs* (Vol. 39, No. 2; April 1975), p. 57.

65 Gowrie to DO, 10 October 1941, DO121/50.

66 Cranborne to Churchill, 24 November 1941, PREM3/155; ibid., note by Churchill, 25 November 1941.

67 Churchill to Eden, 23 November 1941, PREM3/156/6; Richard Grace, 'Whitehall and the Ghost of Appeasement: November 1941', *Diplomatic History*, (Vol. 3; 1979), pp. 173–91.

68 Cumpston, *Lord Bruce of Melbourne*, pp. 188–9; HCWM, 12 November 1941, DO121/11; WCM(41)109, 5 November 1941, CAB65/24; Cranborne to Fadden, 12 September 1941, DAFP V, pp. 109–11; ibid., Cranborne to Fadden, 19 September 1941, pp. 116–17.

69 HCWM, 24 November 1941, DO121/11.

70 Diary, 18 November 1941, Page Papers.

71 Attlee to Churchill, 20 November 1941, DO121/10B.

72 WCM(41)122, 1 December 1941, CAB65/24; de-cyphered Japanese document, 30 November 1941, HW1/288; Gilbert, *Finest Hour*, pp. 1259–67.

73 Brigadier Ivan Simson to Liddell Hart, 26 June 1968, Liddell Hart Papers, LH9/31/41a.

74 H. Martin and N. Orpen, *South Africa at War, Vol. 7* (Cape Town, 1979), pp. 124–5, 132–3; J. C. Smuts, *Jan Christian Smuts* (London, 1952), pp. 415–16; A. M. Pollock, *Pienaar of Alamein* (Cape Town, 1943), pp. 75–86; Carel Birkby, *Uncle George: The Boer Boyhood, Letters and Battles of Lieutenant-General George Edwin Brink* (Johannesburg, 1987), pp. 242–4; Harlech to Churchill, 2 October 1941, PREM4/44/1; Harlech to DO, 28 January 1942, DO35/588/3.

75 Beloff, *Dream of Commonwealth*, pp. 348–60; Pickersgill, *The Mackenzie King Record*, pp. 268–95.

76 Day, *The Great Betrayal*, pp. 192–202; Horner, *Inside the War Cabinet*, pp. 75–7; Henry Probert, 'British Strategy and the Far East War, 1941–1945' in Nish (ed.), *Anglo Japanese Alienation, 1919–1952* (London, 1982), p. 161; Mansergh, *Problems of Wartime Cooperation*, pp. 120–3.

77 Ross, *John Curtin*, pp. 236–9.

78 Curtin to Cranborne, 4 November 1941, DAFP V, pp. 162–3; Churchill to Curtin, 27 November 1941, DO121/119; Curtin to Churchill, 29 November 1941, DAFP V, pp. 237–8.

79 Brooke-Popham to Sir Arthur Street, 28 October 1941, Brooke-Popham Papers; Duff Cooper to Cranborne, 31 October 1941, Cranborne Papers; ibid., Duff Cooper to Churchill, 1 December 1941.

80 Horner, *Defence Supremo: Sir Frederick Shedden and the Making of Australian Defence Policy* (Sydney, 2000), pp. 95–6.

81 Churchill, *The Grand Alliance*, pp. 475–7; Ismay to Harry Hopkins, 12 January 1941; Diary, 7/21 December 1941, Waterson Papers.

82 Gilbert, *Road to Victory: Winston S.Churchill, 1941–1945* (London, 1986), pp. 1–3; Charmley, *Churchill: The End of Glory*, pp. 475–9; Robertson, 'Australia and the "Beat Hitler First" Strategy', pp. 310–31.

83 Mansergh, *Problems of Wartime Cooperation*, p. 128.

Notes to Chapter 7: The 'First' Dominion

1 Any study of this question begins with Roger Louis' *Imperialism at Bay* and Thorne's *Allies of a Kind* and it is difficult to surpass them so great and compelling are the two volumes. The first remains the definitive examination of American and British wartime planning for the future of the colonial world, it being rightly acclaimed shortly after its publication as 'one historical study that will not need to be done again'. Among the main themes it sought to explore, one of its foci was the examination of the interaction between Whitehall and the Dominion governments. It recognized at the beginning that Americans generally did not distinguish between the Empire and Commonwealth. But what it was not able to do – because the government documents were not available at the time – was to consider fully the opening questions posed by this chapter. Thorne, with his third chapter looking exclusively at the Anglo-American relationship prior to the Pearl Harbor attack, provides a 37-page synthesis of affairs leading up to 1941 before going forward to conclusively detail events as they happened in the Pacific theatre. To these there should be added Orde's *The Eclipse of Great Britain*. Written nearly 20 years later it traces the origins of the relationship and takes them forward to their nadir at Suez. The fifth chapter, however, provides an excellent and succinct encapsulation of the many themes and issues that affected the wartime relationship, neatly summarizing the two imposing works that had gone before her.

2 J. Ellis Barker, 'The British Empire and the United States', *Current History* (Vol. 15, No. 2; November 1921), pp. 258–62; Admiral Mark Kerr, 'Understanding and Friendship Between English-Speaking People', *Empire Review* (No. 463; August 1939), pp. 76–7.

3 This supplement, *Current History*, was the oldest United States publication devoted exclusively to world affairs and had been founded in 1914 in order to provide detailed coverage of what was then known as the Great War. It subsequently has proven to be one of the most distinguished of American journals.

4 Alastair Buchan, 'Mothers and Daughters (Of Greeks and Romans)', *Foreign Affairs* (Vol. 54, No. 4; July 1976), pp. 651–3; D. C. Watt, *Personalities and Policies*, pp. 37–8.

5 Peter Carlson, 'Raiding the Icebox: Behind Its Warm Front, the United States Made Cold Calculations to Subdue Canada', *Washington Post*, 30 December 2005; the Dominions were all shades of Red – Canada was Crimson, New Zealand was Garnet, Australia was Scarlet (India was included as Ruby).

6 Robert Stewart, 'Instruments of British Policy in the Sterling Area', *Political Science Quarterly* (Vol. 52, No. 2; June 1937), pp. 176–81. This of course was not a new idea, Leo Amery, one of the leading supporters of Imperial Preference, had noted before the meeting began that it would 'register either the final triumph or the failure of nearly fifty years of continuous effort to secure the practical acceptance of the principle that the unity and the strength of the Empire and the welfare of each part of it depend upon mutual economic cooperation'; L. S. Amery, 'The Imperial Economic Conference', *International Affairs* (Vol. 11, No. 5; September 1932), p. 678.

7 Most notable amongst these were Sweden, Denmark and Argentina; Andrew McFadyean, 'International Repercussions of the Ottawa Agreements', *International Affairs* (Vol. 12, No. 1; January 1933), pp. 37–59.

8   Lord Beloff, 'The End of the British Empire and the Assumption of Worldwide Commitments by the United States' in Roger Louis and Bull (eds), *The 'Special Relationship'*, pp. 250–2.

9   H. G. Nicholas, *The United States and Britain* (London, 1975), p. 57.

10 'Howe y. England', *Time*, 5 December 1938; following the fall of France and the growing understanding that the Nazi threat would not necessarily skirt American shores, whilst recognizing the extremes of some his previous argument *Time* praised Howe for being a 'cultured, loquacious, birdlike Bostonian with a famous father (Pulitzer Prize Biographer Mark Antony De Wolfe Howe), a shrewd editorial sense, a mercurial mind'; 'Howe Behind the News', *Time*, 25 November 1940.

11 John Harvey (ed.), *The Diplomatic Diaries of Oliver Harvey, 1937–1940* (London, 1970), pp. 67–86.

12 F. M. Leventhal, 'The Projection of Britain in America before the Second World War' in Wm. Roger Louis, *Still More Adventures with Britannia* (London, 2003), pp. 198–204.

13 Arnold Toynbee and Frank T. Ashton-Gwatkin (eds), *Survey of International Affairs: The World in March 1939* (London, 1952), p. 1; from 1925 Toynbee had served as Director of Studies at Chatham House – and would do so for 30 years – plus he worked within the FO during the war, attended the post-war peace talks and still found time to produce a monumental twelve volume study of the rise and fall of civilizations ('A Study of History').

14 Douglas Fairbanks Jr to Eden, 18 October 1939 (University of Birmingham Special Collections) AP20/7/81; he spent part of his childhood in London, as a result of which he became a passionate Anglophile who was well connected in British society. During the war, as a lieutenant commander in the US Navy, Fairbanks had participated in several combined Anglo-American operations. Having witnessed (and participated in) British training and cross-channel harassment operations emphasizing the military art of deception, he attained a depth of understanding and appreciation of military deception then unheard of in the United States Navy (his experiences were recalled in his memoirs, *A Hell of a War*) and in 1949 he was made an Honorary Knight of the British Empire; Obituary, *The Guardian*, 8 May 2000.

15 Lothian to Halifax, 14 December 1939, FO800/397; Vansittart to Halifax, 31 December 1939, FO800/324.

16 'Memorandum', CP161(38), September 1938, CAB24/277, pp. 1–7; he would later go on to help edit the Royal Institute for International Affairs' *Survey of International Affairs for 1939*.

17 Trevor Reese, *Australia, New Zealand and the United States: A Survey of International Relations, 1941–1968* (London, 1969), pp. 7–9, 10–31; P. G. A. Orders, *Britain, Australia, New Zealand and the Challenge of the United States, 1939–1946: A Study in International History* (London, 2003), pp. 17–27.

18 Neville Chamberlain to Ida Chamberlain, 27 January 1940, Neville Chamberlain Papers, NC18/1/1140.

19 John Simon Rofe, 'Prescription and Remedy: Lord Lothian's Influence upon the Tensions in Anglo–American Relations in Early 1940', *The Round Table* (Vol. 96, No. 389; April 2007), pp. 162–70.

20 David Reynolds, *The Creation of the Anglo–American Alliance 1937–1941* (London, 1981), pp. 63–102.

21 R. A. C. Parker, 'The American Treasury and British Preparations for War, 1938–1939', *English Historical Review* (Vol. 98, No. 387; April 1983), pp. 261–79; Alan Milward, *The Economic Effects of the Two World Wars on Britain* (London, 1972), pp. 66–70.

22 S. Pollard, *The Development of the British Economy, 1914–1990* (London, 1992), pp. 157–8; Ritchie Overy, 'Cyclops' in Reynolds et al., *Allies at War* (New York, 1994), pp. 114–15.

23 'Memorandum on Financial Situation', Treasury document, 9 July 1939, CAB24/287.

24 'Memorandum of Conversation with Churchill', 12 March 1940, Welles Report (1940), Part II (Roosevelt Library), PSF 6; Constance Howard, 'The United States of America and the European War, September 1939 to December 1941' in Toynbee and Toynbee (eds), *The Initial Triumph of the Axis*, pp. 454–6; Christopher D. O'Sullivan, *Sumner Welles, Post-War Planning and the Quest for a New World Order, 1937–1943*, (Columbia, 2007) 'Record of conversation between Secretary of State for Dominion Affairs and Mr Sumner Welles, 13 March 1940', DO35/1000/3/58.

25 Reynolds, *The Creation of the Anglo–American Alliance*, pp. 122–3.

26 Lothian to Halifax, 27 February 1940, DO35/998/7/1; ibid. Halifax to Eden, 15 March 1940; ibid., Stephenson to Parkinson and Machtig, 18 March 1940; ibid., Machtig to Parkinson and Eden, 19 March 1940.

27 Martin Gilbert, *In Search of Churchill* (London, 1994), pp. 276, 263; he had first visited the United States in 1895, his last visit would come 65 years later. There was even some suggestion that the British wartime leader might have been 1/16th Native American Indian.

28 Colville, *The Fringes of Power: Vol. 2, Oct 1941–April 1955* (London, 1987), 2 May 1948, p. 624.

29 Warren F. Kimball (ed.), *Churchill and Roosevelt: The Complete Correspondence* (Princeton, 1984), p. 23.

30 In December 1940 Churchill had prepared a draft message for Roosevelt complaining about the defects in these destroyers but was persuaded by the FO that it should not be sent. While it is certainly true that most of the newly acquired vessels served only about three years of active service with the Royal Navy and the Royal Canadian Navy, it is not true that they made no militarily important contribution, either in terms of what their presence in the North Atlantic made possible, or in the direct effect of their escort duties on the merchant convoys plying those waters; Charmley, *End of Glory*, p. 439.

31 The heavy cruiser *Louisville* (CA–28) departed Simonstown for New York on 6 January 1941, having taken on board $148,342,212.55 in British gold for deposit in American banks; Reynolds, *The Creation of the Anglo–American Alliance*, p. 154; minute by Pitblado, 29 December 1940, DO35/1028/7; ibid., Clutterbuck, 30 December 1940.

32 Cranborne to Mrs Evans, 8 November 1940, Cranborne Papers.

33 WHC, 11 February 1941, DO121/9.

34 Minute, 30 January 1940, FO371/24252; see Fred Pollock, 'Roosevelt, the Ogdensburg Agreement and the British Fleet: All Done with Mirrors', *Diplomatic History*, (Vol. 5; 1981), pp. 203–5.

35 Minute by Hadow, 17 September 1939, FO371/23963.

36 Harding to DO, 27 May 1940, DO35/1003/2/11/1/1B; Menzies to DO, 16 June 1940, DO35/1003/11/3/3; Batterbee to DO, 18 June 1940, DO35/1003/11/4/4; WHC, 6 February 1941, DO121/11.

37 Cited in Ponting, *Churchill*, p. 212.

38 Charmley, *Churchill: The End of Glory*, p. 18.

39 Cited in Gilbert, *In Search of Churchill*, p. 688.

40 Warren F. Kimball, 'Lend-Lease and the Open Door: The Temptation of British Opulence, 1937–1942', *Political Science Quarterly* (Vol. 86, No. 2; June 1971), p. 242.

41 Minute by Liesching, 2 August 1941, DO35/1075/3.

42 Stuart Ball (ed.), *Parliament and Politics in the Age of Churchill and Attlee: The Headlam Diaries, 1935–1941* (London, 1999), p. 234, 31 December 1940.

43 John Robertson, 'Australia and the "Beat Hitler First" Strategy 1941–1942', *Journal of Imperial and Commonwealth History* (Vol. XI, No. 3; 1983), pp. 301–8.

44 Minute by Pitblado, 25 March 1941, DO35/1075/279/67; minute by Pitblado, 30 May 1941, DO35/1075/279/91.

45 Comment by Pitblado at Treasury meeting, 11 December 1941, DO35/1076/1; WHC, 28 October 1941.

46 Machtig to Cranborne, 8 December 1941, DO35/1014/5; ibid., Cranborne to Machtig, 8 December 1941.

47 Minute, February 1941, DO35/1074/279/47; notes by Ashton-Gwatkin (FO) for R. A. Butler, April 1941, Conservative Research Department Papers (Bodleian Library, Oxford), CRD2/28/2; Casey to Department of External Affairs, 11 October 1941, DAFP V, pp. 131–2.

48 Cranborne to Kingsley Wood, 12 August 1941, DO35/1075/3.

49 Orde, *The Eclipse of Great Britain*, pp. 129–59; conversation between Churchill and Roosevelt, August 1941 cited in R. Palme Dutt, *Britain's Crisis of Empire* (London, 1949), p. 44.

50 Minute by Liesching, 19 August 1941, DO35/1075/3.

51 Minute by Liesching, 22 September 1941, DO35/1075/4.

52 'Discussion with Mr Winthrop Brown at the 10 o'clock meeting at the Treasury on December 11th (1941)', DO35/1076/1.
53 V. S. Swaminathan, 'America's Aid to Britain', *Empire Review* (No. 481; February 1941), p. 63.
54 Ritchie Diary, 21 April 1941, *Siren Years*, p. 100.
55 Reynolds, *The Creation of the Anglo–American Alliance*, pp. 140–6.
56 Churchill told the British public in a radio broadcast following his return, that the declaration was in fact 'a simple, rough and ready statement of the goal towards which the British Commonwealth and the United States meant to make their way'; 'Mr. Churchill on a Symbolic Meeting', *The Times*, 25 August 1941.
57 Harvey (ed.), *The Diplomatic Diaries of Oliver Harvey, 1941–1945*, 12 August 1941.
58 Louis, *Imperialism at Bay*, p. 123.
59 WM(41)89, CAB65/19; 'House of Commons Statement by Mr. Churchill', *The Times*, 9 September 1941.
60 Viscount Samuel, 'Thoughts on the Atlantic Charter', *Contemporary Review* (No. 913, January 1942), pp. 1–2.
61 Rt Hon. George Peel, 'Atlantic Charter No. 2', *Contemporary Review* (No. 917, May 1942), p. 264; many of the Americans at the conference remained convinced that imperial trade preferences such as the Ottawa Agreement had contributed strongly to the economic and political malaise of the interwar years.
62 John Barnes and David Nicholson (eds), *The Empire at Bay: The Leo Amery Diaries, 1929–1945* (London, 1987), p. 710.
63 Headlam, 14/15 August 1941, *The Headlam Diaries*, p. 270.
64 Machtig to Cranborne, 23 August 1941, DO35/1002/48/2; Garner to Martin, 29 August 1941, DO35/1002/48/3; Attlee to Churchill, 12 August 1941, CAB66/18/13.
65 Minute by Liesching, February 1941, DO35/1077/281/11.
66 Halifax to Amery, 1 May 1941, Amery Papers, AMEL2/1/33; ibid., Halifax to Amery, 20 May 1941.
67 The source was David Eccles, later Viscount Eccles; Dalton Diary, 25 August 1941, *The Dalton Diaries*, p. 272.
68 Ibid., Dalton Diary, 29 August 1941, p. 277.
69 Cited in Pearson, *Through Diplomacy to Politics*, p. 218.
70 Sir Ian Kershaw, 'Hitler Versus America', *BBC History* (Vol. 8, No. 6; June 2007), p. 20; see also Sir Nicholas Henderson, 'Hitler's Biggest Blunder', *History Today* (April 1993), pp. 35–43.
71 Wm. Roger Louis, 'Sir Keith Hancock and the British Empire: The Pax Britannica and the Pax Americana', *English Historical Review* (Vol. 120, No. 488; September 2005), pp. 932–62.
72 Writing about the *Survey* he cautioned the potential reader about its scope and size, 'I certainly shouldn't recommend it to anybody of feeble health and weak determination', W. K. Hancock, *Argument of Empire* (London, 1943), pp. 7, 9–10.
73 Hancock to Colin Badger, 9 March 1943, cited in Louis, 'Sir Keith Hancock and the British Empire', p. 956.

Notes to Chapter 8: Rupture?

1 Page to Curtin, 8 December 1941, DAFP V, pp. 289–93.
2 Brooke-Popham to Sir Arthur Street, 28 October 1941, Brooke-Popham Papers.
3 Cranborne to Churchill, 12 December 1941, PREM3/206/1–3; Curtin to Churchill, 13 December 1941, DO121/119; Page, *Truant Surgeon*, pp. 319–23; Cumpston, *Lord Bruce of Melbourne*, pp. 189–91.
4 WCM127(41), 12 December 1941, CAB65/20; Memorandum on 'Machinery of Consultation', Page Papers, Item No. 642 (1942); 'Note by Shedden', 17 March 1943 cited in Day, *The Great Betrayal*, p. 219.
5 'Australia is Right', 21 December 1941, *Sunday Express*; 'Blunt Words from Dominions', 23 December 1941, *Daily Mail*.

6 Attlee to Churchill, 23 December 1941, PREM3/63/3.
7 Dalton Diary, 19 December 1941, p. 337.
8 Attlee to Churchill, 23 December 1941, PREM3/63/3.
9 Edwards, *Bruce of Melbourne*, pp. 324–5; Coral Bell, *Dependent Ally: A Study in Australian Foreign Policy* (Melbourne, 1988), pp. 25–6; Eric Baume, 'Australia's Political Trend', *The Fortnightly* (No. 151; January–June 1942), pp. 97–106.
10 Menzies Radio Broadcast, 26 April 1939 in R. G. Neale (ed.), *Documents on Australian Foreign Policy, 1937–1949: Vol. 2, 1939* (Canberra, 1976).
11 P. G. Edwards, 'R.G. Menzies' Appeals to the United States', *Australian Outlook* (No. 28; 1974), pp. 64–70.
12 DO to Whiskard, 21 June 1940, DO35/1003/11/3/7.
13 Gwendolen M. Carter, 'New Trends in British Commonwealth Relations', *Pacific Affairs* (Vol. 17, No. 1; March 1944), p. 71.
14 'Empire War Cabinet – Oral Answers', 18 December 1941, *House of Commons Official Report* (Vol. 376), pp. 2072–3; WCM (41)137, 29 December 1941, CAB65/20. A flurry of letters on the subject published by *The Times* had produced a number of broadly sympathetic responses, largely drawn from those most actively involved in the debate about the role of the Empire. Sir John Marriott was amongst those who strongly endorsed the 'most opportune and just plea' for a revival of an Empire War Cabinet' 'Empire War Cabinet – The Dominions and Strategy', *The Times*, 8 January 1942; 'Planning of War Strategy – Dangers in the Pacific' (Lord Denman), *The Times*, 10 January 1942.
15 Cited in Raymond Callahan, *Worst Disaster: Fall of Singapore* (Delaware, 1977), p. 234; Jacob to Ismay, 24 January 1959, Ismay Papers, ISMAYI/14/69a.
16 'Mr Curtin Explains', 29 December 1941, *The Times*; 'Dominions and Strategy' (Keith Murdoch), 29 December 1941, *The Times*; 'A Word to Mr Curtin', 30 December 1941, *Daily Mail*.
17 Cross to Cranborne, 3 November 1941, DO35/587/89/137; ibid., minute by Machtig, 29 December 1941; minute by Cranborne, 31 December 1941; John Gooch, 'The Politics of Strategy: Great Britain, Australia and the War against Japan, 1939–1945', *War in History* (Vol. 10, No. 4; 2003), pp. 436–8.
18 Cranborne to Churchill, 1 January 1942, DO35/1002/48/7A.
19 Memorandum on 'Machinery of Consultation' (1942), Page Papers, No. 642; 'Note of a Meeting between Lord Cranborne and Sir Earle Page', 31 December 1941, FO954/4.
20 'Lord Cranborne's comments on Sir Earle Page's proposals', 2 January 1942, FO954/4.
21 'Memorandum on Machinery of Consultation', Page Papers; Curtin to DO, 1 January 1942, DO35/1002/48/7A.
22 Cranborne to Eden, 7 January 1942, FO954/4.
23 Ibid., Note by Cavendish Bentinck, 12 January 1942.
24 Ibid., minute from unknown to Sir Orme Sargeant, 13 January 1942.
25 WCM137(41) and WCM138(41), 29 December 1941, CAB65/20; Gilbert, *Road to Victory*, pp. 32–3.
26 Batterbee to Attlee, 19 February 1942, CAB66/24.
27 Diary, 9 January 1942 cited in Lord Moran, *Struggle for Survival* (London, 1966), p. 21; there have been some doubts raised about the accuracy of some of the comments attributed by Churchill's surgeon.
28 Curtin to Churchill, 1 January 1942, DAFP V, pp. 396–8; ibid., Churchill to Curtin, 3 January 1942, p. 399; ibid., Curtin to Churchill, 6 January 1942, pp. 417–20; ibid., Churchill to Curtin, 8 January 1942, pp. 423–6; Evatt to Casey, 7 January 1942, pp. 420–1; Casey to Evatt, 8 January 1942, pp. 421–3.
29 COS(40)592, 15 August 1940, CAB80/15; Churchill to Ismay, 7 January 1941, PREM3/157/1; Churchill to Mrs Churchill, 21 December 1941 cited in Mary Soames (ed.), *Speaking for Themselves: The Personal Letters of Winston and Clementine Churchill* (London, 1998), p. 460; Christopher M. Bell, '"Our Most Exposed Outpost": Hong Kong and British Far Eastern Strategy, 1921–1941', *The Journal of Military History* (Vol. 60, January 1996), pp. 75–88.
30 Gilbert, *Road to Victory*, pp. 45–7; Churchill to Curtin, 14 January 1942, DO121/19; Curtin to Churchill, 17 January 1942, DAFP V, pp. 441–3; Churchill to Curtin, 19 January 1942, DO121/19.

31 WCM8(42), 17 January 1942, CAB65/25.
32 Churchill to Curtin, 19 January 1942, DAFP V, pp. 445–7; Cranborne to Churchill, 17 January 1942, PREM3/167/1; Churchill to Fraser, 17 January 1942, DO35/1010/476/124; Curtin to Churchill, 21 January 1942, DO35/1010/476/128.
33 Cross to Cranborne, 21 January 1942, PREM4/50/7A; ibid., Cranborne to Churchill, 22 January 1942; Cross to DO, 14 January 1942, DO121/50; Cranborne to Emrys-Evans, 31 August 1941, Emrys-Evans Papers.
34 Cross to Cranborne, 9 August 1941, Cranborne Papers; ibid., Duff Cooper to Cranborne, 1 December 1941; Cross to Cranborne, 13 January 1944, DO121/11; 'Sir Ronald Cross Rebuked', *Daily Mail*, 18 July 1941.
35 Memoranda by Cranborne, WP(42)29 and WP(42)30, 21 January 1942, CAB66/21.
36 Note by Bentinck, 12 January 1942, FO954/4.
37 WCM8(42), 17 January 1942, CAB65/25.
38 Alexander Hardinge to Churchill, 22 January 1942, PREM3/167/1.
39 Churchill to The King, 22 January 1942, PREM3/167/1.
40 Ibid., Hardinge to Churchill, 26 January 1942.
41 Note by Cadogan, 23 January 1942, FO954/4; Newton to DO, 25 November 1942, DO35/1002/52/10.
42 WHCM, 14 January 1942, DO121/12; ibid., WHCM, 15 January 1942; Waterson to Smuts, 15 January 1942, Waterson Papers.
43 WHC, 26 January 1942, DO121/12.
44 Diary, 22 January 1942, Waterson Papers; ibid., 26 January 1942.
45 Ibid., Diary, 28 January 1942; Waterson to Smuts, 27 January 1942.
46 Ibid., Smuts to Waterson, 29 January 1942.
47 Fraser to Churchill, 25 January 1942, DO35/1010/476/129.
48 Fraser to Churchill, 22 January 1942, DO35/1010/476/124.
49 Ibid., Peck to Garner, 26 January 1942; Churchill to Roosevelt, 27 January 1942, DO35/1010/476/128.
50 Baume, 'Australia's Political Trend', *The Fortnightly*, p. 98; R. G. Menzies, 'We Don't Turn From You', *Daily Express*, 6 January 1942.
51 Curtin to Churchill, 24 January 1942, Chartwell Papers, CHAR20/69.
52 Gilbert, *Road to Victory*, pp. 48–9; Edwards, *Bruce of Melbourne*, p. 329.
53 Churchill to Curtin, n.d. (Not sent), PREM3/150/3.
54 Diary, 24/25 January 1942, Harvey Papers; ibid., 1 February 1942.
55 Diary, 28 January 1942, Woolton Papers.
56 'Commonwealth Control', *The Round Table* (Vol. 32; December 1941–September 1942), p. 221; 'Editorial', *The Times*, 19 January 1942.
57 'Letter from Hubert Gough to Editor', *The New Statesman and Nation* (7 February 1942), p. 92.
58 'Is Australia Threatened?', *The New Statesman and Nation* (Vol. 23, No. 568; 10 January 1942), p. 20; under the editorship of the leading left-wing figure Kingsley Martin, this was one of the most popular weekly British journals.
59 DO to Australia, 28 January 1942, PREM4/43A/14; DO to Australia, 2 February 1942, Chartwell Papers, CHAR20/69A.
60 Diary, 27 January 1942, Waterson Papers.
61 'Imperial War Cabinet', 14 February 1942, *The New Statesman and Nation*; ibid., Letter to the Editor from Hubert Gough, 21 February 1942.
62 J. A. R. Marriott, 'An Empire Cabinet', *The Nineteenth Century* (Vol. 131, No. 781; March 1942), p. 128.
63 'Situation in the South-West Pacific', 29 January 1942, *House of Lords Official Report* (Vol. 71), p. 569–78.
64 DO to Dominion governments, 28 January 1942, DO35/1010/476/141.
65 'Curtin is Blunt to Churchill', 27 January 1942, *Daily Mail*.
66 'Australians Stirred – Warm Praise for Mr Churchill', *The Times*, 30 January 1942; only two weeks later the same source for the story in *The Times* – the *Melbourne Argus* – was recommending that it

was no time for 'a one–man band' and urging Churchill to listen to his critics; "'Our Honeymoon is Finished" – Mr Curtin Warns Australia', *The Times*, 17 February 1942.

67   Garner, *The Commonwealth Office*, pp. 213–15; Diary, 9 February 1942 cited in Dilks, *Diaries of Sir Alexander Cadogan*, p. 432; Page, *Truant Surgeon*, pp. 328–9; Harvey, *Consultation and Cooperation in the Commonwealth*, pp. 96–7.

68   Diary, 16 January 1942, Page Papers.

69   'Situation in the South West Pacific', 28/29 January 1942, *House of Lords Official Report* (Vol. 71), pp. 497–510, 537–41, 551.

70   Headlam Diaries, 8 February 1942, p. 294.

71   'World View – Anxiety in Australia', *Manchester Guardian*, 17 February 1942; Harvey to Eden, 13 February 1942, Harvey Papers; Diary, 16 February 1942 cited in Pimlott, *The Dalton War Diary*, pp. 369–70.

72   Diary, 16 February 1942 cited in Eden, *The Reckoning*, p. 321.

73   Minute, 17 February 1942, Bruce Papers.

74   Diary, 23 January 1942, Waterson Papers; Bruce to Curtin, 17 February 1942, DAFP V, pp. 530–1; see Day, *Menzies and Churchill at War*, p. 241.

75   Diary, 19 February 1942, Waterson Papers; 'Debate in the House of Commons (War Situation, Ministerial Changes)', comments by Prime Minister, 24 February 1942.

76   Machtig to Bridges, 12 February 1942, DO35/1010/476/141; Diary, 19 February 1942 cited in Dilks, *Diaries of Sir Alexander Cadogan*, p. 435.

77   'Speech at United Warden's luncheon of the City of London', 23 February 1942, Attlee Papers (Department of Western Manuscripts, Bodleian Library), dep. 4, fol.209–220; Dixon Memoirs, Batterbee Papers, Box 20/5.

78   Diary, 26 July 1943, Massey, *What's Past is Prologue*.

79   Diary, 19 May 1942, Ritchie, *Siren Years*; Diary, 3 March 1942, Waterson Papers, ibid., Diary, 28 April 1942. It is perhaps almost ironic therefore that it would be Attlee, now as prime minister, who in October 1948 promulgated the demise of the terms 'Dominion' and 'Dominion governments' to be superseded by 'Commonwealth country' or 'member of the Commonwealth'; 'Dominion Status' was dropped in favour of 'fully independent Member of the Commonwealth'; see McIntyre, 'Commonwealth Legacy' in OHBE4, p. 696; the department had already been renamed in July 1947 as the 'Commonwealth Relations Office' (CRO).

80   Waterson Diary, 5 June 1942; ibid., 25 June 1942.

81   'Imperial War Cabinet', *The New Statesman and Nation* (14 and 21 February 1942).

82   Churchill to Curtin (Telegram), 20 February 1942, DO121/10B; ibid., Cross to DO, 21 February 1942; Cross to DO, 14 July 1943, DO121/10B; 'Draft of Message from Prime Minister to Mr Curtin', n.d. This incident returned to haunt both governments the following year. During the 'No Confidence' debate precipitated by the Opposition at the end of June 1943, various references were made to Burma and to the earlier decision to withdraw troops from the Western Desert. The DO was so concerned that a telegram was sent in Churchill's name urging Curtin to try 'to prevent embarrassing and possibly dangerous disclosures' in order to avoid 'public political controversy'.

83   Diary, 30 March 1942, *Diaries of Harold Nicolson*, p. 219.

84   'Evidence as to Behaviour of Australian Troops in Malaya', n.d., DO35/1010; minute by Boyd-Shannon, 20 May 1942; Richard Wilkinson, 'Ashes to Ashes', *History Today* (February 2002), pp. 39–41.

85   Headlam Diaries, 10 March 1942/pp. 302–3.

86   Minute by Machtig, 31 August 1942, DO35/1010; ibid., Attlee to Churchill, 2 September 1942; Churchill to Attlee, 6 September 1942.

87   Robert Menzies, 'This is What Australians are Thinking', *Daily Express*, 7 April 1942.

88   Cross to Attlee, 16 September 1942, DO35/1010.

89   G. M. Brown, 'Attitudes to an Invasion of Australia in 1942', *RUSI Journal* (Vol. 122, No. 1; March 1977), pp. 27–31; Air Commodore A. D. Garrisson, 'Darwin 1942', *Australian Defence Force Journal* (No. 122; January/February 1997), pp. 41–77. Overall 64 Japanese air attacks were

conducted against Darwin, the last of these in mid-November 1943 but it is the first which is most remembered.

90   'South Australia Bans Horse-Racing', *The Times*, 26 February 1942. In South Africa also petrol rationing, trial blackouts and the curtailment of long distance rail services were all seen as responses to Japanese penetration into the Indian Ocean; 'Defence Measures in South Africa', *The Times*, 13 March 1942.

91   Noel Annan, 'How Wrong Was Churchill?', *The New York Review of Books*, 8 April 1993 (Vol. 40, No. 7); Gilbert, *Road to Victory*, p. 128; Andrew Stewart, '"The Klopper Affair": Anglo–South African Relations and the Surrender of the Tobruk Garrison', *Twentieth Century British History* (Vol. 17 No. 4, 2006), pp. 516–54.

92   Auchinleck to Alanbrooke, 25 July 1942, Alanbrooke Papers (Liddell Hart Archives), 6/D/4f/E; 'Notes on Freyberg and Auchinleck', n.d. (July 1955?), Liddell Hart Papers, LH1/242/417.

93   'Notes on Alanbrooke, Churchill and Tobruk', 3 April 1957, LH1/242/429; Dorman-Smith described Dominions troops as 'semi-independent expeditionary forces ... whose commanders had a definite responsibility to remote Dominion governments'; Dorman-Smith to Liddell Hart, 15 April ??, LH1/242/370.

Notes to Chapter 9: Holding the Imperial Line

1   John Deane Potter, *Fiasco: The Break-out of the German Battleships* (New York, 1970).

2   'The Dieppe Raid', *The Times*, 20 August 1942; 'Dieppe and Cherbourg – Experience Gained from Landings', *The Times*, 5 August 1944; General Denis Whitaker and Shelagh Whitaker, *Dieppe: Tragedy to Triumph* (London, 1992), pp. 23–8; C. G. Roland, 'On The Beach and In The Bag: The Fate of the Dieppe Casualties Left Behind', *Canadian Military History* (Vol. 9, No. 4), pp. 6–25; C. P. Stacy, *The Canadian Army, 1939–1945* (Ottawa, 1948), p. 80.

3   Cited in Roger Louis, *Imperialism at Bay*, p. 200 and Gilbert, *Churchill: A Life* (London, 1992), p. 734; according to John Charmley such rejoinders were, by this stage, pointless as 'the Empire was already on the way to liquidation, with the Americans taking the role of receiver to the bankrupt concern', Charmley, *End of Glory*, p. 431.

4   'Debate on the Address', 12/18 November 1942 and 2/3 December 1942, *House of Commons Official Report* (Vol. 385), pp. 134–8, 201–2, 265–7, 293–4, 398–9.

5   'Dominion Prime Ministers (Cooperation)–Oral Answers', 11 June 1941, *House of Commons Official Report* (Vol. 372), pp. 187–9; the exchange included one of Churchill's more celebrated rejoinders. When assured by Granville that he was trying to hinder the prime minister in the conduct of the war but was 'merely following the writings and precepts of Winston Churchill', the prime minister responded, 'I am afraid that at times that gentleman was very annoying'.

6   'Dominion High Commissioners (War Meetings)–Oral Answers', 24 June 1941, *House of Commons Official Report* (Vol. 372), pp. 936–7; 'Empire and United States–Oral Answers', 22 July 1941, *House of Commons Official Report* (Vol. 373), pp. 761–2; 'Empire War Collaboration–Oral Answers', 9 September 1941, *House of Commons Official Report* (Vol. 374), pp. 28–9; Churchill was still being asked much the same questions by these two as late as February 1944.

7   'War Situation', 20 May 1942, *House of Commons Official Report* (Vol. 380), pp. 290–2.

8   Graham Stewart, *His Finest Hours: The War Speeches of Winston Churchill* (London, 2007), pp. 299–301.

9   'Ol' Man River', *Time*, 2 September 1940.

10   Claude Bissell, *The Imperial Canadian: Vincent Massey* (Toronto, 1986), p. 126.

11   Diary, 12 and 19 October 1942, Massey Papers.

12   John Colville, *The Fringes of Power: Vol. 1*, p. 148.

13   Miller, 'Special Relationship', p. 380.

14   Robert Rhodes James, 'The Politician' in A. J. P. Taylor et al., *Four Faces and the Man* (London, 1969), p. 94.

15   Malcolm MacDonald Papers, pp. 122/123.

16 'The Empire', 21 July 1942, *House of Lords Official Report* (Vol. 123), pp. 933–77.

17 Cranborne to MacDonald, 6 June 1942, MacDonald Papers, 14/5/29.

18 Cranborne to Emrys-Evans, 18 March 1943, Emrys-Evans Papers.

19 Hector Bolitho, 'This Empire of Ours', *Empire Review* (No. 304, January 1943), pp. 10–11; born in New Zealand, the prolific writer served as a wartime intelligence officer in the Royal Air Force Volunteer Reserve. He was also said to be well connected with the royal family as a result of a popular account he wrote of the H.R.H. Duke of York's 1927 tour of New Zealand; I. G. Wilkinson, *Journalese* (Wellington, 1934), p. 47.

20 Kenneth O'Morgan, 'Imperialists at Bay: British Labour and Decolonization' in King and Kilson (eds), *The Statecraft of British Imperialism*, pp. 234–6.

21 'Empire or Commonwealth', *Time*, 25 January 1943.

22 'As England Feels …', *Time*, 13 April 1942.

23 Of the 895 correspondents polled just 29 per cent of them understood the distinction between 'Dominion' and 'Colony'; 'The British Empire', BBC Listener Research Department, 22 February 1943, FO371/34088.

24 Frank Heinlein, *British Government Policy and Decolonisation 1945–1963* (London, 2002), pp. 8, 64.

25 Unknown newspaper clipping, 15 May 1940, Pearson Papers, MG26, N8.

26 Pickersgill, *The Mackenzie King Record*, pp. 663–4.

27 Halifax, *Fullness of Days*, p. 273; also in Roger Louis, *Imperialism at Bay*, p. 16.

28 Hancock, *Argument of Empire*, pp. 9–13.

29 Clement Attlee, 'Wartime Cooperation in the British Commonwealth', *United Empire* (Vol. 34, No. 1; January–February 1943), pp. 7–12. The *Royal Empire Society* was founded in 1869 with 174 members; by the end of 1941 this had risen to 18,002. Its splendid buildings on Northumberland Avenue in central London suffered extensive damage in April and May 1941, virtually the entire library was destroyed by a huge bomb and water damage from the efforts of the fire brigade, a total of 232,353 volumes in all; 'The Royal Empire Society – Report of the Council', 17 June 1942; *United Empire* (Vol. 33, No. 4; July–August 1942).

30 A. Duff Cooper, 'The Future Development of the British Empire' (12 January 1943), *United Empire* (Vol. 34, No. 2), p. 33.

31 Richard Law, 'The British Commonwealth as a World Power' (19 January 1943), *United Empire* (Vol. 34, No. 2; March–April 1943), pp. 35–8.

32 Lord Elton, 'Post-War Role of the Empire', *Empire Review* (No. 505, June 1943), pp. 13–16; ibid., Lord Hailey, 'The New Attack on "British Imperialism"', pp. 44–8; Sir Charles Petrie, 'At the Peace Table – And Afterwards', pp. 30–2.

33 Sir Arthur Salter, the Independent MP for Oxford University, who was closely involved at this stage in shipping questions and had visited the United States as part of the Lend-Lease negotiations; Diary, 8 July 1942, *Dalton Diary*, p. 465.

34 Richard Akwei to Sir Alan Burns, 18 January 1943, Swinton Papers (Churchill Archives), Swin II 5/5.

35 Swinton to Cranborne, 17 October 1942, Swinton Papers, Swin II 5/5.

36 'Alleged Indiscretion of US Cabinet Minister', 21 February 1944, FO371/38522; Cross to Attlee, 22 December 1942, DO35/1628.

37 Greenway (DID) to DO Premiers, draft telegram 'Most Secret and Personal', 13 March 1943, FO371/36606.

38 'The Campbell is Coming', *Time*, 27 January 1941.

39 Campbell to Cadogan, 6 August 1942, FO371/39695; minute by Sir David Scott, 26 August 1942, FO371/39695.

40 Cited in Roger Louis, *Imperialism at Bay*, p. 198. The author's brother penned a much less critical piece which appeared as an editorial in the January 1944 edition of *Fortune* magazine and was warmly welcomed both by Lord Halifax in Washington and the FO back in London; John Davenport, 'The British Empire and the United States', *Fortune*, January 1944; Halifax to Eden, 3 January 1944, FO371/38522; ibid., minute by Mason, 14 January 1944.

41 Amery to Cranborne, 27 October 1942, Amery Papers, AMEL2/1/34; ibid., Cranborne to Amery, 3 November 1942.

42 It was not merely anti-imperialism that Wilkie suffered from; there was also more than a hint of defeatism on display during his tour. During a stopover in West Africa he had met the British Resident Minister, Lord Swinton, who recorded that he had been 'frightfully gloomy' about the Allied position in North Africa until he had seen the position in Egypt which 'entirely changed his outlook', Swinton to Cranborne, 11 September 1942, Swinton Papers, Swin II 5/5.

43 Attlee to Churchill, 16 June 1942, DO121/10B.

44 Waterson to Smuts, 2 October 1942, Waterson Papers.

45 Massey Diary, 29 July 1942, Massey Papers.

46 Bissell, *Imperial Canadian*, p. 186; Diary, 2 July 1943, Massey Papers.

47 Cited in David Day, *John Curtin: A Life* (Sydney, 2000), pp. 522–6.

48 'Curtin Advocates Body to Govern Whole Empire', *The Courier Mail* (Brisbane), 16 August 1943; 'Empire Council Plan Supported', *The Herald* (Melbourne), 3 September 1943; 'British Interest in Empire Government Plan', *Daily Telegraph* (Sydney), 7 September 1943; 'A Council for Empire', *The Times*, 7 September 1943; 'Doubtful on Empire Parliament Plan', *Daily Telegraph*, 16 August 1943; 'Curtin's Scheme Not New', *Daily Telegraph*, 16 December 1943.

49 Sir Earle Page, 'Australia and the War', *United Empire* (Vol. 33, No. 2; March–April 1942), pp. 36–8; Wing-Commander the Hon. T. W. White, 'Australia's Outlook', *United Empire* (Vol. 34, No. 4, July–August 1943), pp. 97–101; Sir Ernest Fisk, 'The Empire as an Australian Sees It', *United Empire* (Vol. 34, No. 6; November–December 1943), pp. 167–70.

50 Emrys-Evans to Wakehurst, 4 June 1943, Emrys-Evans Papers.

51 For example Lord Elton, 'Post-War Role of the Empire', *Empire Review* (No. 505; June 1943), pp. 13–16; Keith Newman, 'New Trends in Anglo–Australian Relations', *The Fortnightly* (October 1943), pp. 241–7; Samuel Storey MP, 'Australia Wants Closer Cooperation', *Empire Review* (March–May 1944), pp. 35–40; L. C. Key, 'Australia in Commonwealth and World Affairs, 1939–1944', *International Affairs* (Vol. 21, No. 1; January 1945), pp. 60–73.

52 Smuts, *Jan Christian Smuts*, pp. 440–8.

53 'Peace and Power', *Time*, 13 December 1943; Kenneth Ingham, *Jan Christian Smuts: The Conscience of a South African* (London, 1986), pp. 223–30.

54 High Commission, Pretoria to DO, 18 March 1944, DO34/1204; Garner to Pugh, 20 January 1944, DO35/1205 – there was also, not unexpectedly, considerable anger at the questioning of France's position; 'Reactions to FM Smuts Recent Speech', 15 December 1943, FO371/34411.

55 Diary, Monday 24 January 1944; Halifax Papers; I am grateful to Professor Greg Kennedy for supplying this reference.

56 Pickersgill, *The Mackenzie King Record*, pp. 636–41; Andrew Roberts, *The Holy Fox: A Life of Lord Halifax* (London, 1991), pp. 294/5; Diary, 8 February 1944, Mackenzie King Papers.

57 Halifax to Cranborne, 30 January 1944, DO35/1485.

58 Ibid., Cranborne to Halifax, 9 February 1944.

59 'The Four-Power Plan', Memorandum by the Secretary of State for Foreign Affairs, 8 November 1942, CAB66/30/46.

60 Handwritten comment, 'Foreign Affairs', 17 July 1942, DO35/998/7/48.

61 'The United Nations Plan', Memorandum by the Secretary of State for Dominion Affairs, 28 January 1943, CAB66/33/44.

62 'The Relation of the British Commonwealth to the Post-war International Political Organisation', Memorandum by the Secretary of State for Dominion Affairs, 15 June 1943, CAB66/37/44.

63 'Discussion on status and representation of the Members of the British Commonwealth in the International Sphere', Thursday 1 April 1943, DO35/1838.

Notes to Chapter 10: The Private Anzac Club

1 McIntyre, p. 49; Ian Wards, 'Peter Fraser – Warrior Prime Minister' in Margaret Clark (ed.), *Peter Fraser: Master Politician* (Palmerston North, 1998), pp. 155–6.
2 Alan Watt, *Evolution of Australian Foreign Policy 1938–1965* (London, 1968), pp. 73–7; Robin Kay (ed.), *The Australian New Zealand Agreement 1944* (Wellington, 1972), pp. xxviii–xxxii; Wm. Roger Louis, *Imperialism at Bay*, pp. 409–21; Thorne, *Allies of a Kind*, pp. 480–6; Orders, *Britain, Australia, New Zealand and the Challenge of the United States*, pp. 95–101; Roger J. Bell, *Unequal Allies, Australian–American Relations and the Pacific War* (Melbourne, 1977), pp. 146–56; Hasluck, *Diplomatic Witness*, pp. 112–24.
3 Hankinson to Cranborne, 18 February 1944, CAB66/48/19.
4 Peter Lyon, 'Great Britain and Australia' in H. G. Gelber (ed.), *Problems of Australian Defence* (Melbourne, 1970), pp. 70, 76.
5 Hankinson to Stephenson, 26 May 1944, DO35/1118; he would later become British Ambassador in Dublin.
6 Hasluck, *Diplomatic Witness*, p. 117.
7 Minute by Cranborne, 11 December 1943, DO35/1118.
8 Malcolm McKinnon, *Independence and Foreign Policy: New Zealand in the World since 1935* (Auckland, 1993), p. 44.
9 Attlee to Churchill, 11 March 1943, DO121/10B.
10 Batterbee to Cranborne, 22 February 1944, DO35/1119.
11 Lt. T. A. Gibson, '"Bayonets About the Crown": The Record of the Australian Army in the Second World War', *The Army Quarterly* (Vol. 56; April and July 1948), pp. 167–70; Grey, *The Military History of Australia*, pp. 177–80; David Dilks, 'Britain, the Commonwealth and the Wider World 1939–1945', Paper Given at the 'International Conference on the Contribution of the Commonwealth to the War Effort, 1939–1945', Oxford, April 1998, pp. 12–13 (I am grateful to Dr Ashley Jackson for sharing this paper).
12 Cross to Cranborne, 27 January 1944, DO35/1993.
13 Speech by Curtin, 17 January 1944, WO106/3419; ibid., Speech by Fraser, 17 January 1944; 'Defence of the South-West Pacific Region', Press Statement by the Prime Minister of Australia, Canberra, 18 January 1944.
14 'Charter for Down Under', *Time*, 31 January 1944.
15 On a map prepared within the WO the Australian 'offer' to police territories until such time as the United Nations organization was established was laid out: Java, New Guinea, the Solomon Islands and the New Hebrides chain were all clearly marked, forming a security umbrella that stretched along the entire northern Australian littoral.
16 Cross to DO (telegram), 18 January 1944, WO106/3419; Curtin had also assured the high commissioner, and told him that he should repeat the same to London, that the next stage to the talks would be to discuss the initial findings with the British government, most likely at the prime minister's conference, before discussing them with anybody else. The final post-conference announcement failed to include any reference to discussions with the British government.
17 Cross to DO (telegram), 26 January 1944, WO106/3419.
18 'Impressions of a New Zealand Official in his Return from the Australia–New Zealand Conference at Canberra, 31st January 1944', Note by F. E. Cuming-Bruce, 7 February 1944, DO35/1993; ibid., Batterbee to Machtig, 9 February 1944.
19 Sir A. D. McIntosh Papers (Alexander Turnbull Library, Wellington), MS–Papers–6759–459, p. 486.
20 Cross to Cranborne, 13 January 1944, DO121/11; Evatt visited London in mid-1942 and was so charmed by the prime minister that he subsequently 'would not hear a word against him'. His return to Canberra with the news that Churchill was 'a very great man' swept Australia and feeling towards Britain began to abate. Cross to Cranborne, 13 January 1944, DO121/11; Cross to DO (Telegram No. 74), 19 January 1944, WO106/3419; T. B. Millar, 'The Australia–Britain Relationship', *The Round Table* (Vol. 67; 1977), p. 195.

21 Batterbee to DO (Telegram), 1 February 1944, WO106/3419; McIntosh to Bernedsen, 3 February 1944 in Ian McGibbon (ed.), *Undiplomatic Dialogue, Letters between Carl Berendsen and Alister McIntosh 1943–1953* (Auckland, 1993).

22 'Australia–New Zealand Agreement of 21st January 1944', Memorandum by Cranborne, 2 February 1944, CAB66/46/20; 'Extract from the Conclusions of the 17th(44) Meeting of the War Cabinet', 9 February 1944, WO106/3419.

23 DO to Australian and New Zealand governments, 12 February 1944, WO106/3419.

24 Cross to DO (telegram), 18 February 1944, WO106/3419.

25 Minute by Greenway, 12 February 1944, FO371/42677.

26 Minute by Clarke, 2 February 1944, FO371/42681.

27 Ibid., minute by Butler, 5 February 1944; minute By Butler, 16 May 1944, FO371/42678.

28 Ibid., minute by Ashley Clarke, 16 May 1944.

29 Minute by Greenway, 2 February 1944, FO371/42681.

30 Minute by Boyd-Shannon, 1 March 1944, DO35/1215; ibid., Garner to Costar, 21 February 1944.

31 Ibid., Holmes to Boyd-Shannon, 10 March 1944.

32 High Commission, Ottawa to DO (telegram), 27 January 1944, WO106/3419.

33 Ibid., Australian High Commission to DO (telegram), 25 January 1944, WO106/3419; Australian High Commission to DO (telegram), 8 February 1944; New Zealand High Commission to DO (telegram), 25 January 1944.

34 Batterbee to DO (telegram), 9 February 1944, WO106/3419.

35 Ibid., Batterbee to DO (telegram), 14 February 1944 (No. 66).

36 'Australia–New Zealand Agreement of 21st January 1944', WP(44)107, 14 February 1944, CAB66/47/7.

37 Batterbee to DO (telegram), 14 February 1944 (No. 62).

38 Ibid., DO to Cross (telegram), 26 February 1944, WO106/3419.

39 Watt, *The Evolution of Australian Foreign Policy*, p. 77.

40 Minute by Greenway, 2 March 1944, FO371/42677; there was also some thanks for the attitude adopted with regard to French aims which 'should put the President in a very prickly mood on this subject for some little time'.

41 Ronald Campbell to Cadogan, 8 May 1944, DO35/1994; there was some suggestion that this 'informant' was actually Sir Owen Dixon, the Australian Minister in Washington.

42 Minute by Greenway, 18 February 1944, FO371/42681; ibid., Campbell to Butler, 6 March 1944.

43 Minute by Ashley Clarke, 2 March 1944, FO371/42677.

44 Ibid., minute by Newton, 4 April 1944.

45 Ian McGibbon, 'The Australian–New Zealand Defence Relationship since 1901', *Revue Internationale d'Histoire Militaire* (No. 72, 1990), p. 139.

46 William Johnstone, 'Australian and New Zealand Agree', *Far Eastern Survey* (Vol. 13, No. 4; 23 February 1944), pp. 31–5.

47 David Jenkins, 'Implementing the Canberra Pact', *Far Eastern Survey* (Vol. 14, No. 1; 17 January 1945), pp. 8–9.

48 Paul Emrys-Evans, 'Relations of the Dominions to the Colonial Empire', 13 January 1943, DO35/1896.

49 Batterbee to DO (telegram), 7 November 1944, DO35/1900.

50 'New Zealand–Australia Conference', Memorandum by Secretary of State for Dominion Affairs, 10 November 1944, CAB66/57/41.

51 Hankinson to Harvey, 28 March 1939, FO800/310.

52 DO minute, 10 November 1944, DO35/1214.

53 DO minute, 10 November 1944, DO35/1215.

54 Batterbee to DO, 30 October 1944, DO35/1214.

55 McIntosh to Berendsen, 29 November 1944 in McGibbon, *Undiplomatic Dialogue*.

56 Minute by Cranborne, 29 October 1944, DO35/1215.

57 Batterbee to Machtig, 8 November 1944, DO35/1214.

58   Ibid., Batterbee to Machtig, 27 November 1944.
59   Ibid., Batterbee to DO, 24 November 1944.
60   Minute by Machtig, 5 December 1944, DO35/1215.
61   Ibid., Batterbee to Machtig, 27 November 1944; minute by Cranborne, 3 December 1944.
62   Ibid., Batterbee to Machtig, 6 November 1944.
63   Evatt to Cranborne, 19 November 1944, DO35/1899; ibid., Cranborne to Evatt, 21 November
      1944; Evatt to Cranborne, 25 November 1944; Cranborne to Evatt, 1 December 1944.
64   Batterbee to Machtig, 8 November 1944, DO35/1215.
65   McIntosh to Berendsen, 10 November 1944 cited in McGibbon (ed.), *Undiplomatic Dialogue.*
66   Ibid., McIntosh to Berendsen, 21 December 1944.
67   Ibid., McIntosh to Berendsen, 29 November 1943.
68   David Day, *Reluctant Nation*, pp. 181–6; Watt, *The Evolution of Australian Foreign Policy*, p. 103.
69   Professor Vincent Harlow, 'Can the British Commonwealth Keep Together After the War?', *Evening
      Standard*, 27 January 1944; ibid., 'Speak with One Voice', 28 January 1944; 'States in Unison',
      Commonwealth and Empire Review (September–November 1944), p. 82.

Notes to Chapter 11: A Family Council

1   'Meeting of Dominion Prime Ministers', Memorandum by the Secretary of State for Dominion
      Affairs, 4 June 1941, CAB66/16.
2   'Brief History of Attempts to Arrange a Meeting During the War – Meeting of Dominion Prime
      Ministers, May 1944', n.d., DO35/1480.
3   Minute by Churchill, 8 April 1943, DO35/1470.
4   Ibid., Churchill to Attlee, 11 April 1943.
5   Cranborne to Churchill, 5 November 1943, DO121/10A.
6   Attlee to Churchill, 27 April 1944, DO121/10B; Cranborne to Churchill, 15 October 1943,
      DO121/10A; ibid., Cranborne to Churchill, 1 November 1943.
7   Ibid., Cranborne to Churchill, January 1944.
8   'Meeting with Dominion Prime Ministers', Memorandum by Cranborne, 7 January 1944,
      DO35/1473.
9   Ibid., 'Extract from the conclusions of a meeting of the War Cabinet held at 10 Downing Street,
      on Thursday 20 January 1944'.
10   Minute by Greenway, 7 February 1944, FO371/42677.
11   Minute by Boyd-Shannon, 9 December 1943, DO35/1473; ibid., minute by Machitg, 5 January
      1944; Machtig to Cranborne, 20 January 1944.
12   The Whitehall body was to consist of five Ministers supported by three secretaries. The chair
      would be taken by Cranborne with Bevin, Amery, Colonel Stanley and the FO Minister of State,
      Richard Law.
13   'Minutes of a meeting held on the DO on 15 February 1944', DPM(44) 1st Meeting,
      DO35/1488.
14   Minute by Newton, 14 February 1944, FO371/42681; ibid., minute by Greenway, 12 February
      1944; minute by Newton, 17 March 1944.
15   'Cooperation in the British Commonwealth', Memorandum by Cranborne, 7 April 1944,
      FO371/42682.
16   'Minutes of meeting held on 12 April 1944', DO35/1488.
17   Minute by Newton, 13 April 1944, FO371/42682; ibid., minute by Greenway, 11 April 1944.
18   Minute by Machtig, 12 February 1944, DO35/1474; ibid., Bevin to Cranborne, 1 February 1944;
      Amery to Cranborne, 25 January 1944.
19   Cranborne to Chiefs of Staff, 3 March 1944, DO35/1473.
20   'The Coordination of Defence Policy within the British Commonwealth in Relation to a World
      System of Security', Memorandum by the Chiefs of Staff Committee, 31 March 1944, DO35/1744;
      Lt. Colonel G. S. Cole (MO1) to Colonel W. Ray, 27 March 1944, CAB121/156; the first draft had

been undertaken by Brigadier Jacob and was submitted at the beginning of March 1944; 'Note by Brigadier Jacob', 8 March 1944, CAB80/81.

21 'Secretary's Note for the Chairman', 11 April 1944, DO35/1474; ibid., 'Secretary's Note for Chairman', 20 April 1944.

22 Minute by Butler, 12 February 1944, FO371/42677; ibid., minute by Jebb, 14 February 1944; Jacob to Greenway, 10 March 1944; minute by Brigadier Jacob, 1 April 1944.

23 Ibid., Smuts to Churchill (Telegram), 20 March 1944; minute by Greenway, 21 March 1944.

24 Greenway to Eden, 26 April 1944, FO371/42678.

25 'Growing Unity of the Empire', *Empire Review* (June–August 1944), pp. 69–71; Cranborne to Churchill, 20 April 1944, DO121/10A; ibid., 'Notes for Debate on Motion Regarding Empire and Commonwealth Unity', n.d.

26 'Empire and Commonwealth Unity', *House of Commons Official Report* (Vol. 399), 20/21 April 1944, pp. 390–486, 497–586.

27 'Mother England', *Time*, 1 May 1944.

28 'Note of Arrangements for Air Passages for Dominion Prime Ministers', 18 April 1944, DO35/1204.

29 Ibid., 'List of Accommodation Reserved for Dominion Prime Ministers', n.d.; note to Colonel Sir Eric Crankshaw, 16 April 1944.

30 'Arrangements for Meetings with Dominion Prime Ministers', Memorandum by the Prime Minister, 25 April 1944, CAB121/156.

31 'Meeting of British Commonwealth Prime Ministers, May 1944 – Notes on Administrative Arrangements', n.d., DO35/1480.

32 Lascelles to Cranborne, 1 April 1944, DO35/1475; ibid., minute by Stephenson, 22 April 1944.

33 'List of Social Engagements', n.d., DO35/1204; Cranborne to Churchill, 3 April 1944, DO121/10A.

34 'Social Engagements – Meeting of British Commonwealth Prime Ministers, May 1944', n.d., DO35/1480.

35 Cranborne to Churchill, 8 May 1944, DO121/10A.

36 'Publicity Arrangements', Note by Joint Secretaries, 5 April 1944, FO371/42682; 'Publicity Engagements – Meeting of British Commonwealth Prime Ministers, May 1944', n.d., DO35/1480.

37 'Commonwealth Faces the Future', *The Times*, 2 May 1944; 'Common Counsel', *The Round Table* (No. 134; March 1944), pp. 103–107; 'The Conference', *The Round Table* (No. 135; June 1944), pp. 195–8.

38 Minute by Cadogan, 12 June 1944, FO371/42678.

39 'Report of Speeches made at the Opening Meeting of the Prime Ministers', 1 May 1944, DO35/1854.

40 A. L. Kennedy to Newton, 4 May 1944, FO371/42681.

41 Minute by Greenway, 24 May 1944, FO371/42678.

42 Duff to Cranborne, 5 June 1944, DO35/1204; Holmes to Machtig, 29 June 1944, DO35/1476.

43 Minute by Newton, 17 May 1944, FO371/42682.

44 Cranborne to Churchill, 11 May 1944, DO121/10A.

45 McKinnon, *Undiplomatic Dialogue*, p. 77.

46 Boyd-Shannon to Antrobus, 18 August 1944, DO35/1854; ibid., minute by Machtig, 18 May 1944; minute by Stephenson, 18 May 1944.

47 Ibid., Churchill to Eden and Bridges, 21 May 1944; 'Future World Organisation – Meeting on 17 May 1944'; Eden to Churchill, 2 June 1944.

48 Minute by Compton, 7 July 1944, FO371/42682.

49 'Impressions of a New Zealand Official on his Return from the Australia–New Zealand Conference at Canberra, 31st January 1944', Note by F. E. Cuming-Bruce, 7 February 1944, DO35/1993; Cross to Cranborne, 13 April 1944, DO35/1476; ibid., Cross to Cranborne, 1 July 1944. Cross also took the opportunity to provide Whitehall with a detailed verbal picture of Curtin. This began with the comment 'If Mr Curtin were to be put on a clerical collar and stock he would appear to be a typical

middle-aged Church of England clergyman but offered a positive conclusion of a man who was committed to his country, filled with "right purpose" and, more significantly perhaps, convinced that Australia's future was "as a partner of the Commonwealth of Nations"'; 'Note by Cross', 2 April 1944, DO35/1476.

50 Cross to Cranborne, 10 June, DO35/111.
51 Cross to Cranborne, 26 July 1944, DO35/1118.
52 Pickersgill, *The Mackenzie King Record*, pp. 663–96.
53 Ritchie Diary, 2 February 1944, *Siren Years*, pp. 163/164.
54 Minute by Campbell, 31 May 1944, FO371/42682; ibid., minute by Campbell, 25 May 1944.
55 Garner to Cranborne, 26 May 1944, DO35/1204.
56 Minute for Prime Minister, 27 April 1944, CAB120/813; ibid., Colville to Brigadier Jacob, 1 May 1944.
57 Smuts, *Jan Christian Smuts*, p. 452.
58 Thorn, *Peter Fraser*, pp. 222–4; W. D. McIntyre, 'Peter Fraser's Commonwealth' in A. D. McIntosh et al., *New Zealand in World Affairs, Vol. 1* (Wellington, 1972), pp. 47–8.
59 'Meeting of the King's Prime Ministers of the United Kingdom, Canada, Australia, New Zealand and South Africa', 16th May 1944, DO118/24.
60 'Commonwealth Consultations', *Commonwealth and Empire Review* (March–May 1945), p. 38–9.
61 'Prime Minister's Conference: A Milestone in History', *Empire Review* (June–August 1944), pp. 11–14.
62 'Family Council', *Time*, 17 April 1944; 'The Brothers', *Time*, 22 May 1944.

Notes to Chapter 12: Losing an Empire

1 Ashley Jackson, *The British Empire and the Second World War* (London, 2006), pp. 21–40.
2 'The Conference of 1944', *The Round Table* (No. 136; September 1944), pp. 311–12.
3 Halifax to FO, 7 May 1944, FO371/42682; ibid., minute by Campbell, 8 May 1944; minute by Butler, 10 May 1944; minute by Butler, 30 May 1944; minute by Campbell, 16 June 1944.
4 Ibid., minute by Mason, 19 May 1944.
5 Memorandum (WP(43)115), 22 March 1943, DO35/1838; ibid., Archer to Maclennan, 20 April 1943.
6 Memorandum prepared by MacDonald, 'Methods of Achieving Imperial Unity', April 1944, DO35/1489.
7 Minute by Cranborne, 12 November 1944, DO35/1204; ibid., minute by Emrys–Evans, 6 November 1944; Garner to Machtig, 15 April 1944.
8 Professor H. L. Stewart, 'A Closer Empire Unity', Speech at the Empire Club of Canada, 27 April 1944.
9 Charles Luke, 'Plan for Commonwealth Unity', *Empire Review* (March–May 1944), p. 72.
10 Minute by Campbell, 25 May 1944, FO371/42682; ibid., minute by Newton, 1 June 1944.
11 Halifax to Eden, 14 April 1944, DO35/1204.
12 Ibid., Circular from Eden, 3 October 1944; Machtig to Emrys-Evans, 24 July 1944; Garner to Costar, 4 February 1944; Batterbee to Machtig, 14 April 1944.
13 'Civil Aviation', 1 June 1943, *House of Commons Official Report* (Vol. 390), pp. 90–143.
14 WHCM, 9 June 1942, DO121/12; WHCM, 28 November 1944, DO121/14; Bissell, *Imperial Canadian*, p. 130; Orders, *Britain, Australia, New Zealand and the Challenge of the United States*, pp. 22–3.
15 Minute by Machtig, 9 January 1945, DO35/1236; ibid., minute by Cranborne, 14 January 1945; Boyd-Shannon, 'British Commonwealth Delegations to Chicago Conference, November 1944', n.d. (December 1944).
16 Minute by Boyd-Shannon, 2 April 1945, DO35/1891; 'After Chicago', *The Round Table* (No. 138; March 1945), pp. 130–6.
17 E. J. Hughes, 'Winston Churchill and the Formation of the United Nations Organisation', *Journal of Contemporary History* (Vol. 9, No. 4; October 1974), p. 193.

18 Adam Roberts, 'Britain and the Creation of the United Nations' in Roger Louis (ed.) *Still More Adventures with Britannia* (London, 2003), p. 231; Hughes, 'Winston Churchill and the Formation of the United Nations Organisation', p. 193; *Memoirs of Lord Gladwyn* (London, 1972), pp. 118, 121–2; 'Something for a Name', *Time*, 6 July 1942 – the name was first used officially on January 1, 1942, when 26 states joined in the 'Declaration by the United Nations', pledging to continue their joint war effort and not to make peace separately.

19 'Proposed Four-Power Declaration', Memorandum by the Secretary of State for Dominion Affairs, WP(43)412, 22 September 1943, CAB66/41/12.

20 Woodward, *British Foreign Policy in the Second World War*, pp. 135–72.

21 Op. cit., Woodward, pp. 282–300.

22 Holmes to Stephenson, 2 April 1945, DO35/1891.

23 Cranborne to Churchill, 7 December 1944, DO121/10A.

24 Ibid., Cranborne to Churchill, 2 April 1945.

25 Ibid., minute by Cranborne, 23 March 1945.

26 'British Commonwealth Meeting', 4 April 1945, DO35/1213; 'British Commonwealth Meeting April 1945 – Minutes of Meetings and Memoranda', CAB133/325.

27 Dilks, *The Diaries of Sir Alexander Cadogan*, 4 and 9 April 1945, pp. 726–7.

28 Colonel Oliver Stanley, 'International Aspects of Colonial Policy', 21 December 1944, DO35/1900; this document was produced by the CO with the DO being allowed to see drafts at various stages but not being invited to comment.

29 Ibid., Churchill to Eden, 31 December 1944; Eden to Churchill, 8 January 1945.

30 Roger Louis, *Imperialism at Bay*, pp. 455–8; describing this intervention Louis opined that 'rhetorically it must rank high in the annals of British imperialism as an extemporaneous and uninhibited defence of the Empire'.

31 'International Aspects of Colonial Policy', Memorandum by Secretary of State for the Colonies, 19 March 1945, CAB66/63/55.

32 'International Aspects of Colonial Policy', Memorandum by the Secretary of State for Dominion Affairs (as Chairman of the British Commonwealth Meetings on World Organisation), 10 April 1945, CAB66/64/28.

33 'Note on Trusteeship for Mr Bottomley by Mr Boyd-Shannon', 15 October 1946, DO35/1912.

34 William Hardy McNeill, *Survey of International Affairs: America, Britain and Russia – Their Cooperation and Conflict, 1941–1946* (London, 1953), pp. 592–4.

35 Minute by Butler, 31 August 1944, FO371/38721; 'Note of conditions of appointment of Mr B. Cockram on attachment to HM's United Kingdom Embassy, Washington', 3 November 1944.

36 Minute by Machtig, 12 July 1945, DO35/1884.

37 Ibid., Cockram to Machtig, 28 April 1945.

38 Ibid., Cockram to Stephenson, 15 May 1945.

39 'International Aspects of Colonial Policy', Memorandum by the Secretary of State for the Colonies, WP(45)300, 14 May 1945, CAB66/65/50.

40 Cockram to Stephenson, 15 May 1945, DO35/1884. He was not alone in this view, Cadogan agreed, Evatt was 'the most frightful man in the world; he makes long and tiresome speeches on every conceivable subject, always advocating the wrong things and generally with a view to being inconvenient and offensive to us, and boosting himself. However, everyone by now hates Evatt so much that his stock has gone down a bit and he matters less'; Dilks (ed.), *The Diaries of Sir Alexander Cadogan*, 21 May 1945, p. 745.

41 Smuts, *Jan Christian Smuts*, pp. 474–5, 482–3.

42 Cockram to Stephenson, 2 June 1945, DO35/1884.

43 Ibid., Cockram to Stephenson, 16 June 1945.

44 Cockram to Gladwyn Jebb, 20 March 1945, DO35/1891.

45 Paul Hasluck, 'Australia and the Formation of the United Nations', *Royal Australian Historical Society Journal and Proceedings* (Vol. 40, No. 3; 1954), p. 167.

46 David Tothill, 'Evatt and Smuts in San Francisco', *The Round Table* (Vol. 96, No. 389; April 2007), pp. 178/9, 181, 183, 187–9.

47   Cockram to Stephenson, 23 June 1945, DO35/1884; this was an example of a wider malaise largely resulting from the statements made during the signing of the Anzac Pact. The American military had decided it did not need any help from the Dominions during the final phases of the Pacific war and the result was that British Commonwealth forces played only a peripheral role. In reality the United States appeared to have grown weary of Australian-led demands for a greater say in post-war planning for the Pacific region; Orders, *Britain, Australia, New Zealand and the Challenge of the United States*, pp. 129–30; Bell, *Unequal Allies*, pp. 159–203.
48   UK Delegation San Francisco to FO, 23 June 1945, DO35/1884; ibid., Cockram to Stephenson, 18 June 1945.
49   Telegram from DO Section, San Francisco Conference to DO, 26 June 1945, DO35/1883; ibid., 'Summary of Reports on Dr Evatt's Press Conference for the United Kingdom Press, Friday 22 June', 23 June 1945.
50   Telegram from Australia HC to DO, 29 June 1945, DO35/1883; ibid, 4 July 1945; Eggleston, who had been a member of the Australian delegation and was not noted for his admiration for Evatt, thought that there was something in the Australian complaint. Whilst he agreed it was difficult to accuse Halifax of being 'disingenuous', his claims that the British had effectively been responsible for the chapter on trusteeship that developed were unfair on Evatt and did not reflect the work he had had put in on the issue, not just at San Francisco but in the years before, Frederic Eggleston to Stanley Bruce, 9 July 1945 (National Archives, Canberra) M100, July 1945.
51   Cranborne to Evatt, 25 June 1945, DO35/1883; ibid., Evatt to Cranborne, 26 June 1945; ibid., Cranborne to Evatt, 26 June 1945.
52   Minute by Charles Welsley (FO), 24 August 1945, FO371/50371.
53   Cockram to Stephenson, 2 July 1945, DO35/1883; ibid., minute by Cockram, 2 July 1945.
54   'Debate on the Address', *House of Commons Official .Report* (Vol. 406), 1 December 1944, pp. 211–12.
55   Batterbee to Cranborne, 20 July 1945, DO35/1119.
56   Cranborne to Emrys-Evans, July 1945, Emrys-Evans Papers; Emrys-Evans lost his Derbyshire South seat at the 1945 general election – he was in good company as so did 31 other ministers or junior ministers in one of the largest ever changes of elected government.

Notes to Conclusion: Brave New World

1   R. G. Casey, *Double or Quit* (Melbourne, 1949), p. 104.
2   Ritchie Diary, 25 December 1940, *Siren Years*, p. 81.
3   Speech given at luncheon, 23 February 1942, Attlee Papers, MS.Attlee dep. 4, fol.209–20.
4   Diary, Lt. Colonel C. A. de Candole Papers (Imperial War Museum), 98/35/1.
5   Porter, 'What Did They Know of Empire?', p. 47; Denis Judd, 'Britain: Land Beyond Hope and Glory', p. 20.
6   John O'Sullivan, 'The History of Empire Can Reunite This Divided Nation', *Daily Telegraph*, 1 September 2007.
7   Cited in H. Duncan Hall, 'The British Commonwealth as a Great Power', *Foreign Affairs*, July 1945; comments by Heathcote-Smith, 21 August 1945, FO371/50371; McIntyre, 'Clio and Britannia's Lost Dream: Historians and the British Commonwealth of Nations in the First Half of the 20th Century', *The Round Table* (Vol. 93, No. 376; September 2004), pp. 521–2.
8   Diary, 14 December 1940, *Hugh Dalton*, pp. 121–2; Bell (ed.), *The Headlam Diaries*, 24 September 1942, p. 334.
9   'Situation in the South-West Pacific', *House of Lords Official Report* (Vol. 71), 29 January 1942, p. 578.
10 B. J. C. McKercher, 'The Foreign Office, 1930–39: Strategy, Permanent Interests and National Security', *Contemporary British History* (Vol. 18, No. 3; Autumn 2004), pp. 95, 87.
11 Garner to Costar, 4 February 1944, DO35/1024/75/23.
12 Campbell to Batterbee, 20 May 1940, Batterbee Papers, Box 6/2.

13 Holland, *Britain and the Commonwealth Alliance*, p. 172.

14 Amery to Cranborne, 4 February 1944, DO35/1485; Amery to Cranborne, 28 January 1942, Amery Papers, AMEL2/1/34.

15 Churchill (ed.), *Never Give In!*, pp. 299–301.

16 Eden to Whiskard, 4 February 1940, DO35/1003/3/43; Churchill to Curtin, 21 March 1942, PREM3/206/1–3; ibid., Curtin to Churchill, 22 March 1942; 'Australia and the Empire', *The Times*, 24 March 1942; minute by Machtig, 19 February 1943, DO35/1896/213/3; A. J. Stockwell, 'The Audit of War', *History Today* (March 2006), pp. 52–3; Arnold L. Haskell, *The Dominions – Partnership or Rift* (London, 1943), pp. 5–32; Jeffrey Grey, 'Australia and Allied Relations in the Post-War Period, 1945–1972', *Revue Internationale d'Histoire Militaire* (No. 72, 1990), p. 168.

17 Ritchie Diary, 18 March 1941, *Siren Years*, p. 96; 'We Remain in Commonwealth after War', *Daily Chronicle*, 23 June 1942 .

18 'South Africa: Notes for Lecturers', War Office, 25 February 1942, FO371/34088.

19 'Empire and the War', November 1939, DO35/99/24/3; Harlech to Attlee, 20 July 1942, FO954/4B; Gann, 'South Africa and the Third Reich', p. 518; Smuts to Theron, 21 July 1942, Smuts Papers; Grundlingh, *The King's Afrikaners*, p. 354; Annette Seegers, *The Military in the Making of Modern South Africa* (London, 1996), pp. 58–9.

20 Batterbee to Machtig, 21 December 1941, DO121/116; Cranborne to Churchill, 2 February 1942, PREM3/150/2; 'Notes on New Zealand's War Effort and Future Participation in Pacific War', 5 May 1944, DO35/1631; by the 28 November 1945 final casualty figures stood at 9,334 dead and 27,413 wounded. This compares with 16,302 dead and 41,702 wounded during the Great War – 'British Empire War Casualties', CAB106/305.

21 'Recall Without Repining', W. G. Stevens Papers, p. 217.

22 Arnold Toynbee, 'The British Commonwealth' in Toynbee and Ashton-Gwatkin (eds), *Survey of International Affairs 1939–1946*, pp. 28–9.

23 Lawrence James, 'Nailing the Lie of the Evil Empire', *The Sunday Times*, 18 June 2006; a provocative account of the British response to the Mau Mau uprising in Kenya in the 1950s was condemned by the renowned reviewer who described its author as an 'heir of the war of independence and schooled to believe that all empires are intrinsically evil'.

24 Nicholas Mansergh (ed.), *The Constitutional Relations between Britain and India: The Transfer of Power, 1942–1947* (London, 1971), p. 253.

25 'Sub-Committee 1 on American Opinion, Preliminary Report', 27 January 1943, FO371/34086; minute by Attlee to Churchill, 16 June 1942, DO121/10B; Mansergh, *The Commonwealth and the Nations*, pp. 66–75.

26 A. Duff Cooper, 'The Future Development of the British Empire' (12 January 1943), *United Empire* (Vol. 34, No. 2), p. 33; Howe, *Have We Bonds*, p. 245.

27 For an excellent review see Niall Ferguson, 'Hegemony or Empire?', *Foreign Affairs* (September/October 2003), pp. 154–61.

28 Heinlein, *British Government Policy and Decolonisation*, p. 11–12; 'A Record of Great Achievement', *The Commonwealth and Empire Review* (Vol. 79, No. 513; June–August 1945), p. 20; Ovendale, *English Speaking Alliance*, pp. 17–18; David Sanders, *Losing an Empire, Finding a Role: British Foreign Policy Since 1945* (London, 1990), pp. 47–9.

29 'British Empire War Casualties', Cohen to Brigadier General Edmonds, 7 June 1945, CAB106/305; Glen St J. Barclay, *The Empire is Marching* (London, 1976), pp. 214, 217.

30 Francine McKenzie, 'In the National Interest: Dominions' Support for Britain and the Commonwealth after the Second World War', *The Journal of Imperial and Commonwealth History* (Vol. 34, No. 4; December 2006), pp. 553–76; John Gallagher, *The Decline, Revival and Fall of the British Empire*, pp. 143–8; Ritchie Ovendale, *The English-Speaking Alliance: Britain, the United States, the Dominions and the Cold War 1945–1951*, pp. 17–25; D. K. Fieldhouse, 'The Labour Governments and the Empire–Commonwealth, 1945–1951' in Ritchie Ovendale, *The Foreign Policy of the British Labour Governments, 1945–1951* (Leicester, 1984), pp. 83–120; Heinlein, *British Government Policy and Decolonisation*, pp. 8, 64–7, 72–3; Eugene P. Chase, 'Government by Consultation in the British Commonwealth', *The Journal of Politics* (Vol. 9,

No. 3; May 1947), pp. 198–210; K. C. Wheare, 'Is the British Commonwealth Withering Away?', *The American Political Science Review* (Vol. 4, No. 3; September 1950), pp. 545–55; 'Dominions Now Seen in Key Role of Empire's Power and Preservation, *The Dominion* (Wellington), 25 November 1947; 'Britain at the End of an Era. Dominions Now in Key Role', *The New York Times*, 24 November 1947; James L. Sturgis, 'What's In A Name?: A Perspective on the Transition of Empire/Commonwealth 1918–1950', *The Round Table* (No. 334, 1995), p. 203; Halifax to Eden, 25 April 1944, DO35/1204.

31   Barnett, *The Collapse of British Power*, p. 232; Correlli Barnett, 'Imperial Overstretch, from Dr Arnold to Mr Blair', *RUSI Journal* (August 2005), pp. 27–8.

32   'Man of England', *Time*, 6 March 1944.

33   'King's Speech – Debate on the Address', *House of Commons Official Report* (Vol. 457), 28 October 1948, p. 242.

34   'Foreign Affairs', *House of Lords Official Report* (Vol. 81), 25 May 1944, pp. 953–4, 998–9, 1011.

35   John Bierman and Colin Smith, *Alamein: War Without Hate* (London, 2003), p. 334.

36   'Note of a Talk with Mr Bruce at 10.00am on the 23rd of October [1945] at Shoreham Hotel, Washington', DO35/1491.

Bibliography

PUBLISHED SOURCES

Addison, Paul (1994) *The Road to 1945*, London: Pimlico.

Alport, C. J. M. (1937) *Kingdoms in Partnership: A Study of Political Change in the British Commonwealth*, London: Lovat Dickson Ltd.

Amery, L. S. (1953) *My Political Life: Vol. 2, War and Peace, 1914–1929*, London: Macmillan.

——(1964) *Thoughts on the Constitution*, London: Oxford University Press.

Andrews, E. M. (1970) *Isolationism and Appeasement in Australia*, Canberra: ANUP.

——(1987) *The Writing on the Wall: The British Commonwealth and Aggression in the East, 1931–1935*, Sydney: Allen and Unwin.

Armstrong, H. C. (1937) *Grey Steel: J.C. Smuts, A Study in Arrogance*, London: Arthur Barker Ltd.

Atkin, Ronald (1980) *Dieppe 1942, The Jubilee Disaster*, London: Macmillan.

Attlee, Clement (1954) *As It Happened*, London: Heinemann.

Avon, Earl of (1965) *The Eden Memoirs: Vol. 3, The Reckoning*, London: Cassell and Co. Ltd.

Balfour, Harold (1973) *Wings over Westminster*, London: Hutchinson and Co.

Ball, Stuart (ed.) (1999) *Parliament and Politics in the Age of Churchill and Attlee: The Headlam Diaries, 1935–1941*, London: Cambridge University Press.

Barclay, Glen St J. (1976) *The Empire is Marching*, London: Weidenfeld and Nicolson.

Barnes, John and David Nicholson (eds) (1987), *The Empire at Bay: The Leo Amery Diaries, 1929–1945*, London: Hutchinson.

Barnett, Correlli (1984), *The Collapse of British Power*, Gloucester: Sutton.

——(1986), *The Audit of War: The Illusion and Reality of Britain as a Great Nation*, London: Macmillan.

——(1995), *The Lost Victory: British Dreams, British Realities 1945–1950*, London: Macmillan.

Barr, Niall (2005), *The Pendulum of War: The Three Battles of El Alamein*, London: Pimlico.

Barris, Ted (1992), *Behind the Glory*, Toronto: Macmillan Canada.

Baxter, Chris and Andrew Stewart (eds) (2008), *Diplomats at War*, Leiden: Brill.

Beevor, Antony (1991), *Crete: The Battle and the Resistance*, London: John Murray.

Bell, Coral (1988), *Dependent Ally: A Study in Australian Foreign Policy*, Melbourne: Oxford University Press.

Bell, P. M. H. (1974), *A Certain Eventuality*, London: Saxon House.

——(1986), *The Origins of the Second World War*, London: Longman.

——(1997), *France and Britain, 1940–94*, London: Longman.

Bell, Roger J. (1977), *Unequal Allies, Australian–American Relations and the Pacific War*, Melbourne: Melbourne University Press.

Beloff, Max (1970), *Imperial Sunset: Vol. 1, Britain's Liberal Empire, 1897–1921*, New York: Alfred A. Knopf.

——(1989), *Imperial Sunset: Vol. 2, Dream of Commonwealth, 1921–42*, London: Macmillan.

Bennett, George (ed.) (1953), *The Concept of Empire*, London: Adam and Charles Black.

Berriedale, Keith A. (1932), *Speeches and Documents on the British Dominions, 1918–1931*, London: Oxford University Press.

Bierman, John and Colin Smith (2003), *Alamein: War Without Hate*, London: Penguin.

Birkby, Carel (1987), *Uncle George: The Boer Boyhood, Letters and Battles of Lieutenant-General George Edwin Brink*, Johannesburg: Jonathan Ball Publishers.

Bissell, Claude (1986), *The Imperial Canadian: Vincent Massey*, Toronto: University of Toronto Press.

Blainey, Geoffrey (1988), *The Causes of War*, 3rd edn, London: Macmillan.

Blake, Robert and Wm Roger Louis (eds) (1993), *Churchill: A Major New Reassessment of His Life in Peace and War*, London: Oxford University Press.

Bolitho, Hector (ed.) (1947), *The British Empire*, London: B. T. Batsford Ltd.

Bond, Brian (1980), *British Military Policy between the Two World Wars*, Oxford: Clarendon Press.

Bourne, K. and D. C. Watt (eds) (1967), *Studies in International History*, London: Longman.

Boyce, Robert and E. M. Robertson (eds) (1989), *Paths to War: New Essays on the Origin of the Second World War*, New York: St Martin's Press.

Brett, Judith (1992), *Robert Menzies' Forgotten People*, Australia: Macmillan.

Bridge, Carl (ed.) (1991), *Munich to Vietnam: Australia's Relations with Britain and the United States since the 1930s*, Melbourne: Melbourne University Press.

Broad, Lewis (1955), *Sir Anthony Eden: The Chronicles of a Career*, New York: Thomas Crowell.

Brown, J. M. and Wm Roger Louis (eds) (1999), *The Oxford History of the British Empire: Vol. 4, The Twentieth Century*, Oxford: Oxford University Press.

Brown Scott, James (1921), *Autonomy and Federation within Empire: The British Self Governing Dominions*, Washington DC: Carnegie Endowment.

Butler, J. R. M. (1957), *Grand Strategy: Vol. 2*, London: HMSO.

Cain, Frank (ed.) (1998), *Menzies in War and Peace*, Sydney: Allen and Unwin.

Cain, P. J. and A. G. Hopkins (2002), *British Imperialism 1688–2000*, Harlow: Pearson Education Ltd.

Callahan, Raymond (1977), *Worst Disaster: Fall of Singapore*, Delaware: University of Delaware Press.

——(1984), *Churchill, Retreat from Empire*, Wilmington: Scholarly Resources Inc.

Campbell, Alexander (1943), *Smuts and the Swastika*, London: Victor Gollancz Ltd.

Campbell, Gerald (1949), *Of True Experience*, London: Hutchinson and Company Ltd.

Canndine, David (2002), *Ornamentalism, How the British Saw Their Empire*, London: Penguin Books.

Canny, Nicholas (ed.) (1998), *The Oxford History of the British Empire: Vol. 1, The Origins of Empire*, Oxford: Oxford University Press.

Careless, J. M. S. and R. Craig Brown (eds) (1967), *The Canadians 1867–1967*, Toronto: Macmillan Canada.

Carlton, David (1981), *Anthony Eden*, London: Allen Lane.

Carter, G. M. (1947), *The British Commonwealth and International Security*, Toronto: Ryerson Press.

Casey, R. G. (1949), *Double or Quit*, Melbourne: F. W. Cheshire.

——(1962), *Personal Experience*, London: Constable and Company Ltd.

'Cato' (1940), *Guilty Men*, London: Victor Gollancz Ltd.

Lord Chandos (Oliver Lyttelton) (1962), *Memoirs*, London: Bodley Head.

Chanock, Martin (1977), *Unconsummated Union: Britain, Rhodesia and South Africa, 1900–1945*, London: Macmillan.

Charmley, John (1989), *Chamberlain and the Lost Peace*, London: Macmillan.

——(1993), *Churchill: The End of Glory*, London: BCA.

Chisholm, Anne and Michael Davie (1992), *Beaverbrook: A Life*, London: Hutchinson.

Churchill, Winston (1949), *The Second World War: Vol. 1, The Gathering Storm*, London: Cassell and Co. Ltd.

——(1949), *The Second World War: Vol. 2, The Finest Hour*, London: Cassell and Co. Ltd.

——(1949), *The Second World War: Vol. 3, The Grand Alliance*, London: Cassell and Co. Ltd.

Churchill, Winston S. (ed.) (2004), *Never Give In! The Best of Winston Churchill's Speeches*, London: Pimlico.

Clark, Margaret (ed.) (1998), *Peter Fraser: Master Politician*, Palmerston North: The Dunmore Press.

Clayton, Anthony (1986), *The British Empire as a Superpower 1919–1939*, Athens, GA: The University of Georgia Press.

Collier, Richard (1993), *The Years of Attrition*, London: Allison and Busby.

Colville, John (1981), *Winston Churchill and His Inner Circle*, New York: Wyndham Books.

——(1985), *The Fringes of Power: Vol. 1, 1939–41*, London: Hodder and Stoughton.

——(1987), *The Fringes of Power: Vol. 2, Oct 1941–April 1955*, London: Sceptre.

Commonwealth Relations Handbook, 1952 (1951), London: HMSO.

Commonwealth Relations Handbook, 1967 (1966), London: HMSO.

Constantine, Stephen (ed.) (1992), *Dominions Diary: The Letters of E. J. Harding, 1913–1916*, Halifax: Ryburn Publishing.

Cowan, John (1952), *Canada's Governor-Generals, 1867–1952*, Toronto: York.

Cowie, Donald (1941), *War for Britain: The Inner Story of the Empire in Action, September 1939–September 1940*, London: Chapman and Hall Ltd.

Cowman, Ian (1996), *Dominion or Decline: Anglo–American Naval Relations in the Pacific, 1937–1941*, Oxford: Berg.

Creighton, Donald (1976), *The Forked Road: Canada 1939–57*, Canada: McClelland and Stewart.

Crisp, Dorothy (1944), *Why We Lost Singapore*, London: Dorothy Crisp and Co. Ltd.

Cross, Colin (1968), *The Fall of the British Empire*, London: Hodder and Stoughton.

Cross, John A. (1967), *Whitehall and the Commonwealth: British Departmental Organisation for Commonwealth Relations, 1900–1966*, London: Routledge and Kegan Paul.

Crozier, Andrew (1988), *Appeasement and Germany's Last Bid for Colonies*, London: Palgrave Macmillan.

Cruickshank, Charles (1976), *Greece 1940–41*, London: Davis-Poynter.

Cumpston, I. M. (ed.) (1973), *The Growth of the British Commonwealth 1880–1932*, London: Edward Arnold Publishers Ltd.

——(1989), *Lord Bruce of Melbourne*, Melbourne: Longman.

Curtis, Lionel (1942), *Decision and Action*, London: Angus and Robertson Ltd.

Darby, Phillip (1987), *Three Faces of Imperialism: British and American Approaches to Asia and Africa, 1870–1970*, Yale: Yale University Press.

Darwin, John (1991), *The End of the British Empire, The Historical Debate*, Oxford: Basil Blackwell Ltd.

Davenport, T. R. H. (1991), *South Africa – A Modern History*, London: Macmillan.

Davis, Lance E. and Robert A. Huttenback (1986), *Mammon and the Pursuit of Empire, The Political Economy of British Imperialism, 1860–1912*, Cambridge: Cambridge University Press.

Robert MacGregor Dawson (ed.) (1965), *The Development of Dominion Status 1900–1936*, London: Frank Cass and Co. Ltd.

Day, David (1988), *Menzies and Churchill at War*, New York: Paragon House Publishers.

——(1988), *The Great Betrayal, Britain, Australia and the Onset of the Pacific War 1939–42*, Melbourne: Oxford University Press.

——(1992), *Reluctant Nation, Australia and the Allied Defeat of Japan 1942–1945*, Melbourne: Oxford University Press.

——(2000), *John Curtin: A Life*, Sydney: HarperCollins Publishers.

Deane Potter, John (1970), *Fiasco: The Break-out of the German Battleships*, New York: Stein and Day.

Dilks, David (ed.) (1971), *The Diaries of Sir Alexander Cadogan, 1938–45*, London: Cassell and Co. Ltd.

——(1978), *Britain, Canada and the Wider World*, Canada House Lecture No. 4.

——(ed.) (1981), *Retreat from Power: Vol. 1*, London: Macmillan Press.

——(ed.) (1981), *Retreat from Power: Vol. 2*, London: Macmillan Press.

Dockrill, M. L. and B. McKercher (eds) (1996), *Diplomacy and World Power, Studies in British Foreign Policy 1890–1950*, Cambridge: Cambridge University Press.

Dockrill, Saki (ed.) (1994), *From Pearl Harbor to Hiroshima*, London: Macmillan.

Donaghy, Greg (1995), *Parallel Paths: Canadian–Australian Relations Since the 1890s*, Ottawa, ON: Department of Foreign Affairs.

Douglas, Roy (1986), *World Crisis and British Decline, 1929–1956*, London: Macmillan.

Douglas, W. (1986), *The Creation of a National Air Force: The Official History of the RCAF, Vol. 2*, Toronto, ON: University of Toronto Press.

Dugdale, Blanche E. (1936), *Arthur James Balfour, First Earl of Balfour, 1906–1930*, London: Hutchinson.

Duncan Hall, H. (1971), *Commonwealth: A History of the British Commonwealth of Nations*, London: Van Nostrand Reinhold Co.

Duncan Hall, H. and William Elliot (eds) (1943), *The British Commonwealth at War*, New York: Alfred A. Knopf.

Dunmore, Spencer (1994), *Wings for Victory*, Toronto: McClelland and Stewart Inc.

Dunn, David (1997), *Anthony Eden*, London: Arnold.

Dunn, Michael (1984), *Australia and the Empire 1788 to Present*, Sydney: Collin.

Eade, Charles (ed.) (1954), *Churchill by His Contemporaries*, New York: Simon and Schuster.

Eayrs, James (1965), *In Defence of Canada*, Toronto, ON: University of Toronto Press.

Edwards, Cecil (1965), *Bruce of Melbourne: Man of Two Worlds*, London: Heinemann.

Edwards, P. G. (1983), *Prime Ministers and Diplomats, The Making of Australian Foreign Policy, 1901–49*, Melbourne: Oxford University Press.

Elliott, W. Y. (1932), *The New British Empire*, London: McGraw-Hill Book Company Inc.

Lord Elton (1946), *Imperial Commonwealth*, New York: Reynal and Hitchcock.

Empire Information Service (1946), *Origins and Purpose: A Handbook on the British Commonwealth and Empire*, London: HMSO.

English, John (1989), *Shadow of Heaven: The Life of Lester Pearson: Vol. 1*, Toronto, ON: Lester and Orpen Dennys.

Estorick, Eric (1949), *Stafford Cripps: A Biography*, London: Heinemann.

Evatt, H. V. (1945), *Foreign Policy of Australia*, London: Angus and Robertson Ltd.

Fadden, Sir Arthur (1969), *They Called Me Artie*, Melbourne: Jacaranda.

Farrell, Brian P. (2006), *The Defence and Fall of Singapore 1940–1942*, Stroud: Tempus,

Ferguson, Niall (2004), *Empire, How Britain Made the Modern World*, London: Penguin Books.

Fiddes, Sir George (1926) *The Dominions and Colonial Offices*, London: G. P. Putnam.

Forbes, Avery H. (1911), *A History of the British Dominions Beyond the Seas*, London: Ralph, Holland and Co.

Foot, M. R. D. (ed.) (1973), *War and Society: Historical Essays in Honour of J. R. Western*, London: Elek Books.

Gallagher, John (1982), *The Decline, Revival and Fall of the British Empire*, London: Cambridge University Press.

Gannon, F. R. (1971), *The British Press and Germany, 1936–1939*, Oxford: Clarendon Press.

Garner, Joe (1978), *The Commonwealth Office, 1925–68*, London: Heinemann.

Gelber, H. G. (ed.) (1970), *Problems of Australian Defence*, Melbourne: Oxford University Press.

Geyser, O. (2001), *Jan Smuts and His Contemporaries*, Johannesburg: Covos Day.

Gilbert, Martin (1983), *Winston Churchill: Finest Hour, 1939–1941*, London: Heinemann.

——(1986), *Winston Churchill: Road to Victory, 1941–1945*, London: Heinemann.

——(1992), *Churchill: A Life*, London: Minerva Books.

——(1994), *In Search of Churchill*, London: HarperCollins Publishers Ltd.

Lord Gladwyn (1972), *Memoirs of Lord Gladwyn*, London: Weidenfeld and Nicolson.

Golley, John (1983), *Aircrew Unlimited*, London: Patrick Stephens Ltd.

Gordon, Donald (1965), *The Dominion Partnership in Imperial Defence, 1870–1914*, Baltimore: John Hopkins.

Granatstein, J. L. (1975), *Canada's War*, Toronto, ON: University of Toronto Press.

Grant, Bruce (1972), *The Crisis of Loyalty, A Study of Australia Foreign Policy*, Sydney: Angus and Robertson.

Grey, Jeffrey (1990), *A Military History of Australia*, Cambridge: Cambridge University Press.

Griffiths, Sir Percivale (1969), *Empire into Commonwealth*, London: Ernest Benn Limited.

Grigg, Sir Edward (1943), *The British Commonwealth, Its Place in the Service of the World*, London: Hutchinson and Co. Ltd.

Earl of Halifax (1957), *Fullness of Days*, London: Collins.

Hall, Walter Phelps (1928), *Empire to Commonwealth, Thirty Years of British Imperial History*, New York: Henry Holt and Co.

Hancock, Kenneth (1946), *New Zealand at War*, Wellington: A. H. and A. W. Reed.

Hancock, W. K. (1937), *Survey of British Commonwealth Affairs: Vol. 1, Problems of Nationality, 1918–1936*, London: Oxford University Press.

——(1942), *Survey of British Commonwealth Affairs: Vol. 2, Problems of Economic Policy, 1918–1939*, London: Oxford University Press.

——(1943), *Argument of Empire*, London: Penguin Books.

——(1968), *Smuts: The Fields of Force, 1919–1950*, Cambridge: Cambridge University Press.

W. K. Hancock and M. M. Gowing (eds) (1949), *British War Economy*, London: HMSO.

Hankey, Maurice (1961), *The Supreme Command, 1914–1918: Vol. 2*, London: Allen and Unwin.

Harvey, Heather (1952), *Consultation and Cooperation in the Commonwealth*, London: Oxford University Press.

Harvey, John (ed.) (1970), *The Diplomatic Diaries of Oliver Harvey, 1937–1940*, London: Collins.

——(1978), *The War Diaries of Oliver Harvey, 1941–1945*, London: Collins.

Haskell, Arnold (1943), *The Dominions, Partnership or Rift*, London: Adam and Charles Black.

Hasluck, Paul (1952), *The Government and the People, 1939–41*, Canberra: Australian War Memorial.

——(1980), *Diplomatic Witness*, Melbourne: Melbourne University Press.

Hatch, F. (1983), *The Aerodrome of Democracy*, Ottawa, ON: Department of National Defence.

Hazlehurst, Cameron (1979), *Menzies Observed*, Sydney: George Allen and Unwin.

Heaton Nicholls, G. (1961), *South Africa in My Time*, London: Allen and Unwin.

Heinlein, Frank (2002), *British Government Policy and Decolonisation 1945–1963*, London: Frank Cass.

Hetherington, John (1973), *Blamey: Controversial Soldier*, Canberra: Australian War Memorial.

Hill, Christopher (1991), *Cabinet Decisions on Foreign Policy, 1938–1941*, London: Cambridge University Press.

Hilliker John (1990), *Canada's Department of External Affairs: Vol. 1, 1909 to 1946*, Montreal, QC: McGill-Queen's University Press.

Hillmer, Norman (1978), *'The Outstanding Imperialist': Mackenzie King and the British*, Canada House Lecture Series No. 4.

Hodson, H. V. (ed.) (1939), *The British Commonwealth and the Future*, London: Oxford University Press.

——(1942), *The British Empire*, London: RIIA.

Holland, Robert (1981), *Britain and the Commonwealth Alliance, 1918–1939*, London: Macmillan.

——(1996), *The Pursuit of Greatness: Britain and the World Role, 1900–70*, London: Fontana Press.

Horne, Alistair (1969), *To Lose a Battle: France, 1940*, London: Macmillan.

——(1988), *Macmillan: Vol. 1, 1894–1956*, London: Macmillan.

Horner, David M. (1978), *Crisis of Command: Australian Generalship and the Japanese Threat 1941–43*, Canberra: Australian National University Press.

——(1982), *High Command, Australia and Allied Strategy*, Sydney: George Allen and Unwin Australia.

——(1984), *The Commanders*, Sydney: George Allen and Unwin Australia.

——(1996), *Inside the War Cabinet: Directing Australia's War Effort, 1939–1945*, NSW: Allen and Unwin Australia.

——(2000), *Defence Supremo: Sir Frederick Shedden and the Making of Australian Defence Policy*, Sydney: Allen and Unwin Australia.

Howard, Michael (1972), *The Continental Commitment*, London: Temple Smith.

Howarth, Patrick (1973), *Intelligence Chief Extraordinary: Victor Cavendish Bentinck*, London: Bodley Head.

Howe, Stephen (2002), *Empire, A Very Short Introduction*, Oxford: Oxford University Press.

Hudson, W. J. (1986), *Casey*, Melbourne: Oxford University Press.

Hudson, W. J. and H. J. W. Stokes (eds) (1980), *Documents on Australian Foreign Policy, 1937–1949: Vol. 4, July 1940–June 1941*, Canberra: Australian Government Publication Service.

——(eds) (1982), *Documents on Australian Foreign Policy, 1937–1949: Vol. 5, July 1941–June 1942*, Canberra: Australian Government Publication Service.

Hurst, Sir Cecil (ed.) (1928), *Great Britain and the Dominions*, Chicago: University of Chicago Press.

Hyam, Ronald (1972), *The Failure of South African Expansion, 1908–48*, London: Macmillan.

Ingham, Kenneth (1986), *Jan Christian Smuts, The Conscience of a South African*, Johannesburg: Jonathan Ball Publishers.

Irving, David (1987), *Churchill's War: Vol. 1*, Australia: Veritas.

Lord Ismay (1960), *Memoirs*, London: Heinemann.

Jackson, Ashley (2006), *The British Empire and the Second World War*, London: Hambledon Continuum.

James, Lawrence (1994), *The Rise and Fall of the British Empire*, London: Little, Brown and Company.

James, R. (ed.) (1976), *Victor Cazalet*, London: Collins.

Jeffries, Charles (1938), *The Colonial Empire and its Civil Service*, Cambridge: Cambridge University Press.

Jeffries, Sir Charles (1956), *The Colonial Office*, London: George Allen and Unwin Ltd.

Jenkins, Roy (2001), *Churchill*, London: Macmillan.

Joll, James (1984), *The Origins of the First World War*, London: Longman.

Joske, Sir Percy (1978), *Sir Robert Menzies: A New Informal Memoir*, Sydney: Angus and Robertson.

Judd, Denis (1968), *Balfour and the British Empire: A Study in Imperial Evolution, 1874–1932*, London: Macmillan.

——(1996), *Empire: The British Imperial Experience*, London: Harper Collins.

——(2004), *The Lion and the Tiger, The Rise and Fall of the British Raj, 1600–1947*, Oxford: Oxford University Press.

Judd, Denis and Peter Slim (1982), *The Evolution of the Modern Commonwealth*, London: Macmillan.

Kay, Robin (ed.) (1972), *The Australian New Zealand Agreement 1944*, Wellington: A. R. Shearer.

Kennedy, Greg (ed.) (2007), *The British System of Imperial Defence, 1856–1956*, London: Taylor and Francis.

Kennedy, Paul (1981), *The Realities Behind Diplomacy: Background Influences on British External Policy 1865–1980*, London: Fontana Press.

——(1989), *Strategy and Diplomacy, 1870–1945*, London: Fontana Press.

Kent, John (1993), *British Imperial Strategy and the Origins of the Cold War, 1944–49*, Leicester: Leicester University Press.

Kenway, H., H. J. W. Stokes and P. G. Edwards (eds) (1979), *Documents on Australian Foreign Policy, 1937–1949: Vol. 3, January–June 1940*, Canberra: Australian Government Publication Service.

Kiernan, R. H. (1944), *General Smuts*, London: George C. Harrap Ltd.

Killingray, David (ed.) (1986), *Africa and the Second World War*, London: Macmillan.

Kimball, Warren F. (ed.) (1984), *Churchill and Roosevelt: The Complete Correspondence*, Princeton: Princeton University Press.

King, Michael (2003), *The Penguin History of New Zealand*. Auckland: Penguin Books.

King, Robert D. and Robin Kilson (eds) (1999), *The Statecraft of Imperialism, Essays in Honour of Wm. Roger Louis*, London: Frank Cass Publishers.

Kinvig, Clifford (1996), *Scapegoat, General Percival of Singapore*, London: Brassey's.

Kirk-Greene, Anthony (1999), *On Crown Service: A History of HM Colonial and Overseas Services, 1837–1997*, London: I.B. Tauris Publishers.

Kitchen, Martin (1996), *The British Commonwealth and Empire*, London: Macmillan Press.

Knaplund, Paul (1956), *Britain, Commonwealth and Empire, 1901–1955*, London: Hamish Hamilton.

Kraus, Rene (1941), *The Men Around Churchill*, New York: J.B. Lippincott and Co.

Kruger, D. W. (1969), *The Making of a Nation, A History of the Union of South Africa, 1910–61*, Johannesburg: Macmillan.

Langhorne, Richard (ed.) (1985), *Diplomacy and Intelligence during the Second World War, Essays in Honour of F.H. Hinsley*, Cambridge: Cambridge University Press.

Lawlor, Sheila (1994), *Churchill and the Politics of War, 1940–41*, Cambridge: Cambridge University Press.

Lee, J. M. and Martin Petter (1982), *The Colonial Office: War and Development Policy*, London: Institute of Commonwealth Studies.

Lewin, Ronald (1973), *Churchill as Warlord*, London: B.T. Batsford Ltd.

Lissington, M. P. (1972), *New Zealand and Japan, 1900–41*, Wellington: A. R. Shearer.

Lloyd, Lorna (2007), *Diplomacy with a Difference: the Commonwealth Office of High Commissioner, 1880–2006*, Leiden: Brill.

Lloyd, T. O. (1986), *Empire to Welfare State, English History 1906–1985*, Oxford: Oxford University Press.

Long, B. K. (1945), *In Smuts Camp*, London: Oxford University Press.

Lowe, Peter (1977), *Great Britain and the Origins of the Pacific War*, London: Oxford University Press.

Lyon, Peter (ed.) (1976), *Britain and Canada, Survey of a Changing Relationship*, London: Frank Cass.

MacDonald, Callum (1993), *The Lost Battle: Crete, 1941*, London: Macmillan.

MacDonald, Malcolm (1972), *Titans and Others*, London: Collins.

Macintyre, Stuart (1986), *The Oxford History of Australia: Vol. 4, 1901–42*, Melbourne: Oxford University Press.

Macleod, Iain (1961), *Neville Chamberlain*, London: Muller.

Madden, A. F. and W. H. Morris-Jones (eds) (1980), *Australia and Britain: Studies in a Changing Relationship*, London: Frank Cass.

Madden, Frederick and John Darwin (eds) (1993), *Select Documents on the Constitutional History of the British Empire and Commonwealth: Vol. 6, The Dominions and India Since 1900*, London: Greenwood.

Malherbe, Captain Janie (1944), *Complex Country – South Africa*, London: Longman, Green and Co. Ltd.

Manchester, William (1988), *Winston Churchill: The Caged Lion*, London: Oxford University Press.

Mansergh, Nicholas (1948), *The Commonwealth and Nations*, London: RIIA.

——(1952), *Survey of British Commonwealth Affairs: Problems of External Policy, 1931–39*, London: Oxford University Press.

——(1953), *Documents and Speeches on British Commonwealth Affairs 1939–1952 (Vols 1 and 2)*, London: Oxford University Press.

——(1958), *Survey of British Commonwealth Affairs: Problems of Wartime Cooperation and Post-War Change, 1939–1952*, London: Oxford University Press.

——(1969), *The Commonwealth Experience*, London: Weidenfeld and Nicolson.

——(ed.) (1970), *The Constitutional Relations between Britain and India: The Transfer of Power, 1942–1947*, London: Her Majesty's Stationery Office.

——et al. (1958), *Commonwealth Perspectives*, London: Cambridge University Press.

Marder, A. J. (1974), *From the Dardanelles to Oran*, London: Oxford University Press.

Martin, A. W. (1993) *Robert Menzies: A Life, Vol. 1, 1894–1943*, Melbourne: Melbourne University Press.

Martin, A. W. and Patsy Hardy (eds) (1993), *Dark and Harrying Days, Menzies' 1941 Diary*, Canberra: National Library of Australia.

Martin, H. and N. Orpen (1979), *South Africa at War; Vol. 7, Military and Industrial Organization and Operation in Connection with the Conduct of the War*, Cape Town: Purnell.

Massey, Vincent (1963), *What's Past is Prologue*, Toronto, ON: Macmillan.

McCarthy, John (1976), *Australia and Imperial Defence 1918–1939*, Queensland: University of Queensland Press.

McDermott, Geoffrey (1969), *The Eden Legacy*, London: Leslie Frewn Publishers.

McGibbon, Ian (ed.) (1993), *Undiplomatic Dialogue, Letters between Carl Berendsen and Alister McIntosh 1943–1953*, Auckland: Auckland University Press.

McIntosh, A. D. et al (1972), *New Zealand in World Affairs, Vol. 1*, Wellington: New Zealand Institute of International Affairs.

McIntyre, W. David (1977), *The Commonwealth of Nations: Origin and Impact, Vol. 9*, Minneapolis: University of Minnesota Press.

——(1979), *The Rise and Fall of the Singapore Naval Base*, London: Macmillan.

——(1988), *New Zealand Prepares for War*, Canterbury: University of Canterbury Press.

McKenzie, Francine (2002), *Redefining the Bonds of Commonwealth, 1939–1948: The Politics of Preference*, Basingstoke: Palgrave Macmillan.

McKinnon, Malcolm (1993), *Independence and Foreign Policy: New Zealand in the World since 1935*, Auckland: Auckland University Press.

McNeill, William Hardy (1953), *Survey of International Affairs: America, Britain and Russia – Their Cooperation and Conflict, 1941–1946*, London: Oxford University Press.

McNeish, James (2003), *Dance of the Peacocks: New Zealanders in Exile in the Time of Hitler and Mao Tse-Tung*, Auckland: Vintage Books.

Menzies, Sir Robert (1967), *Afternoon Light*, London: Macmillan.

Merchant, Sir James (ed.) (1954), *WSC: Servant of Crown and Commonwealth*, London: Cassell and Co.

Middlemas, Keith (1972), *The Diplomacy of Illusion: British Government and German, 1937–1939*, London: Weidenfeld.

Millar, T. B. (1978), *Australia in Peace and War*, London: C. Hurst and Co.

Miller, J. D. B. (1966), *Britain and the Old Dominions*, London: Chatto and Windus.

Milward, Alan S. (1972), *The Economic Effects of the Two World Wars on Britain*, London: Macmillan Education.

Mommsen, Wolfgang J. and Lothar Kettenacker (eds) (1983), *The Fascist Challenge and the Policy of Appeasement*, London: Allen and Unwin.

Monroe, Elizabeth (1981), *Britain's Moment in the Middle East, 1914–71*, London: Chatto and Windus.

Lord Moran (1966), *Struggle for Survival*, London: Constable.

Morris, James (1979), *Farewell the Trumpets, An Imperial Retreat*, London: Penguin Books.

——(1979), *Pax Britannica, The Climax of an Empire*, London: Penguin Books.

——(1979), *Heaven's Command, An Imperial Progress*, London: Penguin Books.

Morton, Desmond (1981), *Canada and the War*, Toronto, ON: Butterworth and Co. Ltd.

Mowat, C. L. (ed.) (1968), *The New Cambridge Modern History: Vol. 12, The Shifting Balance of World Forces 1898–1945*, Cambridge: Cambridge at the University Press.

Murfett, Malcolm et al. (1999), *Between Two Oceans, A Military History of Singapore from First Settlement to British Withdrawal*, Oxford: Oxford University Press.

Murray, David R. (ed.) (1974), *Documents on Canadian External Relations: Vol. 7, 1939–41*, Ottawa, ON: Department of External Affairs.

Nash, Walter (1944), *New Zealand: A Working Democracy*, London: J. M. Dent and Sons Ltd.

Nasson, Bill (2004), *Britannia's Empire, Making a British World*, Stroud: Tempus Publishing Ltd.

Neale, R. G. (ed.) (1976), *Documents on Australian Foreign Policy, 1937–1949: Vol. 2, 1939*, Canberra: Australian Government Publishing Service.

Neilson, Keith and Greg Kennedy (eds) (1997), *Far Flung Lines, Studies in Imperial Defence in Honour of Donald Mackenzie Schurman*, London: Frank Cass and Co. Ltd.

Neilson, Keith and Roy Prete (eds) (1983), *Coalition Warfare: An Uneasy Accord*, Canada: Wilfred Laurier University Press.

Nicholas, H. G. (1975), *The United States and Britain*, London: University of Chicago Press.

Nicolson, Nigel (ed.) (1967), *Harold Nicolson: Diaries and Letters, 1939–1945*, New York: Athenaeum.

Nimocks, Walter (1970), *Milner's Young Men, The 'Kindergarten' in Edwardian Imperial Affairs*, London: Hodder and Stoughton.

Nish, Ian (ed.) (1982), *Anglo-Japanese Alienation 1919–52, Papers of the Anglo-Japanese Conference on the History of the Second World War*, London: Cambridge University Press.

Nolan, Brian (1988), *King's War: Mackenzie King and the Politics of War, 1939–45*, Toronto, ON: Random House.

Lord Normanbrook (ed.) (1968), *Action this Day: Working with Churchill*, London: Macmillan.

Oliver, W. P. (ed.) (1981), *The Oxford History of New Zealand*, Wellington: Open University Press.

Orde, Anne (1996), *The Eclipse of Great Britain: The United States and British Imperial Decline*, London: Macmillan Press.

Orders, P. G. A. (2003), *Britain, Australia, New Zealand and the Challenge of the United States, 1939–1946: A Study in International History*, Basingstoke: Palgrave Macmillan.

O'Sullivan, Christopher D. (2007), *Sumner Welles, Post-War Planning and the Quest for a New World Order, 1937–1943*, Columbia: Columbia University Press.

Ovendale, Ritchie (1975), *Appeasement and the English Speaking World*, Cardiff: University of Wales Press.

——(1984), *The Foreign Policy of the British Labour Governments, 1945–1951*, Leicester: Leicester University Press.

——(1985), *The English Speaking Alliance, Britain, the United States and the Dominions, 1945–51*, London: Allen and Unwin.

Page, Sir Earle (1963), *Truant Surgeon*, Sydney: Angus and Robertson.

Palme Dutt, R. (1949), *Britain's Crisis of Empire*, London: Lawrence and Wishart.

Palmer, Alan (1996), *Dictionary of the British Empire and Commonwealth*, London: John Murray.

Palmer, Gerald (ed.) (1934), *Consultation and Cooperation in the British Commonwealth*, London: Oxford University Press.

Parker, R. A. C. (1993), *Chamberlain and Appeasement, British Policy and the Coming of the Second World War*, London: Macmillan.

Parkinson, Cosmo (1947), *The Colonial Office from Within*, London: Faber and Faber.

Pearson, Lester B. (1973), *Through Diplomacy to Politics: Memoirs, 1897–1948*, London: Victor Gollancz Ltd.

Perkins, Kevin (1968), *Menzies, The Last of the Queen's Men*, Adelaide: Rigby Ltd.

Perry, F. W. (1988), *The Commonwealth Armies, Manpower and Organisation in Two World Wars*, Manchester: Manchester University Press.

Peters, A. R. (1986), *Anthony Eden at the Foreign Office, 1931–1938*, Aldershot: Gower.

Pickersgill, J. W. (1960), *The Mackenzie King Record: Vol. 1, 1939–44*, Toronto, ON: University of Toronto Press.

Pienaar, Sara (1987), *South Africa and International Relations between the Two World Wars*, Johannesburg: Witwatersrand University Press.

Pimlott, Ben (ed.) (1986), *The Second World War Diary of Hugh Dalton, 1939–1945*, London: Jonathan Cape.

Playfair, Major-General I.S.O. et al. (1954), *Official History of the Second World War: The Mediterranean and Middle East Vol.1: The Early Successes Against Italy, to May 1941*, London: HMSO.

——(1956), *Official History of the Second World War: The Mediterranean and Middle East Vol. 2: The Germans Come to the Help of Their Ally, 1941*, London: HMSO.

Pollock, A. M. (1943), *Pienaar of Alamein*, Cape Town: Cape Time Ltd.

Ponting, Clive (1994), *Churchill*, London: BCA.

Porrit, Edward (1922), *The Fiscal and Diplomatic Freedom of the British Overseas Dominions*, Oxford: Clarendon Press.

Porter, A. N. and A. J. Stockwell (1987), *British Imperial Policy and Decolonization, 1938–1964: Vol.1, 1938–1951*, New York: St Martin's Press.

Porter, Bernard (1975), *The Lion's Share: A Short History of British Imperialism, 1850–1983*, London: Longman Group.

——(2004), *The Absent-Minded Imperialists, What the British Really Thought About Empire*, Oxford: Oxford University Press.

——(2006), *Empire and Superpower: Britain, America and the World*, London: Yale University Press.

Rea, J. E., (1997) *T.A. Crerar, A Political Life*, Kingston: McGill-Queen's University Press.

Reese, Trevor (1969), *Australia, New Zealand and the United States: A Survey of International Relations, 1941–1968*, London: Oxford University Press.

Reitz, Deneys (1943), *No Outspan*, London: Faber and Faber Ltd.

Reynolds, David (1981), *The Creation of the Anglo-American Alliance, 1937–41*, London: Europa Publications.

——(1991), *Britannia Overruled, British Policy and World Power in the Twentieth Century*, London: Longman Group.

——et al. (1994), *Allies at War: The Soviet, American and British Experience 1939–1945*, New York: St Martin's Press.

Rhodes James, Robert (ed.) (1967), *Chips: Diaries of Sir Henry Channon*, London: Weidenfeld and Nicolson.

——(1986), *Anthony Eden*, London: Weidenfeld and Nicolson.

Rice, Geoffrey W. (ed.) (2002), *The Oxford History of New Zealand*, Melbourne: Oxford University Press.

Ritchie, Charles (1974), *The Siren Years: Undiplomatic Diaries, 1937–45*, London: Macmillan.

Robbins, Keith (ed.) (2002), *The British Isles, 1901–1951*, Oxford: Oxford University Press.

Roberts, Andrew (1991), *'The Holy Fox': A Life of Lord Halifax*, London: Macmillan.

Robertson, John and John McCarthy (1985), *Australian War Strategy, 1939–45*, Brisbane: University of Queensland Press.

Rock, William R. (1988), *Chamberlain and Roosevelt, British Foreign Policy and the United States, 1937–40*, Colombus, OH: Ohio State University Press.

Roger Louis, Wm (1978), *Imperialism at Bay: The United States and the Decolonization of the British Empire*, London: Oxford University Press.

——(1992), *In the Name of God Go! Leo Amery and the British Empire in the Age of Churchill*, London: W. W. Norton and Co.

——(ed.) (2003), *Still More Adventures with Britannia*, London: I. B. Tauris and Co. Ltd.

——(ed.) (2005), *Yet More Adventures with Britannia*, London: I. B. Tauris and Co. Ltd.

Roger Louis, Wm and Hedley Bull (eds) (1986), *The 'Special Relationship': Anglo-American Relations since 1945*, Oxford: Clarendon Press.

Rose, Norman (1994), *Churchill: An Unruly Life*, London: Simon and Schuster.

Roskill, Stephen (1960), *The Navy at War, 1939–1945*, London: Collins,

——(1974), *Hankey: Man of Secrets, Vol. 3, 1931–63*, London: Collins.

Ross, Lloyd (1977), *John Curtin*, Melbourne: Macmillan.

Rothwell, Victor (1992), *Anthony Eden: A Political Biography*, Manchester: Manchester University Press.

Sanders, David (1990), *Losing an Empire, Finding a Role: British Foreign Policy since 1945*, London: Macmillan.

Sanger, Clyde (1991), *Malcolm MacDonald: Bringing an End to Empire*, Montreal, QC: McGill-Queen's University Press.

Scott, James Brown (ed.) (1921), *Autonomy and Federation within Empire, The British Self-Governing Dominions*, Washington DC: Carnegie Endowment for International Peace.

Seegers, Annette (1996), *The Military in the Making of Modern South Africa*, London: Tauris Academic Studies.

Shakespeare, Geoffrey (1949), *Let Candles be Brought In*, London: MacDonald.

Sheffield, Gary and Geoffrey Till (eds) (2003), *The Challenges of High Command, The British Experience*, Basingstoke: Palgrave Macmillan.

Sinclair, Keith (1959), *A History of New Zealand*, London: Penguin Books.

——(1977), *Walter Nash*, Auckland: Auckland University Press.

Smuts, J. C. (1952), *Jan Christian Smuts*, London: Cassell and Co.

Soames, Mary (ed.) (1998), *Speaking for Themselves: The Personal Letters of Winston and Clementine Churchill*, London: Doubleday.

Soulter, Gavin (1976), *Lion and Kangaroo: The Initiation of Australia 1901–1919*, Sydney: Collins.

Stacy, C. P. (1948), *The Canadian Army, 1939–1945*, Ottawa, ON: King's Printer.

——(1983), *Canada and the Age of Conflict, 1921–48*, Toronto, ON: University of Toronto Press.

Stevenson, William (1981), *The Origins of the British Commonwealth Air Training Scheme from 1923 to December 1939*, University of London [unpublished manuscript].

Stewart, Graham (2007), *His Finest Hours: The War Speeches of Winston Churchill*, London: Quercus.

Stewart, I. (1966), *The Battle for Crete*, London: Oxford University Press.

Stirling, Alfred (1974), *Lord Bruce: The London Years*, Melbourne: The Hawthorn Press.

Stokes, Robert (1930), *New Imperial Ideas, A Plea for the Associate of the Dominions in the Government of the Dependent Empire*, London: John Murray.

Strawson, John (2004), *The Battle for North Africa*, London: Pen and Sword Military Classics.

Sweetman, John (ed.) (1986), *Sword and Mace: Twentieth Century Civil–Military Relations in Britain*, London: Brassey's Defence.

Tangye, Derek (1944), *One King: A Survey of the Dominions and Colonies of the British Empire*, London: George G. Harrap and Co. Ltd.

Tarling, Nicholas (1993), *The Fall of Imperial Britain in South-East Asia*, Oxford: Oxford University Press.

Taylor, A. J. P. (1964), *The Origins of the Second World War*, London: Penguin Books.

——et al. (1969), *Four Faces and the Man*, London: Allen Lane.

(1940), *The Colonial and Dominions Office List, No. 79*, London: HMSO.

Thompson, Andrew S. (2000), *Imperial Britain, The Empire in British Politics c.1880–1932*, Harlow: Pearson Education Ltd.

——(2005), *The Empire Strikes Back? The Impact of Imperialism on Britain from the Mid-Nineteenth Century*, Harlow: Pearson Education Ltd.

Thompson, Peter (2005), *The Battle for Singapore*, London: Portrait.

Thompson, Willie (1999), *Global Expansion, Britain and its Empire 1870–1914*, London: Pluto Press.

Thorn, James (1952), *Peter Fraser, New Zealand's Wartime Prime Minister*, London: Odham's Press Ltd.

Thorne, Christopher (1978), *Allies of a Kind: The United States, Britain and the War against Japan, 1941–1945*, London: Hamish Hamilton.

Thurston, Anne (1995), *Records of the Colonial Office, Dominions Office, Commonwealth Relations Office and Commonwealth Office*, London: The Stationery Office.

Toynbee, Arnold and Frank T. Ashton-Gwatkin (eds) (1952), *Survey of International Affairs: The World in March 1939*, London: Oxford University Press.

Toynbee, Arnold and Veronica Toynbee (eds) (1958), *Survey of International Affairs 1939–1946: The Initial Triumph of the Axis*, London: Oxford University Press.

Tree, Ronald (1975), *When the Moon Was High: Memoirs, 1897–1942*, London: Macmillan.

Turner, John (ed.) (1988), *Britain and the First World War*, London: Oxford University Press.

Tute, Warren (1973), *The Deadly Stroke*, London: Collins.

Underhill, Frank H. (1956), *The British Commonwealth: An Experiment in Cooperation Among Nations*, Durham, NC: Duke University Press.

Van den Heever, C.M. (1946), *General J.B.M. Hertzog*, Johannesburg: A.P.B. Bookstore.

Van der Poel, Jean (ed.) (1973), *Smuts Papers: Vol. 6, December 1934 to August 1945*, London: Cambridge University Press.

Visser, George (1979), *Ossewa Brandwag, Traitors or Patriots*, Cape Town: Macmillan South Africa.

Walker, Eric (1944), *The British Empire: Its Structure and Spirit*, London: Oxford University Press.

Walker, Patrick Gordon (1962), *The Commonwealth*, London: Secker and Warburg.

Warren, Alan (2002), *Singapore 1942, Britain's Greatest Defeat*, London: Hambledon Continuum.

Watt, Alan (1967), *The Evolution of Australian Foreign Policy, 1938–1965*, Cambridge: Cambridge University Press.

Watt, D. C. (1965), *Personalities and Policies*, London: Longman.

——(1989), *How War Came*, London: William Heinemann.

Webster, Wendy (2005), *Englishness and Empire 1939–1965*, Oxford: Oxford University Press.

Wheare, K. C. (1942), *The Statute of Westminster and Dominion Status*, London: Oxford University Press.

Whitaker, General Denis and Shelagh Whitaker (1992), *Dieppe: Tragedy to Triumph*, Toronto: McGraw-Hill Ryerson.

Wigmore, Lionel (1957), *Australia in the War of 1939–1945: Army Vol. 4, The Japanese Thrust*, Canberra: Australian War Memorial.

Williamson, James (1945), *Great Britain and the Commonwealth*, London: Adam and Charles Black.

Wills, Clair (2007), *That Neutral Island, A Cultural History of Ireland during the Second World War*, London: Faber and Faber.

Wood, F. L. W. (1971), *The New Zealand People at War: Political and External Affairs*, Wellington: A.H. and A.W. Reed.

Woodburn Kirby, S. (1957), *History of the Second World War: Vol. 1, The War Against Japan*, London: HMSO.

Woodward, Sir Llewellyn (1970), *British Foreign Policy in he Second World War, Vol. 1*, London: HMSO.

Youngson, A. J. (1960), *The British Economy*, London: Allen and Unwin.

Zimmern, Sir Alfred (1941), *From the British Empire to the British Commonwealth*, London: Longman, Green and Co. Ltd.

ARCHIVAL HOLDINGS

Abrams Papers (Churchill College, Cambridge)

Alanbrooke Papers (Liddell Hart Archives, King's College London)

Lord Attlee Papers (Bodleian Library, Oxford: Dept. of Western Manuscripts) MS.Attlee

Australian Government Cabinet Minutes: Vol. 7 (National Archives of Australia, Canberra) CRS A2697

Lord Avon Papers (Birmingham University)

Sir Harry Batterbee Papers (Rhodes House Library, Oxford)

Carl Berendsen Papers (Victoria University, Wellington, New Zealand)

British Conservative Party Archive (Bodleian Library, Oxford: Dept. of Western Manuscripts) X.Films 63/5

Brooke-Popham Papers (Liddell Hart Archives, King's College London)

Lord Bruce Papers (National Archives of Australia, Canberra) AA1969

Sir Alexander Cadogan Papers (Churchill Archives, Cambridge) ACAD

Lt. Colonel C.A. de Candole Papers (Imperial War Museum, London)

Neville Chamberlain Papers (University of Birmingham)

Chartwell Papers (Churchill College, Cambridge) CHAR

W.H. Clark Papers (London School of Economics)

W.H. Clark Papers (Cape Town University)

Colville Papers (Churchill College, Cambridge) CLVL

Conservative Research Department Files (Bodleian Library, Oxford: Dept. of Western Manuscripts) CRD 2/28/2

Duff Cooper Papers (Churchill College, Cambridge) DUFC

Hubert Cowell Papers (Rhodes House Library, Oxford)

Sir G.S. Cox Papers (Alexander Turnbull Library, Wellington)

Sir Lionel Curtis Papers (Bodleian Library, Oxford: Dept. of Western Manuscripts) MS.Curtis

Sir Patrick Duncan Papers (Cape Town University) BC294

Frederic Eggleston Papers (National Library of Australia, Canberra) MS423

Paul Emrys-Evans Papers (British Library) ADD.MS.58240

Peter Fraser Papers (National Archives, Wellington) Series One

Eighth Viscount Galway Papers (Nottingham University)

Lord Hankey Papers (Churchill College, Cambridge) HNKY
Oliver Harvey Papers (British Library) ADD.MS.563998
C.D. Howe Papers (Library and Archives Canada, Ottawa) MG27
Sir Thomas Inskip Papers (Churchill College, Cambridge) INKP
Lord Ismay Papers (Liddell Hart Archives, King's College, London)
William Jordan Papers (New Zealand High Commission, London)
Capt. Sir Basil Liddell Hart Papers (Liddell Hart Archives, King's College London)
Malcolm MacDonald Papers (Durham University)
Malcolm MacDonald Papers (Rhodes House Library, Oxford)
William Mackenzie King Papers (Library and Archives Canada, Ottawa) MG26
John Martin Papers (Churchill College, Cambridge) MART
Vincent Massey Papers (Toronto University) B87-0082
Massey Family Papers (Library and Archives Canada, Ottawa) MG32
Sir A. D. McIntosh Papers (Alexander Turnbull Library, Wellington)
Sir Robert Menzies Papers (National Library of Australia, Canberra) MS4936
National Archives, London:
- ADM199
- AIR2, 8, 19, 20
- CAB2, 21, 27, 63, 65, 66, 67, 68, 99, 101, 102, 104, 120, 123
- CO429, 430, 532, 877, 881, 882, 886, 918
- DO1, 3, 35, 114, 119, 121
- FO371, 372, 800, 954
- HW1
- INF1
- PREM1, 3, 4
- PRO30
- WO106, 208, 216
Oxford Colonial Records Project: Interview with Malcolm MacDonald (Rhodes House Library, Oxford) MSS Brit.Emp.s.533
Sir Earle Page Papers (National Library of Australia, Canberra) MS1633
Lester Pearson Papers (Library and Archives Canada, Ottawa) MG26
Fifth Marquess of Salisbury [Lord Cranborne] Papers (Hatfield House)
Sir John Simon Papers (Bodleian Library, Oxford: Dept. of Western Manuscripts) MS.Simon
Thomas Skinner Papers (National Archives, Wellington) Series One
Jan Smuts Papers (National Archives, Pretoria)
Oliver Stanley Papers (British Library) ADD.MS.56398
W.G. Stevens Papers (Alexander Turnbull Library, Wellington)
Lord Swinton Papers (Churchill College, Cambridge)
Charles Te Water Papers (National Archives, Pretoria) A78
Sydney Waterson Papers (Cape Town University) BC631
Lord Woolton Papers (Bodleian Library, Oxford: Dept. of Western Manuscripts) MS.Woolton

JOURNALS, MAGAZINES AND NEWSPAPERS

Australian Defence Force Journal
Australian Journal of Politics and History
Australian Outlook
BBC History
Diplomacy and Statecraft
Diplomatic History
Canada House Lecture Series

Canadian Military History
Commonwealth and Empire Review
Contemporary British History
Current History
Daily Chronicle (London)
Daily Mail (London)
Daily Telegraph (London)
Daily Telegraph (Sydney)
Empire Review
English Historical Review
Evening Standard (London)
Far Eastern Survey
Foreign Affairs
Historical Studies
History Today
Institute of Commonwealth Studies Seminar Papers
Intelligence and National Security
International Affairs
International History Review
Journal of African History
Journal of Canadian Studies
Journal of Commonwealth Political Studies
Journal of Contemporary History
Journal of Imperial and Commonwealth History
Journal of Strategic Studies
Life
London Illustrated News
Military Affairs
Pacific Affairs
Political Science Quarterly
Public Administration
Punch (London)
Revue Internationale d'Histoire Militaire
Reynolds Illustrated News (London)
Royal Australian Historical Society Journal and Proceedings
RUSI Journal
Sunday Express (London)
Survey
The American Political Science Review
The Contemporary Review
The Courier Mail (Brisbane)
The Economist (London)
The Fortnightly
The (Manchester) Guardian
The Herald (Melbourne)
The Historical Journal
The Journal of Military History
The Journal of Politics
The New Statesman and Nation
The New York Review of Books
The New York Times
The Nineteenth Century
The Quarterly Review

The Quarterly Review of Commerce
The Round Table: The Commonwealth Journal of International Affairs
The Times (London)
The Washington Post
Time
Twentieth Century British History
United Empire
War and Society
War Illustrated
War in History

Index